A Modern Bestiary

Ars Poetastrica

A Modern Bestiary
Ars Poetastrica

Alessandro Gallenzi

Translated by J.G. Nichols
Illustrations by Luis Fanti

HERLA PUBLISHING

Published by Herla Publishing
Herla is an imprint of Hesperus Press Limited
4 Rickett Street, London SW6 1RU

Bestiario moderno and *Ars poetastrica* © Alessandro Gallenzi, 2002
English language translation © J.G. Nichols, 2004
Illustrations © Luis Fanti, 2004
This edition first published by Herla Publishing, 2004

Designed and typeset by Fraser Muggeridge
Printed in Jordan by the Jordan National Press

ISBN: 1-84391-777-7

Contents

A Modern Bestiary

Le arpie

Non fanno il loro nido tra gli sterpi,
come diceva Dante: è dentro i chiostri
della felicità che questi mostri
depongono le loro vive serpi.

E non gli basta immergere gli artigli
nei cuori dei nemici, ma si avventano
con ferocia (e non credo se ne pentano)
persino contro i loro stessi figli.

Sopra le poche gioie che offre il mondo,
sopra candidi sogni e sentimenti,
gettano i loro luridi escrementi.

E non sono contente fino in fondo
se poco prima di volare via
non lanciano un'orrenda profezia.

The Harpies

They do not make their nests in undergrowth,
as Dante said: it is inside the cloisters
of happiness itself that these foul monsters
are pleased to bring their brood of snakes to birth.

For them it's not enough to sink their claws
in hearts of enemies: they go berserk
(never, I think, regretting the attack)
even against their own poor sons and heirs.

On those few joys which our small world holds out,
on the most innocent dreams or sentiment,
they love to drop their filthy excrement;

and never reach the peak of their delight
unless, sometime before they fly away,
they hit us with some hideous prophecy.

Il mulo

Io pensavo che il mulo qualche volta,
arrancando gravato dalla soma
(ne ho visto proprio ieri uno a Roma),
fosse invaso da un senso di rivolta,

che in lui si riaccendesse almeno un po'
l'eredità materna, cavallina,
salendo su per la gravosa china
bastonato e umiliato. E invece no:

il mulo nasce, cresce e muore mulo:
con il sole, la pioggia o la tempesta,
non lo vedrete alzare mai la testa.

Nemmeno se lo pizzicasse al culo
il becco acuto e caustico di un gallo
farebbe un'impennata da cavallo.

The Mule

I thought: at least occasionally the mule,
stumbling under the loads that weigh him down
(I saw one only yesterday in Rome),
would have a feeling that he must rebel;

some spark of his heredity must show,
drawn from his mother's background as a horse,
always climbing, always in such distress,
humiliated, given stick. But no:

the mule is born, grows up, and dies a mule:
whether it rains, or shines, or storms are brewed,
you will not see him ever raise his head.

Not even if a caustic cockerel
should peck him critically upon the arse
would he once rear and bridle like a horse.

Il camaleonte

Arrampicato sui più alti rami
dell'albero che gli dà vita e forza,
cambia continuamente la sua scorza,
benché per fare questo non si squami

come il serpente quando muta spoglie,
ma in gioiosa armonia con la natura
fonda la sua mimetica figura
con la scena cangiante che l'accoglie.

Al riparo dal grigio sublunare,
questo fratello dell'arcobaleno
sempre nuovi colori ospita in seno.

Uomini bui, lasciatelo sognare
lassù nella sua altezza solitaria
e variopinta, e banchettare d'aria!

The Chameleon

Perched up upon the very top of those
branches from which his life and strength are drawn,
he spends all of his time changing his skin,
although there are no scales he needs to lose

(he's not like snakes casting their clothes away);
no, in a joyful harmony with nature
the appearance of this imitative creature
is based upon his changing scenery.

Responding to sublunary grey gloom,
this brother of the rainbow-coloured sky
always has novel tones that he must try.

Mankind with all your darkness, let him dream
in many-coloured loneliness up there
and feast upon a banquet of pure air!

Le falene

Se si accende una luce nella notte,
state pur certi che ben presto attorno
a quella falsa immagine del giorno
accorreranno le falene, a frotte.

E tanto gireranno intorno al lume
che l'avido calore a poco poco,
come la fiamma di un ardente fuoco,
consumerà le loro ceree piume.

Ora domando a voi: cosa le induce
a icareggiare in quella folle danza
di morte, senza avere altra speranza

che il martirio? L'amore della luce,
il desiderio d'essere scaldate
o la brama di essere abbagliate?

Moths

If you put on a light when all is dark,
you may be sure that very readily
round that deluding image of the day
the rushing moths will gather, in a flock.

And they will twist around that light and turn
until eventually the greedy heat,
like naked flame from a fire that's blazing bright,
consumes their waxen plumes and all are gone.

I ask you this: what makes them so delight,
Icarus-like, in dancing like a fool
that dance of death, and with no hope at all

but martyrdom? Is it mere love of light,
the wish perhaps to be warmed in the glow,
or lust for dazzlement, makes them act so?

Il ramarro

Ci sono bestie molto più insensibili
della pietra al calore della vita,
che dalla loro bocca inaspidita
lanciano solo velenosi sibili.

E tra queste il ramarro è la peggiore:
nemmeno il mezzodì canicolare,
con i suoi raggi vivi, può scaldare
un po' il suo sangue, freddo di livore.

Ricordi, Mirco, quando da bambini
lo cacciavamo con le nostre fionde
tra i rovi in mezzo ai quali si nasconde?

Ora, se incrocio i suoi occhi viperini
o per caso passando lo calpesto,
sono io che me la batto lesto lesto.

The Lizard

There are some beasts which are less tender even
than stone towards life's warmth and eagerness,
so cold that nothing from their viperous
mouths ever comes but hisses filled with venom.

And I believe the very worst of these is
the lizard: even noon when dog days blaze
can add no touch of warmth, with living rays,
to its cold blood where livid envy freezes.

Remember, Mirco, how in childhood days
we used to hunt it down with slings, waylaid
among the brambles where a beast can hide?

Now, if I come across its viper's eyes,
or step upon it accidentally,
I am the one who turns and runs away.

La pecora

A chi non viene voglia di aggreggiarsi
vedendo com'è comoda la vita
delle pecore d'oggi? Come invita
quel gioioso belevole obliarsi,

quel placido brucare ininterrotto
sui pascoli che ha scelto il buon pastore,
quel ruminìo mansueto, quel torpore
da gatto cittadino da salotto!

Per vivere così, senza fatica,
senza avere il bisogno di pensare,
anch'io mi farei mungere e tosare.

Sbaglia di grosso la saggezza antica:
meglio cent'anni e più da pecoroni
che un giorno tribolato da leoni.

The Sheep

Who does not see being herded as sheer bliss,
noticing life is oh so comfortable
for sheep today? Who does not feel the pull
of blessed bleating self-forgetfulness

on meadows the good shepherd has picked out;
to graze uninterruptedly and browse,
and tamely ruminate, and even drowse
like a domesticated fireside cat.

To live this way – no trouble to be taken,
and with no need for thinking in the least –
I would be happy to be milked and fleeced.

The ancient wisdom's very much mistaken:
better a hundred years spent sheepishly
than live as lions do one troubled day.

L'asinibbio

Se non credete all'asino che vola,
guardate un po' più spesso verso l'alto:
forse, staccati gli occhi dall'asfalto,
vedrete pure voi questa bestiola.

Passeggiavo tranquillo quando: 'Cribbio!'
esclamo, 'che è quel coso che mulina
lassù nell'aria?' E il coso si avvicina
e fa ragliando: 'Io sono l'asinibbio,

perfetta, naturale macedonia
di spirito rapace e zucca vuota,
ed ho per dio il bastone e la carota.'

E chi pensa sia favola o finzione,
ricordi come spesso la fortuna
libri gli asini fin sopra alla luna.

The Asshawk

If you can't credit there's an ass that flies,
lift up your eyes unto the highest height:
and then, perhaps, instead of mere asphalt,
you too will see this jackass in the skies.

Strolling in peace I hear myself exclaim:
'Good lord! What is that whirling in the air,
up in the sky?' The thingummy draws near,
and brays in answer, 'Asshawk is my name

(that portmanteau describes me to perfection):
rapaciously inclined, empty of head,
I take the stick and carrot for my god.'

And anyone regarding this as fiction
ought to recall what fate has often done,
promoting asses way above the moon.

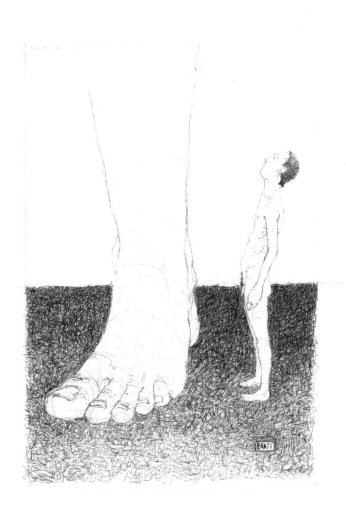

Il lombrico

Che tristezza mi viene quando acciacco
casualmente un lombrico camminando...
'Chissà se anche tu soffri,' mi domando,
ripassandoci sopra con il tacco.

'Che cosa fai laggiù nel fango nero?
Che scopo ha la tua vita, questa guerra
combattuta in silenzio nella terra,
tuo unico alimento giornaliero?

Tiri avanti così, strisciando piano
e allungandoti anello dopo anello...
che ci trovi, in quest'incubo, di bello?

Al mondo non c'è nulla di più vano,
povera creaturina spiaccicata,
della tua assurdità celenterata.'

The Earthworm

What a great melancholia I feel
squashing an earthworm accidentally...
I wonder, 'Do you suffer, just as we?'
treading it down once more under my heel.

'What do you do down there in that black mud?
What is the purpose of your life, the end
of this war fought in silence in the ground,
the earth which is your daily only food?

You get along somehow, you slowly crawl,
stretching your self cautiously ring by ring...
what does this profit you, worth mentioning?

The world has nothing less effectual,
miserable little exiguity,
than your coelenterate absurdity.'

Lo stercorario

Questo nero animale ci ha insegnato
come si può trascorrere una vita
sisifeggiando lungo una salita
con la rassegnazione di un forzato.

Non so cosa lo spinge a andare avanti,
ad adorare ciò che gli altri aborrono,
a trascinarsi mentre gli altri corrono,
incurante di tutto e tutti quanti.

Su immense solitudini di sabbia,
lui porta la sua croce puzzolente
verso un brullo calvario inesistente.

Chissà se prova un minimo di rabbia
quando si imbatte in api indaffarate
a commerciare ambrosie profumate?

The Dung-beetle

We are all taught by this black animal
how we may spend what days we have to live
with all the resignation of a slave
rolling, like Sisyphus, stones up a hill.

I do not know what drives it to persist,
to go on worshipping what others shun,
to drag itself along while others run,
as nothing else could possibly exist.

Over a boundless sandy solitude
it bears its cross that's stinking to high heaven
towards a Calvary that's not there even.

Perhaps it feels a little bit annoyed
coming by chance on where some busy bee
trades in fragrant ambrosia day by day?

Il cane

Stare a catena e sgranocchiare un osso,
leccare mani e piedi alle persone,
scodinzolare a un cenno del padrone,
ringhiare ed abbaiare a un pettirosso,

fiutare feci, tendere il guinzaglio
per lasciare qua e là una pisciatina,
lanciarsi, sciolto, in una sgroppatina
per poi tornare mite nel serraglio:

questa, cane, al tuo sguardo impecorito,
velato di servile ottusità,
appare la più gran felicità.

Forse piangi quel lupo ormai ammansito
incatenato al fondo del tuo cuore
quando ululi alla luna il tuo dolore?

The Dog

Being chained up and gnawing on a bone,
licking everyone's hands and feet all over,
wagging your tail at one nod from your master,
snarling and barking when a robin's come,

sniffing faeces, and straining at the leash
to make sure that some piss is left behind,
then, once released, making a sudden bound
to go off home, meekly as one could wish:

all this, dog, in your eyes, humiliated
and dimmed by your slavelike stupidity,
appears the acme of felicity.

Perhaps you mourn that wolf, domesticated
by now, but in your heart still, on a chain,
when you are howling sadly at the moon?

La piovra

Triste colui che cade nei tentacoli
di questa bestia dei fondali bui,
così golosa della vita altrui
che non ammette alle sue brame ostacoli.

Prende tutto, anzi arraffa, a dieci mani
e ingoia ciecamente: il suo palato
non distingue più il dolce dal salato,
tanto è avvezzo agli intingoli più strani.

La sua fame è infinita, senza fondo:
se avesse mille bocche da sfamare,
spopolerebbe terra, cielo e mare.

E svuotato e annientato tutto il mondo,
inizierebbe poi come un'ossessa
a mordere e a inghiottire anche se stessa.

The Octopus

Woe betide him who's in the tentacles
of this beast of the dark unfathomed sea,
so greedy for other people's lives that she
is undeterred by any obstacles.

And all she takes with all her hands – no, snatches –
she swallows blindly, since her taste cannot
distinguish any longer sour from sweet,
being so accustomed to the strangest dishes.

Her hunger's infinite, interminable:
had she a thousand mouths to satisfy
she would depopulate earth, sea, and sky.

Then, having emptied out the world and all,
she would at once, like one possessed, begin
to chew herself up ready to gulp down.

La lumaca

Ieri è venuta a cena una lumaca,
sobria come un pastore luterano,
ha sorseggiato un po' del mio trebbiano
ed è strisciata via mezza ubriaca.

Di fronte alle mie irsute verità
ritraeva le corna intimorita,
per poi fissarmi, mezza sbigottita,
dietro il guscio di eburnea ottusità.

Ma quella casa che ha innalzato a tempio
della sua lenta, viscida esistenza
è sicura soltanto in apparenza.

Basta appena un nonnulla per far scempio
del suo fragile tetto, e un bestemmione
la trasforma in un nudo lumacone.

The Snail

A snail arrived for dinner yesterday,
as sober as a preaching Lutheran;
it sipped a sip of my Trebbiano down,
then crawled a little tipsily away.

Under the harsh home truths I had to tell
it drew its horns in, for it was afraid,
and then gazed at me, almost stupefied,
under the smooth obtuseness of its shell.

But that house it has built up as a shrine
in honour of its slow and sticky life
is only on the face of it quite safe.

It takes the merest trifle to smash in
the fragile dwelling, and a good round curse
transforms the snail to sluggy nakedness.

Il gatto

È l'animale che più odio al mondo,
forse in parte perché un po' mi ci specchio,
a mano a mano che divento vecchio
e il mio ventre borghese si fa tondo.

Furbo, approfittatore, ti si posa
prepotente sul grembo miagolando
e facendo le fusa, specie quando
ha intenzione di chiederti qualcosa.

E sceglie bene chi può arruffianarsi:
a che pro, infatti, farsi accarezzare
da chi non può passargli da mangiare?

E se un giorno si stanca di strusciarsi,
aspettatevi pure un voltafaccia,
e che vi renda fiele per focaccia.

The Cat

This is the beast whom most of all I hate:
a glass in which I find myself revealed
a little at a time as I grow old
and see my bourgeois belly rounding out.

A cunning profiteer, she sinks to rest
on someone's useful lap, arrogantly,
to miaow and mew and purr, especially
whenever she has something to request.

She's very careful in her choice of friend:
what point in being fondled and caressed,
if one gets nothing out of it at last?

And, if she tires of stroking in the end,
a swift volte-face is always de rigueur:
she'll bite the hand that feeds, with no demur.

I castori

Non lontano da me c'è una colonia
di pasciuti castori che prolifica
beatamente in seno alla munifica
selva oscura accademica d'Ausonia.

Passano tutto il tempo a rosicchiare:
ognuno rode ingordo il suo tronchetto,
non lo abbandona mai, lo tiene stretto
tra i denti per non farselo rubare.

Il cacciatore un tempo li cacciava,
si racconta, per togliergli i testicoli,
ma loro, per non correre pericoli,

con un morso, di ciò che gli pesava
si sono con piacere liberati,
e ora vivono placidi e castrati.

Beavers

Not far from where I live's a colony
of well-fed beavers: they proliferate,
enjoying the best benefits of that
dark academic wood that's Italy.

They gnaw and gnaw all day and every day,
each one of them on his own bit of tree,
gripping it in his teeth, lest it should be,
if he but let it go, stolen away.

Men used to hunt them once upon a time,
to take their testicles, so people say;
in order to avoid such jeopardy,

they took off what was growing burdensome
with one neat bite; being thus liberated,
they carry on contentedly, castrated.

La pecora nera

Se avete modo di vedere un gregge,
fateci caso: in mezzo a quella schiera
bianca uniforme c'è una macchia nera
che sembra contrastare con la legge

della natura, anche se bela e bruca
come chi le sta intorno e mite mite
segue le sue compagne albicrinite
ovunque il buon pastore le conduca.

Chi pensa che ci sia una differenza
tra lei e le sue consimili si sbaglia:
anche in lei brucia un'anima di paglia.

Non fidatevi mai dell'apparenza:
nonostante il suo vello non sia bianco,
è comunque una pecora del branco.

The Black Sheep

If you should come upon a flock, then pause
and notice: in that uniformly white
assembly there will be just one black spot
that seems a contradiction of the laws

of nature, even if she browses, bleats
just like the others all around, and follows
as gently, mildly as her milk-white fellows
to anywhere where the good shepherd leads.

He's wrong who thinks that there are differences
between the others of the flock and her:
in her also there burns a soul of straw.

You should not judge things by appearances:
she is, although she has no pure white fleece,
one of the same old herd, nevertheless.

L'uomo

Eccomi dunque all'animale umano,
il vertice e l'abisso del creato,
che passa il poco tempo che gli è dato
ad affannarsi e arrovellarsi invano

in cerca di un nonsenso e di uno scopo
coi quali illuminare i propri ieri,
riempiendo il mondo d'ossa e di pensieri
mentre il tempo con lui fa a gatto e topo.

Il Dio che lo ha innalzato da animale
a bestia prediletta gli ha concesso
di farsi vile schiavo di se stesso.

Spera in un'altra vita, e vive male
tra una polvere e l'altra, tra la culla
e la bocca famelica del nulla.

Mankind

So finally I reach the human beast,
the summit and abyss of all creation,
who spends the little time that is his portion
beating his useless brains, never at rest,

searching for stuff and nonsense, and some aim
which will illuminate his time that's gone,
filling this world of ours with thought and bone
while time itself plays cat and mouse with him.

The God who raised him from mere animal
to this most favoured creature also gave
the gift to make himself his own base slave.

In hopes of a better life, he still lives ill,
caught between dust and dust, between his birth
and nothingness with greedy gaping mouth.

Ars Poetastrica

Da quando hanno inventato il verso anarchico,
la poesia non è più un regno oligarchico,
ma si è a tal punto democratizzata
che è diventata ormai una baggianata,
tanto che non esiste analfabeta
che oggi non possa dire: 'Io son poeta.'

Il secolo oramai volge alla fine
e seppellisce nelle sue rovine
orde d'opere indegne di memoria
10   di poeti senza arte e senza gloria,
milioni di milioni di parole
che svaniranno come brina al sole.

Spesso mi chiedo con malinconia:
'Dove è andata a finire la poesia?'
Viene rabbia a pensare che qui intorno,
sopra questo deserto, fiorì un giorno
un rigoglio di cime verdeggianti,
come Dante, l'Ariosto o Cavalcanti!

Forse da qualche parte è sotterrato
20   il loro seme, e se non si è seccato
di certo prima o poi germinerà –
magari tra due secoli, chissà –
ma intanto sulla terra desolata
non si raccoglie neanche l'insalata.

Quando mi guardo intorno vedo solo
un infinito e brulicante stuolo
di gente persa su binari morti
(o lungo i labirinti più contorti
che l'intelletto umano può creare)
30   in cerca di qualcosa da trovare.

Soon as anarchic writing came to hand,
verse, now no more an oligarchic land,
became so democratic as to be
a paradise for sheer tomfoolery;
so that, by now, there's no illiterate who
does not declare: 'I am a poet too.'

This century is drawing to its end.
Beneath the ruins it will leave behind
are works of poets without art, unnumbered,
10   inglorious, and not fit to be remembered,
millions of words that came and now are gone
as snowdrifts vanish at a touch of sun.

I wonder in my melancholy way:
'What has it come to now, this poetry?'
It is a staggering thought that all around
there used to flourish in this desert land
clusters of laurel wreaths, poets in plenty,
like Dante, Ariosto, Cavalcanti.

Now maybe underground somewhere or other
20   their seed is buried; if it does not wither,
sooner or later it will germinate,
perhaps two hundred years hence it will sprout;
meanwhile throughout this desolated region
no one can hope to harvest lettuce even.

As I look all around I come upon
nothing except a never-ending swarm
of lost souls moving on to some dead end
or (such the contortions of the human mind
in subtle mazes that still lead nowhither)
30   looking for something that they can discover.

Vedo gente che fa versacci orribili,
gente che scrive porcherie illeggibili,
gente che si nasconde nei nonsensi,
o in brodi acquosi o in minestroni densi,
gente che scrive ma non sa perché,
gente che cita Eraclito e De Andrè.

Questi poetastri sono così tanti,
e sono così tossici e inquinanti,
che col tempo potrebbero causare
dei disastri ambientali in terra e in mare,
ma per fortuna il tempo li setaccia
e di loro non lascia alcuna traccia.

Quelli che adesso chiamano poeti,
come L***, Z*** o S***,
se lasciate passare qualche anno
vedrete che destino oscuro avranno:
i loro nomi se li porta il vento
e spariranno in meno di un momento.

Ma per me oggi il guaio principale
non è tanto una crisi generale
di qualità, quanto il fraintendimento
di cosa è la poesia, l'atteggiamento
nei confronti dell'arte e, soprattutto,
la mescolanza adultera del tutto.

Cerchiamo dunque di capire bene
che cosa è la poesia e se le catene
di verso e rima servono a qualcosa
o se al contrario è giusto che la prosa,
con le sue schiere caotiche e confuse,
invada la regione delle Muse.

Some are producing nasty scraps of verse,
writing what is illegible, or worse,
hiding in nonsense like a sort of cloak,
or soup that's watery or far too thick,
people who write but do not know the reason,
who quote both Heraclitus and Bob Dylan.

The thing is that there are so many such,
and they're so poisonous and pollute so much,
that, given time enough, they might well be
40   the cause of some worldwide catastrophe,
except that time will always sieve and sift
until no trace of them at all is left.

Those who for poets nowadays do duty,
as do L***, Z***, or S***,
if you just let one or two years go by
you'll find they end up in obscurity,
their very names borne off by some light breeze
in less time than it takes to tell you this.

Today for me, however, the salient vice is
50   not after all the universal crisis
of quality, so much as the mistake
over what poetry is, the line they take
towards the art, and most of all this stew,
this mishmash, *mélange adultère de tout.*

Let us therefore try hard to understand
what poetry is, and see what worthy end
is served by all the chains of rhyme and verse,
or whether rather it is right that prose
should, with its lawless ill-assorted forces,
60   invade this region sacred to the Muses.

La poesia è innanzi tutto ispirazione,
fiamma che non conosce gestazione
ma divampa improvvisa e repentina,
invisibile forza che trascina
la nostra mano docile sul foglio
come l'onda del mare sullo scoglio.

Chi non ha mai sentito questo fuoco
ardere dentro il petto, anche per poco,
chi non ha mai provato questa gioia,
70   ma scribacchia per calcolo o per noia,
oltre a essere un uomo sfortunato,
non può dirsi un poeta, ma un castrato.

Perché l'ispirazione sgorghi pura
deve però trovare una natura
che sia imbevuta della lingua viva
e che conservi fresco nella stiva
della memoria il carico pregiato
dei più grandi poeti del passato.

C'è chi scrive, in maniera disonesta,
80   la prima cosa che gli salta in testa
e senza preoccuparsi di vagliare
le proprie idee si mette ad imbrattare
quanti più fogli può: tremendo mostro
che di continuo inghiotte carta e inchiostro.

Non dico che bisogna soffocare
l'ispirazione in schemi o deformare
in modo innaturale le parole
gettandole qua e là come si vuole
per fare undici sillabe e la rima:
90   io dico che lo schema viene prima.

Above all, poetry is inspiration,
a flame that does not issue from gestation
but blazes out quite unexpectedly,
an unseen power that irresistibly
draws the tame hand across the pure white sheet,
as a wave of the sea is drawn across a reef.

He who has never ever felt this flame
blaze in his breast, if but for a short time,
he who has never known this wild elation,
70   but scribbles from ennui or calculation,
apart from being a man no luck can gladden,
cannot be called a poet, but a capon.

For inspiration to issue without taint
it has however to find a temperament
thoroughly soaked and steeped in the living tongue,
and one that has preserved from perishing
precious remembrance of the legacy
left by the greatest poets of times gone by.

There's one who writes (to me his name is mud)
80   all the first things that come into his head
and, never taking any care at all
to winnow his ideas, sets out to soil
as many sheets as possible: drinks ink
and swallows paper faster than you think.

I do not mean that anyone should smother
inspiration in patterns, or disfigure
words in a way that is unnatural,
flinging them round him at his own sweet will
to make ten syllables and one poor rhyme:
90   simply the pattern must come first in time.

Chi si è a lungo nutrito di poesia
sente naturalmente l'armonia
di un verso e, quando scrive, la sua mente
organizza le idee spontaneamente
nella forma che più gli è congeniale
senza fare nessun salto mortale.

Ogni forma, se imposta dal di fuori,
porterà senza dubbio a degli orrori
(e nel passato, ahimè, ne abbiamo visti:
100   basta solo pensare ai petrarchisti),
ma se agisce da dentro non dà impaccio,
anzi ci aiuta e funge da setaccio.

Senza nessun ostacolo formale
la poesia si riduce a una banale
ginnastica del polso e della mano
o, come ha detto il poeta americano
Robert Frost, che voi tutti conoscete,
a una partita a tennis senza rete.

La metrica pertanto ha la funzione
110   di guidare la nostra ispirazione
e di filtrare le acque del reale
scartando tutto ciò che è inessenziale:
di trovare, in sostanza, la pepita
nel fango in mezzo al quale è seppellita.

Questa pepita poi va raffinata
al fuoco del buon gusto e lavorata
a colpi di limetta e di cesello
per innalzarla al rango di gioiello,
per trasformare il grezzo minerale
120   in un'opera d'arte originale.

To him who has been fed on poetry
it's natural to hear the harmony
of verse, and, when he writes, his mind at once
puts his ideas into perfect sense
in the pattern most congenial to him:
he doesn't go through hoops to achieve this aim.

A pattern forced upon us from outside
will give results that no one can abide
(no shortage of examples in the past:
100   needs but recall so many a Petrarchist);
but if the pattern rises from within
it helps us like a sort of winnowing-fan.

Without an obstacle to overcome
poetry comes down at last to some humdrum
physical jerks of hand and not of head,
or, as a great American has said
(whose poems I am sure you will have met),
a game of tennis but without a net.

Metre, it follows from all this, must function
110   as a Virgilian guide to inspiration,
a filter for the waters of the real
rejecting what's not indispensable,
a way of finding out, when all is said,
the nugget that is buried in the mud.

This nugget must be afterwards refined
in fires of good taste, taken well in hand,
and filed and cut and polished to become
what it was meant to be – a dazzling gem,
to make from the raw unprocessed mineral
120   a work of art that is original.

Certo, c'è anche chi acquista abilità
nel cesellare versi ma non ha
quel fuoco, quella sacra ispirazione
che è la principale distinzione
tra il semplice artigiano e il grande artista
e tra il poeta e l'arido enigmista.

Ma non per questo vanno ripudiate
le regole e le forme tramandate
dai nostri padri antichi, non per questo
130   non bisogna tentare un nuovo innesto
sul tronco della nostra tradizione,
che non è secco come si suppone.

Certo, è molto più comodo affidarsi
all'arbitrio e al capriccio che adeguarsi
a norme che richiedono esperienza
e una massiccia dose di pazienza,
ma non si illuda l'improvvisatore:
non esiste poesia senza sudore.

Non esiste poesia senza fatica,
140   senza difficoltà, senza l'ortica
delle incertezze e dei ripensamenti,
non esiste poesia senza tormenti,
senza scontento, senza arrabbiature,
non c'è poesia senza cancellature.

La metrica ha anche il merito di offrire
dei criteri coi quali stabilire
un punto saldo di riferimento,
per non parlare poi dell'elemento
di sfida e di confronto, che va perso
150   se si sceglie la prosa e non il verso.

It's true, some do acquire the ability
to polish verses who are utterly
devoid of fire – that sacred inspiration
which constitutes the principal distinction
between a tradesman's work and artistry,
poetry and enigmatography.

And yet this is no reason we should scorn
the precepts and the verse forms handed down
by our great predecessors, and no reason
130   we should not try a grafting operation
of something new upon tradition's trunk
(which is not dry and withered as some think).

It's certainly much easier to give in
to every whim and fancy than conform
to rules which call upon experience
and endless patience; easier, but the dunce
deceives himself who merely plays about:
there is no poetry where there's no sweat.

There is no poetry without great trouble,
140   hard nuts to crack; without grasping the nettle
of afterthoughts and great uncertainties;
no poetry without great agonies
and discontent; without rage bursting out;
no poetry without much blotting out.

Metrics has too this merit: it can shape
criteria with which we may set up
some certain solid points of reference;
not to speak of the useful elements
of challenge, confrontation – all that goes
150   when we do not choose verse, but simply prose.

Nel caso in cui si accetti come norma
la più assoluta libertà di forma
e si scarti ogni regola poetica,
viene a crearsi un'anarchia estetica,
in quanto non può essere distinta
una vera poesia da quella finta.

Bisogna ricomporre l'armonia
o non avremo più vera poesia;
la poesia adesso è in mano a dei cialtroni
160   che blaterano versi da Caproni:
occorre ricondurli a bastonate
dentro l'ovile delle forme usate.

Non c'è mai stata nella storia umana,
da quando l'uomo attinge alla fontana
dolceamara che sgorga in Elicona,
un'epoca più vandala e piagnona:
un'epoca che ha ucciso e infranto tutto
e ora incoccodrillita piange a lutto.

Diamo una botta al cerchio e una alla botte:
170   l'avanguardia fu un faro nella notte
al tempo in cui regnava Carduccione,
re rimaiolo della stagnazione;
ma ora che più di un secolo è passato,
perché sfondare un muro già sfondato?

Ho visto gente fare i burattini
recitando poesiole da bambini,
altri muggire come buoi al macello
facendo smorfie e gesti da bordello,
e la cosa più triste è che ogni volta
180   trovano chi li applaude e chi li ascolta.

If we accept – indeed make it a norm –
the greatest possible liberty of form,
discarding every rule of poetry,
we move towards aesthetic anarchy,
because it gets so very hard to tell
pretended poetry from what is real.

We need to recompose this harmony
or there will be no more true poetry;
poetry now is in the hands of such as
160   blather such verses as Caproni butchers:
they should be beaten back into the fold
of those great verse forms that we know of old.

In all the history of the human creature
there never was, since men drew sweet and bitter
waters out of the springs on Helicon,
an epoch more disposed to smash and moan,
one more destructive, more inclined to kill,
and then weep for it like a crocodile.

Now let's be fair and square: I do admit
170   the avant-garde was a beacon in the night
in the days when King Carducci ruled the nation,
the rhyming monarch of a great stagnation;
but, now that time is out of sight and mind,
why mine a wall already undermined?

I have seen those who cut a sorry figure
reciting rhymes at which the kiddies snigger,
others mooing like cattle to the slaughter,
making a face and many an obscene gesture;
and every time the thing I find most sad
180   is, some applaud – some even pay them heed!

La poesia futuristica ha stufato:
tutto il dadà e dudù dove ha portato?
Già il gran Guittone ha eretto col suo verso
un monumento eterno al tempo perso:
eppure anche oggi esistono gli arguti
che aspirano alla lista dei caduti.

Le avanguardie nascondono soltanto
confusione e ignoranza sotto il manto
della modernità: questi mercanti
190   di false novità tirano avanti
a casaccio e preparano il terreno
a chi sa sempre più di sempre meno.

Lo gnomo sulle spalle del gigante
si è fatto presuntuoso ed arrogante,
e invece di mostrare il suo rispetto
medita come fargli lo sgambetto;
ma il gigante lo lascia macchinare:
sa che il pigmeo non lo potrà atterrare.

Un tempo la poesia seguiva i ritmi
200   dell'armonia, non certo gli algoritmi
della corrente critica imperante:
la musica era l'unico collante
delle parole, non l'ideuzza stitica
di qualche mattacchione della critica.

Oggi invece è regina la teoria,
alfa ed omega di ogni malattia
che infetta il verso, canchero ghiottone
che distrugge ogni nostra sensazione
alla fonte, smorzandone il colore
210   e succhiandone via tutto l'ardore.

The Futurists have left us merely bored –
Dada – Mummy – whatever! They're all dead.
Guittone has already raised in rhyme
a lasting monument to wasted time,
and yet today we still find clever men
aspiring to the 'honoured list' of slain.

The avant-garde means merely those who seek
to hide their ignorance beneath the cloak
of what seems modern, and quite thoughtlessly
190   deal in vain novelties, and so get by,
and so prepare the ground for this and this
man who knows more and more of less and less.

The dwarf upon the shoulders of a giant
has turned presumptuous, even arrogant;
and now he'd like (who once was reverent)
to put the giant's nose quite out of joint;
the giant simply lets him plot and plan:
he knows a pigmy cannot bring him down.

Poetry followed once the rhythmic track
200   of harmony, and not the arithmetic
ordained by critics who are in the news;
and only music's power could join and fuse
our words, and not the constipated whim
of criticism and its last buffoon.

Today instead we're ruled by theory,
the root and branch of every malady
infecting verse, greedy and cancerous,
destroying every feeling that is ours
at the very root, making it lose its colour,
210   and sucking from it all its glow and ardour.

Basta dunque teoremi, basta ismi,
basta con cervellotici aforismi
che esprimono in astratto tutto e niente
e lasciano il lettore indifferente,
basta montaleggiare aridi e assorti,
e basta dare vita a versi morti.

La poesia non deve essere un lamento,
ma un inno alla bellezza, un monumento
virile a luci e ombre della vita:
220 deve cantare a festa l'infinita
famiglia tra l'inferno e il paradiso,
senza perdere il gusto del sorriso.

Finirà mai questo piagnucolio
intellettuale, il flebile pio pio
da pulcini impauriti, i singhiozzucci
di tutti i leopardini e i leoparducci
che posano a ginestre nel deserto
e sono invece fogne a cielo aperto?

Risuonerai mai più, grido sublime,
230 capace di percuotere le cime
più alte, di vibrare così forte
da svegliare le nostre lingue morte?
Sì, sono certo che ritornerai:
la fiamma antica non si è spenta mai.

Può restare per secoli assopita,
ma poi ritorna prepotente in vita
e divampa improvvisa in qualche cuore
ispirando un eroico furore:
se il cuore non è paglia, il fuoco dura
240 e illumina anche l'epoca futura.

So let's have done with theorems and with isms,
have done with those eccentric aphorisms
expressing in the abstract all and nothing,
leaving the reader in sheer boredom yawning,
have done with following Montale's lead,
and lending life to verses that are dead.

Poetry should not be a mere lament,
but a hymn to beauty, a strong monument
to life in all its glorious shade and light:
220   poetry ought to sing and celebrate
the whole creation – hell to paradise –
and still delight in smiling through all this.

Where is the end of intellectual weeping,
where is the end of all the feeble cheeping
of frightened chicks, the sobbing and the sighs
of those who would write Leopardi-wise,
posing as brooms in the desert, but really are
sewers and cesspools in the open air?

Will you resound once more, sublimest shout,
230   you who can reach up to the highest height,
you whose vibrations are so strong and deep
they can wake language from its deathly sleep?
Yes, I am certain you'll resound again:
the ancient flame has never yet died down.

That can, I know, flicker through centuries,
but then return to sudden life and blaze
out irresistibly, and so inspire
some fit though few hearts with heroic fire:
in hearts not made of straw that fire burns on
240   to light up all the ages still to come.

Fu senza dubbio questa fiamma viva
lo spirito guerriero che ruggiva
nel petto di quel grande che hai lasciato
morire come un figlio ripudiato
nel gelo dell'esilio, folle Italia,
che nutri la gramigna e non la dalia!

Mentre il grasso poetastro prosperava,
e rimirando l'ètra sospirava
un altro deh, innalzando la sua lagna
250   sulle tue magre costole di cagna,
lui trascinava stanco tra i Cimmeri
il suo muto travaglio di pensieri.

Quanti, anche oggi, sfiatano i polmoni
per soddisfare cuori da pavoni?
Non si va in cerca più di gloria vera,
ma si aspira a una fama passeggera:
si strizza l'occhio all'oggi, e del domani
fa comodo lavarsene le mani.

Le nostre pance sono troppo piene
260   e dappertutto cantano sirene
che attirano la nostra navicella
sugli scogli del pane e mortadella:
non c'è un Orfeo che col suo canto assordi
le lusinghe di questi mostri ingordi.

Quanto è facile perdersi oggigiorno
e imboccare una via senza ritorno!
Non abbiamo più tempo di pensare,
perché occorre produrre, lavorare,
fare quadrare i conti a fine mese
270   e innalzare altarini al dio borghese.

There is no doubt at all this living flame
became the warlike spirit that found a home
in his great breast whom when he was exiled
you left to die, a disinherited child,
whom you froze out, O foolish Italy,
growing not blooms, but weeds, in your nursery!

And while the portly poetaster thrived,
and looking to the highest heaven sighed
alas, venting those lamentations which
250   rise where he battens on your ribs, lean bitch,
that great man dragged through the Cimmerii
his silent thought in all its misery.

How many today must breathe out what's inside
to satisfy the peacock of their pride!
They do not look for glory worth the name,
aspiring to mere transitory fame:
today they smile and wink at, and they borrow
Pontius Pilate's handwashing for tomorrow.

Our paunches are already full, and more,
260   while Sirens everywhere attempt to lure
with their attractive singing our small boat
onto the rocks and shoals of bread and meat:
we have no singing Orpheus to allay
these greedy monsters and their flattery.

How easy nowadays to go off track
and take a road that leaves us no way back!
No longer have we time for taking thought
if we're to work and prosper as we ought,
square our accounts, as people say we should,
270   and raise a temple to the bourgeois god.

D'altronde, chi non guarda con orgoglio
la propria pianticina di erbavoglio
salire verso il cielo, chi si stanca
di governare il proprio conto in banca
come un pollo all'ingrasso, chi non gode
se un asino gli assegna dieci e lode?

Ma il problema non è tanto legato
all'avvento dell'intellettualato
di massa, quanto all'imborghesimento
280   del gusto, delle idee, del sentimento:
pochi nutrono nobili passioni
e ancora meno nobili ambizioni.

Chi passa tutto il tempo a zappicchiare
il suo orticello, potrà mai trovare
nascosto tra le zolle un gran tesoro?
È impossibile assurgere all'alloro
ingoiando ogni giorno avidamente
le scorie avvelenate del presente.

Tanto più che viviamo in un'età
290   sovrabbondante di volgarità,
un'età che si fonda sull'immagine,
che tesse e tesse sopra la voragine
del nulla fili di esili speranze
su cui l'uomo conduce folli danze.

Regna il brutto, l'effimero, il banale,
tutto è immerso in un caos universale:
non esistono più leggi o valori,
la morale è un gingillo da amatori,
e in mezzo al dilagante puttanesimo
300   la bellezza non vale più un centesimo.

Besides, who does not look with pride to see
his beanstalk growing taller every day
until it hits the sky? Who does not want
to go on feeding his own bank account
as geese are fattened? Whom does it not please
when asses give us ten on ten and praise?

The problem is not really bound up with
the advent of mass intellectual death
so much as with the vast *embourgeoisement*
of tastes, ideas, and feelings that goes on:
there are so few who nourish noble passions,
and even fewer nourish high ambitions.

Will he who only lives to hoe and weed
in his own cabbage patch lift up a sod
and find a treasure hidden in the earth?
One cannot well assume the laurel wreath
if all the time one swallows avidly
polluted scoria from the present day.

All the more as we're living in an age
when crass vulgarity is all the rage,
an age which takes the image as its base,
which goes on weaving over the abyss
of nothingness thin threads of thinner hope
on which we play the fool and hop and skip.

The ugly, ephemeral, and banal reign;
there is no doubt 'chaos is come again';
there are no values any more, no laws,
morality's a toy for connoisseurs,
and while such filthy whoredom spreads apace
true beauty is not worth a penny piece.

280

290

300

Il poeta, che un tempo era cantore
del bello, ora è sommerso dal rumore,
e se pure cantasse a squarciagola
non troverebbe più un'orecchia sola
in grado di ascoltarlo e di capire
ciò di cui parla e ciò che vuole dire.

Oggi i poeti innalzano peana
alla squadra di calcio brasiliana,
parlano di politica o di sesso,
310 o descrivono ciò che gli è successo
cinque minuti prima in un caffè
o hanno appena sentito al TG3.

Si fa a gara a chi versa più brodaglia,
a chi scende più in basso, a chi più raglia:
il pudore non serve da confine,
si attinge sempre più dalle latrine:
si cerca di stupire con l'osceno,
si scrive sempre più, si dice meno.

E in mezzo a tutta questa confusione,
320 la legge eterna dell'evoluzione
ha plasmato creature totalmente
adattate alle asprezze dell'ambiente:
questi quattro fratelli, bene o male,
troneggiano nel mondo intellettuale.

A partorirli, pare, fu l'Accidia
(secondo altri invece fu l'Invidia)
fecondata dal seme dell'Orgoglio,
e vennero svezzati a fiele e loglio.
Furono concepiti nella notte
330 nella profondità di oscure grotte.

The poet, a great singer when time was,
is overwhelmed these days by the mere noise,
and even if he sang out loud and clear
he would no longer find a single ear
able to hear him and to comprehend
what he was speaking of and what he meant.

The poets nowadays shout out hosannas
for the Brazilians (their team has the honours),
they talk of politics, they talk of sex,
310   or else they talk about what happened next
in some café a little time before
or what they've heard about on Channel 4.

There's rivalry in pouring out dishwater,
in who can get more low, who brays the louder;
since shame no longer serves to draw the line,
they draw their matter up from the latrine;
they try to stun us with lasciviousness,
and, as they write the more, they say the less.

Right in the middle of all this confusion
320   the everlasting law of evolution
has fashioned beings adapted totally
to the environment's asperity:
and these four brothers now, for good or ill,
dominate all that is intellectual.

They were all born, it seems to me, of Sloth
(though others think that Envy gave them birth),
with Pride no doubt the father of them all;
and they were weaned on tares and bitter gall;
and they were all conceived in pitch-black night
330   deep down in caverns with no hint of light.

Nacquero, si racconta, senza cuore
e genitali: verdi di livore
sin dalla culla, sfogano la rabbia
dell'impotenza come tigri in gabbia:
dove passano bruciano il terreno,
e se mordono iniettano veleno.

Il primo vive e vegeta a catena,
rumina libri, con la testa piena
di aforismi e di belle citazioni,
340   che rivomita in turgidi centoni,
dispensando giudizi a destra e a manca
come un santone dalla barba bianca.

Presi a dispetto i voti letterari,
ha la sua parrocchietta e aviti lari
da venerare con i confratelli,
a cui immola saggetti e trattatelli
nella speranza di un'apoteosi
tra tomi bibliografici gloriosi.

Il secondo trascorre la sua vita
350   procariote da vile parassita.
Travasa col suo imbuto la poesia
mutilandone il senso e l'armonia.
Sa di essere sconfitto già in partenza,
odia tradurre e non sa starne senza.

Sputa continuamente nel suo piatto
e sbuffa, eternamente insoddisfatto,
guardando la bellezza di lontano:
non riuscendo a toccarla con la mano,
si strugge in malinconici languori,
360   in haiku, pensierini e ghirigori.

They were born, people say, without a heart
or genitals; always livid with spite
even in the cradle; and they vent their rage
at impotence – a tiger in a cage;
the earth is scorched to a cinder where they pass;
and when they bite, their bite is poisonous.

The first one vegetates, kept on a lead,
and ruminates on volumes, with his head
full of divine quotations and wise saws
340   which turn to turgid matter which he spews,
dispensing judgements to the left and right.
(A bigot's surely wise whose beard is white?)

In all bad faith he's vowed himself to words.
He has his parish, and the household gods
whom he, with his few cronies, venerates,
to whom he offers essays and tractates
in hopes of future glory and high praise
in many-volumed bibliographies.

The second has unindividual life
350   and spends it as a worthless parasite.
Through his own funnel he pours poetry,
spoiling its sense and all its harmony;
he knows he's beaten at his setting out;
he loathes translation but can't do without.

He fouls his own nest all and every day,
and snorts, unsatisfied eternally,
looking at beauty only from afar:
not managing to touch it, or get near,
he is consumed in listless melancholy,
360   scribbling haikus, doodling – suchlike folly.

Il terzo è destinato a vagolare
in eterno tra terra, cielo e mare.
Si guarda sempre intorno, eppure è cieco,
grida la notte e il giorno, come l'eco.
Striscia a faleneggiare intorno a un lume:
striscia perché non ha gambe né piume.

Ruffiano, senza fede, sempre ingordo
di falsità e di denaro lordo
di sangue umano, agita la coda
370   e ti lecca, ti sbrodola e ti loda
per fame, ma alla minima occasione
può trafiggerti come uno scorpione.

Con la stessa pietà con cui il carnefice
stringe il nodo sul collo dell'artefice
di un assassinio, scrive un trafiletto
se muore una regina del balletto
o spreme una commossa colonnina
per una strage o un terremoto in Cina.

Il quarto invece fa da capoccetta,
380   dopo una lunga, umile gavetta,
nella melma accademica italiana,
dove il sapere va di rana in rana,
dove si studia e suda e si ricerca,
e dove Dante tutto dì si merca.

Un tempo valvassore, poi vassallo,
prima fantoccio a piedi, poi a cavallo,
alla morte del suo predecessore
fu incoronato e fatto professore.
Ora è barone e quindi sbaroneggia
390   come un tiranno dentro la sua reggia.

The third has wandering as his destiny –
wandering for ever between earth, sky, and sea.
He looks about, though he has lost his sight,
and shouts, as echo does, all day and night.
He crawls about a lamp in a mothlike way:
crawls since he has no legs and cannot fly.

A faithless go-between, chock-full of ardour
for lots of filthy lies and filthy lucre –
filthy with human blood – he wags his tail
370   and licks your hand, and praises in fine style
as hunger urges him, but when need is
he stings your heel, just as a scorpion does.

With the same pity as executioners
tighten the knot round necks of murderers,
he writes a little piece (one paragraph)
about a ballet dancer's 'tragic death',
or squeezes out sad inches all about a
Manchurian earthquake or some senseless slaughter.

The fourth's a bossman, working his way up
380   after a long and hard apprenticeship
in the Italian academic bog,
where knowledge travels on from frog to frog,
where people study, research, and sweat away,
where Dante's bought and sold the livelong day.

A vassal first, and then his lord's liegeman,
a pawn on foot, and then a mounted pawn;
when death arrived and claimed his predecessor
he was crowned in his place – a full professor.
A baron now, he barons all around,
390   a petty tyrant in a barren land.

E dietro a lui già fanno capolino
il prode paggio e il baldo valvassino,
che un giorno ahimè lontano lotteranno
fino alla morte per l'ambito scanno
da cui poter dettare norme e leggi
a sempre nuove e più mansuete greggi.

Questa è la scena che oggi si presenta
al povero nostalgico che tenta
di riscoprire il lume del buon senso
400   nel mondo odierno, avvolto in fumo denso,
questa è l'empia progenie umanimale
che abita il sottobosco culturale.

Stando così le cose, non sorprende
che oggi imperi la legge del 'chi vende'
e che ormai la poesia sia relegata
in un cantuccio oscuro, sbaragliata
da altri generi e obbrobri letterari
e da pastrocchi e polpettoni vari.

Questa è l'età di ferro del romanzo,
410   dei busillis lanciati da Costanzo,
dei flussi di incoscienza, di Henry Miller,
degli io, dei super-io, dei *serial killer*,
della pornografia innalzata ad arte,
di sproloqui alla James o alla Roland Barthes.

Non si pensa che ai numeri e alla vendita,
non si sogna che vivere di rendita
con i diritti: scrivere è un mestiere,
e a tutti piace fare il romanziere.
Il ludibrio dei posteri non conta
420   e il meritato oblio non è più un'onta.

Behind him are already to be seen
the valiant page and the bold hanger-on,
who will one day (one day long lusted for)
fight to the death for the alluring chair
from which to issue laws with their mere words
to always new and always tamer herds.

This scene is what presents itself today
to any poor nostalgic who might try
to bring to bear the light of common sense
400   on this day's world, blacked out in ignorance;
this is the iniquitous half-human brood
inhabiting our cultural underwood.

In these circs obviously the golden rule
always and everywhere is 'Will it sell?'
So poetry by now is relegated
to some dark corner, having been defeated
by every other wordy mess and botch
and literary jumble and hotchpotch.

We find the novel in this Iron Age:
410   nothing to brag about is all the rage –
streams of unconsciousness, and Henry Millers,
and egos, super-egos, serial killers,
pornography regarded as an art,
and ramblings à la James or Roland Barthes.

All everyone can think of is his returns,
all everyone can dream of is what he earns
with all his fees; writing's just one more trade:
being a novelist is rather good.
No fear of our descendants and their scorn;
420   no shame in well-deserved oblivion.

Io non ritengo che il romanzo sia
un genere inferiore alla poesia,
ma non credo nemmeno che, al contrario,
sia il più alto cimento letterario:
taccia perciò chi chiama l'estinzione
della poesia una giusta evoluzione.

La poesia fu la lingua originaria
di qualsiasi altra forma letteraria:
prima del gran diluvio universale
430   delle prose selvagge, era normale
rivestire una storia con il manto
dei versi, delle rime o del bel canto.

Senza tali ornamenti, anche il racconto
più sublime è ridotto a un resoconto
insipido di azioni e avvenimenti.
Spogliato della forma e degli accenti,
anche l'amore tra Romeo e Giulietta
diventa una banale favoletta.

Oggi conta la trama, o meglio il *plot*,
440   come dicono i figli di Nembrot
laggiù a Milano, i plausi tributati
da illustri recensori prezzolati
o l'alloro dei premi letterari,
da cui spuntano orecchie da somari.

Contano, come ho detto, sangue e sesso
e sesso e sangue, mescolati spesso
a qualche altro ingrediente da due soldi.
Quello che conta, per quei manigoldi
degli editori, è spingere la massa
450   come moschini attorno alla melassa.

The novel is not something that I find
a lesser thing than poetry in its kind;
yet neither have I ever once professed
that it's, as writing goes, the acid test:
let no one ever say the dissolution
of poetry is a natural evolution.

Poetry was the language at the dawn
of every other literary form:
and long before the universal flood
430   of barbarous prose, it was well understood
a story should be decked out in the dress
of verse and rhyme and every artifice.

Even a lofty story, full of point,
without such helps comes down to an account,
a mere account, a bare account, of deeds.
Without some shape and metre to the words
the fate 'of Juliet and her Romeo'
becomes a tale that simply is so-so.

It is mainly the plot that counts today,
440   or so the sons of Babel like to say
down in Milan, and all the wild applause
when mercenary reviewers clap their paws,
or laurel leaves of literary prizes
from which the ears that sprout look like an ass's.

What counts, as I have said, is sex and blood
and blood and sex, to which they sometimes add
some other very cheap ingredients.
For reprobates that publish all that counts
is something to attract 'the much-too-many'
450   to swarm like flies around a pot of honey.

Sì, sono loro i veri responsabili
delle mostruosità biodegradabili
furoreggianti in libreria o alle fiere.
Mercanti, in cuore, di patate o pere,
per qualche strano scherzo di natura,
si ritrovano a vendere 'cultura'.

Per loro il libro è un bene di consumo
da appioppare ad allocchi e mangiafumo,
perciò, abbassando il gusto dei lettori,
460   crescono i potenziali compratori:
ben venga dunque l'idiozia totale,
e ci sommerga il buio universale!

Ben vengano i B*** e i C***,
e la schiera degli altri romanzieri
che invece di buscarsi la pagnotta
in modo onesto sfornano una frotta
di efemeridi ad alta tiratura,
in copertina rigida e in brossura!

Ma ora torniamo al tema principale
470   del poema, e cioè il caos generale
che ha travolto gli stili, i gusti e l'arte
e, mettendo i prosipari da parte,
cerchiamo di affrontare con coraggio
la barbarie di generi e linguaggio.

L'arte è unica, è una, e non dipende
dalla forma specifica che prende.
Un dipinto, una statua o una poesia
possono sublimare in sinfonia:
l'arte autentica appaga tutti i sensi
480   e prescinde da critiche e consensi.

Yes, they're the ones who are responsible
for the uncouth, biodegradable
monstrosities in bookshops and book fairs.
Born traffickers in apples, spuds, and pears,
by some strange freak or joke of Mother Nature
they find themselves engaged in flogging 'culture'.

They see a book as what they're offering
to those who are glad to swallow anything;
and so, by lowering their readers' taste,
460   the number of their buyers is increased:
let foolishness be taken at the full,
and universal darkness bury all.

So welcome C*** and B***,
and other novelists their very echo,
who do not work to earn their bread and butter
by honest means, but have a mind to litter
our streets with gibberish and jibber-jabber,
with some in paperback, some in hard cover!

But now let's get back to our chief concern:
470   poems, and how 'chaos is come again'
upon the styles required, the taste, the art;
let's leave prose-breeders for a while apart,
and boldly make the attempt to take in hand
the barbarism of language and of kind.

All art – being one, unique – does not depend
on the specific form in which it's found.
A painting, piece of sculpture, poetry
may be sublimed into a symphony:
authentic art satisfies all the senses
480   and has no need of critics or consensus.

Mescolando le arti alla rinfusa
si ottiene una farragine confusa,
un ibrido deforme, falso, muto,
un pasticciaccio senza contenuto:
l'artista è solo un tramite d'azione,
l'arte si fa da sola, non si impone.

Ma in ogni era di decadentismo
impazza un insensato sincretismo:
e anche oggi si cerca solamente
490   di trascinare a forza ogni ingrediente
nel crogiolo dell'arte, non importa
per quale viuzza ripida o contorta.

Si parla molto di virtualità,
di arte totale e interattività,
di villaggi o discariche globali,
di esperienze o follie multimediali.
Poveri noi! La gente guarda al nome,
si lascia imbambolare e non sa come.

Due persone che saltano invasate
500   sopra un letto facendo a cuscinate
sono da galleria o da manicomio?
E merita una critica o un encomio
la tela impiastricciata di poesiole
su cui è affissa una falce e un girasole?

Tale degrado artistico è aggravato
dall'uso, anzi l'abuso incontrollato
di materiale sempre più composito.
Ad ogni istante spunta uno sproposito,
ad aumentare la vergogna eterna
510   esposta nei musei d'arte moderna.

Throwing the various artforms all together
gives a farrago that's not worth the bother,
a monstrous hybrid that is false and dumb,
all sheer perplexity without a theme:
the artist's but a road, a path, a way:
art cannot be imposed: it comes *per se*.

In times of decadence, like our own age,
a wild syncretism is all the rage;
and so today we see the one attempt
490   is to force who cares what ingredient
into art's crucible, without a care
whether the ways are narrow, steep, obscure.

There's talk of virtual reality,
of total art and interactivity,
of global villages and atmospherics,
of multimedia trials and hysterics.
Poor people! Names alone inspire them so
they are bewildered: why, they do not know.

Two madmen have a sort of pillow-fight,
500   leaping about a bed: is that a sight
made for a gallery, or a mental home?
And is this worth the least encomium:
a canvas where some doggerel is smeared
and which is all besickled and sunflowered?

This artistic decay only gets worse
with every effort that is made to press
such disparate materials into one.
At every instant a fresh blunder's born,
and every blunder lives to aggravate
510   the shame of galleries of modern art.

Tutto è esaltato ad arte, dal letame
in scatola alla fetta di salame.
Tutto va ad arricchire la poesia,
anche i fumetti o la fotografia.
Non c'è più distinzione, il niente è tutto
e tutto è niente: bello, scialbo o brutto.

Il problema sta a monte, è la mancanza
di basi, il vecchio mostro, l'ignoranza,
è la paura di sembrare 'vecchi',
520   che spinge a arrampicarsi sugli specchi
del nuovo senza usare nessun metro
e senza voler mai guardarsi indietro.

Stesso discorso vale per i generi:
ci si cosparge il capo con le ceneri
del 'tutto è stato fatto, detto e scritto',
e si proclama a ogni ora un nuovo editto
che autorizza i più astrusi esperimenti,
spacciati per mirabili portenti.

Ho letto di recente una poesia,
530   una sorta di audace allegoria
in forma meta-lirico-teatrale,
che degenera in farsa nel finale:
è scritta parte in prosa e parte in rima
e si chiama *Divina pantomima*.

Apre la scena un coro di vestali,
a cui risponde un coro di animali,
poi c'è un coro di forze, e infine il coro
delle anime perdute e di coloro
che vorrebbero vivere in eterno
540   ma sono esclusi anche dall'inferno.

Now anything is art – boxes of dung,
a slice of salami – I mean anything!
Anything helps to enrich our poetry –
comics even, even photography.
No more distinctions made! Nothing is all,
and all is nothing: lovely, ugly, pale.

The problem's basic – that there is no base,
only the same old monster, ignorance,
the dreadful fear of seeming out of date
520   which makes men try to prove that black is white,
'making it new' without a hint of metre,
and never looking back at what was better.

Of every art the selfsame thing is said:
men whine, while scattering ashes on the head,
'All has been said already, written, done';
and every day fresh edicts have their run
where wild experiments are authorised
and given out as portents in the skies.

I read a poem very recently,
530   a sort of wildly way-out allegory,
part lyrical and part theatrical,
and ending up in fact quite farcical:
written partly in prose, partly in rhyme,
called *The Divine* (believe it!) *Pantomime*.

A chorus of vestal virgins leads the way,
to which an animal chorus makes reply;
a chorus of abstract forces then; and last,
after the souls of all those who are lost,
those who would love to live *in aeternum*
540   but find that even Hell is barred to them.

Dai cori si diffonde una preghiera,
una specie di assorta tiritera,
per scongiurare la maledizione
scagliata contro il mondo da Plutone:
tutto viene descritto in uno stile
da cui zampilla un'ironia sottile.

La scena poi si sposta all'improvviso
presso la sommità del paradiso,
dove un coro di insetti e invertebrati,
550   insieme a un'ampia schiera di beati,
innalza un inno fallico in falsetto,
mentre gli angeli inscenano un balletto.

In questo gran cancan un pipistrello
va stridendo nell'aria uno stornello,
mentre in basso una vecchia tartaruga
legge, sopra due foglie di lattuga,
un cantico liturgico in latino,
per poi scolarsi un calice di vino.

La scena quindi cambia un'altra volta
560   e ci si trova in una landa incolta
dell'aldilà, dove un ragazzo imberbe
va strappando e succhiando certe erbe.
Una fata compare e gli domanda
perché si aggiri solo in quella landa.

Il giovane risponde che in sé sente
un impulso vitale travolgente
e di cercare quindi in quelle piante
l'oblio, o il sonno, o almeno un tranquillante.
Tutto è sempre descritto con un tono
570   di parodia e di ironico abbandono.

The choruses are praying all this while –
a self-absorbed and rambling rigmarole
intended to ward off the dreadful curse
that Pluto hurled against this world of ours;
and all is rendered in that sort of style
where subtle irony's discernible.

Then suddenly the scene shifts: in a trice
we're on the very peak of Paradise;
there insects and invertebrates are placed
550 together with the legions of the blest;
falsettos raise a phallic hymn of praise,
while angels put a ballet on the stage.

A bat, through all this dreadful racket, sings,
or rather shrieks and squeaks, some comic songs,
while down below an ancient tortoise reads,
out of what seem to be two lettuce leaves,
something in Latin from the liturgy,
then takes a glass of wine and drains it dry.

The scene thereafter changes once again,
560 to what is an uncultivated plain
of the beyond, where there's a beardless boy
plucking up herbs and sucking them away.
A fairy asks, having come upon the scene,
why he goes wandering through that barren plain.

The youth replies that he is overcome
by a vital impulse: it's too much for him;
he wants – and seeks some herb as the provider –
oblivion, sleep, at least a tranquilliser.
All's rendered in a tone of parody,
570 of wild abandonment to irony.

D'un tratto irrompe su un cavallo nero
una fanciulla dallo sguardo fiero,
dietro alla quale sfilano pazienti
orrende moltitudini di genti.
La fanciulla è una chiara incarnazione
della morte, a cui aspira ogni nazione.

Infine, nella scena conclusiva,
le genti si disperdono ed arriva
una razza più cinica e crudele
580   che edifica una torre di Babele,
cantando laudi alla modernità
e auspicando una nuova umanità.

Quando ormai è terminata anche la cima,
ritorna in scena il giovane di prima,
che guida gli altri al sommo della torre,
al di là delle nubi, per deporre
il tiranno dei cieli dal suo trono
e restituire il regno al vecchio Crono.

Dio, spodestato, scappa in modo buffo:
590   messo il paracadute, con un tuffo
si getta a capofitto nell'abisso,
ma viene preso al volo e crocifisso.
Gli uomini nuovi intanto, tutti in coro,
salutano la nuova età dell'oro.

Ma ora passiamo ad altre malebolge,
dove non solamente si stravolge
il genere o la forma, ma la stessa
essenza del linguaggio, dove è messa
alla berlina e in croce la parola
600   e dove la stoltezza regna sola.

Then suddenly there bursts upon the scene
a youth on a black horse, with a proud mien,
behind whom marches, patient on parade,
a sad innumerable multitude.
This youth is obviously an incarnation
of death, the aim and goal of every nation.

Then ultimately, the last scene of all,
another race, more harsh and cynical,
takes over from the sad and patient herd;
580   they come to Babel where a tower's to build,
singing the praises of modernity,
and prophesy a new humanity.

When this is finished and the roof is on,
we see the youth I mentioned first return,
to guide the others to the tower's top
above the clouds, in order to cast off
the tyrant of high heaven from his throne
and to restore old Chronos to his reign.

God, having been dethroned, escapes alive
590   at first, in a strange way: He takes a dive,
and parachutes headlong in the abyss,
where He is caught and crucified, of course.
And all the chorus of new men, meanwhile,
salute the coming Age of Gold in style.

Let's pass to other pits of ill report,
where men not only wrench, distort, contort
the kinds and forms, but shatter at its core
language itself; where every word is sure
of being crucified and put to scorn,
600   and where stupidity is king alone.

Là si aggirano turbe balbettanti
di poeti, poetastri e dilettanti
che di continuo vomitano corpi
straziati di parole e verbi storpi,
frasi già fatte, prestiti alla moda
e neologismi senza capo o coda.

Intorno a loro giacciono confusi
hapax geniali, simili a refusi,
e buttati qua e là in fosse comuni
610 cadaveri esumati da volumi
della Crusca si mischiano ad aborti
gergali e altri idiotismi nati morti.

Là striscia una stentata forzatura,
là cola una vistosa sbavatura,
là scoppiano deliri di impotenza,
là si libra un'illecita licenza.
Ah, lingua mia, che cosa ti hanno fatto?
Non c'è proprio più scampo? È scacco matto?

Il linguaggio, da mezzo di espressione,
620 va degradando in comunicazione.
L'anelito all'estetica si è spento
e il contenuto ha preso il sopravvento.
E il senso senza forma fugge via:
il senso è muto senza l'armonia.

Questo secolo scende nella tomba
avvolto in un silenzio che rimbomba.
Intorno a noi fluisce, si diffonde,
lungo cavi sinuosi e radioonde,
una torma di dati e di segnali
630 che va crescendo a ritmi esponenziali.

There is a Pit of Discord worse than Dante's,
where poets, poetasters, dilettantes
wander continually and vomit words
that have been torn and tortured into shreds,
set phrases, borrowings in the modern style,
neologisms without head or tail.

Hapax legomena, most like misprints,
lie heaped around them, smart but very dense,
and, thrown down here and there into a ditch,
610   bodies of academic phrases which
lie mixed with slangy abortions, all long gone,
and other idiocies which were stillborn.

There crawls some wretched forced and laboured thing,
there drools some showy dribbling slavering,
there bursts out such ecstatic emptiness,
there hover unacceptable licences.
And, O my language, is there no escape?
What have they done to you? Is this checkmate?

Language, from being a matter of expression,
620   declines to nothing but communication.
The study of aesthetics is in tatters:
the content now is all that really matters.
And without form sense simply seeps away:
the sense is silent without harmony.

This century descends into the tomb
wrapped up in silence like a dull dull boom.
Around us flows, and spreads itself, and heaves
a mass of sinuous cables, radio waves,
a swarm of data and signals rhythmically
630   seething and growing exponentially.

La massa di parole aumenta, aumenta,
ed arginarne l'impeto diventa
un'impresa impossibile, già persa.
La lingua vera soffoca, sommersa
dal profluvio di lingue artificiali
di TV, radio, cinema e giornali.

Questo frastuono non ci dà respiro:
siamo continuamente sotto tiro.
E ora c'è anche l'*Internet*, che dona
640   un pulpito virtuale a ogni persona,
offrendo a cani e porci l'occasione
di inquinarci con altra informazione.

Troppe sono le voci, troppi i galli
che aprono a vuoto i loro becchi gialli
perché si faccia veramente giorno.
Nessuno riesce più a orientarsi intorno,
ogni guida ci addita la sua via:
così il sapere sfuma in diceria.

E il linguaggio, riusato e riciclato,
650   diventa sempre più indeterminato,
non riesce a colpire, ad evocare,
come vino che a forza di annacquare
perde gusto e colore al punto tale
che si trasforma in acqua minerale.

Eppure è così semplice obbedire
al buon senso e all'orecchio, riscoprire
la forza pura della lingua viva,
invece di seguire la deriva
del linguaggio volgare o, peggio ancora,
660   martoriare la lingua che ci onora.

si ciba di ombre e fantasie
riverà solo fumo e non poesie:
poesia non è frutto di catarsi
ascesi, ma deve rinfrescarsi
ontinuo nelle acque del reale,
perdersi in un mondo intellettuale.

che pro perdo tempo e spreco il fiato?
rto non è a me che fu assegnato
imere i mali del presente.
rerà una voce più potente
risorga la morta poesia
se del *sì* e del *mamma mia*.

! Se la lunga carestia
a spinto a abiurare la poesia,
hanno cacciato dalla vetta
na e rimpiazzato in fretta
he altra ninfetta più lasciva,
a una nobile invettiva!

lungo e in largo lo Stivale,
ni poetico animale
na tra la spazzatura
risei della cultura,
tà a un Savonarola
un gran falò della parola.

e questo tempo indegno
rado di lasciare un segno
insulsi e false rime
o fare da concime:
del secolo ventesimo
i un nuovo umanesimo.

The mass of words just goes on swelling, swelling;
and to dam up its impetus is calling
for powers beyond our power. Our mother tongue
is always overwhelmed and foundering
in the flood of artificial languages
from papers, cinemas, TV, radios.

This hullabaloo hardly lets us respire,
like soldiers who are always under fire.
And now there is the Internet: this is
640   a pulpit for what anybody says,
which gives pig ignorants their best occasion
to foul our wells with extra information.

Too many voices – like too many cooks
spoiling the broth, or like too many beaks
crowing out orders – for the day to break.
One cannot even see what road to take,
there are so many guides to show the way:
knowledge fades into gossip and hearsay.

And language used again and yet again
650   becomes more and more vague as we go on;
it does not hit the spot, does not evoke,
as wine when watered is not merely weak
but flavourless, and really is no better,
having lost its colour too, than mineral water.

And yet it is not really hard to hear
the sound and sense of words; the careful ear
catches the purity of the living tongue,
instead of drifting carelessly along
with trashy kinds of talk, or, what is worse,
660   racking the language that should honour us.

Per lingua viva intendo le strutture
più profonde, le lievi sfumature
che elevano la parola dal suo rango
ordinario, strappandola dal fango
della trivialità, dandole un manto
di nobiltà che può innalzarla al canto.

Quanti invece riversano di peso
nei loro scritti il chiacchiericcio preso
dai discorsi banali di ogni giorno,
670   credendo che un linguaggio disadorno,
crudo, sciatto, realistico e corsivo
sia in qualche modo significativo?

Quanti stendono i loro panni neri
come qualcosa di cui andare fieri?
Quanti sfoggiano eloqui traboccanti
di improperi, bestemmie e ammazzasanti?
Ah, chi ha il coraggio di chiamare arte
le oscenità di questi imbrattacarte?

Non dico che bisogna idolatrare
680   il verbo come il prete sull'altare,
ma nemmeno trattarlo con disprezzo.
Cercando di seguire il giusto mezzo,
rifuggendo bassezze e puzze al naso,
si avrà una lingua degna del Parnaso.

E il poeta deve essere ruspante,
non trincerarsi in una delle tante
torri d'avorio estetiche settarie
soggiogate alle mode letterarie:
deve calarsi a pieno nell'agone
690   della vita, e lì trarre ispirazione.

By 'living tongue' I mean
structures, the shades o
to raise beyond itself th
pulling it by its boot s
of triviality, giving it
which it may welcon

And yet how many
into their writing
they hear in conv
670   believing langu
realistic, rough
must be signif

How many h
as it were so
How many
chock-full
But who (
public d(

Not th;
680   as tho
but n
Tryi
avo
we

T

690

C
sc
la
o (
di (
non

Ma a
Di ce
di re(
700   Occor
Perch(
nel pa(

O Muse
non vi h
se non v
dell'Elic(
con qual(
date voce

Correte in
710   scovate og
che si rinta
dei templi f
date la pote(
che accenda

Possa brucia(
che non è in g
e che versacci
possano almer
720   che il tramont(
annunci l'alba (

Who feeds his heart on shades and fantasy
will write on smoke and vapour: poetry
is not what comes from mere purification,
or even from divine intoxication:
it needs reality to make it real,
not merely what seems intellectual.

But why waste breath, and why waste all this time?
For it is not my mission to redeem
the present day and all that's wrong with it.
700 We need a voice more powerful than that
for exiled poetry to reappear
in the sweet land of *sì* and *mamma mia*.

O Muses! If protracted scarcity
has not forced you to abjure all poetry,
if you have not been driven from the peak
of Helicon in favour of a pack
of loud lascivious nymphs, then clear your throats
for strong expostulation and grim taunts!

Course up and down the whole Peninsula;
710 flush out each beast of poetry from its lair,
hiding among the sweepings of a street
where Pharisees of culture hold their court;
bring Savonarola back and give him power
to heap their words upon one great bonfire.

May this unworthy age be smashed and burned
till hardly a trace of it is left behind;
its last stupidities thrown on a midden –
dung upon some cosmic market garden;
our twentieth century, as its sun goes down,
720 announce new humanism, a new dawn.

The mass of words just goes on swelling, swelling;
and to dam up its impetus is calling
for powers beyond our power. Our mother tongue
is always overwhelmed and foundering
in the flood of artificial languages
from papers, cinemas, TV, radios.

This hullabaloo hardly lets us respire,
like soldiers who are always under fire.
And now there is the Internet: this is
640   a pulpit for what anybody says,
which gives pig ignorants their best occasion
to foul our wells with extra information.

Too many voices – like too many cooks
spoiling the broth, or like too many beaks
crowing out orders – for the day to break.
One cannot even see what road to take,
there are so many guides to show the way:
knowledge fades into gossip and hearsay.

And language used again and yet again
650   becomes more and more vague as we go on;
it does not hit the spot, does not evoke,
as wine when watered is not merely weak
but flavourless, and really is no better,
having lost its colour too, than mineral water.

And yet it is not really hard to hear
the sound and sense of words; the careful ear
catches the purity of the living tongue,
instead of drifting carelessly along
with trashy kinds of talk, or, what is worse,
660   racking the language that should honour us.

Per lingua viva intendo le strutture
più profonde, le lievi sfumature
che elevano la parola dal suo rango
ordinario, strappandola dal fango
della trivialità, dandole un manto
di nobiltà che può innalzarla al canto.

Quanti invece riversano di peso
nei loro scritti il chiacchiericcio preso
dai discorsi banali di ogni giorno,
670   credendo che un linguaggio disadorno,
crudo, sciatto, realistico e corsivo
sia in qualche modo significativo?

Quanti stendono i loro panni neri
come qualcosa di cui andare fieri?
Quanti sfoggiano eloqui traboccanti
di improperi, bestemmie e ammazzasanti?
Ah, chi ha il coraggio di chiamare arte
le oscenità di questi imbrattacarte?

Non dico che bisogna idolatrare
680   il verbo come il prete sull'altare,
ma nemmeno trattarlo con disprezzo.
Cercando di seguire il giusto mezzo,
rifuggendo bassezze e puzze al naso,
si avrà una lingua degna del Parnaso.

E il poeta deve essere ruspante,
non trincerarsi in una delle tante
torri d'avorio estetiche settarie
soggiogate alle mode letterarie:
deve calarsi a pieno nell'agone
690   della vita, e lì trarre ispirazione.

By 'living tongue' I mean the more profound
structures, the shades of meaning we can find
to raise beyond itself the living word,
pulling it by its boot straps from the mud
of triviality, giving it clothes
which it may welcome as its singing robes.

And yet how many pour out helter-skelter
into their writings all the banal chatter
they hear in conversations every day,
670 believing language that is slovenly,
realistic, rough, completely unadorned,
must be significant and more profound!

How many hang their dirty washing out
as it were something to be proud about!
How many like to flaunt an oratory
chock-full of insults and foul blasphemy!
But who can give the name of art to these
public debauches and obscenities?

Not that we ought to reverence the *word*
680 as though it were the very Word of God;
but neither should we treat the *word* with scorn.
Trying to find the happy medium,
avoiding filth and snotty, snobby poses,
we find a language worthy of the Muses.

The poet ought to know his way about,
and not take refuge from the fuss and fret
of life in any ivory tower of those
raised by some current literary craze:
but let himself go down in the abyss
690 and draw his inspiration out of this.

Chi si ciba di ombre e fantasie
scriverà solo fumo e non poesie:
la poesia non è frutto di catarsi
o di ascesi, ma deve rinfrescarsi
di continuo nelle acque del reale,
non perdersi in un mondo intellettuale.

Ma a che pro perdo tempo e spreco il fiato?
Di certo non è a me che fu assegnato
di redimere i mali del presente.
700 Occorrerà una voce più potente
perché risorga la morta poesia
nel paese del *sì* e del *mamma mia*.

O Muse! Se la lunga carestia
non vi ha spinto a abiurare la poesia,
se non vi hanno cacciato dalla vetta
dell'Elicona e rimpiazzato in fretta
con qualche altra ninfetta più lasciva,
date voce a una nobile invettiva!

Correte in lungo e in largo lo Stivale,
710 scovate ogni poetico animale
che si rintana tra la spazzatura
dei templi farisei della cultura,
date la potestà a un Savonarola
che accenda un gran falò della parola.

Possa bruciare questo tempo indegno
che non è in grado di lasciare un segno
e che versacci insulsi e false rime
possano almeno fare da concime:
che il tramonto del secolo ventesimo
720 annunci l'alba di un nuovo umanesimo.

About the Author

Bernie Crosthwaite has written plays for radio and theatre and won awards for her short stories. Her crime writing has been shortlisted for the Crime Writers' Association New Writing Awards and for the Sunday Times Crime Story Competition. She has been a journalist, teacher and tour guide, and currently works with children with special needs. She lives in North Yorkshire.

Thanks to Ruth Bowes, Marcus Corazzi, Jim Dolan, Penny Dolan, Douglas Hill, Simon Hulme, Neville Hutchings, Mike Jones, Alfie McKay and Ian Ward.

For James Joseph Woods

Prologue

Footsteps clattered along the high metal walkway. They echoed around the vast cavern of the press hall, a space packed with machinery, capable of producing thousands of copies of the Ravenbridge Evening Post six days a week, not to mention the weekly free newspaper and all types of private contracts – the presses were hardly ever still. But this was Saturday night, and for once the huge reels of paper had stopped turning. There was no night shift on Saturdays. Everything was silent but for the clang of heavy-soled boots on iron.

Despite the cold I was basted with sweat. My bra felt like a band of steel crushing my ribs at each painful intake of breath. An ancient Nikon camera, as heavy as a bag of stones, bumped painfully against my hip as I ran.

There's nothing to fear but… nothing to fear but… The words kept turning in my head like a mantra. Blood pounded in my ears. My jeans were sticking to me like clingfilm. *Nothing but…* Nothing but what? Who said it, anyway? Some American president. Eisenhower? Kennedy? No, not them. Roosevelt. Of course. The one who'd had polio. The one they were only allowed to film from the waist up to hide his withered legs.

The only thing we have to fear is fear itself. That was it. I muttered it again and again and felt calmer. My headlong rush slowed to a trot. The clanging footsteps slackened too. With a rush of relief I realised they were made by my own boots, the sound amplified and distorted by the echo chamber of the press hall.

Nothing to fear. Just fear itself.

A draught of air breezed through the cavernous space, chilling my neck. The door from the plate-making room closed softly. Someone leaving? I held my breath, listening for every sound, but my ears detected nothing.

A second later came a clattering noise as someone stumbled in the dark. I swore under my breath, and the curse was eerily echoed aloud by my invisible pursuer. Clearly I wasn't the only one who didn't know their way around this unfamiliar territory.

I expected the racket of shoes on metal, as noisy as mine had been, but there was silence once more. My follower was standing still, waiting until they got their bearings in the profound gloom. Or so I thought. After a few seconds I sensed a vibration running along the metal floor and passing through my body.

It was easy to run noiselessly. It was simply a matter of removing your shoes.

Two could play at that game.

I bent down to unzip my boots and shoved them aside. In bare feet I pattered quietly along the upper walkway that encircled the press hall. It was almost pitch dark. Below me the presses were shadowy sleeping giants. I reached the end wall and took the narrow metal staircase to the lower level, the rail cold under my slippery hands.

Down here the blackness was as thick and tangible as velvet. I twirled round, disorientated. Then I caught a faint glow from Stan's control room. That was where I would find what I was looking for.

A crash, a stumble and a loud expletive from somewhere above me. I cheered mentally that my boots had played their own small part.

As my eyes adjusted I could see the low square arches

made by the legs of the conveyor belt that carried the river of newsprint around the works. The floor was littered with open tubs of ink and sticky with oil. Dipping under the arches, testing every step before moving on, at last I came to an open aisle, flanked by machinery on both sides. I broke into a run.

There was a thud in front of me, then another. I stumbled and fell headlong. Crawling on my knees, I felt around blindly. I could smell them – sodden with snow and sweat – before I touched them. I had fallen over my own boots, tossed contemptuously from the walkway above.

The only thing we have to fear is… nothing to fear but… I tried to chant it but breathing had become too complicated. Who was I trying to kid? A person who had killed before wouldn't hesitate to do it again. I was certain of it.

Old FDR was right. Fear made your imagination go haywire, scrambled your thought processes, made you lose control.

I mustn't lose control.

I moved forward into the gloom. The glow of Stan's glass booth was fifty metres away, forty, thirty…

"Come out!"

The cry boomed from somewhere above me. It bounced from wall to wall. The silence that followed was ear-splitting.

I sank back into the maze of machinery.

"I know you're down there."

A wheel of white paper loomed up like an iceberg. It was bounded by a mesh cage on three sides, but there was a pocket of space between paper and wire. I squatted down, my back wedged against the roll of paper, and became foetal, arms tight around my knees.

Although I could hear nothing I felt a disturbance in the

air as someone passed by. My head dropped with exhaustion but not the kind that leads to sleep. My nerve endings were wired to detect danger and humming like tuning forks. In any case, it was bloody uncomfortable – something with sharp edges was digging into my side.

"I'm going to find you."

The voice was much closer now.

"Can't you see there's no point in this?" The voice was distorted by anger, almost unrecognisable.

"We have to talk!"

Too late for that, I mouthed silently.

When I did talk it would be front-page stuff, headline news. I was a photographer, not a reporter, but I'd tracked this story down like the keenest tabloid hack, and in the process I'd risked everything. The presses I was surrounded by would roll out every sordid detail. My boss, the editor of the Evening Post, would demand an exclusive, but this story was too big for a provincial paper alone. Within an hour nationwide TV and radio would include it in their bulletins. The national dailies wouldn't be far behind. The headlines would shriek *Press snapper Jude Baxendale in Printworks Horror.* A picture of me, exhausted and traumatised, would flash on the collective retina of the nation.

Of course I had to get out of here alive first.

No problem.

I began to giggle hysterically then slapped a hand over my mouth. Don't lose control, remember?

The pressure at my side was becoming painful. It was my camera. I eased it forward. My faithful old Nikon. Not the neat digital model I used for work, but a 1978 Nikon F, a cumbersome black box with manual focus. Great for high-definition stuff and distance shots, especially for the kind of pictures I took when I wasn't at work, just for myself. I never went anywhere without it, even though it weighed a ton.

I traced the familiar buttons with my fingers. I probably wouldn't be in such deep shit if it wasn't for this thing. A few days ago I had been in the dark about the whole business. I had been blind and stupid. But truth, like a photographic image, had taken time to develop. Even now the picture was murky, the details lacked sharpness, but I knew enough. If I reached the exit before it was too late, I would tell the world about it.

If I didn't, no one would ever know.

One

That morning, the day it began, I was woken by the cold, on the verge of losing my nose to frostbite. I pulled the duvet up to my eyebrows and lay listening to the tap with the loose washer dripping into the bath. Then the central heating spluttered into life and began its daily struggle to heat my draughty Victorian semi.

I ought to get up, I told myself. I was on early shift, which meant I had to be there by eight. As chief photographer of the Ravenbridge Evening Post I should be setting a good example to my team on our first day back after the New Year break. There had been no paper yesterday, and the edition for today, Tuesday January 2nd, was pretty much sorted, so we only had four more editions to pump out this week. The trouble was, there was never much news at this time of year, so it was going to be a struggle to cobble together a decent paper each day. Which meant more work for my department because pictures take up more space. But they weren't all processed yet. In fact I knew there was a large backlog to catch up on. I groaned and rolled over.

As I lay there I reflected that, on the whole, despite a crap boss, long hours and constant pressure, I really liked my job. It was getting up I hated most, the thought of padding across the chilly floor, groping for the staircase, staggering into the cold kitchen to be greeted by the sight of last night's dishes piled in the sink.

Nothing for it. I fumbled for the dressing gown that I took to bed with me in winter. A little trick I'd learnt.

It was at least one degree warmer than if I'd left it exposed to the night air. I wriggled into it and tied the belt quickly to trap any residual warmth, then stepped into a pair of scruffy sheepskin slippers.

Standing bleary-eyed on the landing, scratching my head through its spiky crop to wake myself up, I could see that Daniel had left his lamp on all night. I crept into his room. The dim light made the pictures on his wall flicker and dance. Like the room of any typical eighteen-year-old male, there was lots of female flesh on show. But these weren't posters of movie stars or pop princesses. The pictures were Daniel's own work, mainly nudes, done in charcoal, pastels, oils. The best ones were of a girl called Lara, a wisp of a figure with a cloud of reddish-golden hair. She worked as an estate agent during the day, and occasionally as an artists' model at night. Daniel had been drawing her for months, then a few weeks ago they started going out together. She was twenty, an older woman. My Mrs Robinson, Daniel called her.

Even in the gloom the pictures of Lara had a luminous quality. One in particular stood out, a new one I hadn't seen before, that glowed as if lit by some inner light. Daniel had used oils to capture the pale pearly skin and hair like fine twists of copper wire. There was a lot of green and blue in the skin tones – that accounted for the unearthly glow. I touched the picture gently. The paint was still wet.

It was serious, then. Daniel had had girlfriends before, had even drawn or painted them, but I'd never seen anything of this intensity. The picture shimmered with something more than mere technique. I felt a little stab, the way mothers do when their children take yet another step into adulthood. It quickly evaporated. I wanted him to be happy, that was all that mattered.

Anyway, it might not last. In my experience, the relationships you had at his age were as transitory as snow. Then I remembered overhearing the pair of them on Christmas Eve, wrapping presents and giggling and talking about the future. Lara was thinking about giving up being an estate agent. After doing the job for three years she was bored. Maybe she could move in with Daniel when he went away to art college in September? I hadn't taken the idea seriously then; now it seemed I should. I wiped the sticky oil paint on my dressing gown. I just hoped Lara didn't break his heart.

Leaning down to switch off the lamp I saw there was a smudge of green across Daniel's cheek. I gently removed the glasses that were perched crookedly across his temples, aware that I wouldn't have him around much longer. My son the artist, my son the genius, my son the next big thing. Not that I was biased or anything.

He coughed. Was that a wheeze at the end of it?

My son the asthmatic.

I shook him roughly awake.

"Do you need your inhaler?"

"What? What time is it?"

"You were coughing and wheezing."

He stared at his clock. "Five past seven? For god's sake, Mum. I don't go back to school till tomorrow."

"Where's your inhaler?"

"I'm fine. Bog off."

He disappeared under the quilt.

"Right," I said. "I'll do that."

The path was so icy with frost I was glad of my thick-soled boots. The three steps down to the gate were even more treacherous. I nearly went down on my backside a couple of times. I was dragging the gate shut when I heard shouting. I glanced up at the house that was the Siamese twin of my own, the grey-gold stone slightly forbidding when not mellowed by sun. The light was on in the front bedroom, and I could clearly hear raised voices, one deep and angry, the other high and defensive. My heart sank. Rob and Denise were a lovely young couple but they'd been having a rough time lately, ever since Rob's accident, and the slanging matches were becoming more frequent and intense. I hoped they could hold it together – they were friends as well as neighbours, and I worried what would happen to their little girl Hayley if her parents split up.

I got in the car and flung my camera bag on to the back seat of my beloved red Triumph Herald. Daniel had customised it for me as a birthday surprise by painting a shark's mouth with razor-sharp teeth all over the bonnet and sides. When I switched on the ignition the engine wouldn't start. Yet again. Despite Daniel's wonderful artwork, on cold mornings like this, when it hawked and spluttered but wouldn't move, I cursed the car with a passion.

The best thing to do was to get out and give it a few kicks. I was just about to slide back behind the steering wheel when I caught sight of Hayley running out of her gate. She shot across the road, heedless of traffic, her short legs cutting the air like scissors. She turned on to Weavers' Field, a sloping patch of land too scruffy to be called a park, where owners walked their dogs and boys played football. It led down to the River Raven, at a point just past one of the weirs, where the water was often high and full, especially after heavy rain, racing over jagged rocks to create treacherous whirlpools.

"Hayley! Wait!"

I sprinted after her. She was running frantically round the frosty grass.

I caught her by the arm. "Hayley! What's wrong?" She looked pinched and drawn, as if she hadn't slept well.

"It's my ferret! It's escaped!"

"From that big cage? How did that happen?"

"There was a hole in the wire mesh." She pulled away, nearly in tears. "There, look!"

She pointed at a flash of silky gold and brown fur undulating through a mulch of leaves. It took a drunken zigzag path, almost impossible to track, then disappeared.

"Where's the damn thing gone?" I muttered.

"It's climbing that tree!"

"Ferrets don't climb trees, Hayley."

"This one does. Dad says it's been crossed with a polecat."

"Great."

We peered up into the bare branches.

"There he is," whispered Hayley. The ferret was clinging to the top of the trunk, its short legs spread out so that it looked like a skinned pelt hung up to dry. "You'll have to climb up and get it." She looked at me with wide trusting eyes.

"I suppose I will," I said, like someone hypnotised.

I dropped my leather jacket on the ground. Gripping the tree with both hands, I began to climb, aware that Hayley was watching my every move. Luckily the trunk was gnarled and knotty, providing plenty of footholds, and the branches were close enough together for me to haul myself from one to another. As I inched upwards I knew no one was going to give me any marks for speed or grace, but once I'd started, nothing was going to stop me retrieving the pesky thing, whatever it cost. I was a metre or so away from the creature when I felt the front of my white shirt snag and heard it rip. The cost of a new shirt for one thing.

My heart was hammering by the time I came level with the rigid ferret. Extending my left arm I reached out to grab it. But I was a touch slow. It gave a sudden twist and sank its needle teeth into my hand.

"Bugger!"

The next time I was lightning-fast and got a grip on its neck. It dangled from my outstretched left arm, turning its lithe body and baring its tiny fangs. Now what?

"You got it?"

"Yes, Hayley, I've got it."

"Come down then."

"Give me a chance."

I was tempted to drop the ferret into Hayley's waiting arms – but what if I missed or she dropped it and it ran away and the whole thing started over again? There was no alternative but to climb down one-handed. A few more rips, a scraped chin, arms and legs twanging with the unaccustomed exercise, and I was down. Hayley took the animal from me, plunging her face into its rank fur.

"I thought I'd lost him forever," came her muffled voice.

"Let's get you both back home."

I picked up my jacket, noticing that beads of blood were seeping from the bite on my hand. Holding Hayley lightly by the shoulders, I guided her across the busy road. She trotted through her gate, the ferret limp and docile in her arms.

I glanced at my watch. "Dammit." No time to change my shirt. I was going to hit the worst of the rush-hour congestion as it was. I jumped into the Triumph Herald. At the first turn of the key the engine coughed into life, proving my theory that most machines like a good kicking every now and then.

I screeched down Weaver Street. By the time I had forced my way into the near-solid stream of traffic on the main road I was already half an hour late and counting.

The buildings that made up the outer reaches of Ravenbridge looked as if they'd been flung against the hills, and the lucky ones had stuck. They rose in tiers on both sides of the River Raven, old and new, stone and brick, mixed together to create an untidy chaotic jumble, which was one of the things I loved about the place.

As I crawled towards the traffic lights on East Bridge, I could see up ahead the ruins of the fourteenth-century castle and the tangle of medieval streets that led up to it. The lights changed and I shot across the bridge before they flicked back to red. I turned left into the wide Georgian market square, then took the right fork at the war memorial. Paper and linen mills had made Ravenbridge rich in Victorian times, and the grand ebullient architecture here on Queen Street – the town hall, the central library, the Hutchinson Art Gallery, and the shops with their ironwork canopies – were evidence of this past wealth. There were only a couple of working mills left now, and Ravenbridge had gone through some hard times before its current revival. These days new office blocks and housing estates and shopping centres seemed to be going up all over the place.

There was gridlock at the roundabout at the end of Queen Street. I tapped my steering wheel impatiently. This was the downside of the town that planning forgot – it was hell during the rush hour. My Triumph juddered at the edge of the roundabout, like a dog straining on a leash.

At last a small gap opened up and together we shot forward, swinging round in a wide arc and exiting on to Millhouse Lane, a straight stretch of comparatively fast-moving traffic. Nearly there. Just after nine o'clock. Not bad, only an hour late.

The Ravenbridge Evening Post had its offices in an ornate redbrick building. It was linked to the noisy print-works next door by a glassed-in walkway at first floor level. I drove under this glass bridge to the car park. Hurrying to the staff entrance, I swiped my key card to get in; then, unzipping my leather jacket as I went, I took the stairs two at a time to the second floor.

I burst through the swing doors into the newsroom where a battery of computer screens blinked and hummed. About a dozen reporters were slumped in their swivel chairs, most of them looking wrecked. They'd obviously had a better holiday than me. On New Year's Eve I rented a video and ate a whole drum of popcorn on my own, and I spent New Year's day working. The only chemical stimulants I'd seen had been in dishes in my basement darkroom. It wasn't that I didn't have friends. But I'd found out about my partner's infidelity at one raucous New Year's Eve party and I'd turned my back on that particular celebration ever since.

There were a few muttered greetings, one or two meaningful looks at the clock, nothing I couldn't handle.

The venetian blinds of the editor's office snapped open as I approached. Tony Quinnell glared through the slats at me. He came to his door.

"Nice way to start the New Year, Jude." He spoke in a grainy London accent, deepened and roughened by nicotine.

"Sorry, Tony. Had to climb a tree and rescue a ferret."

He noted my bloody chin, then his eyes flickered down to my torn shirt, lingering there for a moment. I guessed my bra was showing. I tugged my jacket closed.

"Staff meeting. Conference room. Fifteen minutes." He backed into his office and closed the door. The blinds snapped shut.

At the far end of the newsroom was the photographic department, essentially one cramped windowless space with rows of computers and scanners on clinical white benches, and walls dotted with enlargements of our work.

Raymond, our sports photographer, swivelled his chair to face me. "Happy New Year, Judith."

There was no point telling Raymond not to call me Judith. There was no point telling Raymond anything.

"Thanks."

"Did you, by any chance, see the latest test match down under?"

"Sadly I didn't catch that one, Ray," I replied, getting my retaliation in. He hated his shortened name even more than I hated my full one.

"England had to get 256. They were on 253 for nine, took four off the last ball of the over and beat Australia with an unbroken last-wicket partnership of 45."

"Fascinating."

"Victory snatched from the jaws of defeat." He pursed his lips and shook his head, making his jowls wobble. "You missed a tremendous sporting occasion."

The bags under his eyes looked even heavier than usual. It always amused me that sports snappers were usually the most overweight, wheezy and downright unfit members of the team, and Raymond was no exception. His pictures were notorious for being blurred (*an action shot*, he would explain). Quite often there was no sign of the ball (*it's a close-up, what do you expect?),* or the heads would be missing (*sport happens from the neck down, dear girl).*

I blew him a kiss. "I'll try and get over it." I dumped my bag on the workbench. I took out a carton of milk and put it in the fridge, the same one that had contained boxes of film in the old pre-digital days. Then I put my Nikon F camera in the stationery cupboard. I always brought it to work for the occasional job that needed a really high-definition picture, but it was too heavy to lug around everywhere in my workbag.

In the chair next to mine sat a long thin under-nourished figure. He was staring at his screen through a curtain of dead-straight mousy hair, cut shorter on one side than the other, and absently fiddling with a star-shaped pendant on a leather thong around his neck.

"Morning, Harrison."

He turned slowly and grunted, "You're late."

"Perhaps I'm on second shift, and am, in fact, incredibly early."

Harrison glanced at the rota on the wall and muttered something in a Neanderthal dialect I wasn't familiar with.

I booted up my machine and began dealing with the backlog of pictures. I worked fast, erasing scratches, removing anything unsightly, brightening the colour, all with a twitch of my mouse. Who said the camera never lied?

"Where's Buzz?" I asked.

"Chatting up that Danish girl in telesales," said Raymond.

"That figures."

I got up and made coffee in my favourite mug, the Photographers Do It In The Dark one with the hairline crack. Just as I took my first reviving sip, Burhan Hussein, known to his colleagues as Buzz, arrived at top speed. Buzz did everything at top speed. Immediately, the energy level in the room shot up, the air fizzing with his infectious vitality.

"Hi, Buzz…" I did a double take. "Nice trousers." They were leopard skin, worn with a tight black top. The effect should have been utterly tacky, but on Buzz's lithe body everything looked good. From his glossy black hair to his shiny shoes he was so well-groomed you could have eaten your dinner off him, and I knew several women who would love to have done just that.

"Thanks, Jude. It's nice to be appreciated."

It wasn't difficult to read Buzz's mind as he conducted a high-speed scan of the three of us, taking in Raymond's defeated-looking tweed jacket, Harrison's grubby hooded top, and my stained shirt, complete with ventilation holes. His eyebrows rose eloquently before he turned and bustled with his computer.

"Raymond says you've been chatting up Birgitta," muttered Harrison, still staring at his screen.

"Dirty work but somebody has to do it," said Buzz.

"Result?" asked Raymond.

"Taking her for a drink tonight." He punched the air. "Yes!"

"What do you do, hypnotise them?"

"OK, guys," I intervened. "Can we get on with some work?"

For a while the only sound was the humming of the machines and the soft clicking of keys and mouse. I opened up the business supplement file and made a start on that. Buzz grabbed a batch of job tickets and headed out on the road. Raymond tagged along, but he was only going as far as the coffee shop down the street for his usual late breakfast of muffins and hot chocolate with whipped cream. When I glanced at my watch, I noticed that the beads of blood on my hand had congealed in a jagged line and the bite itself looked inflamed. I'd have to clean it up and put some antiseptic on it later.

I leaned across to Harrison. "I've got to go to a meeting in a minute." He looked at me blankly, his mouth hanging open so that I could see the stud piercing his tongue. "If anyone rings or brings in a photo order, make sure you write it down. OK?" Harrison had been known to bodge the simplest tasks. He had a diploma in photo journalism, or so he said. I found it hard to believe.

Then I remembered an extra job. "Can you do something for me while I'm in the meeting?"

Harrison grunted.

"Don't worry, it won't take you long." I pulled a folder of prints from my bag. "I processed several rolls of film over the holiday, stuff I've had hanging round for ages. Can you scan and file these three pix into the system? They could be useful for the picture bank."

I spread the black and white prints on the workbench. I'd taken them in my free time with the Nikon. One was a view of gridlocked traffic in November when a freak snowstorm had caused chaos on the roads. Then there was a picture of the river in flood, next to the modern housing development that had transformed the run-down riverside area. From the bridge I'd noticed that a For Sale sign on one of the properties had been bent over by the wind so that it nearly touched the rising water. It looked as if the river was up for grabs. The last one was a shot of industrial cranes working on a new cinema complex on King Street, starkly beautiful against a stormy sky. In my opinion, it was one of the best I'd ever done.

Harrison picked up the river picture. "What's this all about?"

I explained the visual joke.

"That's balls."

"Thanks for that critical assessment, Harrison. But *cojones* or not, just get on with the job, will you?"

"Coho-what?"

"*Cojones* – Spanish for testicles."

He made a low sound that was probably Neanderthal for Bog off, then peered at the other two prints. "I like the cranes, though."

"Good choice."

"And the snowed-up traffic. The line of cars against the white background… it's kind of like… abstract."

"Kind of," I said casually, but for the first time ever I was impressed by his intelligence. That didn't last long. I looked back at my screen, called up an image that Harrison had taken and filed as Boringpic. Not exactly a helpful label, when file names were meant to be a kind of shorthand summary so that we could find an image fast. It turned out to be a mug shot of the manager of the estate agents where Lara worked, celebrating the fact the branch had won a productivity award. It was a terrible picture, badly composed and slightly out of focus. I realigned it and burnt in the edges, making it almost passable. But what had Harrison done to make the poor man's skin so raw, as if he'd shaved with a lawn mower? With a few deft swipes of the mouse I gave him a complexion of peachy smoothness. Then I closed the file down, grabbed a notebook and ran.

Two

"Where's Matt Dryden?" Tony was yelling as I slid into the conference room.

Charmaine, the news editor, looked up from her notebook. "He rang in to say he's following up rumours of contaminated blood products being used at the hospital. He's gone straight there and he'll be back as soon as he can."

Tony grunted. When he saw me he stretched backwards in his leather chair and clasped his hands behind his head. Though only in his early forties, his skin was grey from smoking too much. His eyes were dull and sunken, and he had a lean, wolfish look. Despite the chilly day two perfect circles of sweat had formed in the armpits of his shirt.

"Jude. Glad you could spare the time."

"I can't." I sat down next to Charmaine.

"As I was about to say..." Tony released his clasped hands and leaned forward, staring at my torn shirt. I didn't bother to cover up this time. He peeled his eyes away and glowered around the room. "These are not easy days for the newspaper industry. Remember what I told you all before Christmas?"

I sighed. We were in for one of Tony's periodic inspirational talks: New Year, new start, all that stuff. Most of the reporters were there, plus representatives from the other departments – telesales, advertising, printworks, and me from Photographic. Looking across the table I made eye contact with Stan, the legendary number one from the press hall. He winked at me and I grinned back.

It was hard not to smile at Stan's cherubic imperturbable face. I reminded myself that he was Lara's uncle, so if she and Daniel were going to get together that would make Stan and me practically family. I mouthed *Happy New Year* and he gave me a double thumbs-up.

Tony was ranting on. "This paper is barely holding its own. Circulation is rocky and therefore so is advertising, and as we all know, that's where the real money comes from. We've all got to work harder to make the Ravenbridge Evening Post a more exciting read."

Sensational tabloid stuff was what he meant, not always easy to come by in a town like Ravenbridge. Last year our biggest stories were the blowing up of a block of flats which had been an eyesore for years, and a student protest over the opening of a strip club. The gossip was that Tony had come here from London two years back, all for the sake of love. There was a picture of a smiling red-haired woman on his desk, who we assumed was his partner. He never talked about her, just occasionally stared wistfully at the photo. But love, if that's what kept him here, was a false friend, since Tony clearly found Ravenbridge about as exciting as an old people's home.

He thumped the table with the flat of his hand. "It's up to each and every department to pull its weight, or else… you know the consequences." He was referring to his habit of sacking people he didn't feel were taking his mission statement seriously enough. He leaned back again. "Right. What have we got for today's second edition?" There was no response. "How about tomorrow? Charmaine?"

Charmaine was a tall graceful woman with skin the colour of burnt sugar. Normally cheerful and outgoing, now she was tugging nervously at a strand of beaded hair.

"Typical post-Christmas drought, I'm afraid. If it turns

out to be true, the contamination rumour at the hospital is a possible lead story. Like I say, Matt's chasing that up. Traffic-calming measures, dog fouling…" She sounded desperate.

I spoke up. "I've got plenty of picture fillers – Christmas parties, cheque presentations, that sort of stuff."

"What else?" Tony barked.

No one spoke.

"Well?"

Nick, one of the chief reporters, said quietly, "I might have something…"

"What?"

"Doggy story. You know – dog jumps into a van, gets taken fifty miles away. Kids heartbroken because they don't know where it's gone. But the dog makes its own way home in time for Christmas."

Tony received this in grim silence.

"Great," said Charmaine brightly. "Nice feel-good piece. Big picture of the children hugging the dog…"

Tony's jaw was working. "Jesus wept," he muttered.

The door opened and Matt Dryden walked in, wearing a long dark coat. He'd been with the paper for nine months or so, having worked on a weekly in Manchester before. He was a good young journalist, keen and ambitious, ready to take on any job that Tony threw at him, even the shitty ones.

"Sorry I'm late," he said. He took a seat next to Stan.

"You haven't missed much," said Tony. "What did you get from the hospital?"

"Nothing."

"What?"

"They closed ranks. Nobody would talk to me. No press release. Nothing."

"Not even a quote from the hospital manager?"

"Zero. It's just rumour and hearsay at the moment. So, no story."

"Do you know what you are?" Tony paused for effect. "You're an arsehole."

Matt ran a hand through his curly dark hair. I saw his ears turn pink.

I kicked my chair back and stood up. "Now just a minute — "

"Moving on," said Tony.

"No. Rewind to that last comment. Matt is not an arsehole. He's a good reporter trying to do an honest job. The question I want to ask is this – who really is the arsehole round here?"

Some people stared at me with shocked expressions, others suddenly found their notebooks rivetingly interesting. Stan was the only one who nodded with approval.

"Perhaps there's more than one," said Tony quietly. He began to study his fingernails. "I was only saying to the managing director the other day that the photographic department is over-staffed."

"What? Are you crazy? We're rushed off our feet!"

"So how come, on the first day back, you're over an hour late? Some bullshit about a ferret when it's obvious you had a late night with your bit of rough, whoever he is." He gestured at my rips and scratches.

"That's rubbish! I'm not even in a relationship at the moment and what's more…" I stopped before I revealed to everyone in the room how long it was since I'd had sex.

"One-night stand, eh? And you're questioning my judgement?"

"Somebody has to."

Before he could answer, his mobile phone began to trill.

Tony picked it up on the second blast.

"Yeah?"

He listened intently, then sat bolt upright. He mouthed to Charmaine the single word *Fred*. Everyone knew that Fred was Tony's contact at the police station. He gave us advance warning of anything newsworthy. No one knew what Tony gave him in return.

He scribbled something on his pad. "Right. Cheers."

He switched the phone off. A half-smile appeared on his face.

"The police have received a phone call about a body. A young woman."

The atmosphere in the room, already charged, crackled with electricity, the way it always did when a real story came in. In the skewed world of journalism, death, especially violent death, was good news. I saw a frown cross Stan's face. Like me, he didn't share the hacks' delight at other people's misery.

"Any details?" asked Charmaine.

"She was found sitting on a bench in Jubilee Park."

The electricity in the room fell by a few volts. People started talking at once. *Hypothermia? Or heart attack maybe? Drug-related, probably. Still a good story, though. Definitely front-page stuff…*

Tony held up his hand to silence them.

"They don't know the cause of death yet. But it's definitely not natural causes. There's a lot of blood." He couldn't help himself. His half smile spread until it reached from ear to ear. "Looks like murder."

Three

The babble of excited voices stopped when Tony pointed a finger at Matt Dryden.

"Think you can handle it?"

"Just give me the chance. I won't let you down. I'll need a photographer."

"Don't try and teach me my job, smart-arse." He looked at me. "Who's free in your department?"

"I'd like Jude to come," said Matt.

Tony considered that for a moment. "Looks like you've got a chance to redeem yourself, Jude. Don't mess up this time." His face glistened as he addressed the room. "You know what they say – *if it bleeds, it leads*. If this pans out we've got a front-page story, and one with legs. I don't want anyone involved to cock it up. Do I make myself clear?" No one spoke. "Well, get on with it," he spluttered, flapping his hands at me and Matt. "I want you there before the TV and radio turn up."

"I'll drive," I said as we hurried under the glass bridge.

"I've been here nearly a year now. I do know my way around."

"And all the short cuts?"

Matt hesitated when he saw my car, complete with shark's teeth. "I've always meant to ask, did you do this yourself?"

"My son painted it for me. It's great for camouflaging the rust."

He looked doubtful. "It does go, does it?"

"I can usually coax it into a slow chug."

"Why don't we take mine?"

"Get in."

I pulled out of the car park, into Millhouse Lane, a clear straight road where I was able to put my foot down. From the corner of my eye I could see Matt's white knuckles on the dashboard.

"All right. You've made your point. The car goes."

I slowed down. Left into Clarence Street, left again into Jubilee Road.

"Listen, Jude… thanks for standing up for me back there. You put yourself on the line."

"I'm a big softie, me. I've got the evidence to prove it." I lifted my hand from the steering wheel to show Matt the bite, which was now looking angry and swollen.

"Anything to do with a ferret?" He sounded ridiculously cheerful.

"You reporters." I smiled ruefully. "Never happier than when you're chasing a story."

"I really need this, Jude. You heard what Tony said – the story's got to be good."

"Today the Ravenbridge Evening Post, tomorrow the Guardian?"

"Make that the Sun. And next week, foreign correspondent for CNN. I'm a bloody good journalist." He started tapping his thighs with impatience. "When I get the chance." He took out a pack of cigarettes. "Mind if I smoke?"

"Yes, I do mind. It's a filthy habit."

"Don't beat about the bush, Jude. Say what you really mean." He put the fags away.

The iron railings surrounding the park came into view. I pulled up near the main entrance only to find it blocked by a police car and ambulance. The gates themselves were marked off with blue and white tape. I drove round to the entrance on Victoria Street. More tape.

"Shit. They've sealed the place off already."

We got out anyway. I led Matt to a point where the trees and bushes beyond the railings were thin and weedy. I slung my camera bag diagonally across my body. "We used to get in this way late at night when we were teenagers. And I've already had some climbing practice today." I put my foot on the lowest bar of the railing.

"Jude, you can't just…"

I was already halfway up the fence. I looked down at Matt. "Do you want this story or not?"

He breathed deeply. "I'd give my right arm if I didn't need it for writing copy."

"Get up here, then. And mind the spikes at the top."

I had already landed on the other side when I saw Matt jump and heard the rip of tearing cloth.

"Whoops," I said.

Matt held the torn flaps of his wool coat. "Doesn't matter. Go on."

I led the way out of the bushes and headed towards the pond. In the distance people in fluorescent yellow jackets were clustered round a park bench. As we grew closer we could see two scene-of-crime officers in white coveralls, and several uniformed police officers including a WPC. A police photographer was circling the bench taking shots from every angle. As he lowered his camera I saw it was Ben Greenwood, who used to be a mate of mine. Shielded by Matt, I fished a camera out of my bag and slotted in a new digital cartridge.

We were only a short distance away when the WPC saw us. "How did you get in here?"

Matt held up his press pass. "We're from the Ravenbridge Evening Post. I know this is a bit cheeky, but it *is* a local story and we'd like a statement from the officer in charge before the rest of the media get hold of it."

While Matt was talking, the people around the bench shifted their positions. Now I could see the dead girl, although her face was still obscured by a SOCO officer leaning over her. She sat stiffly on the park bench, legs straight out in front. Her denim jacket was open, her T-shirt matted with blood, no longer scarlet but a reddish brown. My camera was in my hand but I didn't lift it. There were limits, whatever Tony Quinnell might think.

"If there's a psycho at large, the people of the town have a right to know as soon as possible," Matt was saying.

The guy in white overalls straightened up, revealing the girl's face. The skin was bluish, the lips bloodless. The only life-like colour was her cloud of sandy-gold hair.

"The whole park is a crime scene," said the WPC, her voice becoming shrill. "And you come tramping all over it! We don't even know the identity of the victim yet."

"Get them out of here," someone said. A couple of uniformed officers started manhandling us backwards.

"The public should be told – there could be a serial killer on the loose!"

I wanted to tell Matt to shut up, but I was shocked into silence by what I had seen. It was as if the earth had suddenly shifted on its axis, throwing me off balance so I could hardly stand up straight.

"Move away, please, sir, madam."

"You need an ID?" I whispered.

"Just leave it to us, madam."

"I know who she is."

They stopped pushing then.

"What?"

"Her name's Lara. Lara Ramsey. She's my son's girlfriend."

They gave us hot coffee while we waited for the detective team to arrive. I tried to contact Daniel at home but he must have gone out. I wasn't going to tell him about Lara's death over the phone, just to stay where he was and wait for me. When I tried his mobile number all I got was his voice mail.

"He's forgotten to switch his phone on," I told Matt. I remembered the light left on all night. "Typical Daniel." Then I thought of something else. "I have to go."

"You can't, Jude. I need you here. And they'll want to talk to you."

"I have to tell Stan Roguski."

"Stan from the printworks?"

"He's Lara's uncle."

"Phone him."

"I'm sorry, Matt, I'm off. There's nothing more I can do here." I gave him a small camera from my bag. "You might need this."

"I'm not a photographer."

"Just point and shoot. But remember to take the lens cap off, OK?"

I took the stairs to the first floor. A heavy swing door led on to the glass bridge, which reeked of stale tobacco. The offices and works were strictly No Smoking zones, so nicotine addicts often came here for a fix.

I reached the matching swing door at the far end, which led into the plate-making room. Zigzagging past the machines I ignored a sign that read Strictly No Admittance and entered the press hall. Immediately the clatter and hum of the machines hit me with full force. This was a modern state-of-the-art printworks but it was still incredibly noisy.

A flight of metal stairs led down to the lower floor. I walked along the aisle between the enormous presses to Stan's control booth. Unauthorised staff were not allowed down here without permission, strictly speaking. Even modern machinery could be dangerous. But I hadn't wasted time getting a permit.

The glass-walled office was the nerve centre of the whole operation. Stan was standing at a panel of buttons, playing it like a silent piano. When I rapped on the door Stan looked round and gestured me to come in.

As soon as I shut the door the clatter of the machinery outside was reduced by half.

"Stan…"

"Hold on, Jude. It looks like there's a problem."

A light was flashing on the control panel.

"Running short of paper on web number sixteen." He peered out of the glass booth. "Just as I thought. That new production assistant hasn't put a fresh reel on standby and he's gone for his lunch. Fancy a walk to the paper store with an old man?"

"No, but I'll come with you."

Stan smiled and my heart contracted. How was I going to tell him?

He handed me a tiny plastic bag containing green foam ear protectors. I stuffed one in each ear, and I was glad of them as we marched towards the paper store.

"What are you printing today?" I shouted. "Apart from the Post, I mean?"

"In-house magazine," he yelled back. "Kerwin and Black."

My heart squeezed harder still. Lara worked for the Ravenbridge sector of the company, which had branches all over the region.

The pages were being printed in their hundreds and carried around on a head-high conveyor belt where they were automatically cut, collated and folded. At the end of the gangway I could see a line of freshly printed magazines pouring into the stitch-and-trim department in an overlapping row like an endless pack of cards.

As Stan turned left into the paper store I grabbed an unstitched copy from the moving belt. Lara's face smiled at me from the cover, her extraordinary Pre-Raphaelite hair surrounding her finely boned face. Underneath I read *Ravenbridge Branch Scoops Productivity Award. Full story on page 6.* It was obvious why the editor of the magazine had chosen Lara to represent her workplace rather than the dull-looking manager. It was a good picture too, but seeing her alive and beautiful, caught in a moment in time that could never be recaptured, was like a punch in the stomach.

I wanted to keep walking forever, but it was all too short a distance to the paper store, which was a large barn-like space backing on to Stan's control room. I followed Stan inside. Huge reels of paper were stacked into fat white columns, nearly up to the high ceiling. Stan gave an order to the store manager, and with the help of a fork-lift truck a reel of blank paper was manoeuvred into the press area.

It was quieter in here. I removed my ear plugs.

"Stan, there's something I've got to tell you."

"Fire away."

"It's about the girl, the one who was found dead."

"What about her?"

I showed him the cover of the magazine.

"This is so hard... The fact is, it's Lara."

His round pink face went completely blank for a moment. "Lara? What do you mean?"

"I'm so sorry, Stan."

He took the magazine from me and stared intently at his niece's face.

"No... it can't be." He clutched the image to his chest as if he was holding on to her. "My lovely Lara? No... there's some mistake."

I swallowed hard. "I saw her, Stan. I was the one who identified her. Unofficially. But there's no mistake."

His face crumpled at last. He sank down on to a bale of paper. I put an arm around his broad shoulders. We stayed like that for some time, rocking to and fro, the eternal rhythm of grief.

"What about your boy – Daniel – does he know?"

"I haven't been able to contact him, but I'm going straight home now."

"She was talking about him only yesterday. She spent the day with me and Carol. I didn't know it would be the last time..." His voice cracked. I held his hand. He gripped me so tight my fingers went numb, but I didn't care. Eventually he was able to go on. "We were joking with her – he's too young for you, you cradle-snatcher." He released my hand and wiped his face with flat palms. "Go on, Jude, go home and tell your son."

"And you too, Stan. You should be with Carol." Stan and his wife had no children and I knew he thought the world of Lara, the only child of Carol's sister.

He nodded. "Tell him he was very special to Lara. Tell him that. At least he'll have that to cling on to when you tell him she's dead."

Four

I didn't need to tell Daniel.

The living room door stood open and the TV was blaring out some daytime soap. I looked in but the room was empty. I switched the TV off. On the sofa I found Daniel's mobile, the display window still lit up. Word gets round fast. One of his friends must have texted him with the news.

I mounted the stairs slowly. Daniel's door was ajar. As I drew nearer I heard a sound that chilled me to the bone. I ran up the last few steps.

He was lying on the floor, his chest heaving. He was breathing in laboured gulps but the oxygen couldn't get far along his rapidly closing airways.

"Where's your inhaler?" I shouted.

Daniel pointed to his desk, too far away for him to reach when catching every breath took all the strength he had. I searched frantically among the jumble of sketch books and paint tubes and old beer cans until I found the small blue periscope.

I lifted his shoulders from the floor and placed the inhaler between his lips.

"Come on, Daniel. You can do better than that."

His breathing was becoming more wheezy by the second. I punched 999 into the mobile still clutched in my hand, then cradled him in my arms while we waited for the ambulance. He hadn't had a full-blown attack like this for ages. Was this going to be the day I'd dreaded all these years, the day I lost him?

They put Daniel in a room on his own and attached him to a nebuliser to help him breathe. I held his hand until he stabilised, only letting go when he slipped into sleep.

At some point in the passing blur of time a nurse looked in, a young man, prematurely bald, with kind eyes. He took Daniel's pulse and checked his heart without waking him.

"He's going to be fine."

"Are you sure?"

"He'll have to stay in hospital for a couple of days." He saw my reaction. "He's in good hands."

"I know. It's just…"

"Talking of hands…" He lifted my left arm. "What happened?"

Only then did I realise how badly the ferret bite was throbbing.

"It looks infected. I'm sending you down to A&E."

"It's nothing."

"Maybe. But it needs checking out."

I had a horrifying thought. "Ferrets don't have rabies, do they?"

"Not as far as I know. Even so, this looks quite bad. When was the last time you had a tetanus injection?"

I shrugged, then looked at Daniel. His eyes were still closed.

"Don't worry. I'll look after him."

First they cleaned and bandaged my hand, then they left me in a cubicle for a while, until someone was available to give me an anti-tetanus shot. When the nurse arrived, a dour middle-aged woman, she twitched the curtain shut in a manner that meant business.

"Right buttock, please," I said. I didn't want anyone to

mess with the tattoo on my left one. I'd had it done when I was seventeen, in the days when I'd been a bit of a wild child, still getting pleasure out of shocking my strait-laced parents. The tattoo was a reminder of those times, not happy ones but formative, and I was still fond of the evidence.

She swabbed my right buttock then plunged the needle in.

I took a sharp intake of breath.

"Leopard, is it?"

"It's a tiger," I said, offended. The design was a little faded but the tattooist had been an artist, the best in Ravenbridge. "A leopard has spots."

"I wouldn't know." She placed the syringe in the kidney dish with a clatter. "I had a snake in the other day. Tattooed all the way round his you-know-what. Quite appropriate, really."

I zipped up my trousers.

"I've even seen a whole body tattoo. Looked like he was wearing a flowery tracksuit."

"Why don't you have something done?" I asked her. "How about a skull and crossbones? Or barbed wire around your neck?"

She actually considered this as a serious proposition. Then without a trace of irony she said, "No. It's not for me. The thing is, I don't like needles."

When I got back to the ward, walking stiffly from the jab, I found Matt Dryden sitting next to the bed. For a moment I was disorientated. Matt didn't know my son, so what was he doing here? Two parts of my life, work and home, seemed to have collided. It took a couple of seconds to remind myself that we were colleagues, working on the same story. The shocking sight of Lara's body flashed

34

across my mental screen. No doubt Matt was here to tell me the latest. Only I wasn't sure I wanted to know.

Matt stood up awkwardly. Daniel was awake and looking slightly brighter. The nebuliser had been moved aside. I hugged him as best I could with all the hissing, bleeping, ticking equipment surrounding him.

"How you doing?"

"I've been better," he whispered.

"I've been trying to cheer him up," said Matt. "Told him a few jokes. And we've been talking football, haven't we, mate? But for some inexplicable reason he doesn't like Manchester United."

Daniel smiled wanly. "They're rubbish. Get yourself a proper team to support."

"Blasphemy!" Matt gently ruffled Daniel's hair. He glanced at the dressing on my hand but didn't comment. He pointed to the vacant chair.

"No thanks, I'll stand."

He sat down again, looking uncomfortable. I could see the cogs going round in his brain. Did Daniel know about Lara? And if he did, what do you say to a young man whose girlfriend has just been brutally murdered? I was grateful to Matt, telling my son jokes, trying to make him smile, a small human defence against the tide of horror that threatened to engulf us.

"It was kind of you to come." I tipped the blind to let in more light. "How did you know where we were?"

"I tried to ring you, but — "

"They don't allow mobiles in here."

"So I went round to your house. Your neighbour – a guy in a wheelchair – he told me about the ambulance. I came as soon as I could. I wanted to see how you were. And Daniel." Matt pulled on his earlobes. "I know what you're

35

going through, mate. I've ended up in hospital a couple of times myself. I'm allergic to peanuts, would you believe." He turned to me. "Is it an allergy with Daniel?"

"It can be. Dog hair's bad, so are things like cleaning solvents. Or it can be caused by shock."

He punched him lightly on the upper arm. "Hang in there, Dan. You've had a rough time, but you'll come through." He stood up, pulling the flaps of his coat together. "I'd better be going."

I followed him into the corridor. Despite myself, I asked what had happened since I left the park.

"The SOCO team took ages but eventually they moved the girl's body to the mortuary. I take it Daniel knows, that's why...?"

"Yeah. The shock of it caused a full-blown attack."

"I hung around in the park until I could get a word with the SIO. A guy called Laverack. Do you know him?"

"I don't think so."

"Bit of a tight-arse. But I got a quote, of sorts. He asked about you, and the ID and Daniel, and the thing is..." He paused, twisting his mouth sideways.

"What?"

"Laverack wants to talk to him. As soon as possible. That's what I was ringing you about. You'd better warn Daniel – to have his story ready."

"Story? He doesn't need a story."

"I didn't mean..." Matt looked stricken. "For god's sake, Jude, I wasn't implying he killed her."

Hearing those words said aloud, even in denial, left me winded.

"Tell Tony I'll be back at work tomorrow," I muttered. "Bye, Matt."

I had barely got back into Daniel's room when there was

a quiet knock at the door. The male nurse leaned in.

"Daniel's got a couple of visitors."

"Have they got trilby hats, belted raincoats and big flat feet?" I asked, looking meaningfully at my son.

"No."

Daniel sank back on to his pillow, looking as pale and ethereal as smoke. He'd understood.

"You'd better show them in," he whispered.

In fact, the man was wearing a beautifully cut grey suit with a bright geometric tie. He held up his ID card briefly. "Detective Inspector Laverack." He spoke softly with a light Tyneside accent. "This is DC Naylor." She was young, chubby, with knotty hockey player's legs.

"I take it you're Jude Baxendale?" said Laverack. "You're the one who identified the murder victim?"

"Yes."

He glanced at the bed. "And this is your son Daniel?"

"We need to ask him a few questions," said Naylor. "In private."

"I'm not leaving. Can't you see this business has made him seriously ill?"

"It's all right, Mum."

I backed out of the room reluctantly.

"Hey, Jude!" It was Matt Dryden. He began to hum the old Beatles song.

I raised my eyebrows.

"Sorry. I suppose everyone comes out with that."

"No, not at all. You're the first," I said drily.

"Point taken."

"I thought you'd gone."

"I saw Laverack and his entourage arrive. I thought you might need some company while they…" He tipped his

37

head towards the closed door.

"You're right."

"Let's grab a coffee."

"How did Daniel get to know Lara in the first place?"

"His art teacher – Mr Keele – he set up life-drawing classes after school. Lara was a regular model. Daniel was really taken with her. It took some time but eventually, a few weeks ago, they started going out."

"Did they sleep together?"

I looked at Matt sharply. "That's none of my business."

"This is exactly what Laverack will be asking Daniel." Matt skimmed the froth from his coffee and sucked it off the spoon. "If they were sleeping together, do you mind?"

"He's eighteen, an adult. He has to make his own choices now."

"I wish my mum had been like you when I was his age." He was about to light a cigarette. I pointed to the *No Smoking* sign. He put the pack away.

"It was Lara's birthday last week," I said. "Daniel made her a beautiful bracelet. He made each stone individually out of clay, glazed and fired them, painted them, then strung them on a silver wire. She loved it."

"Lucky girl." Matt shook his head. "Sorry, that was a stupid thing to say. Did you know her well?"

"Hardly at all. She stayed for a few meals – she was very keen on pasta, which was lucky, as that's about the only thing I can cook. We talked a bit about her work at Kerwin and Black, and about being an artists' model, but she seemed quite reserved with me and I didn't push it." I stirred my tea even though it contained no sugar, trying to recall the real Lara.

"Did Daniel talk about her?"

"Not to me. And I didn't ask. You don't pry at that delicate stage of a relationship. I let them get on with it." I tried to picture Lara sitting at the kitchen table, a pretty girl, striking even, but somehow elusive. "She had a curious aloof quality, like a cat. Do you know what I mean? She wasn't that easy to get to know. But Daniel loved her and that was enough for me. Mind you…"

"What?"

"If she'd hurt him, broken his heart, I think I'd have wrung her neck." I stopped. "How could I have said that? I didn't mean…"

"So you think she was killed by the vengeful mother of a previous boyfriend?"

I smiled despite myself.

"They'll be asking him about the last time he saw her," Matt said.

"That must have been New Year's Eve. Sunday night."

"A party?"

"No, they just went to the pub, a crowd of them. Then just before twelve they all poured into the square to listen to the town hall clock strike midnight."

"Was he drunk?"

"He said not. A lot of them were, of course. He told me about one guy who climbed the statue of Queen Victoria and put a full beer glass on her head." Matt gave me a sidelong glance. "It's traditional."

"And after that?"

"Lara hadn't brought her car into town that night and she'd missed the last bus, so Daniel walked her back to her flat. She was going to see Stan and his wife on New Year's Day and she didn't want to be too wasted."

"Did Daniel go inside with her?"

"No. I think he was slightly pissed off about that.

39

He'd never gone to her flat before and he was curious to see it. You see, she kept telling him it was her own private space, that very few people were allowed in. But she'd given him the impression he would be one of the few, some time soon."

"Did he hang around, go home, what?"

"What did he say… ?" I tapped the spoon against the side of the cup until Daniel's words came back to me. "He went back to the pub, hooked up with some mates and I think they went clubbing. No, wait, they couldn't get in, that's right, so they went to the park and had a few more beers."

"Jubilee Park?"

I nodded. We didn't say anything for a while. I took a few sips of cold tea.

"He didn't see her yesterday?"

"No. We were both home all day. Daniel was working on his A-level art project and I was doing some freelance stuff." Matt looked at me questioningly. "I've got my own darkroom in the basement."

"I'm impressed." He drained his cup. "Are you sure Daniel didn't go out?"

"What is this, Matt? You don't really think he's guilty, do you?"

"Of course not. I told you, I'm just predicting what they're asking him right now. He needs to be sure of his facts. I've seen how the police can manipulate things, get witnesses confused, and they end up accusing them of all sorts of things they had nothing to do with."

"Fair point." I thought back to the day before. "We had lunch together and a meal in the evening and I know he was there the rest of the time because I could hear that pounding music he likes pouring out of his room."

40

"From your basement?"

"It's lightproof but not soundproof."

"All the same, hearing music isn't the same as seeing Daniel, is it?"

I glared at him. He held up his hand.

"I know, I know. But that's how the police mind works." He waited a few seconds before asking, "Are you sure you didn't go out?"

"Quite sure! Hold on… I did pop out to the corner shop in the late afternoon because we'd run out of washing-up liquid. They were closed. Actually it was just an excuse to get some fresh air."

"How long were you gone?"

"A few minutes… maybe a bit longer. I went for a short walk, but definitely no more than half an hour."

"Did you actually see Daniel when you got back?"

"No, but I heard his music, and later we had dinner together. I know he was there."

"Good. Don't let them rattle you, that's all I'm saying."

I pushed my cup away. "Thanks, Matt. I'm beginning to see what we're getting into here." I stood up. "I'd better go back to the ward now."

"Will you be coming into work tomorrow?"

"Yep. Assuming Daniel's OK."

He leaned across and brushed my cheek with his lips. "Take care, Jude."

I realised how uncannily accurate Matt had been when Daniel told me the questions Laverack asked him. Right down to the one about sleeping together.

"That's none of his business!"

"It is now she's dead." He swallowed hard. "I told him the truth. Lara wanted to wait. She wasn't a virgin or anything. I knew that. But she said we were special. She would know when the time was right. Soon, she said…"

I hugged him and felt his thin frame tremble.

"They will catch this bastard, won't they?" he said.

"Of course they will."

"What if they don't?"

"They will." I wasn't as confident as I sounded. After all, murders often went unsolved.

"If we still had hanging," he said grimly, "I'd offer to put the rope round his neck and pull the lever."

"Stop it! This isn't like you, Daniel."

"Can't you try and find out what happened?"

"I think we should leave that to the police."

"But you know loads of people in this town, and everything that's going on."

"Of course I don't! In any case, the killer could be a complete stranger."

"Maybe. Only… I got the impression Lara was worried about something."

"Did you tell Laverack?"

"Yes. He wrote it down but I don't think he took it seriously."

"What made you think she was worried?"

"Difficult to say. I'd known her casually for months and she seemed fine, nothing fazed her. Then soon after we started going out there was a nervousness that I hadn't seen in her before. Not wanting to go out that much. Avoiding certain pubs… I don't know. When I asked her what was wrong she clammed up."

"She didn't mention any names, people she wanted to avoid?"

"No, but it's somewhere to start, isn't it?"

"Start? Daniel, I'm not going to start anything. It would

be stupid to even try. And dangerous."

His face was as pale as his pillow. "Do you want this maniac to kill somebody else?"

"What kind of question is that?"

"I'm just asking you to keep your eyes open, ask around. You work for a news-gathering organisation, for Christ's sake!" He sank back, breathing in short shallow gasps.

"All right!" I passed Daniel the oxygen mask.

"Promise me you'll try."

I thought about Lara's mother, what she must be going through right now. Today I'd nearly lost my son, but all things considered I was damn lucky.

What choice did I have?

Five

"Did you tell Tony I'd be in today?" I had my phone tucked between shoulder and chin while I sprinkled cereal into a bowl.

"Yep, as instructed," said Matt. I could hear the soft clatter of his keyboard.

"Then untell him."

"Why?"

I pulled the fridge door open looking for milk. No milk. I remembered I'd taken the last full carton to work yesterday. Was it only twenty-four hours ago? It seemed like weeks. I began to eat the dry flakes.

"I can't come in."

"Daniel – is he…?"

"He's fine. Physically on the mend, anyway. It's just…" I explained about my promise. In the cold – perishing cold – light of day it seemed crazier than ever. All the same, during a long sleepless night, a vague plan of campaign had begun to form.

"Is that a good idea?"

"I won't try any heroics. I just need to find out what I can, for Daniel's sake. He's really hurting."

"I know. But think about it, Jude. Lara walks in the park late at night and gets attacked. A random act of violence, surely? The police just need to catch the perv who did this."

"See, that's the point. That's what it looks like, but you saw her body, didn't you?"

"Not really. They got us out of the way pretty quick."

44

"She wasn't exactly sitting on the bench. She was sort of leaning in a straight line. What does that suggest to you?"

"I'm not sure."

"I don't think she was attacked in the park. I think she was killed earlier and put there after rigor mortis had set in."

"Bloody hell."

There was silence for a while.

"I think you're on to something, Jude. What are you doing next?"

"I'm going to see Lara's parents. I know her mum slightly. She's Stan's sister-in-law."

"Really? I've been trying to ring them. Nobody's answering. Can I come with you?"

"Matt, this is personal. It's not for the paper."

"Understood. But you waved a red rag at Raging Bull Quinnell for my sake, and I'd like to repay the favour. You know how good I am at asking questions."

I thought about it. I didn't really know what I was going to say to the Ramseys. Pictures were my thing, always had been.

"OK." I gave him the address. "I'll see you there in half an hour."

Everything in the room was bleached of colour, including Patricia Ramsey. She had ash-blonde hair, and a porcelain complexion like her daughter's. She was dressed all in taupe and wore a white gold crucifix round her neck. I knew from Stan that she was a devout Catholic. He and Carol took a much more relaxed approach to their faith, but Patricia was a lay reader and unofficial secretary to the local priest, and Stan had implied that she practically ran the parish. She sat on a cream leather sofa, her knees pinned rigidly together. There was a strong smell of air freshener in the room, which was militarily neat and spotlessly clean.

Patricia hadn't opened the door to us until she'd peeped through her net curtains and recognised me. When she finally let us in she hugged me briefly. I'd felt the tension in her, like a stretched elastic band, and wondered what would happen when she snapped.

Matt took a ballpoint pen from his pocket and started clicking it in and out. I glared at him. He stopped clicking. The silence lengthened like a stain. Even Matt was having difficulty here. It was like talking to a waxwork.

"Is your husband…? Perhaps he could…?" he tried.

"He's on business in Dubai. He's taking the next flight home. He'll have to identify the body. I can't do it." She looked down at her hands then at me. "Your son… sorry, I've forgotten his name. How is he?"

"Daniel. He's upset. We're all very upset," I said.

"I didn't think she was that serious about him. She had so many boyfriends."

"Really?" I realised how little I knew about Lara. How many boyfriends? Was she going out with other people at the same time as Daniel? That certainly wasn't the impression I'd got. They seemed to be together every free minute they had. "Daniel was very serious about her, and I'm pretty sure she felt the same. There was even some talk of them moving in together when he goes away to college in September."

She stiffened. "Leave Ravenbridge? I knew nothing about that."

"How did you and Lara get on?" asked Matt.

"Fine. Why do you ask?"

"It's just that she didn't live at home, and I wondered…"

Mrs Ramsey leaned forward to the coffee table and

picked up a wooden box inlaid with mother of pearl.

"Lara decided she wanted to live in that sordid flat. She looked so sweet and biddable, but in her quiet way she could be very headstrong, even as a little girl. Then from the age of sixteen she was…"

She lifted the box lid. A thin stream of music tinkled out. *Lara's Theme*. Of course. I'd seen *Doctor Zhivago* years ago and hated it, mainly because of that damn tune played endlessly on a high-pitched balalaika.

"I love this theme, don't you?" Patricia murmured.

"Unforgettable," I said. I knew it would be twanging round my brain for days.

"What happened when she was sixteen?" Matt asked.

"She refused to stay at the Sacred Heart and insisted on going to Ravenbridge High to do her A-levels. That didn't last long – she dropped out. But the damage was done."

"Damage?"

"Mixing with the wrong types."

"Isn't that part of growing up?" I asked, remembering my own teenage years.

"Everything we've ever taught her about behaviour and morals – it all went out of the window."

Matt tapped his pen on his knee. "You mean she slept around?"

Mrs Ramsey snapped the lid of the music box shut, opened it and played the tune again. I gave Matt another glare and he looked suitably chastened, shrugging his shoulders to convey this was like slaving in the Siberian salt mines. I nodded briefly in agreement. We waited while the whiny melody tinkled to an end.

"There are so many dangers in the world. She didn't realise her power. A beautiful girl like her… And then she started that modelling business. She didn't tell me. I only found out through someone in the congregation. Taking her clothes off for anyone to ogle her at those art classes – she was a temptation to sinners!" She fingered her crucifix. "I asked Father Thomas to talk to her, but it didn't do any good. She told him there was nothing sinful about the naked human body." She closed her eyes. "She was so naïve and trusting, that's what killed her." There was a long pause. We waited patiently until she came back to us. Eventually her eyelids fluttered open. "Do you work for the paper as well?" she asked Matt. "Is that why you're here?"

"No. I'm here as Jude's friend."

"You can put what I said in the paper if you like."

"Yeah?" He was already pulling out his reporter's notebook. "This will be an exclusive, yes?"

"I don't want to talk to any other journalists if that's what you mean."

"Great." Matt couldn't keep the smirk off his face. "Look, I know this sounds crass, but I have to ask you about your reaction to Lara's death."

"Devastated. That's the kind of word you like, isn't it?

Matt dutifully wrote it down, along with a stream of religious dogma about sinners and tempters, predators and victims, our sick and debauched society.

"Lara stopped attending Mass at St Bridget's when she was fifteen. Then she changed schools. She didn't want to go to the convent any more. She was adamant. In the end, we decided she could go to Ravenbridge High School as long as she worked hard and applied to university, but no, she dropped out of the sixth form and messed around for a while before she got a job at an estate agents. It was only supposed to be temporary."

"She worked there for… three years? It must have been

pretty boring. How come she stayed so long?"

"The money, I suppose. She was determined to leave home and live independently. As soon as she'd saved enough, that's exactly what she did. She went to live alone in a slum. And look what happened to her!"

"It could have happened to anyone," I said quietly.

"No. She was special. Someone picked her out. I'm sure of it."

Matt closed his notebook. "All I need now is a family photo, Lara with you and your husband. A holiday snap, perhaps?"

"No, I'm sorry."

"You don't have any family pictures?" I asked.

"Yes, I have. But I don't want to part with any of them. I gave the police a recent photo, and that's all I'm prepared to hand over."

"It would help the story enormously," said Matt.

"Lara was an only child." She stroked the lid of the music box. "Souvenirs and pictures, they're all I've got left."

Somewhere in the house a phone began to ring. Mrs Ramsey didn't move.

"It could be your husband," said Matt. "Or the police."

She rose slowly out of her seat and left the room. As soon as the door closed Matt began rapidly searching the dresser, the mantelpiece, the windowsill, every surface where ornaments and photographs were neatly lined up.

"What are you doing?"

"Yes!" he cried triumphantly. He held out a silver photo frame.

"Put it back! In all the years I've been a newspaper photographer I've never stooped so low as to steal a picture and I'm not going to start now."

Sighing deeply, Matt put the frame back on the shelf.

A few seconds later Patricia Ramsey returned. "Double glazing," she said.

We were walking down the path when Matt's mobile rang.

"Yeah?" He began to walk faster. "Right. Thanks. I'll be back as soon as I can."

"What is it?"

"Tony. The police have been going through Lara's flat and they've found something."

"What?"

"Blood."

"So I was right. Lara was obviously killed at her flat and moved much later."

"Miss Marple, eat your heart out. This is a good one." Matt pointed at the screen. He had persuaded me to come back to work to scan and file the pictures he'd taken at Jubilee Park. "I'm not trusting anybody else with them," he'd said.

I examined a picture of a black body bag being wheeled away on a trolley. I tried to separate my professional expertise from the feeling of horror that crept over me.

"Depends what you mean by good, " I muttered. He looked crestfallen. "The focus and composition are fine, I don't mean that. For god's sake, Matt, it's a real human being in that bag. It's Lara. The girl Daniel loved."

"Sorry, Jude. I wasn't thinking."

"You journalists never do. I know, don't tell me – you just report the facts. I've heard it all before."

I moved on to the next one, a mug shot of Detective Inspector Laverack. I reduced the red tones and erased a tree branch that seemed to be sticking out of his ear.

"You're good at this." Matt got off the workbench and

looked round at the pictures on the walls. He peered at the three new ones. "I haven't seen these before. Are they yours?"

I glanced up. "Yeah. Harrison must have done some enlargements and put them up."

"They're a bit different."

"I'm not just a gun for hire. I can do arty pix too."

"I can see that. I like this one." He pointed to the 'river for sale' picture.

"It made me smile at the time. Though I'm surprised Harrison bothered with it. He thought it was bollocks." I tapped the screen. "You've got your finger over the lens here."

"Sorry, Jude. We can't all be brilliant."

"Is Tony going to run the interview with Lara's mum?"

"As long as I tone it down a bit, emphasise the 'mother's emotional plea to other vulnerable young girls' angle, and drop the religious stuff, he should be OK about it. Especially when we show him this…" He reached into the deep pockets of his torn wool coat and pulled out a silver frame.

"Please don't tell me you stole that?"

"Borrowed. If you get it processed straight away I'll take it back to the house this afternoon. She won't even miss it, I promise."

"I was just thinking what a nice guy you were."

"I am, Jude, I am. But I'm a journalist. Without a good picture it's only half a story. You should know that. You will do it for me, won't you?"

"No way."

After I'd scanned and filed the picture, I leaned back in my chair and scrutinised it. It showed Lara and her parents sitting on some hot Mediterranean terrace. At first glance there was nothing unusual about it, but looking closely I could see that the three of them sat stiffly in their plastic chairs, their drinks barely touched. Lara, looking about seventeen, had a guarded sullen expression, while her parents wore forced smiles. I guessed some waiter or fellow tourist had offered to take a snap of the apparently happy family. But the resulting image told a different story.

I put the original in a reinforced brown envelope and placed it on Matt's desk. He stopped his feverish tapping for a moment.

"Remember this, Matt Dryden, when I'm out of a job and you're editor of the Sun. You owe me."

He touched my hand lightly, sending a current of warmth right through my body. "Don't worry, Jude. I won't forget."

Six

Tony sent Harrison to cover the police activity on Stonebeck Avenue, the street where Lara lived, taking me off the job as a kind of punishment for turning up so late.

I tried to work but I couldn't concentrate. I kept going over what I knew, attempting to make something out of very little. Considering the amount of blood, I assumed Lara had been attacked with a knife or sharp implement, and this had happened in her own flat. That meant she probably knew her murderer, although it didn't rule out the possibility of an opportunistic attack by a stranger. But stranger or friend, why move her body hours later to such a public place? What time did the park gates open? Had anybody seen anything? It had been a bitterly cold morning after a boozy New Year. The killer might just have got away without being spotted by anybody, damn it.

In the end I couldn't stand it any longer. I knew Matt was busy, so I went on my own.

Stonebeck Avenue was a row of squat terraced houses with tiny front gardens. Most of the properties were well kept up, with new window frames and tubs filled with winter pansies.

Number 15 was an exception. All the brickwork had been painted purple, the windows were thick with grime, and the so-called garden doubled as a rubbish tip. It seemed odd that someone who worked in the property business would choose to live here. It was certainly a massive contrast to Patricia Ramsey's house. Perhaps that was the point.

How well did Daniel really know this girl? He had certainly never been inside her flat. He had walked Lara back here just once, at New Year, and he wasn't invited in that night. It was her own private space, she'd told him. *But one day soon…* That day would never come for Daniel now.

Lara's Theme suddenly started buzzing in my head, wrecking my train of thought.

I glanced at the cars parked along the narrow street but I couldn't spot Lara's white Polo. I wondered where it was. Perhaps the police had taken it away. As if I'd summoned them up, a police van arrived and a pair of SOCO officers in white overalls climbed out and ducked under the blue and white tape that spanned the front gate. Just outside the door they pulled on elasticated overshoes, then disappeared into the gloomy hallway.

There was no sign of Harrison.

A few bunches of flowers had been laid on the pavement, glistening in their cellophane wrapping, the hothouse blooms already wilted and frost-bitten. I was reading the messages when I heard a noise behind me. A boy was trundling a bright yellow bag on wheels towards me. He was delivering the second edition of the Evening Post, the one that came out around 1pm. The first edition came out around half past eleven, and usually not much changed for the final one. But in a case like this, things could develop rapidly from hour to hour. I hadn't seen either edition yet but no doubt, like yesterday, the news of Lara's death filled the front page, probably leading with the interview with her mother, complete with family picture.

The boy trailed up each short path on his round and shoved a paper in the letterbox, leaving it sticking out, or sometimes just dumping it on the doorstep. He took no notice of me as he went by, too busy kicking flowers out of the way. Leaving his trolley, he ducked under the tape and dropped a paper on the front step. He was small, but from his hard knowing face I reckoned he was about fourteen.

I looked at my watch. 2.17pm.

"Shouldn't you be at school?" I asked. "You know, first day back?"

"School sucks."

"Do you know what happened to the girl who lived here?"

"Course I do." He waved a newspaper at me. "I can read."

"Then why deliver the paper?"

"There's a flat upstairs as well."

I hadn't thought of that. He was reaching into his bag for the next copy.

"Did you know the girl who died?"

"Sort of. I've seen her around. Nice tits." He squinted at me to see if I was shocked. I kept my face impassive. "She was the only girl I know who wasn't scared of spiders."

"Did you talk to her?"

"None of your business." He scurried away but I dogged his footsteps as he delivered the Post along the street, tackling him each time he emerged from a gateway.

"If you knew she wasn't scared of spiders you must have known her quite well."

"I told you, I just saw her sometimes when I was doing my round."

"In the afternoons? Wasn't she at work?"

"I'm not usually this early."

"Do you bunk off school much?"

"Sod off." He pushed past, his trolley squeaking behind him.

The street was a cul-de-sac ending in a high stone wall,

the back of a discount carpet warehouse, a decrepit old building that had once been a paper factory. The boy crossed to the other pavement.

"Where did Lara keep her car?"

"There's a yard round the back."

"When was the last time you saw her?"

He turned and faced me like a fox at bay. He glanced back at the police van. "Are you one of them?"

"No."

"Then what's your problem? Get off my back, will you?"

"My son was Lara's boyfriend. He's devastated."

"Shit happens, OK? He'll get over it."

"I don't think so."

"There's nothing I can do about it."

He was walking quickly away, giving up on delivering papers. I had to run to catch up with him, then matched him stride for stride.

"Did you see her on Monday? New Year's Day?"

"There was no paper on Monday."

"No, of course not." I bit my lip. "Have you noticed anything odd? Anyone hanging around here? Acting strangely?"

He snorted.

"What? Who did you see?"

"Don't you ever give up?"

"No, I don't. So you might as well tell me."

"I've got nothing to tell," he said shiftily. We were nearly at the end of the road now.

"I think you have. Who was it? Do you know the name?"

He stopped and began kicking his trolley with the toe of his grubby trainer. "I've seen blokes hanging around."

"Did you recognise any of them?"

He snorted again. "You could say that."

"Who was it?"

"That teacher."

"What teacher?"

"That dickhead, Mr Keele." The kicking became frenzied. "I hate him. He banned me from art last term. I hate school. Teachers are wankers. At least I get paid for doing this."

He turned away abruptly.

"Wait." I was frantically trying to think. Of course Adam Keele knew Lara. He was the one who set up the life-drawing classes and hired the models. But why would he be hanging round her flat?

"When did you see Mr Keele?"

"Dunno. Mostly he was just sitting on the wall waiting for her. I reckon he fancied her. Maybe he killed her." The boy grinned. "I'd like to see him get into trouble for a change. Yeah, I'd like that a lot."

At the end of the street he dumped his remaining papers in the bin. He picked up the empty trolley and bolted round the corner. I was too shocked by what he had said to follow him. And much too slow.

Someone stepped in my path.

"Harrison? Where've you been?"

"It was bloody cold so I went to get a coffee. What were you doing talking to Lee Maddox?"

"He's a little bugger, isn't he?"

"If you think he's hard you should see his older brother Scott. He was in the same year at school as me and Lara."

"You knew Lara?"

"Everybody knew Lara. She kind of stood out."

"Listen, I'll talk to you later. There's something I need to do."

"I thought Tony had sent you to take over from me."

"No way. It's all yours, kiddo."

The art rooms at Ravenbridge High were open-plan, with a long straight corridor linking the separate teaching areas. I'd been here often enough for parents' evenings and exhibitions, and breathed in the familiar smell of freshly mixed paint and wet clay. I stopped outside Adam Keele's room. It was oddly quiet. Peering in, I saw that there was no class going on here.

Adam had his back to me, washing his hands in a deep china sink. He'd taken an interest in Daniel's work right from Year 7, encouraged him and nurtured his talent. He was an inspiring and gifted teacher, with a wife and two young children. I'd always thought of him as one of the good guys.

"Adam?"

He twisted round, a haunted look on his face. His unkempt hair and glittering eyes suggested he hadn't had much sleep.

"Jude." He looked relieved. He wiped his hands on his stained black shirt. "How's Daniel? I heard he was poorly."

"He's all right. It's Lara I want to talk about."

He slumped back against the sink. "I can't believe it. She was such a lovely girl. Who'd do a thing like that?"

"Adam, there isn't much time – your next class will be here in a minute." I sat down on a stool. "The fact is, you've been seen hanging around outside Lara's house."

"Who told you that?"

"A boy called Lee Maddox."

"Him? You can't believe anything he says. He's constantly in trouble. I wouldn't say this about kids normally, but he's a complete no-hoper."

"Actually, I did believe him."

He didn't say anything, just stared at the floor.

"You were seeing her, weren't you?"

"No! Not like that." He wrapped his arms around his body as if trying to hold himself together. "I did go to her house a few times. Sometimes she wasn't there."

"And when she was?"

"We never… we just sat on the wall outside and talked. Once, when it was pouring with rain, she let me in."

"What happened?"

"I tried it on – I didn't mean to – but she was so…" His knuckles whitened as he squeezed himself hard. "She said I was a good friend and she didn't want to spoil it. So we just drank coffee and chatted. She'd been badly messed up by her home life – all that religious fervour stuffed down her throat from birth. I just wanted to help her work her way through it."

"Were you in love with her?"

"She was Daniel's girlfriend, for god's sake!"

"They only started going out a few weeks ago." I paused for a moment. "How did you feel about that?"

"It wasn't easy," he said, so quietly I could hardly hear him.

"How long had you felt this way about Lara?'

'Since I first saw her. When I started the life-drawing sessions for A-level students last spring, I rang this model called Annie. Only she couldn't do it – we start straight after school and she was modelling for the Fine Art students at the university until six. Anyway, she said she knew someone, and it was this girl's day off so…"

"It was Lara?"

He nodded. "She'd never done it before, but she was great. The kids all wanted her to come back the next week, and she became a regular. We tried a few other models for variety, but she was the best. She had this incredible quality, a kind of stillness."

"And she was beautiful, with fantastic tits."

"Don't talk about Lara like that!"

"Tell me the truth. Did you kill her?"

Adam raised his haggard eyes to mine. "Of course not. I was at home. The baby wasn't well and I was up and down with him all that night. Check it out with Ruth, ask the neighbours if you don't believe me. They must have heard Shaun crying and me trying to pacify him."

"Of course I believe you. But I had to ask. For Daniel's sake."

He nodded. "I understand."

I stood up to go. "This model you mentioned, the one who sent Lara to you, where does she live?"

"Annie? She lives in the flat above Lara's."

Someone spoke from the doorway.

"Adam Keele?"

I turned round.

It was Detective Inspector Laverack.

I pretended to leave, but hung around in the corridor. From the next room I could hear the busy sounds of an art class clearing up towards the end of the lesson, so I had to strain to catch what Adam and Laverack were saying.

The word *Lara* was repeated many times, and *Monday night* was mentioned more than once, along with *alibi* and *obsession*. Laverack's voice remained level but Adam's rose with each reply until he was almost shouting. Several times I clearly heard him say, "I had nothing to do with it!"

I peeped into the room. Laverack was perched on the edge of a table, making notes in a small book. Adam's arms were still tightly wrapped around his body, which was bent over in a hollow curve as if he couldn't take the weight of the onslaught.

"I think you should come down to the police station so we can continue this interview there. You don't want your next class seeing you in this state."

"But I've got nothing to say!"

Laverack rose to his feet, twitching his suit trousers back into their razor-sharp creases. He extended his arm, indicating the doorway. Adam shrank back, and so did I.

"I'm not going anywhere!"

"Then I've no alternative. Adam Keele, I'm arresting you on suspicion of –"

I heard an anguished cry, then rapid footsteps crossing the hard floor. Everything happened very fast after that. Adam shot past me. I stepped back into the room to remonstrate with DI Laverack.

"Why are you still here? Get out of my way!" Laverack pushed me aside as he ran after Adam.

A bell clanged just above my head, nearly deafening me. Hordes of children in the familiar navy and plum uniform streamed into the corridor. I couldn't see Adam at all, just Laverack's head bobbing through the crowd, a mobile phone pressed to his ear.

As the classrooms filled up and the congestion eased I caught up with him.

"For Christ's sake!" he was saying. "Get the fire brigade!"

"What's happening?"

"He's on the roof and he's threatening to jump."

We took the first exit we could find and ran round the exterior of the school, scanning the rooftop as we went.

"There!" I shouted. From the car park at the front of the school I could see a figure standing right on the edge of the parapet, three storeys up. A man in a black shirt, arms spread wide, his mouth open in a silent howl.

Moments later a fire engine swung into the car park. There was a burst of feverish activity, and soon an extending ladder was manoeuvred into place against the rooftop. A fireman stood poised on the bottom rung.

Adam was pacing up and down, shaking his hands in an agitated manner, muttering to himself, then calling out, but I couldn't hear what he was saying.

"I don't think this is a good idea. Let me speak to him."

"Please don't interfere. This is a police matter."

I looked up. Adam had stopped pacing, now swinging his head to and fro as if he was debating with himself. The fireman began to climb the ladder. Adam leaned dangerously out, watching what was going on.

Then he shouted, loud enough for everyone to hear, "I loved her, but I didn't kill her!"

With arms flung wide he launched himself into the air, spinning like a broken-ribbed umbrella, and smashed on to the hard ground.

Seven

"What do you mean, no pictures?"

I held my mobile half a metre from my head in case Tony's voice ruptured my ear drums.

"For god's sake, Tony. I knew the man."

I didn't tell him that for those moments, as I stood watching Adam plummet from the roof, I'd felt myself split in half – news photographer and human being – and for the life of me I hadn't been able to reconcile the two. That's why I was paralysed. That's why the camera stayed down by my side. It was happening to me increasingly these days.

"Got any pictures at all? A pathetic huddle of traumatised children? Elderly teacher collapsed with a heart attack? Keele's distraught wife and kiddies being held back from seeing the body?"

I kept quiet, hoping that Tony could hear my thought loud and clear, the one that included the word *sicko*. He must have read my eloquent silence.

"Yeah, well, I'm entitled to the occasional tabloid fantasy." He rallied. "Have we got a mug shot of Adam Keele on file?"

"Probably. He's had quite a few one-man shows at the art gallery."

"What about the head teacher?"

I cringed. Relations between the paper and Ravenbridge High School had been sensitive ever since Tony, as the new editor, went overboard on a leaked drugs story. Two boys from Year 11 had been found with a tiny cube of cannabis resin, that was all. But he had made the school sound like some crime-infested dump from the seediest, most drug-ridden part of an inner city. Mr Carpenter was a decent hard-working head and had quite rightly objected to the coverage.

"Yes, we've got one of Mr Carpenter, but why?"

"The murder of Lara Ramsey will be front page again tomorrow, obviously. But the Keele suicide will make a good page three lead. I want pictures of Adam and the head, and underneath, a photo caption saying something like, *The boss who allowed teacher to bonk pupil* – you get the gist of it."

"Tony, that's outrageous! It's complete balls. Lara wasn't a pupil at the school. She left a couple of years ago. And there's absolutely no proof she was having an affair with Adam. That's just malicious gossip. You can't blame the head for any of this. Remember the cannabis story? Remember how furious he was about that? We've only just got back on good terms with the school."

"Yeah, yeah." He sighed deeply. "Sometimes I wonder if you should be in the newspaper industry, Jude."

"Sometimes I wonder too."

I thought I could hear a strangled gurgle of frustration.

"Where are you now?" he rasped.

"I'm going to the hospital to see my son."

There was silence.

"Right," he said at last, at normal volume. "Matt told me Lara Ramsey was Daniel's girlfriend, and about the asthma attack. You should have said."

"Would you have listened?"

Another silence. "Anyway. Get back here as soon as you can."

"You know I will."

"See you, Jude."

I threw the mobile on the passenger seat, unnerved by the faint suggestion of sympathy from my boss. Did Tony have a heart after all? I started the engine, shaking my head in disbelief.

The route to the hospital took me past Jubilee Park. I slowed down, cruising along to check on police activity. There didn't seem to be any. I pulled into a layby near the main entrance. The short wintry day was already fading. They'd be closing up soon.

As I passed through the tall wrought-iron gates I checked the opening time. Six-thirty in the morning, winter and summer. Presuming that the killer brought Lara's body through one of the two legitimate entrances, they must have done so some time after that. Of course there were illegal ways into the park, but they involved fences or thick hedges, and carrying a body at the same time would have been extremely difficult. Either way, legal entry or not, it would have been pitch dark and bitterly cold. Only the most dedicated joggers or dog walkers would have been around. The police had appealed for witnesses, but my strong instinct was that Lara's attacker would have been far too careful to risk being seen.

I made my way across the park towards the pond, the surface of which was beginning to freeze over. The bench nearby, where the body was found, was pretty much equidistant from the two gates so there was no clue as to which one the killer had used. The ubiquitous blue and white tape marked out the immediate crime scene, otherwise the park had returned to its normal tranquil state. It was almost deserted now. The only person I could see was a plump middle-aged man walking slowly around the pond.

There were more flowers here, a whole florist's shop of them. I stared at this strangely inadequate expression of grief. I had never understood why people placed bouquets where someone had died. Most of them didn't even know Lara, had just read about her in the paper or seen the story on TV. Was it an attempt to prettify something ugly? A way to vent their outrage? Or were they simply saying sorry? I bent my head to read some of the cards. *Dear Lara, you were just unlucky. Rest in peace. Beautiful flowers for a beautiful girl,* and bizarrely, *Take care.* Talking to the dead, that's what it was all about. Though I doubted Lara could hear them.

In my peripheral vision I was aware that the plump man was on my side of the water now and edging his way towards me. I stood my ground, hoping he would pass by and leave me in peace to gather my thoughts before I went to the hospital to tell Daniel the terrible news about Adam Keele, but he stopped a few metres from me.

"Shocking business, isn't it?"

I nodded, silently willing him to go away.

"I've visited a lot of crime scenes."

I glanced sideways. He didn't look like a weirdo. He wore a padded coat and one of those fur hats with ear-flaps tied on the crown. He seemed utterly conventional and ordinary. Then I reminded myself that that was exactly what you'd expect a certain kind of weirdo to do – cultivate the appearance of normality.

"This one gives me a very strong sense of evil."

I began to make space between us, but I didn't walk off. There was something oddly compelling about him. It was his voice, which was deep and clear and very sure of itself.

"What else would you expect?" I challenged him.

"Murder isn't always a matter of wickedness. Sometimes

I pick up anger, fear, desperation, passion, revenge. There is an element of all of those, but mostly this place gives me a terrible sense of cold."

"That's hardly surprising, in this weather."

He looked at me directly for the first time. I felt trapped by his penetrating gaze. "That's not what I mean. I'm talking about emotional coldness. Whoever did this calculated every move. But there is passion here too, heat that has turned cold."

I forced myself to back away. "What are you, a medium or something?"

"Some people call it that. I prefer psychic detective."

I tried to mask my spluttering with a fit of coughing. He wasn't deceived.

"I can tell you're not a believer."

"No, since you ask. I think that psychic stuff is all rubbish, just a substitute for religion."

Somehow he had moved near without me realising. "This isn't a matter of faith," he said quietly. "It's a gift. Or to be more accurate, a curse. What I see and feel here is just as real to me as what your five senses tell you." He took another step towards me. "What do you do for a living?"

"I'm a photographer. For the local paper."

He smiled. "Then you have a very highly developed sense of sight."

"I suppose so."

"What I do is just another kind of seeing."

"If you say so. I'd better go… I have to get to the hospital."

"Don't you want to know how this girl died?"

"Of course I do."

"You knew her, didn't you?"

"How did you…?"

"I can't explain how I see it, but I do. She was special to

67

you… or someone near to you." His eyes had a glazed look.

"If you really do know something, you should go to the police."

He frowned, looking down at his gloved hands. "I've tried, but they weren't interested."

I wasn't entirely surprised by that. I couldn't see the likes of Laverack and Naylor welcoming a psychic detective on to their team with open arms. I stared around the park, bleakly beautiful in the fading light.

He edged closer. "Perhaps if you put something in the paper?"

"About you?"

"If I turn out to be right, then next time the police will have to take notice of what I say. And it will be a scoop for the Ravenbridge Evening Post."

"But you haven't said anything. Just some stuff about cold and evil. That's hardly a prediction. I thought you psychics could tell what colour car was used, whether the killer had a limp or a birthmark on their left cheek." As I spoke I realised Matt probably would want to interview this guy. "Be honest, have you picked up any other vibe about this place? Or about the girl who died?"

"The devil is involved."

That stopped my glimmer of interest in its tracks. "The devil?" I asked sceptically.

"There's Satanism in this, but some corrupt form, some imitation of the real thing."

I began to feel slightly nauseous. Trauma and exhaustion and lack of food were taking their toll.

"You've lost me there. You've spun off into the stratosphere and left me way behind. I don't do devils." I walked briskly away but he trotted after me.

"Despite what you say, I see a sympathetic aura around you."

"Is that so?" I kept walking. The Ravenbridge Evening Post could do without a feature headlined *Local Psychic Detective Reveals Satanic Link*. It would make us a laughing stock.

"Take my card." He thrust something into my hand. "My name's Foley, Norman Foley. Ring me if you want to chat. Any time."

I stuffed the card in my pocket and strode towards the gates without looking back.

"Mr Keele is dead." There was no easy way to say it.

Daniel looked bruised around the eyes, as if the terrible things he was being asked to deal with were physical blows.

"What happened?" he whispered.

I told him, leaving out Adam's obsession with Lara, emphasising the fact that simply being a suspect had driven a sensitive grieving man to suicide. I knew it didn't quite add up, but I could tell by Daniel's blank stare that he couldn't make sense of much anyway.

The male nurse came into the room. "Hi," he said cheerfully. Then he saw our stony faces. "Everything OK?"

"Daniel's had another shock." I drew him to the far side of the room near the hand basin, glancing down at his name badge. "Gary, I hate to leave him, but I have to go back to work for a while. My boss is being difficult. But I'm still really worried about Daniel. You know what happened last time."

He nodded. "Leave it to me. I'll check him every few minutes."

I could have kissed him.

"Oh – nearly forgot. There's a woman to see Daniel. She came before —"

"Hockey-player legs?"

"She's wearing trousers."

DC Naylor didn't wait to be invited. She flung the door open and entered the room at speed. "I'd like a quick word with Daniel, if you don't mind." She jerked her head.

I sat down in the chair. "I'm staying."

Gary melted away.

Naylor thought about it. "All right. If you insist." She turned to Daniel. "You mentioned a bracelet. We've searched Lara's flat and we've found various bits of jewellery but nothing like the one you described. So I'd like some more detail."

"Does it matter?" I asked.

"Maybe not. But there again, it could be important. Killers often like to keep a trophy belonging to their victims."

My jaw dropped at her tactlessness. "Do you have to be so graphic?"

"You did ask. Daniel?"

I was about to protest when Daniel said faintly, "It's all right, Mum." He closed his eyes. "I made it out of glazed ceramic stones, every one a different colour, soft tones, like washed pebbles…"

Naylor looked none the wiser.

"Why don't you draw it?" I suggested.

"OK."

I helped Daniel sit up. I tore a sheet from my notebook and gave him a pen. His hand trembled at first then became steadier as he shaded each stone, labelling them as he went – *dove grey, heather mauve, soft grey-green*. Finally he drew the clasp in loving detail.

"There."

Naylor took the piece of paper from him. "Thanks." She tucked it in her shoulder bag. "By the way, have you ever dabbled in black magic, the occult, that sort of thing?"

Daniel frowned. "I think we messed about with a ouija board once, in Year 10. It was rubbish. All in the mind. I don't believe in that shit."

"Why do you want to know?" I asked, remembering what the weirdo in the park had said about the devil. Just a lucky guess. It had to be.

"We haven't been able to do the official post-mortem yet, but it looks like Lara was strangled, that's what killed her, not a stab wound as we thought at first. But after she died something was carved on her, here." She tapped the top of her chest.

An image of Lara's blood-stained T-shirt flashed into my mind.

"And there were marks around her mouth."

"Stop it!"

I looked at Daniel. Now his eyes were rimmed with purple shadows. He was sinking inside himself. With so much horror in the world, where else was there to go?

"Shall we step outside?"

DC Naylor and I stood nearly nose to nose in the corridor as nurses and auxiliaries hurried up and down.

"What was cut into Lara's chest?"

"I can't tell you that."

"Black magic, you said. So what was it? Devil's horns? An evil eye? What?"

She turned her head to watch a man in a wheelchair being trundled past.

"And what about these marks around her mouth?"

"Mrs Baxendale — "

"Ms. I'm not married."

"Whatever. I'm the detective. You've no right to interrogate me."

"We both want to find this bastard, don't we?"

"Of course."

"Have you got any leads at all? Or are you just floundering in the dark?"

I could tell I'd hit a nerve.

"Leave it to us," she said curtly. "We know what we're doing."

She strode down the corridor on her sturdy legs. I wanted to believe her. I wanted more than anything to take my son home, to shut and lock the doors. I longed to huddle safe inside and forget about murder and blood and mutilation.

But what if the police were too slow? What if this monster struck again? I didn't pretend to myself that I could solve this case single-handedly, but surely I could do something to speed things up?

I had to do something.

Eight

"Matt. I know you're busy…"

"Actually, I've just finished."

I tipped my mobile away from my ear to look at my watch. Nearly seven o'clock. I'd lost track of time. There was no way I was going back to Photographic now. I had other plans. "Swot. You should have gone home a couple of hours ago."

"Tony kept me working late on the Adam Keele story. I hear you saw it all. Are you OK?"

"Do you know how I feel?"

"Tell me."

"Angry. Bloody furious in fact. It's like those rows of dominoes – one terrible thing happens, then another and another. The damage this killer's done, it just seems to go on. What if we can't stop it?" My voice grew louder and less steady. I imagined Matt holding the phone away from his ear.

"Cool it, Jude," he said quietly.

"Sorry. But I can't help the way I feel."

"Where are you?"

"I'm going to see the woman who lives in the flat upstairs on Stonebeck Avenue, see if she can tell me anything. I'll never understand what happened to Lara until I find out more about her. My impression of her was obviously quite wrong."

"How do you mean?"

"I thought she was the quiet sensitive type, but her mother was suggesting she was downright promiscuous.

73

And then there's the modelling. When you think about it, not many people can strip their clothes off in front of strangers for the first time and take to it like a duck to water. I'm no prude but I don't think I could do it."

"She actually stripped off in front of them?"

"No! You know what I mean – posing naked for a bunch of sixth-formers. That takes guts, or an amazing ability to overcome inhibition. She was brought up a strict Catholic, remember."

"You think this woman can tell you more about Lara?"

"She knew her. It's not much to go on, but I'm going to talk to anyone who might help. What else can I do? And I was just wondering if you…"

"Give me fifteen minutes. I'll be there."

The alleyway that ran along the back of the houses on Stonebeck Avenue was pitch dark. We had to pick our way carefully to avoid the unseen ruts and frozen puddles.

"Here, hang on to me," Matt said when I slipped and nearly went flying. Clinging to each other, bent over like an elderly couple, we navigated the pitted ground until we reached the rear of number 15. The other houses had garages, high fences and strong wooden gates, but as usual number 15 chose to do its own thing. There had been a fence but it now consisted of a couple of upright posts and a few broken slats. The gate had disappeared completely.

Matt fingered the blue and white tape that blocked our way. "I don't know who manufactures this stuff but they must be making a fortune."

We looked at the tape, looked at each other and nodded. Then with co-ordination as polished as synchronised swimmers we ducked under it.

"Just remind me why we've come round the back and

nearly broken our necks in the process?" asked Matt.

I peered around the yard. A stone sink full of pebbles, bits of driftwood, an old rusty bicycle.

"Lara parked her car here, but there's no sign of it," I said.

"The police have probably taken it away. Perhaps whoever did this used Lara's car to take her body to the park."

"That's just what I was thinking. Is there any way we can find out? What about Fred?"

"Tony's famous police contact? He seems to have dried up as a source. I guess this case is just too sensitive."

"Shame."

The downstairs flat was in darkness. I pointed at a lighted window on the upper floor.

"She's in."

"Good."

We stumbled round to the front. Our footing wasn't much better here. The cold night had made the pavement like a skating rink. I led the way under the tape and up the path of Number 15. The light from the streetlamp allowed me to see the names handwritten on slips of paper. *Flat 1 Ramsey. Flat 2 Molloy.*

I pressed the buzzer for Flat 2 and waited. The ledge at the bottom of the door was fretted with rot as if a small animal had been nibbling it. I touched it with the toe of my boot and several fragments fell away.

As I reached for the buzzer again the door creaked open. In the gloom I could see a small chubby woman with a lot of crinkly grey hair framing her round face.

"Annie Molloy?"

"Yes. What do you want?"

Matt edged forward. "Ravenbridge Evening Post. Can we have a brief word?"

I glared at him. Had he forgotten this was nothing to do with the paper?

He winked back.

"Is it about Lara?"

"That's right. Can we come in?"

"I'm not sure I should…"

"We've already spoken to the police. There's no problem."

The woman pressed her fingers to her temples. "If it's all right with them… I suppose…" She stepped aside to let us in.

We stood in the dark narrow hallway while she closed the door. I stared at the entrance to Flat 1. It was roped off with more blue and white tape.

"Sorry if I seem a bit… to be honest, I'm still in a state of shock," said Annie. Her eyelids were red and swollen.

"We understand," said Matt.

She waved her hand. "Go on up."

We clattered up the steep stairs. The door to Annie's flat was open and led straight into the living room. The walls were covered in pictures. Nudes mostly. There was clutter everywhere. Dirty coffee mugs were balanced precariously on piles of books and magazines. A cat with ears pricked pretended to be asleep on the ragged Persian carpet. I caught the rank odour of cat pee overlaid with the reek of tobacco smoke and joss sticks.

Annie curled up on a cracked leather sofa. She reached shakily for her cigarettes and lighter.

"I don't know what I can tell you." She lit a cigarette and inhaled deeply.

"We'd just like to know a little bit more about Lara, as a person," I said. "She did some modelling, I believe. How did that start?"

Annie nodded. "It was me who got her into it. She used

to come up here sometimes for a drink and a chat, and she saw all these drawings." She waved her arm expansively. Matt stared around him, mesmerised by the sea of naked flesh. "I've been an artists' model for years. I told her, not everyone can do it, but Lara said she'd like to try. So when I got a booking I couldn't do, last spring it was, I sent her off to the high school instead of me." She sighed deeply.

Had she heard about Adam Keele's death? Before I could broach the subject she was off again.

"She took to it straight away. After that first session she worked at the school regularly, and other places too – she was always in demand, but she couldn't do everything, what with working full-time. So I got some of her leftovers." She laughed shrilly. "Not that I minded. I could see why Lara was so popular. She had a lovely body and she was very natural. Some people look stiff and awkward but Annie could fall into a pose like a cat. There wasn't much of her – like a wisp of smoke she was – but she had lovely breasts, a beautiful complexion, and as for that hair…" Annie's face crumpled. "How could anyone…?" She dabbed her eyes with a tissue.

"Are you OK? If you'd rather not talk…"

Now it was Matt's turn to glare at me.

"I'm all right. In fact it helps to talk about her. As far as anything helps."

"She was a good model, then?" Matt pressed on.

"One of the best I've seen. Lara had that gift of stillness, like she was soaking up the attention and loving it. But she quickly learnt how to go into a kind of detached trance at the same time. It isn't just a matter of sitting there, you know. It's a kind of relaxed concentration, an alert stillness."

I nodded. Daniel had often talked about the qualities of the best models. But Matt looked mystified.

"I don't really get it. Taking off your clothes in front of strangers – isn't that downright dangerous, especially if you're as good-looking as Lara?"

"You don't draw, do you?"

Matt shook his head.

"Artists aren't perverts. It 's a sensual experience for them but not an erotic one. It's bloody hard work."

"But there must be the occasional misfit, the pervy type, someone who could get obsessed?"

Annie looked horrified. "Are you saying she was murdered by someone who drew her?" Her hand shook so badly a slug of ash fluttered on to her baggy grey T-shirt. "Oh my god! It was me that introduced her to modelling. Is it my fault she's dead?"

"Of course not," I said. "No one's blaming you."

But tears flowed freely down her cheeks, making her fleshy face look old and ravaged.

"Shall I make you a coffee?"

Annie looked at me through streaming eyes, pointing mutely to the kitchen door.

"Sugar?"

She held up two fingers.

The chilly kitchen was painted bright orange in an attempt to cheer it up, but the colour failed to hide the patches of damp. I found an open jar of coffee among the debris, rinsed out a stained mug, and when the water had boiled, made an oily-looking brew. When I picked up a bowl of lumpy sugar a large spider scuttled across the worktop, making me flinch. It reminded me of what Lee had said, about Lara not being afraid of spiders. I dug out a couple of spoonfuls of sugar and stirred them in. In the fridge there was an inch of milk in a carton.

Stuck to the fridge door was a planner-type diary.

Last year's, of course. I didn't see Annie buying this year's diary till around April. One word kept catching my eye: *Lara* for tea, *Lara* on holiday, *Lara* back home. Then from around late October, no mention of Lara except for one – *Lara's* birthday in December.

Annie was stretched out on the sofa. Her eyes were closed and some of the tension had drained from her tear-blotched face. Matt was talking to her in a low voice. He stopped when I came in, took the cup from me and handed it to Annie.

"You'll feel better for that," he said.

"Thanks, love, you're a godsend." She rested the cup on her ample chest. "I was just telling this young man what a great kid Lara was. I'm twice her age but that didn't matter at all. I've lost a really good friend." She sniffed hard. "We looked out for each other. We had keys for each other's flats. I watered her plants when she went on holiday, and she fed Macavity when I was away." Annie reached down to fondle the cat's ears and was rewarded immediately with a thrumming purr.

"Did she get rid of spiders for you?"

"How did you know that? I'm terrified of them but they didn't bother her a bit. I remember once, there was a massive one in my bed. I was so terrified I started screaming. Lara came running upstairs, calmly picked it up and went down to the front garden with it. The paper boy was walking past, and she showed it to him. I was watching them from the bedroom window. Even he looked a bit taken aback by the size of it. She put it down gently on the ground, and do you know what he did? He stamped on it. She gave him a bit of a lecture about not killing things and he ran off. We had a laugh about it afterwards." She sipped her coffee noisily. "We were always laughing. We used to open a bottle of wine every Sunday night and smoke a bit of weed. We had this toast: three cheers for freedom and excess and the naked body!"

"You'd have missed her when she left?"

"Left?"

"She was thinking of giving up her job and leaving Ravenbridge. Sorry… didn't she tell you?"

"No." Annie stared into space for a while then put the mug on the floor and lit another cigarette. "That's the one thing about Lara I couldn't get on with."

"What do you mean?"

"She was secretive. Me, I'd tell anyone anything. But she held back. Work was taboo – too boring. Parents ditto – too miserable, and as for men…"

"She didn't tell you about her boyfriend?"

"The latest one, you mean? No way. Lara didn't tell me about any of them. She never brought them home. She said her flat was her sanctuary, her private space. I was allowed in there, but only to water her plants when she was away. And she always kept her bedroom door locked."

"She had a lot of boyfriends?"

"Tons, but none of them lasted long. Sometimes it was boys of her own age, often it was older men, even married ones. You couldn't call them relationships. It was just sex. It was as if she was looking for something." Annie shook her head sadly.

"How do you know, if she didn't talk about them?" Matt asked.

"Ah." She tapped the side of her nose. "A mutual friend. Someone she works with."

I was wondering about something else. "If she didn't bring them here, where did they actually do it? Their place? But what about the married ones? A hotel?

Her car?"

"Maybe. But I reckon she took them somewhere. I asked her once, but guess what? She refused to say." She brushed ash from her stomach. "I got the impression this latest one was different. Lara changed when she started going out with him. When was it? Round about last November, I think. She didn't come upstairs so often. I didn't even see her on her birthday. But by then she'd gone soft, less angry – not so much fun, to be quite honest."

"Her new boyfriend was my son."

"Oh shit. I didn't mean…" She gagged on her cigarette and began to cough violently.

"It's all right." Matt patted her hand.

"That's terrible. He must be going through hell," she croaked.

"He is."

Matt leaned forward. "You've been really helpful, Annie. There's just one more thing we need to ask you about. The police believe Lara was murdered in the flat downstairs."

Her eyes widened. "But I thought it happened in Jubilee Park?"

"Now they think she was killed here, then her body was taken to the park and dumped."

"That explains all the police activity downstairs." She waved her cigarette around. "Oh my god," she groaned. "I can't bear it. The thought of it. I must have been here all the time when Lara was… what if he comes back?"

"I'm sure you're not in any danger. But try and remember – it was two nights ago, the evening of New Year's Day. Did you hear anything going on downstairs?"

"Yes."

"What?" Matt was unable to mask his eagerness. I held my breath.

"Music. It was really loud."

"Just music? Nothing else? What time did the music stop?"

"No idea. I turned up my TV in retaliation. I must have drunk a bit too much because I fell asleep, right here on the sofa. I woke up in the middle of the night."

"And everything was quiet downstairs?"

"Yes! How was I to know? The last thing you expect..." Her voice tailed off. She dragged nervously on her fag, reactivating her coughing fit. Her face grew red, her eyes streaming. "No, wait..." She thumped her own chest till the hawking calmed down. "That night it wasn't just her usual music, the kind that makes your head feel like it's being drilled by a Black and Decker – that's one thing that made me realise Lara was definitely not my generation — "

"What kind of music was it?" asked Matt with as much patience as he could muster.

"Hard to describe... the sort that goes with belly dancing."

"Arab music?" I asked.

"Yeah, that's right. Of course it was. I went to Morocco once. I heard the same kind of stuff there."

"Was she interested in belly dancing?"

"She never mentioned it. But then..." Annie blew her nose on the grubby tissue. "I'd hardly seen her for weeks." She lay back limply, her eyes shiny with tears. "I just keep hoping it's all been a terrible mistake, a practical joke that's gone too far. I keep expecting her to come running up those stairs, knock on my door and say Gotcha!" Annie stretched down to pick up the cat, clutching it to her chest. "But she won't, will she?"

I shook my head. "I'm afraid not."

She buried her face in the cat's fur. That's when I

decided I couldn't tell her about Adam Keele. She'd had enough for now, and she would find out tomorrow in any case. Whether it was the Evening Post, local radio or the TV news, the relentless media would reach her somehow.

Matt stood up. "We really appreciate you talking to us."

"When will it be in the paper?"

I looked furiously at Matt. "Actually, I came to see you for purely personal reasons."

"But if it's all right with you, we could include a couple of paragraphs about your friendship with Lara," said Matt smoothly.

"It's fine by me." She smiled up at him.

I had to marvel at the man. First the scary Mrs Ramsey, now Annie Molloy, they were like putty in his hands.

"And we'd like a photo, too. Do you mind?"

"Of course I don't mind." Annie dropped the cat on to the floor. It yowled and slunk off into the kitchen. "Do you want me to take my clothes off?"

Nine

We ducked under the tape on to the frosty pavement.

"Did you believe her?" asked Matt, his arm locked in mine.

"I think so. In fact she seemed a lot more upset than Lara's own mother."

"That's what I mean. All those waterworks. Don't you think it was a bit over the top?"

"You reckon she was pretending?"

Matt skidded on the ice. I yanked him upright.

"Thanks, Jude."

"Now we're quits. Where was I? Oh yeah – if Annie was putting on a show of grief, then all I can say is, she's a bloody good actress."

"I detected a definite whiff of bitterness about her. You know, jealous of the younger, prettier girl."

"Who she fancied."

"You think so?"

"Definitely."

"So there's sexual jealousy too, as well as the fact that Lara was taking a lot of her modelling work."

"What are you saying – you think she killed Lara?" I asked.

"We can't rule anything out."

"I suppose not. But the overwhelming feeling I got from Annie was that she was just plain sad. Lara might have made her feel old and washed up, and when she started going out with Daniel that may have made her jealous – this one wasn't a one-night stand after all – but mostly I think she missed her company, her friendship."

"I'm not convinced, but I'll bow to your feminine intuition on this one."

I dug him in the ribs. "Patronising git."

We reached the end of the lane and headed for the main road where our cars were parked. The pavements had been gritted here, but though there was no danger of falling any more, Matt still held on to my arm, his grip looser now, more companionable.

"There's something I haven't told you," I said. "Apparently Lara had marks around her mouth, and wait, you won't believe this, some sort of black-magic symbol on her chest."

"What, painted on?"

"No. Carved with a knife."

"Christ." He was lost in thought for a moment, then shook himself. "How do you know all this?"

"DC Naylor told me that much, but then she clammed up."

We stopped beside my Triumph Herald.

Matt sighed. "We really could do with some good inside information. You don't know anyone on the SOCO team or CID, do you?"

"Actually…"

"Who?"

"One of the police photographers, Ben Greenwood. He was there in the park, so he must be involved in the case."

"Is he a friend of yours?"

I hesitated. "Yes and no."

"Will he talk to you?"

"Yes… and no."

"For god's sake, Jude. Stop being so enigmatic. Who do you think you are, the Mona Lisa?"

"All right. I'll give him a try."

"Great." He kissed me lightly on the cheek. "See you tomorrow."

"Maybe. I've got stuff to do."

"What?"

"Something Annie said. I need to think it through."

"Don't tell me then, Mona Lisa. Just be careful." He started to walk away. "And don't forget to ring that photographer as soon as you get home."

I nodded, but I was in two minds about that. Ben Greenwood used to work at the Ravenbridge Evening Post and we'd been good friends. For some mad reason I'd been drawn to his gloomy nature and deadpan sense of humour. Then we became more than friends. In fact, we'd lived together for a while. But one New Year's Eve, two or three years back, we broke up. I hadn't spoken to him since.

"Ben? It's Jude."

There was a long lugubrious silence on the other end of the line before I got a response.

"I bet I know what this is about. Climbing over the park fence on to a crime scene. What kind of stunt was that?"

I counted to three. "How are you?"

"Not bad. Apart from the fact my haemorrhoids are giving me hell and I'm going bald."

Four, five, six. Had I really loved this man?

"Listen, Ben, are you still working on the Lara Ramsey story?"

I heard a deep disapproving rumble. "I knew it. Thanks for reminding me why I got out of press photography. This isn't a story. A girl's dead. Just back off, will you?"

"You don't understand. This isn't for the paper. Lara was Daniel's girlfriend."

"Shit. I heard you'd ID'd the body but I didn't realise… How's he taking it?"

"Badly. He had a serious asthma attack. He's still in hospital."

"Is he OK?"

"He'll be fine."

I had a sudden image of Ben and Daniel one cold day playing with a rugby ball in the back garden. Daniel had kicked it too far and it had got lost in the unkempt tangle of bushes down the end. They were laughing as they searched for the ball, their breath pouring out like smoke. It had lodged in my mind because it was so rare to see Ben in a cheerful mood. When I threw him out it had taken Daniel a long time to get over it. Even a pessimistic male role model was better than none.

"Tell him I'm sorry."

"I will. The thing is, he's desperate to know what happened. The police investigation is so damn slow."

"Give us a break, Jude. It's only been a couple of days."

"It feels like years." I swapped the phone to my other ear. "I'm not asking you to steal confidential files or anything."

"Good."

"But any detail would help."

"Such as?" he said cagily.

"Have the police got Lara's car?"

"I don't think so. I certainly haven't been asked to take any photos of a car. What else?"

"I believe Lara had marks around her mouth?"

"Yeah. She had this perfect flawless skin except for those spots."

"Spots? You mean ordinary zits?" I tried to remember if Lara had ever had an attack of acne.

"No. More like blisters."

"That's weird."

"True. Is that it?"

"Hold on. The wound on her chest. What was it exactly?"

"I don't know if I should — "

"It's OK – the police told me it was some sort of black-magic symbol. What sort? I'm just curious."

"It was a pentagram. You know, a five-pointed star?"

"Yeah, I know what a pentagram is, but why…?"

"Can't answer that one."

"Fair enough. You've been a great help. Just one other thing – have they done the post-mortem yet?"

"They're doing it tonight. What with the holidays they've had problems finding a pathologist."

"Will you be there?"

"Yes. But you'll have to wait for the official report like everyone else."

There was silence. Another image flashed up. Ben and a girl called Kirsty from telesales having sex in the bathroom of a friend's house at a New Year's Eve party. The latch was loose, or maybe they were too excited to bolt the door properly. It was just my bad luck – or good fortune – that that was the very moment I needed a pee. I found Kirsty in the sink, her knees gripping Ben's sides while he thrust at her, making the toothbrushes on the shelf rattle in their holder.

"How's Kirsty?" I heard myself say.

"Who?"

"Kirsty. Don't tell me you've forgotten?"

"Oh, her. That didn't last. We broke up soon after… you know… that party."

"Really?" I couldn't stop myself smiling. "Didn't she like the bathroom fittings at your new place?"

"Don't start, Jude."

"Don't worry, I've finished." I felt a small flutter of nostalgia. "We did have some good times, didn't we? Remember that summer when Daniel was away on a school trip, when we camped on the beach at Whitby?"

"How could I forget?"

"That sunset – the way it was reflected in the windows of the church and they blazed red like the building was on fire from within. I've still got the picture I took."

"I remember you getting drunk and being sick. And I remember freezing my balls off in that sleeping bag. You were a lousy hot-water bottle."

The little surge of affection evaporated faster than mist on a summer morning. "Thanks, Ben. See you around."

When I put the phone down I realised I had never done a better thing than dump Ben Greenwood.

Useful contact, though.

It was a long evening. The house felt empty. I even missed Daniel's music, the kind Annie Molloy had so aptly described as making your head feel as if it was being drilled by a Black and Decker. I microwaved a pizza, cracked open a few nuts left over from Christmas and drained the remains of the brandy.

The TV unravelled itself in front of me, an inane parade of quizzes and soaps and so-called reality shows. I let it occupy my eyes while my mind was elsewhere, thinking about what Annie had said, about Lara never bringing her boyfriends to the flat on Stonebeck Avenue. So where did she take them? I'd always encouraged Daniel to bring his friends home. That included the few tentative romantic relationships he'd had, and lately Lara had spent a lot of time here. Not that I saw much of them, apart from a few shared meals. The rest of the time the relentless synthetic beat coming from his room told me when they were in residence. To be honest, I was out a lot of the time, seeing friends, going to films, or holed up in my darkroom in the basement. Now I wish I'd taken more notice.

The national news came on. I held my breath. Lara's murder merited a brief mention well into the bulletin, with no footage. But on the local news that followed, it took top spot, complete with lengthy filming of the bench in Jubilee Park where the body was found. I knew it wouldn't be long before the story became big national news, especially if the killer wasn't found quickly. As a coda, the newsreader mentioned the death of art teacher Adam Keele, the unspoken implication being that he had something to do with Lara's death. I was certain he hadn't.

Longing for some relief from the tragedy, I slumped in front of a documentary about a climber, a man with long hair and aquiline native-American features. I was transfixed by pictures of him climbing vertical rock faces without ropes or a safety harness, like some sort of human fly. After my recent experience struggling up a tree to rescue a ferret, I was bowled over by this man's audacity and skill. The credits came up and as I reached for the remote a voice-over announced that the man had been killed in a climbing accident. Tears welled up and rolled down my cheeks in huge droplets. I didn't know who I was crying for – the human fly, or Lara, or Adam Keele, or Daniel. Or me. In the end I decided I was weeping for the whole damn lot of us, for a world that had tilted on its axis and distorted everything I thought I knew.

The night was even longer. It was so bitterly cold I kept waking up. I was aware of every discomfort – my numb toes, the renewed throbbing in my buttock where I'd had the injection, the scoured feeling in my eyes from crying too much. In the end I swore and got out of bed. I paced about the room, trying to get my blood flowing again, feeling wretched. Why had I lumbered myself with this impossible task? If the police hadn't found an obvious culprit by now my chances were zilch. And why was it so damn cold?

Then I thought of a beautiful young woman lying in the morgue, the irreversible chill of death upon her.

All my whinging slid from me like sand in an egg-timer. I was alive, which made me the most privileged person in the world. I went downstairs and made tea and toast. True, four-thirty in the morning was a touch early for breakfast, but I had thinking to do. I was slapping butter on my second round when it came to me.

I knew where Lara must have taken her men.

Ten

When the sun came up I opened the curtains and saw that a sprinkling of snow had dusted the garden. Across the road a few kids were already sledging on Weavers' Field. Before I set off, I zipped my leather jacket up to my chin and twisted a scarf around my neck.

I thought they might be closed, but the lights were blazing at Kerwin and Black. Pretty naïve of me to suppose that the brutal killing of a colleague would get in the way of making money. When I opened the door the two occupants, a middle-aged woman and a man in his thirties, looked up expectantly from their computers.

The woman pasted on a professional smile. "Can I help you?"

"I'd like to speak to the manager."

The man stood up and crossed the busy carpet towards me. I recognised him at once. In the flesh, his mottled complexion really did look as if he'd shaved with a lawn mower. It wasn't Harrison's fault after all.

"That'll be me." He extended his hand. "Craig Gilmore. What can I do for you?"

I showed him my business card. Matt had the right idea. Presenting yourself as a representative of the media seemed to open people up, even when it wasn't a professional call.

"From the Evening Post? Didn't that picture of me come out? I have to say, that lad with the pierced tongue did seem a bit slack."

"The picture's fine," I said, not mentioning the fact that I'd enhanced it. "It'll be in the business supplement tomorrow."

I unwound my scarf. "I've come about Lara Ramsey."

The woman's smile slithered off her face. Craig Gilmore looked uncomfortable.

"That's all in the hands of the police. I wouldn't want to talk to the media without their permission."

"I'm glad to hear it. I'm here for personal reasons. I knew Lara. So did my son. We're desperately trying to understand what happened, and why."

"It's not for the paper, then?"

"No."

"All the same." He spread his hands and shrugged. "I don't think I can help you. I really didn't know Lara that well."

"I did." The woman swivelled on her chair, which badly needed oiling. At each swivel it screeched as if she was running over a cat.

"Were you friends?"

She stopped swivelling, picked up an emery board and started filing her nails. "Not exactly."

I was mesmerised by her rosy-pink talons, which looked perfectly shaped already. "How do you mean?"

The emery board was thrust into a drawer. "Lara was very good at her job, granted, but in other ways she wasn't quite what she seemed."

"How did she seem?"

"Susan…" Craig said quietly. It sounded like a warning.

The woman ignored him. She picked up a copy of the Kerwin and Black in-house magazine. It was so fresh off the press I could still smell the printing ink. She turned the cover towards me – Lara's face, her cloud of red-gold hair, her enigmatic smile. "Look at her. Butter wouldn't melt." She tossed the magazine on her desk. "Why was she on the cover, I'd like to know. Why not Mr Gilmore? Or one of the other agents? Or all of us? It was supposed to be an award for the whole branch. Why her? They make her look like an angel, don't they? But she was nothing of the sort."

"You mean she had a lot of boyfriends?"

Susan laughed. "You could say that. She never said much about them, but there'd be phone calls and meetings during working hours and long lunches and going home early. They often came here to pick her up. Young men, middle-aged, married ones, even clients – she wasn't fussy."

Susan must be Annie Molloy's friend, I realised, the one who told her all about Lara's colourful love life.

"None of this is relevant," Craig Gilmore butted in. "So, if you don't mind… we do have a lot of work to do." He was twisting the wedding ring on his finger. I could sense his palpable eagerness to see the back of me.

But his colleague was unstoppable. "She took keys from the safe," she blurted out.

"Susan!"

"It's true! I've never told you this, Craig, but I saw her. Several times."

"When was the last time?" I asked.

"A couple of months back. She hasn't done it lately. I think she knew I was keeping a close eye on her. She seemed calmer, more friendly, and the phone calls stopped, so I decided not to say anything."

"Of course she took keys from the safe," Craig said smoothly. "How else could she show clients round properties?"

"I think Susan means she took people there alone," I said.

"No, that's not normal procedure. Agents, especially if they're female, always go in pairs."

"I think she was taking her boyfriends to an empty house," I said patiently.

"That would be highly unprofessional," said Craig. "If head office were to hear about it —"

"She was having sex with them there, wasn't she?" Susan's cheeks were as pink as her nails.

"Probably. Was it always the same key?"

"I'm not sure, but the last time, I checked which key was missing after she'd gone. It was number 47. I remember the number because that's how old —" She stopped abruptly.

"47 what? Where is this house?" I asked.

"It's not a house number, it's a code," said Craig. "We keep the keys and the addresses of properties separate, just in case of a break-in." He returned to his computer. "We number the keys and match them to their addresses on here. I can't remember offhand which property number 47 is but…" He clicked his mouse a couple of times.

I watched Craig's face as he stared at the screen. "Chapel House," he said without a trace of surprise. I had the impression he knew already.

"I should have guessed," said Susan. "It's been on the market so long, the For Sale sign has blown down three times."

"Why hasn't it sold?"

"If you saw it you'd know why. It's not exactly your standard semi."

"It's overpriced," said Craig. "That's why it hasn't found a buyer." He turned to his colleague. "I asked Lara to go out there a few times, Susan, to keep an eye on the place. So that business about the keys was perfectly above board, nothing for you to worry about."

Susan's mouth fell open. It was clear she didn't believe a word of it. Nor did I.

"I'd like to take a look at Chapel House," I said.

"Are you interested in purchasing it?"

"No. I've told you why I'm here."

"Then I'm sorry. We have strict rules. No time-wasters. Head office insists that we follow procedure."

"If you're busy just give me the key. I'll have it back to you within an hour."

"Certainly not."

"I'm not going to smash the place up!"

A little weary smile passed across Craig's face.

"If you don't trust me, come with me and pretend I'm a client."

His gaze skimmed over my worn leather jacket, my frayed jeans. "It's out of the question, I'm afraid."

"At least tell me where it is."

"No can do."

I clenched my teeth. If I had time when I got back to Photographic I was going to restore the mug shot of the branch manager to its former mottled glory.

"OK." I grabbed the Property News from a dump bin by the door. "I'll find it myself."

My mobile rang before I reached my car.

"Where the hell are you?" Tony's gravelly voice blasted in my ear. "Get your arse back here, Jude. The shit's hit the fan."

"Can't you manage without me for an hour or so? There's something really important I need to do."

"*This* is important. What the hell do you think you're playing at? And don't tell me you're visiting your sick son in hospital. According to Matt, he's well on the mend."

"I'm on a job."

"Which job? Give me the ticket reference."

"It's a private job."

"You're doing freelance work on company time?"

"It's nothing to do with photography. I'm following up a hunch I had —"

"A hunch? Who do you think you are? A bloody journalist? I don't believe this. Show your face back here in thirty minutes or else."

"Or else what?"

"You're the investigative reporter now. You work it out."

"Good to know the real Tony is back," I said, but the line was dead.

Tony stood with his hands on his hips, staring at the wall in Photographic.

"What are these doing here?" He jabbed at the enlargements Harrison had mounted. "These aren't news pix. I don't remember any of them." He peered closer. "River for sale? What's that all about? Is this your own arty-farty stuff? Are you using this place as your personal art gallery?"

"I took them in my own time, yes, and now they're logged in the computer. They could be useful. And it wasn't me that put them up."

"Who was it?"

I looked around. Raymond was working at his computer, surreptitiously stuffing his face with chocolate muffin. Buzz, whose leopard-skin trousers had been exchanged for a pair of bright red jeans, was going through the job tickets and entering them in the diary. There was no sign of Harrison. I was about to dump him in it, but I held back. I'd done him a disservice over the Craig Gilmore picture, and to be honest, I was just a little bit flattered that he'd put the prints on display. They stood out against the dreary pictures of cheque presentations and cricket teams, not just in subject matter and composition, but in sheer quality.

I had my old Nikon F and the painstaking work I put in in the darkroom to thank for that.

I floundered, wondering what to say, but Tony had already moved on.

"Never mind. I'll deal with that another time. I want to know exactly where you've been this morning."

"It was about Lara Ramsey. It was something I had to do. When this is all over — "

"You think I'm going to wait that long to get some work out of you? And talking of the Ramsey story, I've had a complaint."

"Who from?"

"Mrs Ramsey, that's who!"

He picked up a copy of yesterday's Post. The Ramsey family smiled in a tight-lipped way from their sun-baked terrace.

"How did you get hold of this photo?"

"I can explain about that."

Two pairs of eyes swivelled in my direction. Raymond stopped chewing, his cheeks as full as a hamster's, while Buzz's sleek dark eyebrows rose nearly to his hairline. Tony glared at them as if to say Mind your own damn business.

"Come to my office. Now."

Tony snapped shut his venetian blinds and sat in the leather chair behind his desk.

"Mrs Ramsey says you stole this picture." He stabbed the image of Lara in the chest with a thick finger.

"But it wasn't me who — " I stopped. I was reluctant to split on Matt and tell Tony that this theft was my colleague's fault. Wasn't I just as much to blame? After all, I had processed the damn thing. "Mrs Ramsey was being difficult. Understandable, of course, but we needed a picture.

It seemed the right thing to do at the time." I shrugged. "I shouldn't have taken it without permission. It won't happen again."

"What a pathetic explanation."

Someone came into the room. I turned round. It was Matt.

"If this is about Lara's picture…" he began.

I warned him with my eyes. "It's all sorted, Matt. I've apologised. Old hands like me shouldn't lead clean-living young reporters into bad ways." I turned to Tony. "I'll take the picture back to Mrs Ramsey and grovel."

"Good. Just as long as I bloody well don't have to do it."

The phone on his desk rang shrilly. "Editor. What? Right. What time?" He banged the phone down. "The police have called a press conference."

"They did the post-mortem last night," I said. "Perhaps there's more information." They both looked at me with something like respect. "Contacts," I explained.

"When is it?" asked Matt.

"Eleven o'clock. You need to get down there straight away."

"Me too," I said, turning to go.

"Just hold on a cotton-picking minute!" Tony exploded. "You're going nowhere, sunshine. There's a pile of stuff waiting to be processed, pix I need for tomorrow's paper."

"Get someone else to do it."

"I'm telling you, Jude. You are not going."

"That's where you're wrong." I leaned across the desk and patted his cheek. "I'll even take some pictures for you."

Eleven

"Did you see his face?" smiled Matt. He drove fast through the town centre, or as fast as the heavy traffic and an unbroken chain of red lights would allow. "By the way, some guy's been ringing you. Someone called Norman Foley? He says he met you in the park."

"Oh, him. He's a complete fraud. Calls himself a psychic detective. He says he can pick up vibes from the place where Lara was found. Can you believe that?"

"Sounds like an interesting angle."

"Forget it, Matt. He just wants his fifteen minutes of fame. He's a con artist, I'm sure of it. Well, fairly sure. But I have got some reliable information." I told him what Susan at the estate agents had said about Lara taking certain favoured clients to properties on her own.

"She was no angel, was she? Downright promiscuous, in fact."

"Only until she met Daniel." I glanced at my watch. "The conference starts in two minutes."

"No problem."

He swerved into a narrow side street, ribbed on both sides with double yellow lines. He slapped a card stating PRESS on the dashboard. "It usually works."

"You're wasted in Ravenbridge, Matt Dryden. It'll be the bright lights of the metropolis for you."

"One day. But right now this place is just fine." He squeezed my hand. I winced. "Sorry. How is it?"

"A lot better, though my bottom's still throbbing."

"That ferret bit you on the arse as well?"

"Tetanus injection."

"That explains why you were walking like a cowboy at the hospital."

He laughed. I grimaced. We both pulled up our collars against the bitter weather. "Come on, Matt, we've got work to do."

The press room at the central police station was packed with reporters and photographers. I recognised local TV and radio staff, and a few stringers for the nationwide titles, but there were several unfamiliar faces too. I knew from last night's TV news that this was now a national story and it wasn't hard to understand why. The brutal murder of a beautiful young girl was the perfect recipe to get the media salivating. Apart from the sensational appeal, this point in the calendar, just after Christmas and New Year, was infamous for its lack of news. It was as if the killer had done the hacks a favour.

Matt and I pushed our way to the standing room only at the front where a conference table bristled with microphones. On the wall behind, a large whiteboard displayed a massive enlarged photo of Lara. Matt and I stared at it wordlessly, immediately sobered up.

"Listen, I want to thank you for what you did back there," said Matt, breaking the silence. "You could have landed me in it with Tony over that stolen photo, but you took the rap. Why did you do that?"

"Guilt."

"It was my fault."

"I colluded with you. I'm equally to blame."

"But Tony thinks it was all down to you."

"You're young, Matt."

"You're not exactly a pensioner."

"No. But I don't have your driving ambition to be big in the media. It would be bad timing if you got into trouble now. This story could be the making of you."

"I can't deny that. That's why I really appreciate what you did." He squeezed my other hand this time. I didn't wince. In fact I felt a rush of electrical energy that was far from painful.

"Where is the photo now?"

He tapped the pocket of his coat. Just then, there was a small commotion at the inner door and all heads swivelled in that direction. Laverack came into the room, followed by a uniformed officer, her shoulder tabs heavy with silver. Mrs Ramsey, walking with a ramrod-straight back, and a man I presumed was her husband, brought up the rear. They all sat behind the desk, dwarfed by the giant picture of Lara.

"I see they've wheeled out the big cheese," whispered Matt.

I nodded. Chief Superintendent Rollins was the chief commanding officer of this division, an area that covered Ravenbridge, a number of smaller towns and all the spaces in between.

Laverack raised a well-manicured hand. "Ladies and gentlemen." The babble of voices ceased at once. The whirr and click of cameras was all that could be heard for several seconds while the detective gathered his thoughts.

"As you know, a young woman, Lara Ramsey, aged twenty, was murdered here in Ravenbridge last Monday night."

A local stringer for the Sun immediately piped up, "Is it true she was a nude model?"

Laverack's hand went up again, a more defensive gesture this time. "Can we leave questions till the end? I have a statement…" He rustled a sheet of paper. "Lara Ramsey was a highly respected member of the community."

I looked at Matt and our eyebrows rose fractionally.

"She left the house of her aunt and uncle, Stanislaus and Carol Roguski, around nine on the evening of January 1st. Our last sighting of Lara is on the bus into the town centre. A few hours later she was murdered in cold blood, almost certainly in her own flat."

"Why did she take a bus?" I whispered. "Why didn't she take her car?" Matt shrugged and put two fingers to his lips to shut me up. He was recording Laverack's words in furious shorthand.

"We believe her body was then left in the park. It was discovered by a man taking an early morning run. I think we can all agree this was a cruel and undignified end to a young person's life." Laverack turned the sheet over. "The police pathologist has now completed the post-mortem and we can confirm that the cause of death was asphyxia caused by strangulation."

A murmur passed like a wave through the room.

"I thought she was stabbed?" Matt said.

"No – didn't I tell you? Sorry, so much to think about. Listen up and keep writing."

"We can also confirm that some, in fact most, of the blood found on the victim's clothing did not belong to her. Nor did the traces of blood found in her flat. DNA testing is underway as we speak. I should point out that the killer made a good job of cleaning up the flat and that very little forensic evidence has been found. This blood sample is vital to our investigation. Therefore we appeal to anyone who might have seen someone, a friend, relative or work-mate, with a bad cut or wound that they can't properly account for, to contact us immediately. We need names, if only to eliminate them from our enquiry."

Patricia Ramsey maintained her iron control, but her husband was openly weeping, head down, shoulders heaving.

Laverack ploughed on. "We can't be sure of the exact time of death – it was an extremely cold night and we don't know how long Lara's body had been left out in the open, but our best estimate is that death occurred around midnight on January 1st."

"Was there evidence of rape?" someone shouted from the back.

"Questions later," he answered sharply. "Lara's parents have agreed to our request to attend this conference and Mrs Ramsey would like to make this statement."

Patricia Ramsey leaned towards her microphone. I could barely watch as she made an appeal for witnesses, or anyone who could help in any way to find the person who had robbed her and her husband of their beloved daughter. Her voice wavered, and everyone in the room held their breath expecting her to break down and pour out her pent-up grief, but she made it to the end, still in control. Mr Ramsey's chin sank even lower on his chest. Remembering my promise to Tony, I raised my camera, but was roughly shouldered aside by a photographer I didn't recognise just as I was taking my shot. There was no alternative but to lift my camera over his head for the next one and, for all I knew, get a fine picture of the ceiling.

Job done, the Ramseys were ushered out, then Laverack and the Chief Superintendent resumed their seats.

"You will all appreciate that we don't want to cause the grieving parents any more distress than absolutely necessary," said Rollins. "There will be a memorial service for Lara Ramsey at St Bridget's Church at seven this evening. But we would ask that the press respect the family's wishes for privacy and keep away." She paused, looking around the room. "So now they've gone, if there are any questions…?" She sounded hopeful that there would be none, but she had underestimated the hunger that was palpable in the room. The restrained appeal from Mrs Ramsey, dramatic in its controlled intensity, had only whetted the reporters' appetite.

"So was Lara raped or not?"

"There was no evidence of sexual assault," said DI Laverack.

"The murderer could have been a woman, then?"

"We can't rule anything out at this stage."

A surge of excitement raised the emotional temperature in the room. Mini tape-recorders were thrust forward, pens flew over notebooks, Matt's included.

"What about the teacher who killed himself? Did he have anything to do with it?"

"We've eliminated Mr Keele from our enquiries."

"How come? Did his alibi check out?"

"Of course," said Laverack testily.

I glanced at Matt. "I knew it," I whispered. "There's no way Adam could have done this."

"Have you liaised with other police forces? Has this killer struck before?"

"There's no evidence of that."

"Are you saying you haven't liaised? What's the point of having a police data base if —"

"We are still at a very early stage in the investigation."

"Do you have any suspects at all?"

"We are following up several possible lines of enquiry."

"Such as?"

"Lara's friends and colleagues have been questioned.

She was an estate agent, and we are looking at her client contacts going back six months. We have conducted house-to-house interviews in the Stonebeck area, plus a fingertip search of the park and other sites. As I explained earlier, we're examining DNA evidence. We've appealed for witnesses – anyone who saw anything suspicious in the early hours of the morning, especially in the vicinity of Jubilee Park."

"Has anyone come forward?"

"Not yet." His stroked his tie. "If there are no more questions…"

I stepped forward. Laverack couldn't miss me. We were practically eyeball to eyeball. I could tell by his cool gaze that he recognised me. "I suggest that you've made barely any progress since Tuesday morning, when Lara's body was found. That was more than forty-eight hours ago."

"An investigation into a serious crime of this nature is rarely simple. Detective work takes hours, weeks, months of painstaking effort."

"What if we don't have that long? What if this killer is planning his next murder right now?"

There were angry mutterings of support.

"Obviously we don't want any more victims," Chief Superintendent Rollins said smoothly. She was looking at me with considerable hostility but I refused to give up. Their united bland front only made me angrier.

"There's a dangerous sadistic psychopath out there. He killed my son's girlfriend and then mutilated her body – a black-magic symbol carved on her chest – a pentagram, I think it's called – and blisters round her mouth. This suggests someone seriously deranged!"

The mutterings became louder. Laverack and Rollins appeared to be in a state of shock.

"You didn't tell us about any mutilation," called out the Sun's local rep.

"How did you know about that?" Laverack asked me quietly through clenched teeth.

"That doesn't matter. What matters is, what are you doing about finding this killer?"

Laverack addressed the room. "We're following up several promising new leads."

"What are they?" shouted several people at once.

"I'm afraid I'm not able to reveal anything that might compromise our investigation." This was greeted by jeers. He gave me a filthy look. The commotion grew to a deafening level so that individual questions were lost in the uproar.

Chief Superintendent Rollins stood up. She waited until the racket stopped. She spoke gravely about the need for everyone, especially women, to take sensible precautions. "But at the same time, it's essential to avoid hysteria. We have no reason to believe this person has been involved in other crimes or will kill again." She quelled the reaction to that with another patient wait.

"I'm calling an end to this conference now," she said eventually. No one argued with her. She gestured to Laverack, who stood up and headed for the door. Realising I'd taken no decent pictures yet I hastily snapped a couple of shots of their departing backs. Tony was going to be thrilled with those. I unscrewed the lens from the camera body.

Matt's mouth hung open.

"What?" I said.

"What have you done?"

"I promised Daniel." Matt was unimpressed by that explanation for my outburst. "I was just trying to wipe the smug self-satisfied looks off their faces."

"You did that all right."

Over Matt's shoulder I could see the stringer from the Sun pushing through the departing crowd towards me.

"Let's get out of here." I led the way up a side aisle. The TV people were blocking the way with their heavy gear and progress was frustratingly slow. I dodged all questions thrown at me about mutilation and ducked through every gap in the crowd I could see. I hoped Matt was close behind.

He was. Out in the street he grabbed my arm.

"Jude, you're letting this business get to you."

"What do you expect? I'm involved in this thing whether I like it or not. I promised Daniel, and all I'm doing is letting him down."

"That's nonsense. You've done your best. Now it's time to stop, for your own sake. Leave it to the police, Jude. They'll get the bastard."

"You heard Laverack. Not exactly a mine of information. What if they haven't got the faintest idea?"

"You really hate this psycho, don't you?"

"Yes. And if the police don't find him, I will."

"Do you know something, Jude? You're amazing." He brushed my lips with his. A brief pause, then another kiss, longer and deeper. "There's just one thing."

"What?" I said unsteadily. It was a long time since I'd been kissed like that.

"You photographer, me journalist. Comprendo?"

"Scared I might be better at it than you?" I pulled his face towards mine once more.

Over his shoulder I saw a two people, escorted by someone I recognised as a family liaison officer, emerge from the police station. They crossed the pavement in front of us and walked towards a waiting car. Lara's parents.

"Have you got that photo?" I demanded.

"Is this the best time?"

"Give it to me."

Matt reached into his capacious pocket and pulled out a brown reinforced envelope. I grabbed it and hurried towards the Ramseys.

Mr Ramsey was tall and stooped. He twisted towards me as I approached, his eyes wild. Patricia Ramsey stood perfectly still, just a pulse beating in her neck like a ticking metronome.

I held out the envelope.

"What's this?" said Mr Ramsey, reaching out a trembling hand.

"It's our picture," said Patricia. "She's the one who stole it."

"Actually, no, I didn't." I was getting heartily sick of covering up for other people. Then I remembered Matt's glittering career, the one he hadn't had yet. "That is, I took it, but I can explain —"

"How could you do such a thing? My wife was heart-broken when she found this picture missing. She searched high and low for it. Never for a moment did she imagine that someone had stolen it. Then when the paper was delivered, and we saw it printed for all the world to see... That was the last holiday we ever had as a family." He angrily brushed his tears away. "Patricia knew it was you who had taken it, someone she thought was a friend. As if we didn't have enough to cope with right now."

"I know, and I'm very sorry. It's just that I..."

He shook his head with weary despair. I'd never believed all that nonsense about auras, but there was a force-field of grief surrounding this man that was almost tangible. It repelled all my feeble excuses.

"No, you're right. It was unforgivable. I know what you

must be going through. I nearly lost my own son."

Mrs Ramsey pulled herself even straighter. "Nearly?"

"He had a very serious asthma attack. He almost died."

"Almost," she repeated. "It's not quite the same is it? *Nearly. Almost.* You nearly lost your son, but he's alive, isn't he? My daughter is dead." Her voice became strangulated, her shoulders slumped forward, then like a dam bursting, her sorrow flooded through the breach. She was bending over and gulping air as if she was retching. Great dry sobs came from deep inside. Her husband caught her before she fell, but she thrust him aside. Her sharp nails reached for my face. I felt the skin tear as she clawed at me. I reared back but she clung to my neck, an astonishing strength in her bony wrists. I had nearly blacked out before Matt, Mr Ramsey and two police officers pulled her off me. I sank to my knees on the ground, gasping for breath.

I heard the car door slam. Her banshee wailing stopped abruptly. Matt knelt beside me.

"Jude – are you OK?"

I couldn't speak.

"You should press charges. She assaulted you. I was a witness. I'll testify."

I shook my head. Let the Ramseys blame me for the small wrong of stealing the photo. It wasn't important. It might even help them cope with the huge and irreversible damage that had been done to them. Patricia Ramsey was right. Daniel was alive, Lara was dead. Even though we were both mothers, we existed in totally different emotional worlds. I was simply grateful I wasn't Patricia Ramsey.

"I think you need a drink."

"No, Matt. I haven't time."

"Don't argue. When did you last eat?"

"Can't remember."

"So what's the best pub round here?"

I took a bite of my tuna sandwich. It tasted like fishy sawdust, but Matt had said I wasn't getting out of The Crooked Man alive until I'd had some lunch.

"To be fair to Laverack, he did say they had some promising new leads," I said. "Apart from the blood they found."

"You don't believe that, do you?" Matt was tucking into an enormous plate of burger and fries. He took a swig from his bottle of Belgian beer. "That's police-speak for we haven't got a frigging clue."

"There's something odd about that blood." I tried to recall Lara's body, lying stiffly against the park bench, her denim jacket wide open and the huge splash of red on her T-shirt. "But I can't put my finger on it."

"And all that stuff about Lara being a pillar of the community." He put his knife down with a clatter. "We know that's not true. I hate it more than anything when people lie to you. I suppose that's why I'm a reporter. I need to know the truth." He ruffled his dark curly hair. "Sorry. I didn't mean to get heavy."

"That's OK. I understand."

"What do you hate most in the world, Jude?"

I didn't need to think about that one.

"Injustice. The big things – the stuff that hits the headlines – racial attacks, the whole Palestinian mess, women falsely accused of murdering their cot-death babies. And the other things too, the ones that don't get reported much. Kids being bullied in school, all day, every day. Animals tortured for fun or profit. People like my neighbour who fell off a ladder at work, got no compensation and lives on benefit." I didn't explain that that was one reason I'd climbed that tree and rescued Hayley's ferret – I knew her dad couldn't. "Actually, those things make me even madder than the big stuff."

Matt put his hand on my arm.

"All right, I know," I said. "*Calm down.*"

"Yes, but I also want to tell you… I think you're amazing."

"So you keep saying."

"I mean it. You're not like most women your age."

"Thanks. I think."

He went back to his meal, dipping each chip in ketchup before eating it with relish. I realised he was just a slightly older version of Daniel. He must have been thinking something similar, probably comparing me to his mother.

"How old are you, Jude?"

"Thirty-seven. And you?"

"Twenty-five."

We looked at each other and I knew we were both doing the maths. Twelve years. It was nothing. Alternatively, it was a hell of a lot.

"We've got so much in common. We seem to see the world through the same eyes."

"Excuse me? I do not approve of stealing photos." I put my hands to my face and felt the raised weals where Mrs Ramsey had raked my cheeks. "How do I look?"

"Like a tribal warrior, complete with battle scars." He sat back in his chair. "You're not going to forgive me for this, are you?"

"I'm just saying, we don't see everything the same way."

"OK, but the important things, like truth and injustice, we agree on those."

"That's not difficult, is it? Doesn't everybody?"

Matt frowned. "No. Think of Tony Quinnell."

We both started to laugh. For a few brief moments I remembered what fun was like. I enjoyed being told I was amazing, but I couldn't totally relax. Not while Lara's killer was still out there somewhere.

"Talking of Raging Bull Quinnell, shouldn't you get back to work?" I asked.

"We're allowed an hour for lunch. That's the law. And you haven't finished your sandwich."

I chewed some more sawdust. "It must seem pretty different here after living in Manchester."

"I like it. I used to open my curtains on a crumbling tower block, all boarded up and derelict. Now every morning I stand at my window looking at the smart new houses opposite, and I can just catch a glimpse of the castle on top of the hill."

"Are you renting somewhere?"

"Nope. I'm buying."

"On a reporter's wages?"

"It's just a small town house. Hardly bigger than a match box. I went to that estate agents in the market square... what's it called?"

"Ravenbridge Properties?"

"That's the one. Luckily for me, the previous owner wanted a quick sale and dropped the price, so I got a bargain. I can just about manage it."

"Then you'd better get back to work and earn the money to pay for it."

"Are you trying to get rid of me?" He stared at my plate. "Come on, Jude, that's pathetic. Now eat the other half."

"It's so dry, and I've finished my beer."

"I'll get you a coffee."

"I really haven't time."

"You look pretty knackered. A shot of caffeine's just

what you need."

I sighed. "Just a quick one, then."

Matt's eyebrows rose.

"Dream on, Matt. I'm too —"

"Don't say you're too old."

"I was going to say I'm too amazing for you."

Over coffee, Matt lit a cigarette and talked about the big stories he had worked on with his previous title. "A lot of small-scale crime stories, especially vandalism, car theft, joy riding – you get the picture. Then there was some shady stuff to do with the council. But nothing as big as this. I've never worked on a story that's gone national before." His eyes shone. He glanced at me. "Sorry. I keep forgetting. That was a crass thing to say."

"At least you're honest."

"I'd never lie to you, Jude."

"Good. Eat up, Matt. You really do need to get back and file the press conference story."

"What about you?"

"Laverack may be lying about new leads, but I've got some ideas I want to explore. There was something Lee Maddox said…"

"Who?"

"Just a boy I spoke to in the street." I drained my cup.

"Jude, you do realise you're getting totally obsessed?"

"Someone has to." I stood up.

"What do I tell Tony?"

"Tell him… tell him I fancy him. That should shut him up."

Twelve

A large Alsatian dog lay on its haunches just inside the rusty wrought-iron gate. It had a drooling mouth, a huge lolling tongue and a manic gleam in its eye. When I whistled, its ears pricked up. I'd probably whistled the command Destroy in dog speak, but I had to do something. It had started to snow while we were in the pub. I couldn't stand out here in the freezing cold all day.

The dog stood up. I whistled again and pushed at the gate. It lumbered backwards, giving me just enough room to squeeze through. I muttered, "Good dog, nice dog, good dog…" all the way up the short path. It followed me like a shadow, growling softly when I knocked on the door.

"Nice dog, lovely dog…" It stood right beside me, staring up, mesmerised, saliva dripping from its jaw, the desire to please me conflicting with the urge to tear me to pieces. I had a few seconds to take in the garden features – a television with a dark hollow where the screen had been, a waterlogged mattress and a motorcycle with no wheels – before the door was pulled open. A rich mix of stale cigarette smoke, stale beer and stale bodies flowed out around the young man with the shaved head who stood there. He was an older, harder version of his brother.

"Scott Maddox?"

His eyes narrowed as he took in my damaged face. "So?"

"My name's Jude Baxendale. I'd like to talk to Lee. Is he in?"

Scott looked furtively up and down the street. "Are you police?"

"No, I'm a photographer. From the paper."

"The Sun?"

"The Ravenbridge Evening Post."

His face fell, and for a moment the hard-man image went with it.

"What's it about?"

"About Lara Ramsey."

"So why do you want to take a picture of Lee?"

"I don't. I just want to talk to him. Privately. It's nothing to do with the paper."

"Waste of time."

I wasn't sure if he was referring to my enquiries or to his brother. The door began to close. "I think he could help."

"Lee? He didn't even know Lara Ramsey."

"He knew her by sight, and he spoke to her at least once."

"So? She knew a lot of people, that bitch."

I remembered that Scott had been in the same year in school as Lara and Harrison. "Including you?"

He worked the saliva in his mouth, and before I could blink, a gob of spit landed a few inches from my right boot.

I took a deep breath. "Were you one of her boyfriends?"

"No. But she had plenty. She'd do it with anyone."

I glanced in the doorway, at the piles of old newspapers, the discarded dirty clothes, the peeling wallpaper. "But not with you?"

"I did ask her out once, when we were in Year 11. Everybody did. But I got knocked back and never bothered with her again. I've got a girlfriend. I didn't need to go after that stuck-up cow." His face hardened. "If you want to know what I think, she had it coming."

"Why do you say that?"

"She wasn't straight."

116

"Straight?"

"I don't mean she was a lezzie. But you never knew what she really thought. She must have got up someone's nose big time and they killed her, that's my opinion." He folded his arms over his broad chest.

"You may be right."

Scott looked surprised, as if he wasn't used to having his views taken seriously. But he had a point. Lara's promiscuity in the past had surely stored up trouble for her. Any number of spurned lovers could have taken their revenge.

"So, is Lee around?"

"He's at school."

"Really? He told me he doesn't go to school any more."

Scott scratched his shaven head. "Oh yeah. He got chucked out of art, had to do extra maths instead. That was the final straw. He'd had enough. It was that teacher's fault – Mr Keele – the one who topped himself."

"Do you know where Lee is?"

"Probably round the back." He jerked a thumb to his left. "In the shed."

The door closed. I followed the path round the side of the house into the back garden, the dog close behind me.

"Good dog, lovely dog, super dog…"

In the far corner was a wooden shed, its door hanging open at an angle. I could hear movement from inside. As I crunched across the whitened grass the sounds fell silent.

I peered in the open doorway. "Hello?"

The barrel of a shotgun was pointing at my chest.

On the other end of it, the small frightened figure of Lee Maddox was backed up against the wall.

"Who were you expecting?" I asked.

"Dunno. Police, teachers, social workers. They're all the same. I don't want nothing to do with any of them."

The muzzle of the gun lowered slightly. "I know you from somewhere…"

"We met yesterday outside Lara Ramsey's flat. You told me about Mr Keele."

"It wasn't my fault he killed himself!"

"No one's blaming you."

He glowered at me, unconvinced. "What happened to your face?"

"I got into a scrap. You should see the other guy."

He slowly put the gun down on the bench then clapped his hands. "Here, Sabre. Here, boy." The dog padded into the shed. Lee bent down to scratch its ears.

This time I followed the dog. Inside the shed I could see fishing rods, traps, lines, all hung on hooks in perfect order. Lee gently pushed Sabre away and turned to the bench.

"What do you want? I'm busy."

"So I see."

He was making fishing flies from wire, beads and feathers. His fingers shaped and threaded the materials with practised skill. If they'd offered Fishing as a subject at school, Lee would have been an academic success instead of an infamous no-hoper.

"There's something I want to ask you. Yesterday you said you'd seen men hanging round Lara's place."

"I saw Mr Keele." He stared defiantly at me, the planes of his face as sharp as blades.

"I know. And I know you were telling the truth. But what you actually said was, I've seen blokes hanging round here. That suggests more than one, doesn't it, not just Mr Keele. What other men did you see?"

"Dunno. Leave me alone! You'll be saying I killed her next!" With sudden ferocity he swept the pile of feathers and wire off the bench. The dog gave a startled bark.

I shook my head. "No, Lee. I'm not suggesting that at all." No one his puny size could have carried Lara into the park. Unless he'd had help, of course. And wheels. Did Scott have a car, or was the disabled motorbike his only form of transport?

"You're just like all the rest. It's not my fault! None of it's my fault!" He chucked the beautifully made flies on the floor and stamped on them. I touched his shoulder, a gesture intended to be reassuring. But Lee flinched, pushed past me and ran out of the shed.

I followed, just in time to see him legging it over the back fence on to the recreation ground. As I climbed after him, Sabre snapped at my heels. "Bloody dog, nasty dog, revolting dog!" I kicked at its drooling fangs. It leapt backwards as if shot. I heard it scrabbling on the fence as I pelted across the snowy field.

Lee was heading towards the derelict cricket pavilion on the far side. It had been abandoned when the cricket club moved to a more salubrious location on the other side of town. It had been regularly vandalised ever since. Now it was a focal point for drunks and druggies. I'd taken several pictures for the paper that charted its decline from a once-handsome wooden clubroom, painted gleaming white, to a tatty tumbledown shed stained green with lichen where it wasn't covered with graffiti.

"Lee! I need to talk to you!"

"Fuck off!" His words floated back to me on the stiff arctic wind.

I was panting heavily by the time I reached the pavilion. Lee had disappeared. His footprints, sharply defined against the white, stopped abruptly at the short flight of steps that led up to the verandah.

"Please, Lee!" I called out. "I'm on your side. If it's any consolation, I hated school as well!" I waited for a response but there was only a profound snow-muffled silence.

I mounted the steps. The door of the pavilion had a padlock attached to it, but it had been sawn through. I put my shoulder to the door and it creaked open. A musty smell hit me – rotten wood and rat droppings. At the shuttered windows, old curtains hung in bleached tatters.

A brisk wind blew through the building, making it almost as cold as outside. I looked up. The ceiling gaped open right up through the loft space, as if a heavy weight had been dropped from the sky and made a direct hit. The room was bare apart from drifts of rubbish in the corners – empty cans, broken bottles, cigarette butts, silver paper, lighters, needles. I walked forward slowly, testing each plank in case it gave way.

There was a faint noise from above. Mice probably, or birds, flying in through the open roof and scratching about in the rafters. Or a boy of fourteen, so distrustful of the adult world he wanted nothing to do with it. Had he climbed up there? I couldn't see any ladders or footholds.

"Lee?" I called softly.

I turned right and made my way gingerly towards the flat-roofed annexe that housed the changing rooms. Two doors faced me, their faded signs reading Home and Visitors. I pushed open each door. The walls were mottled with mould, the low wooden benches blistered and cracked. Further down the corridor, the shower room was even more derelict. The fittings had been ripped off the walls and hung in bizarre twisted shapes. There were pools of ice on the floor, making it too treacherous to walk on.

I heard a clattering and whirled around.

"Where are you?"

No answer.

I hurried back into the main room.

It was empty.

He was here somewhere, I was sure of it.

I went outside. It was snowing more heavily now. I re-examined the footprints. They stopped at the steps, but Lee obviously hadn't gone into the pavilion itself. I walked along the covered verandah, down another short flight of steps, and sure enough, the footprints began again on the grass, leading round the side of the changing rooms. I tracked him to a drainpipe where, once more, the prints came to a halt. The falling snow had already made their outlines fuzzy.

I looked up but I couldn't see him.

"Lee, come down from there. It's not safe." A lean pinched face peered over the gutter. "I need your help."

The face drew back and once again silence descended on us along with the snow.

"Right," I muttered to myself. I spat on my hands. It was years since I'd shinned up a drainpipe. About thirty years, to be exact. Still, how could I have forgotten? It had to be like riding a bike, didn't it? And in any case I'd had some practice lately, even if it was a gnarled tree with plenty of footholds, plus a doddle of a park fence. All I had here were the metal rings that pinned the pipe to the wall every half metre or so. I put my foot on the first one and hauled myself up. So far so good. It got more tricky after that, requiring an awkward squirming movement, gripping with my feet and squeezing with my knees to propel myself upward. Progress was painfully slow. The pipe was icy cold and ripped the skin off my palms. But I kept going. At the top I peeped over the flat roof of the annexe. I knew now how soldiers in the trenches must have felt.

At least Lee hadn't taken his shotgun with him. Or had he?

He was sitting crouched against the pitched roof of the main building, arms clutched round his knees. No gun.

"What do you want? I told you I didn't kill her!"

"I know," I panted. The wind was stronger up here. A sudden flurry of snow blinded me for a moment. As it drifted away I hauled myself on to the roof. Lee pulled his knees in tighter.

"It's all right. I won't come any nearer." I flopped down on the snow-covered roof, just glad to relieve the strain in my limbs. "I really need to know, Lee – how many other men, apart from Adam Keele, did you see calling at Lara's house?"

His eyes screwed up. What if he'd been lying all along? Perhaps he had only seen Adam. Bloke, blokes – singular, plural – wasn't it just semantics, the finer points of which Lee had failed to master?

"Just one other guy, I guess."

My heart leapt. "Who? When did you see him? What did he look like?"

Lee gave me his glowering stare.

Cool it. Slow down. Keep it simple.

"Did you know this person?"

He shook his head.

"Did you see him just once, or several times?"

"Four or five times, I suppose."

"When was the last time you saw him?"

"About a week ago."

I calculated quickly. This was Thursday January 4th. Therefore Lee had seen this man outside Lara's flat some time between Christmas and New Year. I felt a rising sense of excitement.

"This is really important, Lee. Can you describe him?"

"I never saw him properly. I usually deliver the papers after I've had my tea and that can be any time, knowing my mum, so this time of year it's dark by then."

Disappointment made me breathe heavily through my nose. Lee looked at me with alarm.

"OK. Just tell me what he was wearing."

"Can't remember."

"Please try."

"Padded jacket, jeans, trainers. And a woolly hat pulled well down. That last time, I saw him outside Lara's door, but by the time I got there he was walking away."

"Did you speak to him?"

"Course not. Don't you know you're not supposed to talk to strangers, dumbo?"

"Point taken. And you're quite sure it was a man?"

Lee blew on his hands, which looked red and raw with cold. "Think so. Dunno. I suppose it could've been a woman."

I breathed loudly again, sending a plume of mist towards Lee, who watched me warily. I could feel the snow melting under me and the wetness permeating my trousers. My buttocks ached from sitting on the cold hard roof. It was time to go.

"Is there anything else you remember about that evening?"

"No." A foxy look crept into his expression.

"I think there is. What is it, Lee?"

He shrugged.

"Whatever it is, however unimportant it might seem, it could help."

He thought about this, then muttered, "He left something in the letterbox."

"Go on."

"It's a bugger, that letterbox, dead stiff. I could see a corner of a plastic bag sticking out where it had got caught in the hinge. So I put my hand in and pulled it back through."

"What was it?"

"A video. Something called…" His face creased with concentration. "*Scorching Desert*, I think. I thought it was a bit of porn so I took it home and played it."

"And?"

"It was crap. Just these Arabs in tents in the desert, always moving on and riding camels and getting caught in sandstorms."

"Sounds like a documentary."

"No, it was a proper film, with a hero and a pretty girl and all that." He must have caught my doubtful look. "I know what a documentary is. I'm not thick."

"I realise that. So what did you do with it?"

"I fast-forwarded it to the end, but there wasn't any sex so I switched it off."

"Was it a commercial video – you know, with a picture on it, in a proper box?"

"No. It was just a tape with the title written on the spine in pencil."

"Were there adverts every few minutes?"

"Yeah."

"So someone recorded it off the telly. That'll make it harder to track down. Unless you've still got it?"

"I'm not a fucking thief!"

"You gave it to Lara?"

"I put it back through the letterbox."

I eased my frozen bottom.

"Don't come any nearer!"

"I won't, I promise."

We sat in silence for a while. I tried to make sense of what Lee had told me. Lara must have watched the film the night she was killed. That would account for the Arab music Annie Molloy had heard. But did it have anything to do with her murder? It seemed unlikely, a complete blind alley.

"Why didn't you like school?" Lee asked softly.

"What?"

"You said you hated school."

I hesitated, wondering where to begin. "I wasn't any good at anything, except art. I despised most of the teachers. I was bullied by other girls because I preferred to do my own thing. I was always in trouble for speaking out. I loathed school dinners and I was useless at sport. Otherwise it was just fine."

Lee received this speech impassively but I could tell he was digesting each detail, relating it to his own experience. I reckoned times hadn't changed that much for the misfit. After a few minutes he began to shiver.

"Come on, Lee. You need to get home, have a hot bath and something to eat."

He snorted, and I had an image of his home life that didn't include fluffy towels or tasty home-made meals. I got the impression he often crossed the recreation ground and made for this bolt-hole. Maybe here, on top of a freezing-cold roof, he found some small degree of happiness and freedom.

I tentatively extended a hand. "Let's go before bits of us are iced to the floor and get ripped off when we try to stand up." I smiled through stiff lips. "We can talk some more on the way back."

Lee wasn't fooled. "I've told you everything I know. Now leave me alone!"

He scrambled up and bolted for the far side of the roof. Before I had struggled to my feet he had started to clamber down the front of the building. He must have known every escape route in the place. His head disappeared. By the time I reached the edge he was just a tiny figure scurrying across the snow.

Peering down, I could see the drainpipe Lee had used. It looked a lot less secure than the other one, but he seemed to have descended without mishap. I put one leg over the roof, feeling for the first foothold. It held, so I swung the other leg to join it, putting my whole weight on the metal ring. The pipe wobbled. I hesitated, realising that Lee was a lot lighter than me. I contemplated hauling myself back on to the roof, but the pipe didn't like that idea either. When I put pressure on the ring, it expressed itself with an ugly grating sound. I had no choice but descend.

My foot reached for the next ring and after scrabbling about blindly for a while, finally found it. I let the other foot join it, an awkward movement involving a lot of gripping with my thighs. That's when I felt the pipe move. Instinct made me scuttle upwards rather than down. The fierce breeze began to loosen the pipe from the wall. I grabbed the gutter with both hands, and as the pipe gave way, clattering against the brickwork, I was left suspended.

I hung there for what seemed like hours, about three seconds in fact, twisting my neck to see how far it was to the ground. It wasn't that far, but below me was a strip of concrete, cushioned only by a covering of snow. By now my arms had nearly parted from my shoulder sockets. I couldn't hold on much longer. I took a few deep breaths, but before I was ready to let go, a howling gust of wind shook me loose like a tree planted in thin soil. I hurtled downwards, nose, hands and hips in bone-contact with the brick wall.

I hit the ground with a jarring thud. My legs buckled with the force of the drop. My skinned palms stung as if I'd thrust them in a red-hot flame. Eventually I got some air into my lungs. I flexed my ankles carefully. Then the rest of my aching body. No bones broken. But the bruises were going to be spectacular.

I limped the long way round to the street where the Maddox family lived. For some reason I didn't fancy climbing over the fence into their back garden, straight into the jaws of a vengeful Alsatian dog. I pushed open the rusty gate, keeping an eye out for Sabre. But there was no sign of him. I imagined him waiting fixedly by the fence for my re-appearance. I just hoped his sense of smell was as limited as his intelligence, otherwise the reek of sweat and damp that emanated from me would bring him hurtling towards me at the first sniff.

I knocked on the door. After the familiar lengthy interval Scott opened it.

"You again?" He did a double-take. "You've got blood on your face."

I rubbed my nose with a grubby hand. "I slipped on the snow. Is Lee there?"

"Didn't you find him?"

"Yes, I did. But I didn't have a chance to say thanks. He's been a big help."

Scott looked surprised again. Praise and gratitude were clearly on short rations for the Maddox boys. "OK. I'll tell him when I see him." He was about to close the door.

"Can I check something out with you?"

"What?"

"Do you have a car?"

"No. What's it to you?"

"Doesn't matter. I'm sure you've been interviewed by the police already?"

"No way."

"Oh? But I thought you were a friend of Lara Ramsey?"

"I never said that. She was in my year at school, that's all. When she turned me down in Year 11 that was it. I don't think I've spoken to her since. I told you, I've got a girlfriend. And before you ask, the night Lara was killed I was at my girlfriend's house with her mum and dad, two sisters, her cousin and her gran. Ask them, they'll tell you the same thing."

"Was Lee with you?"

"Course not. That little bugger leads his own life. We never know where he is most of the time. Do you think he did it? Or both of us?"

"I wasn't suggesting —"

"Yes, you were."

"I'm sorry if it came out like that."

"Sorry, my arse!" He looked genuinely affronted and I didn't blame him. I seemed to have the knack of blundering about, upsetting people, even someone as apparently hard as Scott Maddox. Though I reckoned the skinhead look was just a front. Underneath, he was as soft as butter, a touch rancid perhaps, but a murderer? I didn't see it somehow. In any case, he had an alibi for that night, and Lee couldn't have done it on his own. Another blind alley.

"Thanks for your time, Scott."

"Are you taking the piss? Get out of here! Or I'll set the dog on you!" He stepped out of the doorway and yelled, "Sabre!"

I heard a throaty growl. The Alsatian trotted round the side of the house. I quickly backed away, then turned and ran down the path and out of the gate, hunting in my pocket for my keys as I went. Where were they?

The dog was so close his hot meaty breath was in my nostrils. I half-twisted and shouted, "Stay!" Some long-forgotten response triggered in his tiny brain. He dropped to the ground, his huge tongue lolling out of one side of his mouth, his whole body throbbing with longing. I found the keys and had slammed the car door shut on him before he realised he'd been had and leapt for me.

"Dream on, sunshine," I mouthed through the window. As I started the engine I heard the sound of unclipped claws scraping the paintwork.

Thirteen

There were no spaces left in the staff car park. I eventually found a gap the width of a wide-screen TV, about half a mile away from the Evening Post building. I manoeuvred into it, then checked my face in the mirror. The skin down the centre of my nose was missing, my lip was cut and already swelling up. These two fresh wounds made a nice matching set with the graze on my chin and the scratch marks down my cheeks. I dabbed at my face with a tissue, then slumped back in my seat. I'd spent most of the day chasing shadows when I was supposed to be at work, and I had absolutely nothing to show for it, apart from bloody hands, bruised limbs and a set of tribal scars. Oh, and a couple of blurred pictures of the ceiling at the police station and DI Laverack's rear end. Tony was going to be ecstatic.

When I got out of the car I saw that Sabre had scored vertical lines through Daniel's beautifully painted shark's mouth.

"Shit."

A black cloud followed me through the streets. I'd never felt so defeated and worthless in my life. Why was I doing this? Matt was right – I was getting obsessed and my obsession was costing me, big time. It simply wasn't worth it. Somehow I had to tell Daniel I was giving up this madness. Lara was dead and we all had to move on. Life was like that, it was just that Daniel was too young and inexperienced to understand it yet.

When I reached the Post building I mounted the stairs

to the first floor with legs that felt as if they were filled with sand. I was halfway down the newsroom when Tony burst out of his office.

"Jude!"

I turned to see him chasing after me, head lowered like an angry rhino. Perhaps Matt really had told Tony I fancied him. Idiot.

"Where have you been? Matt was back from the press conference ages ago, and your bloody mobile's switched off."

"Really?" I said innocently, reaching for my phone and clucking when I saw no light.

"And look at the state of you." His sweeping gaze took in my damaged face and blood-stained clothes. "For god's sake, have your rampant sex romps with your sado-masochistic boyfriend in your own time, not mine!"

"Did you really say *rampant sex romps*?"

"You're in deep shit."

"Anyone would think you were the editor of a tabloid red-top. Perhaps you should be."

"And who do you think you are, the bloody Scarlet Pimpernel? We seek you here, we seek you there, but we can never bloody find you!"

"Some say I'm more like the Mona Lisa."

"Bollocks." He broke into a hacking cough. "Either you're part of this team, Jude, or you're out. This murder is a big story and I need everyone fully on board. No one is going to cock it up. No one!"

Apart from the soft hum and whirr of the computers the newsroom had gone eerily silent.

I kept my voice down, but there was no way I could mask my anger. "Is that really all you care about, your front-page story? For a moment out there, Tony, I thought you had a heart, that you actually cared that my son's girlfriend was dead, that Daniel was seriously ill, that we're going through the worst crisis of our lives. But I can see I was wrong."

"That's it. I've had enough," he croaked. "My office. Now."

I snapped my arm out straight and mouthed to his retreating back, "Ja, mein fuhrer!"

I was aware of the reporters watching me walk the walk of shame. Nick, the one who'd come up with the doggy story, looked anxious, probably thinking it could be him next. I caught Matt's eye. He tipped his head back slightly with the back of his hand as if to say chin up. I nodded, and holding my head high, entered Tony's lair.

He was swivelling back and forth on his chair. When he spoke his voice was like gravel poured from a truck.

"I left a good job in London to come to this shit-hole."

"Do you mind? This is my town and I think it's a great place to live. If you don't like it, there's nothing to stop you leaving."

"Yes, there is." His face softened for a moment as he glanced at the photo of the smiling red-haired woman on his desk. "Anyway, that's not the point. This may be a great place to live, but it's a crap place to sell newspapers, seeing as nothing much happens round here."

"Until now."

"Exactly. Look, Jude, I know you're personally involved, but that's no excuse for your behaviour. It's downright unprofessional."

"That's unfair. For the last couple of days I've had some problems, agreed, but for Christ's sake, I have given years of service to this paper — "

"I've warned you, Jude, and you've taken no notice."

"Are you sacking me?"

He gazed at me stonily.

"Why?" I asked, brimming with anger.

Looking down, he began to count the reasons on his thick fingers. "Persistent lateness, doing private work in company time, using the photographic department as your personal art gallery —"

"That's ridiculous!"

"Disobedience. I told you not to go to the press conference at the police station and you totally ignored me. Did you get any pictures?"

"Sort of…"

"See what I mean? And this comes after the Adam Keele fiasco where you got no pictures whatsoever."

"There were reasons for that."

"I don't accept excuses. Not when your attitude to the job has become inexcusable. And of course, the *piece de resistance*, when you really surpassed yourself by stealing that photo from Mrs Ramsey."

"She got her own back," I said, fingering my scratches.

"What?"

"You'll find out soon enough."

He glared at me, then went through the list of my crimes again. "Lateness, low work rate, lack of pictures, immoral behaviour, poor standard of appearance, lack of co-operation with editorial staff, theft. Need I go on?"

I leaned across his desk. "You needn't bother to sack me, Tony. I resign."

Photographic was empty. I moved my overflowing tray of job tickets along to Buzz's station, with a note to tell him to farm them out among him and the rest of the team. Tony and I had agreed, probably the first time we had ever seen eye to eye, that my resignation should take effect immediately. I binned everything that was useless or out of date. Anything of value I put in a small pile on the workbench. There wasn't much to show for the twelve years I'd worked here, crawling my way up from photographic assistant to head of department – just a folder of recent cuttings, some letters from grateful readers and a cracked Photographers Do It in the Dark mug.

Then I remembered the enlargements Harrison had done. I wasn't going to leave them here. Pearls before swine. Anyway, if I did abandon them, Tony would only tear them down as soon as I'd gone. Harrison had attached them crudely to the wall with blu-tack. Flakes of white paint came away with the photo of traffic in snow, which seemed eerily appropriate. I was more careful with the shot of the industrial cranes, my personal favourite. Large envelopes were always in short supply, so I found some bubble wrap in a cupboard to protect the pictures from the weather.

But surely there'd been three. What was the last one? It took me a while to recall it. Of course. The picture of the River Raven, apparently for sale. I searched the walls but I couldn't spot it. I couldn't even find a gap where it had once hung. Harrison must have re-organised the display and moved my picture, but where?

Raymond shuffled into the room, a sickly look on his face which I thought was probably sympathy. Word travels at the speed of light in a newspaper office.

He spread his arms in a gesture of hopelessness, making his large wobbly stomach stick out.

"Don't say it," I warned him.

"But Judith, if anyone goes it should be me, not you. Let's face it, I'm finished, washed up, pretty much excess baggage round here."

"You didn't steal a photograph."

"And I don't believe you did either."

"Just leave it, OK? I'm going, end of story."

The air seemed to oscillate when Buzz steamed in.

"What's all this about? Jude, you can't be going. No way. It's all just a filthy rumour." He waited a split second for my response. "Isn't it?"

"Leave her be, Buzz," Raymond muttered.

"I can give her a hug, can't I?"

It was a perfunctory squeeze, and not entirely sincere. I knew that Buzz would be in Tony's office the moment I left, staking his claim as the new Chief Photographer.

My colleagues – no, my ex-colleagues, I reminded myself – began filing pix from the day's jobs into the system in unnatural silence. They stole quick glances at me as I stuffed my things into a plastic bag. I covered the two prints in bubble wrap and secured them with sellotape. I glanced around the cramped cheerless room that had been my working home for so long. That was it. All over. Time to surrender my cameras.

"OK, guys. I'm off."

I didn't wait for a reply. I was too choked.

Charmaine, the news editor, was waiting by the lift. She looked embarrassed.

"Jude…"

"Don't say anything."

"Couldn't you at least work out your notice?"

"No way. Like I told Tony, if I'm going, I might as well go now. Seeing as our relationship is at absolute zero, I can't stay on any longer."

"I think it's a shame. We're going to miss you."

That nearly broke through my numbness. "I told you

not to say anything," I said shakily.

She hugged me warmly. Her skin smelt of fresh soap and light flowery perfume. She smelled young and hopeful. She drew back and looked at me sadly. What odour did I give off? Sweat and melted snow and despair.

The lift arrived.

"Going down?" asked Charmaine.

"No. I have to go upstairs to Personnel."

"See you then."

"Probably not," I whispered as the lift doors closed. I waited until the lift returned, then rode up to the fourth floor. I gave in my swipe card and my press badge. The worst part was handing over my photographic equipment. It seemed horribly final, the physical manifestation of the fact that I no longer worked for the Ravenbridge Evening Post. I signed various forms and got out of there as quickly as I could.

Matt was standing outside Personnel. He looked at the plastic bag I was carrying. "What's going on?"

"I am. To new and better things."

"It's true, then?" He sounded incredulous. "You really have been sacked?"

"Of course not."

He scraped a hand through his hair. "Thank god."

"I resigned."

He crumpled slightly as if I'd punched him in the solar plexus. "All because of that bloody photograph?"

"That was mentioned, but it's not why I quit."

"But this is all my fault!"

"Stop it, Matt. This is nothing to do with you. It's between me and Tony. In the end, the gulf between us was too wide. And not forgetting the fact that I did totally mess up and deserved to be fired. I just got my retaliation in first."

"And jumped before you were pushed?"

"Yep."

"Christ, Jude, this is awful."

I reached out and touched his face. "Don't worry, I'll be fine," I lied.

"What are you going to do? Are you going to join another paper?"

"Maybe." Once Daniel went to college in September there was nothing to keep me in Ravenbridge, was there? "In the meantime I'm sure I'll get plenty of freelance work."

Suddenly I was overcome with weariness. I staggered a little. Matt held my shoulders to steady me.

"It's all right, I'm not drunk."

"I wouldn't blame you if you were."

"It's just that… ever since Lara's body was found, my world has sort of… lurched. It's hard to keep my balance." Now it had tilted another few degrees. Soon all horizontals would be vertical and I'd slide off into oblivion, like a mountaineer plunging over a crevasse.

Matt drew me closer.

"Honestly, I'm all right." But I had to admit his chest was comforting. I laid my head there for a moment. He buried his mouth in my hair.

"Jude, you're really special to me."

"That's very sweet of you, Matt, but…"

He wasn't listening. He lifted my face and kissed me, flicking my lips very gently.

We heard the whirr of the lift arriving. He let me drift a little apart from him. The doors opened on an empty space. He pulled me inside. I pressed the button marked G for Ground. The metal cube began to plummet, leaving my stomach just a fraction behind.

Matt's aftershave was very strong in the confined space

– citrus and spice. Tendrils of hair curled over his brow and ears. His tie was at half-mast over a dark shirt. I grabbed the tie and pulled him towards me, running my tongue up his neck to his ear lobe.

We had reached the ground floor. The doors parted. No one waiting. I stabbed another button. Five. Top floor. The doors shut quickly.

I pulled Matt's shirt open and stroked his smooth warm skin. Then his hands were in my hair and on my shoulders, pushing my jacket off and tugging at the buttons of my shirt. I reached for his waist – belt, buckle, zip – undone in seconds.

The lift swished to a halt. The door opened on a man hurrying away from us along the corridor, carrying a briefcase. I punched a button at random. The doors snapped shut.

"Going down," I whispered.

Matt groaned with pleasure, thrashing against the sides of the lift. After a while he pulled me upright. He unhooked my bra in one swift movement. My breasts spilled into his hands. He crouched to lick my nipples, flooding my veins with honey, a sensation intensified by the downward swoop of the lift. The doors opened on the quiet corridors of the third floor. Matt pressed five.

Together we pushed our trousers and pants around our knees. Then came the delicious moment when he slid into me, pounding my buttocks against the metal wall, and I was going up, up, higher than I'd ever been before until there was no more blood in my veins, only sweet sticky syrup.

Fifth floor. The doors opened on an empty corridor. The man with the briefcase had disappeared. We looked at each other and giggled hysterically. I felt blindly for the control panel but my hand never reached it. Matt plunged faster and deeper. My breath came in short gasps. I felt every muscle tauten like a spring until I thought I was going to snap in two. Waves of sweetness broke over me, getting bigger, until one huge wave swept me into deep black water and then back on to land where I juddered like a landed fish. Matt gave a low moan, and a split second later he was swept away too, and then crashed in a heap beside me. Our landing place felt like soft warm sand at first, then quickly turned to a stony beach. But we were too shattered to move and ease our cramped limbs.

I heard voices. I stretched out a trembling hand and banged a button, any button. The doors closed. We struggled up and helped each other back to decency.

I kissed his damp cheek. "That was the stupidest, most reckless thing I've ever done in my life." I licked a pearl of sweat from his chin. "And the most exciting."

Matt held my face in his hands. "Did I ever tell you that you're amazing?"

"Once or twice. But I don't mind hearing it again. And again. And again." I stroked the deflating bulge in his trousers.

Matt whimpered. "Jude… I'm really going to miss you."

Fourteen

The door of St Bridget's was heavy, but glided open without a sound. It was one of those modern Catholic churches, built in the 1960s, very tall and brightly lit, with long thin stained-glass windows and a huge spiky crown of thorns suspended over the altar.

Despite Chief Superintendent Rollins' plea for privacy, I had run a gauntlet of photographers outside the church. Now I no longer worked for the press I had been tempted to shout at them till they backed off in shame, if they knew the meaning of the word. But I restrained myself. It would have been undignified.

The place was packed, though you wouldn't know it from the strangulated murmur that passed for hymn-singing. In the dour stone-built Methodist chapel of my childhood the singing had been so loud the rafters rattled. Not that I did much of it. I stopped believing in God at the age of thirteen when my grandmother had a stroke and became a gibbering rag doll. If God could let that happen he was intolerably cruel. But that was a contradiction in terms, therefore there was no God. Simple. At work I had always tried to palm off holy jobs to Buzz or Harrison or one of the others. I felt nervous going into churches, especially when a service was in progress. It brought back all that childish terror of hell and damnation.

I stayed at the back, hovering around the baptismal font, in case the Ramseys spotted me. I could see them in the front row, Patricia Ramsey standing to attention, in contrast to her husband whose head and shoulders were bent over in a curve, the aura of sorrow still surrounding him. In the same row I spotted Stan's rotund figure and beside him his small neat wife, Carol, a warm, cheerful woman who I'd liked from the first time we met. I couldn't say the same about her sister, however sorry for her I felt.

The singing ended and the congregation, prompted by a gesture from Father Thomas, sat down on the plain wooden benches with a soft concerted thud. All eyes followed the figure in the white robe with a purple cross running the length and width of it, as he slowly made his way to the lectern. He looked as if he was in his early thirties, which struck me as surprisingly young for a parish priest. No doubt he'd been fast-tracked due to a world-wide shortage of men willing to give up sex for their whole lives. He gripped the sides of the lectern, pausing theatrically before he began to speak, ensuring that we hung on every word, delivered in a soft Irish accent.

"We are here today to commemorate the life of Lara Ramsey, beloved daughter of Patricia and Edward. She has been taken from them in such tragic circumstances that it makes God's plan for us, His children, seem mysterious, even bewildering. But we must trust in Him, have faith in Him, give ourselves up to His will."

Even from my position at the back of the church I could hear the smothered groan that came from Edward Ramsey. Father Thomas's words gave me no comfort either.

"Lara was a beautiful girl." There were murmurs of assent from the congregation. "She and I didn't always agree on matters of doctrine." He paused, holding us all in the palm of his hand. Some people call it charisma, others say it's just a matter of timing. Personally, this kind of audience manipulation gave me the creeps. Though I'd been keen on theatre when I was young, disillusion had set in and I began to mistrust the phoniness of it. This was the same kind of trickery.

He had milked the pause and now began again. "But we agreed to disagree. One day, I was certain, she would return to the fold. And on that day she would have been greeted with joy, the prodigal daughter home at last. Instead, God has taken her unto Himself, returned her to the beginning, to the light, to the source of all being. And we must accept it." He raised his arms. "Let us pray."

Heads bowed as one. Even I let my chin sink on to my chest and closed my eyes. After each prayer I found myself chanting Amen along with the rest. It was out of respect for Lara, I told myself. I too needed to commemorate her life, even if I didn't believe her soul lived on in death.

At last the service was over and the congregation, led by Father Thomas, processed down the central aisle, a unified image of misery and grief. If they believed Lara had gone to a better world, why was everyone so bloody miserable? It was a conundrum I'd never been able to work out.

There weren't many hiding places. I made do with turning my collar up and examining the rack of religious literature behind the font. Eventually the noise of passing feet subsided. The door closed silently. Someone had switched the main lights off as they passed, so that the church was illuminated only by the tall candles on the altar and by several trays of small flickering ones, most of them no doubt offered up for Lara.

I walked slowly up the aisle, my footsteps sounding hollow on the polished wooden floor. The smell of incense reminded me of joss sticks. When I reached the altar I turned right and made my way down one side of the church and up the other, stopping to look at the Stations of the Cross. They were bright and primitive like Mexican art. They showed Christ's passion and death, or to be frank, his torture, mutilation and execution. While graphic, they lacked the horror of the real thing. These pictures were sanitised, even beautiful. I'd seen a mutilated body and there was no beauty there. I sighed. It seemed everything came back to Lara.

I was examining the last icon, showing a contorted body nailed to a tree, when I heard a soft click and a door opened somewhere nearby. Father Thomas, in a plain black cassock now, crossed in front of the altar, genuflected, then opened the little gate that led up to the sanctuary itself. One by one he doused the tall candles, casting the church into deep shadow, then, crossing himself, he removed a chalice from the domed receptacle in the centre of the altar.

He came down the steps, still unaware of my presence. He looked tired, spent, as if the performance he'd given during the service had taken it out of him.

"Father Thomas?"

He raised his eyes to me, without fear or surprise. No doubt he was used to being called on at all times of day and night. But there *was* something in his expression – a deep loneliness, shocking in someone even younger than me. I surmised that his life was a contradictory mixture of isolation and a complete lack of privacy. And here I was, yet another supplicant, about to invade his time and space.

"Can I help you?"

I noticed something else. Close-up, he was damned good-looking. He wasn't that tall, but he was compact and graceful. Did he work out, I wondered? I mentally slapped my wrist. I'd just made passionate love to another younger man. Enough, already.

"Yes, I hope so," I said hesitantly.

143

He nodded, and waved a weary hand to the front pew. We sat down side by side.

"Is there something worrying you?"

I wasn't sure what to say. I was reluctant to give my name in case the Ramseys had talked to the priest about me. I was pretty sure he would close ranks and I'd learn nothing.

I found myself saying, "I'm interested in becoming a Catholic."

"I see. What brought you to the Church?"

For a moment I was confused by the question. "I... came by car."

"No." He smiled wanly. "I meant... why Catholicism?"

"Right. How stupid of me." I paused, suggesting deep thought, in fact wondering how on earth I'd got myself into this, and how I was going to wriggle out.

"This murder... it's made me realise... there has to be more to life than just the few years we spend on earth..." I dried up, not daring to look at him.

"God is wonderful, isn't He?"

"Is he? I mean, yes, of course. Or to put it another way, *she* is pretty damn amazing."

"Whether God is male or female, or both, is unimportant. God has brought you here through Lara's death. It goes to prove the old saying, doesn't it? Every cloud has a silver lining. You're the only silver lining I've come across in the last few days and I bless you for it."

"Thanks." I let a decent interval pass. "I came in at the end of the service just now. Did you know Lara Ramsey well?"

"I'd say so, yes. When I first came to St Bridget's she was about fourteen. She sang in the choir, attended the youth club and we got on fine. Things got more difficult when she got older. To be honest, she turned her back on the Church." He gazed at the huge crown of thorns hanging over the altar. "But you… you're reaching out towards it. It's as if God has taken one away and given another one back."

I tried to smile but it froze on my lips. "How do you remember her?"

"How? You mean, my abiding image of her?"

"If you like."

He placed both hands reverently on the top of the chalice as he thought about it. "I remember her hair. That cloud of gold, like a halo. She looked like a madonna." He pointed to a statue of Our Lady, a saccharine, blue-clad plaster saint who looked nothing like Lara.

"Why was she so against the Church?"

"I really shouldn't be talking like this." He gave a huge sigh as if the weight of all the world's sorrow was on his shoulders. "I'm tired out, that's the truth of it. It's been a traumatic few days. Sorry. Let's talk about you. I hold catechism classes at six-thirty every Wednesday evening. If you'll just give me your name and a contact number." He reached into his cassock pocket.

I told him without thinking. "My name's Jude Baxendale, and my mobile number is…"

He stared at me, open-mouthed with horror. "Baxendale? Don't you work for the press – a photographer? The Ramseys told me what you did."

"Shit." I dragged my fingers through my hair. "Look, I've apologised for that. The fact is, I don't work for the paper any more. I resigned. I'm not here to spy, report, take photos or any other media stuff."

"Then why are you here?"

Like a penitent at confession I told him everything, as

honestly as I could.

"I didn't mean to deceive you, but I'm downright tired of coming up against a brick wall. I'm just trying to understand this awful crime. The trouble is, the more I find out about Lara, the less I understand. Before she died I simply thought of her as a quiet sweet-natured girl, but now... I thought you might give me a different perspective."

"You're a photographer, Jude."

"So?"

"Perhaps you tend to go by appearances."

"I suppose I do." Hadn't the psychic detective told me the same thing?

"Sometimes appearances are deceptive and we have to dig deeper."

"You can talk. The thing you remember about Lara isn't her personality or her beliefs, but her hair."

He looked embarrassed, then angry. I could see his patience was wearing thin. Even men of God were human after all. But I persisted.

"OK, I accept we have to go beyond appearances. So what did lie behind Lara's sweet exterior? I think there was something really troubled about her. Her promiscuity was extreme, and that's not normal. Either she was desperately looking for something, or she was trying to forget. My son hadn't known her long enough, so he can't help."

He didn't answer for a while, as if struggling with some inner dilemma. Eventually he sighed and said, "She had an abortion."

"What?"

"She got pregnant when she was fifteen, and terminated the pregnancy, against her parents' advice, my counsel, and the teachings of the Church. Not such a sweet girl, was she?"

"It could happen to anyone,' I said faintly, remembering my own experience of conception when I was eighteen, the result of a hopeless passion and too much alcohol.

"Abortion is wrong. Lara broke the commandments laid down by God."

"She makes one small mistake and she's damned?"

"It doesn't matter how small the transgression is, it is offensive to God. He is merciful, but rules are rules. He does not condone sin."

"Then God – he or she - is an idiot. Why invent sex then tell us humans we mustn't do it?"

"Sex is all very well in the context of marriage —"

"So why invent desire? Why give us that phenomenally powerful feeling, then say back off, no touching? What kind of cruel trick is that?" I was fired up now. And I thought of something else. "Who was the father of Lara's baby?"

"She wouldn't say."

"Do you have any idea?"

He gave me a withering look. "You know what she was like. I'd say she probably didn't know herself."

I felt a sudden surge of closeness to the dead girl. Both she and I had given up on the pointless posturing of religion. Like me, she'd been a troubled teenager, like me, she'd got pregnant. The only difference was that I'd had Daniel, and she'd got rid of her baby. I didn't blame her. I might have done the same but I left it too late. Now I was glad I hadn't had an abortion. I couldn't imagine life without my son. He was the best thing in it. How had Lara felt about the baby she could never hold? It must have been a sorrow that rocked her world for years. And then she met Daniel, who was sweet and unworldly and loved her for herself, not just for sex. Her life began to steady, come together.

Then some maniac killed her.

Father Thomas stood up. "I think you should go now."

"Just one other thing. Did Lara ever dabble in Satanism or black magic?"

"Not that I know of. Though it wouldn't surprise me." His voice had hardened. I wondered why I'd thought him good-looking, charismatic. He was just an ordinary guy, weighed down with overwork, and getting crow's feet round his eyes. I reckoned he would hate that. The toned muscles of his compact body suggested a vain man.

"I'm sorry if I disturbed your rest."

He snorted. "I don't get much of that." He looked at me with a haggard expression. "I'll pray for you, Jude."

"Thanks," I said drily.

I hurried out of the church, away from the cloying smells of incense and polish and candle wax, and into the sharp fresh slap of an arctic wind. If God was to be found anywhere it was here, in the open air, in the beauty of creation. I had found no sign of her in St Bridget's.

Fifteen

There was a screen around Daniel's bed.

My heart raced as I came into the room. I could hear voices coming from behind the curtain. I tugged at it, trying to find the way in. When I succeeded I saw that Daniel had aged by about sixty years and lost all his hair.

An elderly stranger was lying on top of the blankets, white surgical stockings covering his thin bony legs. Two young nurses were giving him some kind of personal attention I didn't even want to think about.

"Sorry. I'm looking for Daniel Baxendale."

"We moved him into the ward," said one of them.

"More company for him," the other one giggled.

"How is he?"

"He's fine."

"We'll be sorry to see him go," said the giggly one.

"I can take him home?" My heart reversed and raced backwards.

"You'll have to speak to the ward sister about it."

"I will."

I rushed out of the room and into the ward. The six beds were occupied by old men in various states of decrepitude, apart from the bed in the corner by the window, on which a tall, thin, gangling figure lay sprawled.

"What are you doing here?"

"Visiting," grunted Harrison. "Dan's gone for a piss, if you're wondering."

"I was, yes." I put my bag on the chair. "How come you know Daniel?"

"Lara."

"Course." Had Harrison been one of Lara's old boyfriends? Knowing her reputation before she met Daniel, it seemed possible, even likely. How much did Daniel really know about Lara's sex life before they started going out? Was I the one who was going to have to tell him?

When Daniel returned I hugged him tightly.

"Hi, Mum," he muttered, trying to extricate himself from my encircling arms. He tugged his dressing gown shut over his pyjamas. "Have a seat."

"Just for a minute. Then I want to see the ward sister about you coming home."

"They're letting me out?"

"Looks like it."

He punched the air.

Harrison reluctantly moved his booted feet to the floor so that Daniel could sit on the bed too. I took the chair. As Harrison shifted his position his pendant swung out. A metal star on a leather thong. I peered closer.

"Nice necklace. Isn't that what they call a pentagram?"

Harrison looked at me through sleepy hooded eyes. "Dunno."

Sweat broke out on my palms. I wiped them on my jeans.

Gary, the male nurse, walked briskly into the ward. "Hey, Daniel. How are things?"

"I'm feeling good. Is it true I'm going home?" His face was more alive than I'd seen it for days.

"Tomorrow, maybe, depending on your breathing test."

"It was fine earlier," said Daniel.

"Can't you let him out tonight?" I pleaded. "He's miles better, and I'm sure you need the bed."

Gary glanced at his watch. "It's a bit late, we don't

usually…" He looked at Daniel's chart thoughtfully. "We have got some urgent cases coming in, though. I'll see what I can do."

"Thanks, I'd really appreciate that."

He hurried away and I slumped back in the chair. Churches, hospitals – they were both places I longed to get out of.

"Mum, are you all right?"

"Fine," I said quickly, before Harrison could butt in with the news that I no longer had a job. No doubt everyone at the Ravenbridge Evening Post knew by now. "I'm just shattered. It's been an eventful day."

I sat very still, listening to Daniel talk idly about football while Harrison grunted his replies. They sounded like old friends. I half-closed my eyes, pretending to be drifting off, but my mind was racing as fast as my heartbeat. Harrison looked like the sort of scary youth that old ladies would shy away from in the street, clutching their handbags. But I'd always assumed he was harmless, just lazy and sullen, and so vacant he was probably on something most of the time. Had he gone too far over the New Year party season and killed Lara in a drug-fuelled frenzy? I gave myself a mental slap for thinking in journalese. All the same, if it was true, then I was sitting a metre away from a murderer.

Harrison must have felt the heat of my attention. He turned to me, blinking behind his asymmetrical curtain of hair. "Bad luck, you getting sacked."

Daniel looked bewildered. "Sacked? What d'you mean?" He turned to me. "Mum?"

"It's not true. I wasn't fired."

Daniel looked mightily relieved. At that moment Gary, bless him, came hurrying towards us, carrying a cardboard flagon for urinating into. "Ward sister says

Daniel can go home tonight. She's doing the discharge forms right now." He waved the peeing pot. "Sorry, got to go. Good luck, Daniel."

"Cheers, mate."

I stood up. "OK, Daniel. You get changed and I'll get the rest of your stuff together." I glared at Harrison, and eventually he retreated beyond the bed so that I could swish the curtain shut around it.

Daniel stripped off down to his underpants. He looked painfully thin. I wanted to hug him again but I was afraid his ribs might break. Looking in the narrow cabinet beside the bed, I found his T-shirt and handed it to him. Someone had hung his jeans neatly on a trouser hanger, almost certainly not Daniel. One of the young nurses perhaps. I pulled them off and hung them over my arm. As I did so something fell out of the pocket. I caught it neatly.

"Oh. Here's that…" I stopped myself. The bracelet felt cool and heavy in my hands. In the gloom of the cabinet I could just see the colours – grey and soft green and mauve.

"Gimme my jeans, will you?"

"Sure. No problem." I slipped the bracelet into my pocket and handed Daniel his trousers.

Then it came again, that sense of slippage, my feet no longer firmly planted on the earth because it was trying to throw me off and hurtle onwards through space without me.

I opened the curtain. Harrison was still there.

"I'm going to speak to the ward sister then we're going home. So… see you around some time."

"I can wait. I'll help you take Dan home."

"There's no need. I can manage."

"It's no problem."

Then Harrison did something I'd never seen him do before. He smiled. And that was truly scary.

To be fair, Harrison made a real effort to be helpful, carrying the plastic bag containing Daniel's clothes and books to the car and chatting to him on the way home in a slightly more fluent version of his usual Neanderthal. They sat together on the back seat while I drove in lonely splendour at the front like a taxi driver. I was preoccupied with my thoughts while they were discussing classic album covers. The names floated over me – Sergeant Pepper, Velvet Underground, Joy Division. But I listened intently when they began to talk about Lara.

"The police came to the hospital a couple of times."

"You were her boyfriend. The odds are you did it, aren't they?" I glanced in the rear-view mirror. Harrison hardly blenched. "I mean, I know you didn't, but from their standpoint…"

"Yeah, yeah."

"Do they really think you killed her?"

"Probably."

"Tough shit."

I couldn't stay quiet any longer. "Don't be ridiculous. Daniel had nothing to do with Lara's death!" The ceramic bracelet lay heavy in my pocket. Lara had given it back to him and he'd forgotten, that was all. Perhaps the clasp had broken and he'd offered to mend it. Absorbed in this thought, I didn't realise the car was veering across the road.

"Mum, watch out!"

I swerved back just in time. The driver of the white van that shot past me raised two fingers, his face contorted with rage and spewing silent obscenities through his side window.

"Hey, Daniel, that would have been ironic, wouldn't it?"

I said as lightly as I could manage. "A few days ago I saved your life. Today I nearly got you killed."

For some reason neither of them seemed to find it hilarious.

Daniel had invited Harrison in before I could stop him.

"It's getting late," I protested. "You should be in bed. I know how hard it is to get any proper rest in hospital."

"Chill, Mum. I'm feeling fine. I'm not even tired."

The two of them disappeared upstairs. In no time I could hear the fast heavy rhythm of one of Daniel's favourite CDs. The high-energy metronomic repetitions began to give me a pounding headache.

I went to the kitchen and made tea – black because I still had no milk. I sat at the beaten-up pine table, sipping the bitter brew, trying to make sense of the last few hours. A series of freeze-frames clicked round my brain – Father Thomas's haggard face, the pentagram round Harrison's neck, the cool stones falling into my hand from Daniel's pocket.

Trying to examine each thought logically, I concentrated first on the priest and his uneasy relationship with Lara. Something troubled me about that. I drummed my fingers on the kitchen table. Of course. Patricia Ramsey had said that Lara went off the rails from the age of sixteen, which meant it all went wrong after the abortion, not before. The pregnancy wasn't the result of promiscuity, it was the cause. So why had Father Thomas lied, suggesting that Lara had had so many lovers she couldn't be sure of paternity?

Father Thomas with his handsome face and muscular body, not to mention his ability to manipulate an audience... Had Lara once thought the priest was wonderful? Had he taken advantage of that? A celibate man with an

154

abiding image of a young girl's beautiful hair…

If the priest had broken his vows and fathered a child, was he capable of turning his back on the sixth commandment too? Illicit sex and murder were not the same thing at all, but perhaps part of the same continuum, the slide away from God. Not small transgressions either. If Father Thomas was a sinner, God would get her own back and make him pay, big time.

And if there was no God, I'd have to do it instead.

But there were other people I needed to think about. Harrison, for one. He wore a pendant that was the same design as the marks scored on Lara's chest. Coincidence? He knew her, he might even have slept with her, and he knew her current boyfriend. The more I thought about it, the less like coincidence it seemed. There had to be a connection here. I tipped the cold tea down the sink. I was trying to find Lara's killer, and guess what, Harrison had inveigled his way into my house. He was upstairs right now. Another coincidence?

And what about Lara's boss, Craig Gilmore? His behaviour had suggested he had something to hide. Father Thomas, Harrison, Craig Gilmore…

But had Lara definitely been attacked by a man? I reminded myself that even DI Laverack admitted the killer could have been a woman. After all, there was no evidence of a sexual assault on Lara, and Lee hadn't been sure if the figure loitering outside Lara's flat had been male or female. Annie's tearful face swam into view. Had she loved Lara enough to kill her when their friendship faded? And what about Patricia Ramsey's disappointment in her beloved daughter? But she was Lara's mother, for god's sake. Could I kill my own son if he'd done something wicked? Never.

Daniel. It was time to think about him.

I took the bracelet from my pocket and examined the clasp. Nothing wrong with it. So why had Lara given it back to him? Or had he taken it, after he'd…? Suppressing that idea, I leaned over the sink, overcome with nausea. Another thought rammed its way in. What if more than one of them – say, Father Thomas and Craig Gilmore, or Annie and Harrison – were in it together? I began to laugh hysterically to stop the terrible images forming in my mind. Two against one? Lara wouldn't have stood a chance. I tried to breathe deeply but ended up hyperventilating, panting as if I'd just run ten miles. It was ridiculous. What possible connection could there be between any of them? Lara. She was the connection. But that got me precisely nowhere.

I made fresh tea to steady myself. Drinking it made me feel a little better. I even smiled wryly as I sipped it. Two days ago no one had any idea who could have killed Lara. Now suspects were falling out of the trees like ripe fruit.

It seemed to have gone quiet upstairs. I went into the hall and listened. There was music, but more subdued this time, something much more mellow. I could also smell smoke. My hackles rose.

I marched upstairs and went straight into Daniel's room without knocking. The room had the same exploded look as when we left it two days ago. Clothes, artist's materials, books and CD cases lay in random tangled heaps. An incense cone burned in a saucer, giving off a heady sickly odour that didn't quite mask the smell of smoke. The noxious fumes emanated from the figure that lay prone on the bed. It wasn't Daniel – he was stretched out on the floor, as still as a corpse.

"What's going on in here?"

Harrison's head rose stiffly from the pillow

"Chill, Mum," Daniel murmured from the floor. His eyes stayed closed. Whatever Harrison was smoking, Daniel was passively imbibing it too.

"Put that spliff out, Harrison. Don't you realise how bad it is for Daniel's breathing?"

"OK." Slowly, almost insolently, he stubbed the joint out in the tin box resting on his chest, no doubt saving the stub for later. Then I remembered something I needed to ask him.

"By the way, what did you do with that print of mine, the one you put on the wall in Photographic, where it looks as if the river's for sale?"

"What?"

I couldn't decide if his blank stare was genuine puzzlement or a put-on.

"The one you said was complete balls."

"Coho- thingy?"

"Cojones, yes. Where is it?"

"I haven't touched it. Why?"

"I was looking for it today." I didn't add that I was clearing my desk, though I knew I'd have to tell Daniel about my resignation soon. "It wasn't there."

"Perhaps it fell off. I only used blu-tack."

"Then who took it?"

"How do I know?"

Exasperated, I marched across to the window, letting in an icy blast of night air. Cold air was bad for asthma but not as bad as smoke. In any case, under the incense and weed, the room smelled rank – paint, papier-mâché, old socks, stale sheets.

"Why don't you two go downstairs while I fumigate the room and change the bed?"

Daniel peeled himself off the floor. Harrison followed him sluggishly. They shambled downstairs.

I must have tugged the sheets off the bed, dumped them in the linen basket, fetched fresh ones from the airing cupboard, but I don't remember any of it. I made Daniel's bed on automatic pilot, only coming back to domestic reality when I had to decide whether to put an extra blanket under the duvet. It was another bitter night and after the fug of a hospital ward I didn't want him to be cold.

I sat down on the bed. I still hadn't faced up to the possibility that my son was a killer. And here I was, worrying about keeping him warm. Then I reflected on what they always said about even the worst criminals – at least his mother loved him.

Sixteen

Daniel was lying on the sofa watching the late-night news. His eyes were heavy and dark-lidded. He was clearly more exhausted than he liked to admit. There was no sign of his friend.

"Has Harrison gone?"

"No, he's in the basement."

"What!"

"I told him about your darkroom and he — "

"You know I don't allow anybody down there, not even you. I've got negs drying and stuff everywhere and all those chemicals."

"I could hardly stop him, could I?"

I ran along the hall and yanked open the door that led down to the basement. My feet thumping on the concrete steps must have announced my arrival, but when I threw the lower door open Harrison was poking through my things on the dry bench as if he had every right to be in my private domain. I got the impression he was looking for something and trying to disguise that as idle curiosity. Despite his denial I was pretty sure he had removed the river print. Was he trying to find the negative so that he could destroy that too? And why did it matter so much?

"Harrison – out!"

"Great place," he muttered. He carried on examining everything as if I simply hadn't heard me ask him to shift his arse. I breathed in the woodpulp smell of soaking paper that pervaded the room, and tried to stretch my patience. Then I noticed he had placed his tin box and lighter on the bench. If he tried lighting up in here I would lose it completely.

"Where do you get your chemicals from?" he asked.

"I buy them wholesale from a specialist. Now will you please — "

"I've always wanted to do this kind of photography. At college we only did a few sessions in the darkroom and I've forgotten nearly all of it. Most of the time we just used computers."

"I'm not surprised. Doing it the old-fashioned way is fiddly and takes ages."

"It's better, though."

"Yeah, the results can be fantastic. But a decent digital camera is just as good."

"So why do you do it?"

I had to think about that. "I guess I like the long slow process. It's satisfying, and to be honest, I always find it really exciting."

"Show me."

"Come on, Harrison. It's late and I'm knackered. This hasn't been the best day of my life, as you well know." In fact, he didn't know the half of it – the unorthodox use of the elevator, the visit to St Bridget's, the jumble of fear and suspicion that had assailed me ever since, not least the possibility that Harrison himself had killed Lara. I held the door open pointedly, desperate to get out of the room. Usually it was my haven. Now it seemed to me a chilly windowless box, a perfect trap. "And for the record, I wasn't fired. I resigned."

"Whatever." Harrison picked up an expensive Leica camera and nearly dropped it.

"Be careful! That cost a fortune."

He put it down with exaggerated reverence. "Can you

handle colour prints down here?"

"Yes. But I don't do them very often. You have to work in the pitch dark. I prefer developing black and white film. It's that thing about watching the image gradually emerge, like clearing steam from a mirror."

"I'd like to do that."

"Another time, perhaps." I jerked my head at the open door. He ignored me.

"No time like the present."

Was there a hint of menace in his tone? Why hadn't I kept quiet about the pentagram? I'd put Harrison on red alert. Now I had to go into reverse, and reassure him by my manner that I had no doubts about him, apart from regarding him as lazy and useless, and he knew that already.

"All right. What do you want to know?"

"The whole process. Have you got some film you need to develop?"

"I suppose so." I closed the door and plunged us into darkness for a split second before switching on the safe light, a naked red bulb that made the room glow ruby.

I picked up the Leica. "There's a finished roll in here." I unloaded it, then demonstrated how to get it into a developing tank, a cylinder about the size of a very large thermos.

"You have to work blind inside a changing bag." This was a cloth bag with little elasticated armholes in the sides. I held it up. "You can see why it's known as granny's knickers."

Harrison looked doubtful. I imagined his acquaintance with female underwear was limited to the G-string and the thong.

"This is the tricky bit. I have to put my hands in the

holes... and they're very cold, which is good in one way – it means I won't leave fingerprints on the film." I didn't tell him that my hands were also clammy with fear and the film was probably ruined anyway. "But it's not so good in another way because it's so bloody difficult to get the film in the spiral." I fiddled for a couple of minutes. "Got it!"

I pulled the tank out of the bag, the film now safe inside it. I moved across to the wet bench and got ready to show Harrison the next process, mixing the developer with warm water then pouring it into the cylinder.

"I'll put the stuff in," he said, with something close to enthusiasm.

I held on to the flagon, trying to remember how caustic the chemical was. "No, I'd better do it this time." I rushed the procedure, turning the tank vigorously like a cocktail shaker to make sure no bubbles spoiled the negs and that each frame was bathed in chemical. I was anxious to get on to the stop bath and the fixer as soon as possible, and raced through those too.

"Now the film has to be washed. But that takes ages." I lowered the tank into the sink and turned on the tap. "We can leave it there for a while. I've got some dry negs over here."

I couldn't afford a drying cabinet so I pegged washed strips of film to an overhead line, each one weighted at the bottom with a metal clip to hold it straight and steady. Even so, they twisted slightly in the air current, like fly papers.

I unpegged a strip at random and placed it on the dry bench. I reached for a pair of scissors.

"I can do this bit." Harrison got to the scissors first.

"OK," I said slowly, masking my leap of panic with a forced smile.

Harrison parked his bottom on a stool and followed my instructions carefully, cutting the long strip into shorter strips of six frames each.

"Now slot each strip on to this grid."

He did so, then with laborious care he placed it under the enlarger and printed up a contact sheet while I finished washing the film in the sink and hung up the wet strip in its turn. I kept my eye on Harrison as I washed the tank and spiral, but he seemed to be totally absorbed in his task.

"Finished." He held up the sheet of tiny pictures.

"Good. I'll put the main light back on, then we can see what we've got."

I examined the prints through a magnifying glass. I'd taken these just before Christmas. Most were exterior shots of bare trees and rock formations, passions of mine. Then I reared back with shock. The last few showed Daniel and Lara in the back garden, chasing each other, posing with the household gnome, holding each other close and smiling into the camera. They seemed lit up from within, radiant. Maybe it was just the cold air making Lara's cheeks unnaturally rosy, but I doubted it.

"I like this one," said Harrison. He pointed to a picture of the couple in profile, just about to kiss.

"We can't print these."

"Why not? Nice present for Daniel."

"I hardly think so."

He sighed, clearly put out.

"All right. Mark the one you want and we'll print it up full size."

Under instruction he slotted the strip into the neg carrier and placed in the enlarger. Underneath went a sheet of resin-coated paper.

"Now expose it to the light for precisely fifteen seconds."

He counted under his breath. "I can't see anything."

"You won't, not yet. It's a latent image. Now for the exciting bit. The pure magic." We returned to the wet bench. "Watch this, Harrison." Despite my misgivings I wanted him to see the steam clearing from the mirror, leaving a perfect image.

After just one minute in the developer the picture began to spread over the paper. But it wasn't ready yet. You had to judge the exact right moment. I showed Harrison how to agitate the paper then handed him the tongs. "Two minutes should do it, but it might need a few seconds more. You decide."

We watched Lara and Daniel emerge. I thought Harrison had messed up by leaving it too long, but just as I was about to speak he lifted the print by the corner and plunged it into the stop bath and fixer. Finally he siphoned it down under the running tap.

As it swirled under the stream of water I saw that Harrison had made a good job of it. Two young lovers, forever suspended in time, glowing with an unrepeatable happiness. It made me want to cry, but a slight flicker round the lips showed that Harrison was pleased with his handiwork.

"You can turn off the tap now. It's finished. It'll take a little while to dry." I began washing my hands.

He unbent his long thin frame and stretched extravagantly.

"That was cool. Thanks, Jude."

I smiled thinly, anxious to get out of the darkroom and see Harrison on his way, but he showed no sign of going. He slumped back on the stool, then seeing something on the floor, he folded himself in half and picked it up.

A short strip of negatives. It must have fallen out of the grid during an earlier session.

He held the strip up to the light. "Hey, here's that picture you were banging on about."

"The river?" I snatched it from him and squinted at it. It was the fourth frame along. I could see the *For Sale* sign leaning over at a crazy angle.

Harrison reached out to take it back.

I jerked away from him, and in a blind reflex, grabbed his lighter and flicked it on. The negative strip burned up in one brief bright conflagration. I dropped the melting mess in the bin. Harrison had wanted this negative for some reason. There was no way he was going to get it now.

He stared at me with blank astonishment. "What did you do that for?"

"I – I – didn't need it any more."

He shrugged. "I just thought... these chemicals... naked flames and all that."

"Don't worry, I'm an expert. I know what I'm doing." My voice sounded shrill and unlike itself. "We're finished here, Harrison. Let's go."

"I can tidy up —"

"No!" I brought my pitch down a key or two. "I'll do it tomorrow. Daniel will be wondering what's happened to us."

"You'll give him the picture, won't you?"

"Yeah...yeah."

I nearly pushed him out of the basement and up the stairs.

Through the open living-room door I could see that Daniel was still on the sofa, nearly asleep.

"Harrison's just going," I called. I hurried down the hall.

"Bye, mate," said Harrison, walking with infuriating

slowness towards the front door, which I was holding open impatiently.

"See you," Daniel called faintly. "Thanks for coming."

"No problem. Get back in the zone soon, won't you, mate? No more skiving."

I shut the door on Harrison's pleasantries and leaned back against it.

Daniel staggered from the living room. "I'm bushed. I'm off to bed now."

My heart went out to him. I couldn't help it. He looked tired and thin, and his face, creased with grief and anxiety, was much older than its years. I could let him go to his rest and suffer a sleepless night myself, or I could tackle him here and get it over with. He might never speak to me again, of course, but that was a risk I had to take.

"Before you go to bed, I need to ask you something."

"What is it?" he said, rubbing his eyes.

"Come and sit down."

I guided him back into the living room where all the familiar objects seemed slightly distorted and too brightly coloured. I told myself it was the effect of working too long under the ruby light, then I told myself that was stupid. I knew what it was. It was fear.

"Will this take long?" Daniel dropped on to the sofa while I took the chair opposite. "Is it about Lara?" He must have seen the look on my face. "Have you found out anything?"

"I've found out lots of things, Daniel. But I'll tell you about those some other time."

"What, then?" He sat up eagerly. "You know who killed her?"

"No. If I knew anything for certain I'd have gone straight to the police."

"But you think you know?"

I paused. "We're getting off the point here."

"What is the point? Come on, Mum, spit it out."

"I need to go back... to when Lara was alive, to when you first met."

"That's easy enough. It was the first time she came to the life-drawing class, last year, around Easter. Mr Keele had booked some other model but she couldn't come that night."

"And Lara became the regular model for the group?"

"We all wanted her to stay. So did Mr Keele. We had a few others, but mostly it was Lara. She was special, in all sorts of ways." His voice vibrated with emotion. "You know all this."

"The fact is I'm a bad mum with the memory of a goldfish. Just remind me when you started going out?"

"Not till November," he said patiently.

"And how did it feel... after you started going out with Lara... when she took all her clothes off to pose in front of the other people in the class, especially the boys?"

He looked mystified. "Fine. I felt fine about it. Life drawing is sensual, but it's not erotic. You're concentrating so hard you just don't think about sex."

He caught my sceptical look. Men were reputed to think about sex every six seconds. With adolescent boys I reckoned you could halve that time span.

"OK. You do think about it sometimes, but you're so busy trying to draw that foot or the shadow of the nose or the exact curve of the breast that you're quickly back to the drawing board – literally." He frowned. "Where is this going?"

"I wish I knew, love." I sighed. There was no way out, only forward. "When you were getting dressed at the hospital, I found this..." I took the bracelet from my pocket and placed it on the coffee table between us. "It fell out of your jeans."

Daniel looked stunned, his eyes flickering from me to the bracelet and back again.

"But I gave that to Lara. On her birthday, just before Christmas."

"She didn't give it back for any reason? To change something on it? For safe-keeping during the New Year pub crawl?" I was aware that I was feeding him ideas, but in my desperation to explain this aberration I couldn't stop myself.

"No."

"So how did it get into your pocket?"

"I've no idea. She wore it all the time. I never saw her take it off, and she definitely didn't give it back." He shook his head. "I just don't understand."

"You know the police have been looking for this bracelet. Their theory is that —"

"That the killer took it from Lara as a kind of trophy. I know. I was there."

I let the silence between us grow, unable to find the right words.

Then Daniel's face crumpled, peeling back the years, making him into a little boy who had fallen over and needed comfort.

"You think… I was jealous, so I killed her?" His voice ended on a thin high note.

"Just tell me the truth, Daniel, however bad it is."

He reached out and picked up the bracelet. He stared at it for a long time. He took a deep breath and began to speak. "Lara was…"

He stopped. He twisted his head towards the door. I heard it too. A clattering noise, coming from outside.

"What's that?"

I stood up. The noise came again. It sounded like someone tripping over dustbins. Daniel struggled up from the sofa. I put out a warning hand.

"No. I'll see to it."

"It's probably just a cat."

"Sure." I was lying. It would have to be a cat the size of a hippo to knock a full dustbin over. "I'll go and check it out. You stay here. In fact…" I put my hands on his shoulders. "Lock the door and don't let anyone else in but me. Understand?"

"Who do you think…?"

"It's just a precaution, right?"

He nodded.

"Give me that torch from the drawer, will you?"

Seventeen

I walked slowly toward the dustbin, waving the torch like an arc light, my boots crackling on frozen snow. As I expected, the bin lay on its side where it had been kicked over. The debris of Christmas lay scattered on the ground – turkey bones and wrapping paper and empty chocolate boxes. Around it was a mash of footprints, impossible to distinguish mine from any intruder's. I shone the torch down to the bottom of the long untidy garden. Beyond the thick tangle of bushes at the end there was a high stone wall and I doubted any intruder would have made their getaway in that direction. Which left the side passage.

I edged along the back of my house, turned into the passage, my torch held out like a weapon. It was deserted, and the five-foot-high wicket gate at the end was bolted. They must have climbed over it. Unless…

I retraced my steps to the back garden and flickered my torch over the grass. There should have been a sheet of virgin white snow, but a diagonal line crossed the lawn, ending at the gap in the fence that I often used to pop next door to see Rob and Denise. On closer inspection I saw the prints ran both ways, the escape route tracks messing up the ones underneath. But at least I knew which way the intruder had come.

I switched the torch off. The snow seemed to give off a bluish fluorescent glow and it was easy to follow the tracks. I reached the fence and peered through the gap. The bedroom light was still on next door and I could hear raised voices. Another argument. If I could hear them,

Hayley could too. She must be lying awake in bed, listening to her parents tearing their family apart.

I stepped into their garden, staring up and down, eyes wide to catch any sign of the intruder. There was no one there. But I could see a dark line of footprints crossing the lawn nearer to the house. I ran quietly along the fence, passing the ferret cage. I could hear the scrabbling of small feet and caught the faint gamey smell of its lair. The light went out in the bedroom. I stopped, letting my eyes adjust to the darkness. Then I ran across the lawn, following the dark track already laid down.

I approached the side entry more cautiously, but like the other one, it was empty. There was no wicket gate at the end, just an ordinary gate with a latch. I ran down the pathway, stopping at the end, peering into the front garden. There was no sound apart from the howling wind. It cut through my thin shirt like a razor. A feeble street lamp cast a pool of hazy light on to the road but I could see no sign of movement anywhere. I waited a few moments. A car came by, driving slowly through the mess of snow and grit, and disappeared in the direction of the main road. Otherwise, nothing.

Whoever had entered my back garden had melted away.

I was about to give up and return home when something caught my eye. A flicker of movement on the other side of the street. A figure running across Weavers' Field. It zigzagged from side to side as it went, recalling the erratic path Hayley's ferret had traced across the same terrain. Then the figure straightened its course, heading down the slope towards the river.

"Scumbag," I muttered under my breath. I had no doubt this was my intruder, and though all I could see was an indistinct shifting shadow I was pretty sure I knew who it was.

I crossed the road and ran on to the field. Marks in the snow were no help at all here. The white stuff had been churned up by children and dog walkers and boys who liked to turn their skateboards into snowboards, leaving great skidmarks across the ground. But it didn't matter. My target was heading for the river and so was I.

I got as far as a lop-sided snowman before I stopped to catch my breath. On this side of the field, well away from the streetlights, it was dark, almost pitch-black. Even so, I didn't want to use the torch. It would mark me out like a spotlight.

I progressed more slowly. Soon I could hear the roaring gush of the river. Having tumbled over one weir, it was racing over rocks towards the next one half a mile downstream, passing through the quieter reaches of the old millpond in its relentless journey. I began to tread carefully, unsure where the ground dropped away. I had no choice but to switch the torch back on, reducing the beam by putting my hand over it. I shivered, deeply regretting my lack of a coat. But I wasn't going to give up now.

I reached the top of the incline and peered over. I shone the beam along the bank, expecting to see a figure huddled there. But there was no one. Puzzled, I slithered sideways down the slope. A few metres along, a massive tree leaned out over the river, its roots exposed like the fingers of a hand. The ground behind had eroded away and left a sheltering space. I let the full beam of the torch play into the hole.

Empty.

I looked along the water in both directions. I could discount the idea of my adversary swimming to safety. A boat? After several weeks of dry cold weather the river was slightly less turbulent than usual, but it was still too dangerous for a small craft, with the hazard of large rocks and another weir not far downstream. Which meant they must have followed the bank. But which way? Muttering obscenities I took one last look – left, right. Every branch and leaf was thickly outlined with hoar frost. For a second I was distracted, wishing I had my camera with me. Then telling myself to concentrate, I looked again for signs of the intruder. But like the temperature, my success rate was well below zero.

I was so cold I could hardly hold the torch steady. Sighing deeply, I realised there was nothing more I could do. The thought of home and warmth and a hot drink began to crowd out my sense of mission. I wasn't really giving up, I told myself. I just needed to recharge my batteries and revise my strategy.

At that moment I felt a sharp shove in my back. My feet left the ground. There was a split second when I was airborne, flying like a thrown stick, before I crashed into the icy water.

I sank like a brick, numb with shock and cold. Flapping my arms, I rose to the surface, gasping, choking, turning in the current. I was hurled against one rock then another. I tried to grab hold of them but they were covered in ice and my fingers were too numb with cold. My brain began to freeze, the synapses shutting down one by one, cells losing power a million at a time. Then, after a few seconds my brain kicked back in. Get out of here, it screamed, you'll die if you don't get out *now*. I fought against the current, trying desperately to reach the bank. But what if my attacker was still there, waiting for me?

Against all instinct I turned back into the flow and, unresisting, was carried along, spinning through whirlpools, trapped in eddies, crashing against protruding rocks. My blood was turning to ice, my limbs to stone. I could hear the distant roar of the weir up ahead. How many times had I walked along here, marvelling at its beauty and tranquillity? How many times had I taken photos? And never for a moment had I thought that being carried along in it was to be as helpless as a leaf blown about by a force-nine gale.

The river began to sweep round in a bend, and from the declining strength of the turbulence, I knew I had reached the calmer stretch where the water changed from millrace to millpond. It seemed even colder here, and I splashed and kicked to move along and to keep my blood above freezing.

My chest hit something hard with a crashing, splintering sound.

Ice.

My arms thrashed, breaking the thin covering up into shards, but the undercurrent here was swirling me further downstream where the ice was thicker, and soon became a solid unbreakable mass. I grabbed the edge of the ice floe and tried to haul myself on to it, but my foot was caught in the treacherous reeds the Raven was notorious for. I slipped away from the flatbed of ice, kicking and twisting, trying to free myself, but it was hopeless. I was dragged back down, down into the liquid world where I didn't belong. The water closed over my head.

It was cold and quiet, appropriate for a grave. I could hear the feeble gurgling of my blood, the fading thump of my heart. I was aware of every tiny capillary as it burst in my lungs. I reached down with both hands and pulled at the reeds. To my surprise they came away and I was floating free, swept along by the strong undertow. All I had to do now was rise to the surface.

I bobbed upwards. My head hit something. I had been swept under the layer of ice. It cut me off from the air like a glass ceiling.

I dived down, turned, hitting my feet on the bedrock, and shot to the surface with all the power I could summon. Arms extended, I punched at the ice. There was a dull grinding sound as it splintered. I punched again. It cracked like crazy paving but still there was no opening. My lungs were about to explode. With one last effort I pummelled at the ice. At last it shattered and I stuck my head through the hole.

I hauled myself on to the remains of the floe, only half-aware of the cracking sounds as it took my weight. I lay gasping and spent for a few seconds, unable to move another inch. I quickly realised I could just as easily die in the open air as under the water. Exposure wasn't fussy that way. There was no alternative but to crawl across the ice and try to reach the bank.

My wriggling movements splintered the fragile surface and I fell through it, back into the river. I thrashed through the sluggish water. As my ears cleared I realised the sound of the weir was very close now. It had a drop of about two metres. I didn't have enough time to get out before I went over. I took a deep breath as the roar became deafening. I tumbled over the stone ledge, a piece of rag on spin cycle. I plunged down and skimmed along under water, then with all my feeble strength I forced myself upwards. My head broke through the drowning liquid and I was whirled along, panting like a dog.

Up ahead I could see West Bridge, smaller than the bottleneck of East Bridge, the main artery into town, but still busy with traffic. Car headlights swept over me and away again in repeated arcs. The sight gave me absurd hope. I just needed to get to the bridge and on to dry land and I stood a chance. With one last effort I propelled myself to the nearest bank, now only a few metres away. When I hit mud and grass and churned snow I flopped, exhausted. For a moment dying seemed the easy option, anything else was just too much effort. An image of my overturned dustbin flashed up, then the running figure, luring me to my death.

Bastard, I thought. No way are you going to have the last laugh.

I got to my feet, trembling in every muscle, as weak as a newborn deer. The bridge loomed up ahead of me. There were steps from the path on to the roadway itself and my feet found these from instinct. Climbing them was more difficult, but dragging myself up the rail I emerged on to the bridge and with a shambling drunken gait made my way across, back to my side of the river. Drivers veered away from me when I was caught in their headlights. I didn't blame them. I must have looked like a zombie.

I began to trot to get the blood flowing again. Sodden, dripping, shivering uncontrollably, I stumbled and staggered my way back to Weaver Street. A man walking his dog crossed the street to avoid me.

The lights were still on at my house. Now I was so close I felt the last few dregs of energy begin to drain away. I collapsed on to the path and half-crawled to the front door. Unable to reach the bell, I battered feebly on the wood.

The light snapped on in the hall.

"Who is it?" Daniel called nervously.

"It's me, let me in." It came out a rusty croak that even I could barely hear. I dragged myself up as far as the letterbox and pushed it open.

"Open the bloody door!"

Then I collapsed. I was vaguely aware of falling into open space, hitting the floor and being dragged over the threshold into billowy clouds of warmth, the kind I thought I would never experience in this world again.

Fragments.

A blanket falling around my shoulders.

Hot sweet tea, stiff with brandy.

Gurgling bathwater.

Stepping gingerly into its shallows, slipping down into the heat of it with care, my head well above the surface, afraid of water touching my face.

The sting of soap on wounds.

Water flowing with streaks of red like ink.

Bed.

A hot-water bottle.

The weight of several duvets.

Sleep.

A tap was dripping somewhere inside my head. I turned my eyes inwards and saw it was dripping blood. The persistent sound moistened my dreams, quarrelled with my erratic heartbeat, drilled my teeth and nagged and nagged at me to wake up.

I dragged my eyes open. The room was filled with the grey light of a wintry dawn. The cold tap in the bath was dripping loudly, but instead of cursing it I welcomed it like a friend. Then the central heating began to crank up. Another old mate. The sounds of home.

Daniel sat slumped in a chair at the end of my bed, wrapped inside a quilt like a cocoon. I struggled to lift my head to tell him off for not getting a proper night's rest in bed. But he beat me to it. His eyes shot open. I saw they were filled with sorrow and pity. And anger.

"What happened?"

"I fell in the river," I whispered.

"How?"

"I slipped. It was an accident."

"You chased a cat to the river and you fell in?"

I had to admit it didn't sound that good.

"It wasn't a cat." He leant forward to hear more. "I don't know who it was exactly."

"Who?"

"Someone knocked over the dustbin to get me outside, then ran off, hoping I'd follow."

"So you did? That was pretty stupid, wasn't it?"

"Yes. I know."

Daniel looked away. But I couldn't take my eyes off him. I was grateful beyond words at the sight of him. Seeing him meant I was alive. There had been several times during the time I was in the river when I thought I would never see him again.

Still staring at the wall, he began to speak. "I've been thinking about what you said last night. About the bracelet and everything…"

I sank into the pillows, holding my breath.

"I didn't kill Lara. And I've no idea who did. Do you believe me?"

I exhaled slowly. "Yes."

The atmosphere cleared a little. Or maybe it was just the radiator beginning to warm the room. I sat up.

"How well do you know Harrison?"

He shrugged. "Not that well. He and Lara were friends – they knew each other from school."

"Had they slept together?"

He took it on the chin. "I'd heard rumours about Lara's reputation, but I didn't grill her about previous boyfriends. It was none of my business. Why are you asking about Harrison?"

"I think he was our intruder last night."

"That's mad."

"Think about it, Daniel. That pendant he wears is a pentagram."

"So what?"

"That's the pattern they found cut into Lara's skin." He caught his breath. "I'm sorry, love."

"It's all right. It can't get any worse. But you can't be serious about Harrison."

"I am. He took a print of mine and I'm pretty sure he was hunting round the darkroom looking for the negative."

"Harrison? He's so laid back he's horizontal. He couldn't plan and execute a murder any more than he could pole-vault. He was just interested in your darkroom – he is a photographer, for Christ's sake."

"That's debatable."

"As for the pentagram – surely that's just coincidence. You see them around everywhere."

I thought about it. Those pendants were available on any self-respecting market stall that sold jewellery, and the design itself was commonplace and easy to imitate. But that didn't prove Harrison was innocent.

"Listen, Mum. We may never know who killed Lara."

"That's rubbish. We'll find out. I won't give up until we do. I'm getting closer all the time."

"You've got to stop!"

"What do you mean?"

"Are you still saying you fell into the river accidentally? Somehow I don't believe that."

"Daniel…"

He pulled off his quilted cocoon and dropped it to the floor. "You have to stop, Mum. It's gone too far. I don't want to lose you as well."

I felt as if I'd been punched in the stomach. "But you're the one who wanted me to find out whatever I could."

"Yes. And look what happened to you. You could have died." He put his head in his hands. "Right at the start you said it was too dangerous and that we should leave it to the police. And that's what we're going to do."

"Then we might wait forever."

"Fair enough."

"You can live with that, never knowing who murdered Lara?"

His face contorted. "I don't know. I just know I couldn't live with the guilt if you… if anything happened to you."

"'Come here." Daniel knelt by the bed and let me hug him. "Don't worry about me. I'll be fine."

"I mean it, Mum. You must stop now. I want you to promise me you won't carry on."

I breathed in his smell, testosterone and sweat, and arising from his clothes, base notes of paint and turps. He was a man now. One day soon I would have to let him go for good. And he'd have to let me go too.

In the meantime, he was right. He needed me. I was pretty much all he had by way of family.

"All right. I promise."

"No more playing detective?"

"Nope." I closed my eyes.

"I hope you're not thinking of going into work today."

My eyes shot open. "No. I wasn't."

"Great. That means we can just chill. I think we both need to. Hey, you could make your fantastic roast veggie lasagne." He knew this was the only decent meal I could make with any competence. "If you're feeling up to it, I mean. Don't worry if you're not. I can do it. And I'll make pancakes —"

"Of course I'm up to it. That's the good news."

"What's the bad news?"

"I won't be going into work tomorrow, either."

Eighteen

"What will you do?"

Daniel was sitting at the kitchen table, eating dry cereal straight from the packet.

"I don't know yet. But we'll manage." I munched my toast without tasting a thing. "Somehow."

"This is all my fault, isn't it? You lost your job because of the time you spent with me in hospital."

"Of course not."

"Chasing up stuff about Lara in working hours, then. That's why he sacked you, I know it is."

"How many times – I wasn't sacked, I resigned!" I poured more tea from the pot with an unsteady hand, splashing some on to my empty plate. "Tony had me in his sights. He wanted to get rid of me, and the fact I didn't have one hundred per cent attention on my work gave him the perfect excuse. It's absolutely not your fault."

He pushed the cereal packet away. It toppled over, spraying a fan of golden flakes across the table.

"Tell me the truth about last night."

I buckled. I gave him a carefully edited version of events. I admitted I was pushed into the river, but I gave the impression I got out as soon as I could, leaving out my prolonged immersion, and especially the bit about being trapped under the lid of ice. I didn't even want to think about that myself.

"You must tell the police."

"Maybe."

"Someone tried to kill you." He took his glasses off,

polished them on his grubby T-shirt and put them back on again. "It has to be the same person who murdered Lara."

"I realise that."

"Then go to the police. You've got vital information."

"I didn't see anything, just a figure in the distance. It could have been Harrison…" Daniel gave me a pained look. "Or anyone, I suppose."

He stood up abruptly. "I'm going to ring them now."

"No. You're going back to bed. You look completely jiggered. I've got some things to sort out, then I'll ring them."

"Promise?"

"Cross my heart."

Daniel's shoulders slumped. He turned to go. But there was something I wanted to ask him, something that intrigued me.

"How long was I gone last night?"

"I'm not sure… about fifteen minutes."

"You're joking! It felt like I was in that water for a lifetime, an hour at least."

"You wouldn't have lasted an hour in an ice-cold river. I reckon you'd have been dead within five minutes."

"No need to sound so calm and matter of fact about it." I saw his hurt expression. "Sorry. That was unfair."

"You have to face it, Mum. You nearly died. So tell the police what happened."

"Message received and understood."

When he'd gone, I swept up the spilled cereal, cleared the dishes away and washed up. I even wiped the cooker and mopped the floor, small tasks to try and mend the frayed fabric of my life.

I remembered the dustbin. Still in my dressing gown I went outside and cleaned up the mess. I tied up the refilled black bag and put a fresh one in the bin.

What now? Not having a job was a huge tear in the fabric, a hole that was going to take a long time to mend. But I couldn't slop around in my nightclothes for hours just because I wasn't going to work. I forced myself to pretend it was a normal day. In the shower I lifted my face to the hot liquid needles, not afraid of the water any more. A small victory. One step at a time.

I peeped into Daniel's room. He was fast asleep, breathing normally. I hadn't forgotten my promise. I was going to ring the police, I really was. But I sensed some resistance in me that I couldn't entirely understand. Of course they needed to know about the attack. It almost certainly had a direct bearing on the Ramsey case. So why was I procrastinating? Was it something to do with getting so close, some desire to finish this thing myself? Once I told the police about it I would hand over all responsibility. But wasn't that exactly what I promised Daniel I would do? I mentally squirmed, torn between instinct and common sense.

I decided to go shopping, a mindless activity that would help me think straight. And not my usual high-speed spin around the supermarket, but a leisurely stroll into town. I made a list – milk, cheese, fresh vegetables, pasta, toilet paper, tea. Ravenbridge had a fine Victorian covered market. I used to love roaming up and down the aisles, getting lost among the stalls. It was as intricate as a maze and full of surprises. I hadn't had time to wander around there for ages. I'd go there, then return home armed with fresh produce and a bargain or two and cook a proper dinner. By then I would be clearer in my mind about what to do next, I was sure of it. I realised that I'd even stopped shaking. Hope was the thing. Hadn't I learnt that last night? Never give up hope.

But I had given up, I reminded myself. I'd given up hope of finding Lara's killer. Another hole in the weave, one that defied darning. But Daniel was right. I couldn't go on acting like some latterday Sherlock Holmes. It was time to stop. So how come I felt so little relief? The truth was, I was eaten up with frustration. I had been so close, I was sure of it.

I left Daniel a note, then I put a thick fleece over my leather jacket and zipped on my boots. I'd leave the car. I wanted to walk, to feel the slap of cold air on my face and the reassuring solidity of the ground under my feet.

I opened the front door. There was something on the doorstep.

A streak of matted brown fur, oozing a slick of blood and guts.

For several seconds I stared at it, uncomprehending. Then I saw what it was.

Hayley's ferret.

A fresh fall of snow had obliterated all the prints across my lawn and across Rob and Denise's too. The door of the empty cage hung open. The cardboard shoe box I was carrying was surprisingly light. I seemed to remember a weighty streak of muscle hanging from my outstretched arm when I rescued the ferret from the tree. But a lot of fluid and organs still lay congealed on my doorstep. I had only picked up what was left of the lifeless body.

Through the kitchen window I could see the top of Rob's head as he bent over the sink. There was no sign of Hayley. It was gone nine o'clock. Denise would have taken her to school before she went on to work. I was glad of that. I worried for the child, recalling the raised voices from last night. If her parents were in conflict she was probably already upset, and then to find her beloved pet missing again this morning when she went to feed it must have broken her heart.

I approached the house. A low ramp had been built over the three steps that led up to the back door. I climbed it slowly. Now I could see Rob clearly. His wheelchair was sideways on to the sink where he was painstakingly doing the washing up. He was twisted from the hips at an awkward angle. His useless legs didn't seem to belong to the powerful upper body. I tapped on the door. He looked up in surprise.

Come in, he mouthed.

"Hi, Rob. How are things?"

"About the same. Can't complain. I'm better off than that young girl who got herself killed anyhow." He jerked a thumb behind him. "I've just been watching the local news. Seems like the police have no idea who did it."

"It's a bad business." I paused, looking helplessly at the box.

"What have you got there?"

"That's what — "

Just then, Hayley's face peeped round the kitchen door. She looked pale and washed-out.

"Hayley… I didn't expect… not at school today?"

She shook her head as she crept into the room.

"She woke up poorly," said Rob. "Denise reckoned she'd better have the day off."

Or maybe she had been woken by her parents shouting and her illness was due to exhaustion and misery. In any case, perhaps she hadn't been out to see to the ferret yet, had no idea it was gone. I slid the box on to the worktop and stood in front of it.

"Dad, can I have a drink of water?" Hayley climbed on to Rob's knee. He held her tenderly while he filled a glass from the tap.

"Back to bed now. I'll be up in a while."

Carrying her drink carefully she wandered out, almost wraith-like, not her normal bouncy self at all.

"How's Denise?" I asked. "I haven't seen her since… when?… Christmas Eve when she popped round with a card."

Rob's face, always pinched with pain nowadays, tightened further. "She's fine. Did you want to speak to her? Only she's gone to work. She'll be home around six. In theory. Come back then."

"No, I just…" I grabbed a tea towel and started drying up. "I hear you've got the stair lift fitted at last."

"Yep. That makes a big difference. It means I can sleep in my own bed and not in the front room any more. Like today, I can go upstairs and see to Hayley when she needs something."

"That's great. Any news about adapting the kitchen?"

"News of a sort. The wrong sort. The council have turned down my application for a grant."

"That's terrible."

"They say my case isn't urgent enough. They've run out of money, more like."

"Are you going to try again?"

"If I can be bothered."

"What about your compensation claim?"

"About the same progress there as the council." He dropped a mug into the soapy water. "It's a bloody mess, Jude, that's what it is."

"I know." I put a tentative hand on his shoulder. Rob once had his own window-cleaning business. He fallen off a ladder and broken his spine. The trouble was, he hadn't got round to renewing his insurance because the premiums had shot up to a ridiculous amount. Now they had to rely on Denise's job as a legal secretary while they waited to see if he would get any kind of compensation payout. I wanted to put my arms around him and tell him everything would be all right. But it would be a lie. We both knew that.

"Fancy a cup of tea?" I asked.

"Don't you have to go to work?" he said, not quite able to hide his envy.

"Morning off. So what do you say?"

He dried his hands, which were red and raw-looking. Real men didn't wear rubber gloves. "Why not?" Gripping the wheels, he swung the chair round.

"Let me —"

"No," he said sharply. "I'll do it."

The kitchen was hopelessly inadequate for a disabled person, everything being too high, too spread out, too awkward. I watched him as he fetched the kettle, and holding it between his knees, trekked back to the sink to fill it. I didn't try to help even though every movement was painfully slow. He put teabags into cups, fetched milk from the fridge, and when the kettle came to the boil with a bad-tempered screech he poured scalding water on them. He put the kettle down with a bang, his shoulders heaving.

"Rob... what's wrong?"

"It's Denise."

"What? Is she ill? She hasn't lost her job, has she?"

"No, thank god. I shouldn't be telling you this..."

I knelt down by the chair. "It looks like you need to tell someone."

"Yeah, I do." He couldn't speak at first. It was like watching the kettle simmer. Finally, when the pressure became too great, he said bitterly, "She's having an affair."

"Rob, I'm so sorry. I had no idea."

"Me neither. Not till she started staying out all night." His cheeks were wet with tears. He swiped them away. "Trouble is, I can't blame her. Look at me, dead from the waist down. Do you know what I'm saying? I can't get it up, Jude. I'm thirty-two and I'm finished. I was finished the day I fell off that ladder. They might as well throw me out with the garbage!"

"You're not finished. Look how much Hayley needs you."

We argued like that for some time, the to and fro of despair and reassurance.

Eventually he reached into his pocket for a handkerchief and blew his nose. "I'm sorry, Jude. I didn't mean to burden you with this. I'm sure you've got better things to do. You get on, I'll be all right."

I stood up. "Is there anything practical I can do to help?"

"No. Wait, there is one thing. You could feed the damn ferret. Hayley wasn't well enough first thing and I haven't got round to it yet."

"About the ferret…" I collected the box from the work-top. "There's been an accident. It must have escaped again and run into the path of a car. I found it on the road outside."

"Oh Christ."

"I put it in this box. I thought Hayley might want to bury it."

"She thought the world of that thing," he said quietly. "Let's have a look."

"It's not a pretty sight."

"I can take it."

I took the lid off and let him see the bloody remains. Neither of us noticed Hayley standing in the doorway until her scream nearly made me drop the box. I pushed the lid back on, but it was too late.

She ran to her dad and buried her face in his chest, sobbing her heart out.

"Listen, I'll bury it for you."

"It's all right," Rob said. "The ground's too hard for digging, anyhow. We'll make a funeral pyre and cremate it. Leave it to us."

I was about to place the box on a high shelf where Hayley couldn't reach it. But then nor could Rob. I put it back on the worktop.

I wanted to tell the truth about the animal's death. It was no accident. But how could I explain that it had been placed on my doorstep, a bloody message to warn me off? I didn't want to drag this innocent family into the sordid world I'd begun to inhabit. I was certain this was the kinder way, even if I hadn't been quite honest.

I was sure of something else too. Promise or no promise, there was no way I was going to stop looking for Lara's killer.

Nineteen

Abandoning plans to walk into town, I took the car, which only stuttered into life after several attempts and a good kicking. As I drove over the East Bridge I glanced down into the icy water, knowing how lucky I was to be alive. Perhaps it was the fact I'd survived that made me so heedless of future danger. Someone had tried to get rid of me. When that didn't work they killed a little girl's pet as an example of what might happen to me if I didn't drop my unofficial investigation. Didn't they realise that when you're dealing with the bloody-minded it just didn't work like that? I remembered reading that during the war Hitler's bombs had made the British even more determined to defeat him. After the Blitz, morale had gone up, not down.

I felt the same way. I'd been pushed too far. Now I was raging with the overwhelming need to see the murderer's face. That was very important. I would risk everything just to look into those eyes and say Gotcha.

As I negotiated the traffic, barely aware of the endless stopping and starting, I made a mental list of any possible leads I could follow. It didn't amount to much: the pentagram and blisters that had mutilated Lara's body, a priest's memory of a young girl's hair, Arab music and a video about the Bedouin, a bracelet that had turned up in the wrong place, a missing print. Only the first of these had any direct link to Lara's death. Were the other things connected? And if so, how? The answer remained as blank as a piece of resin-coated paper before the chemicals got to work. But like the latent image on the paper, it didn't mean the whole picture wasn't there. It meant I had to wait for it to develop.

But if I waited for the truth to emerge, the killer might strike again, and I would never forgive myself.

When they built St Bridget's in the 1960s the parish had bought the much older house next door, and it had been the presbytery ever since. The large villa, built in ugly brown brick, had for several years been the home of one parish priest and at least two curates. Nowadays most churches were lucky to have a priest at all, and I imagined Father Thomas rattled around the empty rooms.

The heavy oak door was opened by a young woman wearing the abbreviated veil and calf-length dress of a modern nun. She looked barely old enough to have left school. Perhaps it was her blameless life that kept her face so fresh and youthful.

"Is Father Thomas in?"

"I'm afraid he's busy right now. If I could take your name?"

I pushed past her into the dark panelled hallway.

"Please," she fluttered, "you need an appointment to see Father."

"I don't need any damn thing."

The house was very hot and smelled of something spicy, incense or oil, and under that I caught the whiff of fried bacon. The raucous sound of some morning TV chat show was blaring from a half-open door down the corridor. I reached it in three strides.

Father Thomas had his feet up on a velvet footstool, eating a late breakfast from a tray, and laughing at the antics of the people on screen. He glanced up when I entered the room and his laughter was switched off at once, along with the TV.

"Jude…"

The young nun was wringing her hands in my wake. "I'm so sorry, Father. She just walked straight in."

"It's all right, Sister." He lifted his slippered feet from the stool and placed the tray on a low table. "Why don't you get on with the filing?"

"Yes, Father." She closed the door softly.

Father Thomas smiled at me. His Irish accent flowed out like honey. "Sadly, Patricia Ramsey isn't available at the moment, so Sister Veronica is helping me out with the admin."

"Does she make your breakfast as well?"

He stared longingly at the plate of congealing bacon and eggs. "No, I made that myself. Very few Catholic priests have housekeepers these days."

"What other duties does she perform?"

"What do you mean?" He frowned. "If you mean what I think you do, that's a disgusting suggestion. She's a nun, a bride of Christ."

"She looks about fifteen." I started to pace around. Heavy brown furniture gave the room a gloomy claustrophobic atmosphere, not helped by the fact that the burgundy velvet curtains were still closed even though it was the middle of the morning. A blazing electric fire and a large corrugated radiator had raised the temperature to greenhouse level. "Lara was fifteen when she had an abortion."

His eyes were pale green chips of marble.

"Why don't you take a seat?" He removed a pile of hymn books from a stiff-backed chair. We sat down facing each other.

"Confession time," I said.

He seemed confused for a moment. "You want me to hear your confession?"

"No. I want to hear yours."

He exhaled as if I'd punched him, disguising it as a mirthless laugh. "I have nothing to confess, not to you anyway. The bishop is the only person who listens to my sins."

"Just imagine you're on a TV show – like the one you've been watching, where people blurt out their darkest secrets. You'll find it easy once you start."

"I told you, I've nothing to say."

The room was stifling. I unwound my scarf and unzipped my fleece jacket. Then I waited.

"Is this something to do with Lara?"

"*Bless me, Father, for I have sinned,*" I murmured. "Isn't that what you're supposed to say first?"

"Don't mock the sacraments!"

I leaned forward. "I'm deadly serious, Father. Tell me about you and Lara."

"That was years ago. Why rake it all up again now? What's the point?"

"The point is, Lara's dead."

"That's not my fault."

"Isn't it?"

The heat was getting to him too. Beads of moisture had appeared on his forehead, his cheeks were beginning to glow. Even though he wasn't wearing a dog collar, he tugged at the open neck of his black shirt.

"Lying is a sin, isn't it, Father?"

"A venial sin, yes. Why do you ask?" He steepled his hands and pointed them under his chin. "Oh, I forgot. You're interested in becoming a Catholic."

"OK. We both lied."

"I didn't."

I stared at him until his gaze shifted to his cold breakfast.

"All right," he said quietly. "Not telling the whole truth is a kind of lying, I suppose. What we call sins of omission."

"And what did you omit?"

"I think you know."

"Perhaps."

His chin sank on to his chest. "God forgive me."

"You can only be forgiven if you admit your guilt. Isn't that right?"

He nodded.

"Then for Christ's sake, get on with it."

"All right!" He got up and walked up and down the room a couple of times, then leant on a glass-fronted cabinet for support, staring at the Waterford crystal and brightly coloured icons that it contained, as if he could draw strength from them. "I was the father of Lara's child," he whispered.

"Louder."

He reared upright, eyes blazing. "Don't push it, Jude."

"Did you encourage her to have an abortion?"

"I… I… it's difficult to explain to someone who…" He tapped his fingernails against the glass door of the cabinet. "Her mother is a good Catholic, so obviously she disapproved of abortion. But she told Lara she couldn't keep the child, it must be adopted."

"Did the Ramseys know you were the father?"

"They had no idea we were… having a relationship."

"How long had it been going on?"

"About six months."

"Jesus Christ! You did realise she was under age, that what you were doing was illegal?"

He slumped on the arm of a chair. "Of course. It was all a terrible mistake, a complete mess, but Lara was so…"

"Beautiful?" He didn't answer. "So you agreed with her

195

parents – the baby must be put up for adoption?" He nodded. "How did Lara take that?"

"Not well. But what was I to do? I could hardly acknowledge the child as mine, could I?"

"In other words, Lara had no support from her parents or from you, the father of her baby. She must have felt so betrayed that abortion seemed the only answer."

Father Thomas nodded. "And when Lara was determined to do something, there was no stopping her."

I stood up and zipped my fleece, feeling vindicated. At least I'd been right about something. There was just one more thing I needed to know.

"What are you going to do?" he asked.

"That depends."

"Are you going to tell the bishop? And then spread it all over the front page of your daily rag?"

"I told you, I don't work there any more."

"That doesn't stop you going to the press."

"No," I admitted. "But like I say, it depends." He shrank a little as I approached him. "Is there anything else on your conscience?"

"Isn't that enough? What Lara and I did was sinful, the result of unchecked desire." He laughed grimly. "At least I understand all about human weakness now – been there and done that. And I've been paying for it ever since."

"Lara was the one who paid, not you!"

"We both did."

"Not good enough, Father Thomas. She was only fifteen when you seduced her. You got her pregnant. Hadn't you heard of contraceptives? No, of course not, you're a Catholic." He bridled at that but I carried on. "Having an abortion at that age must have been traumatic. It was after that she went off the rails, not before. From then on, sleeping around was Lara's way of trying to fill the terrible empty spaces in her life. If one of her ex-lovers killed her, and I think that's very likely, then you're the one who sent her down the road to her death."

He stood up quickly, grabbing the cabinet again to steady himself. The contents rocked and tinkled like wind chimes. "I've been in a long dark tunnel for the last five years. I thought I was just coming out of it. A few weeks ago I saw Lara in the street. She was with a young man. She looked happy, normal. Something lifted from my shoulders, and I could see a chink of light at the end of the tunnel. Then she was killed." He let go of the cabinet, his shoulders slumped. "I'm back in the tunnel, and I don't know if I'll ever come out into the light again."

I rewarded this speech with a slow ironic handclap. "I used to hang around with actors a lot, and quite frankly I can only give that performance C minus."

He shook his head sadly. "That sarcasm will destroy you in the end, Jude."

"It's all you deserve. And you haven't answered my question."

"What?"

"Anything else to confess?"

"Oh, I see. You think I killed Lara?"

"It's a reasonable theory. Her parents had no idea you were sleeping with her. She might have threatened to tell them, or the bishop. She could have destroyed your reputation in this parish, threatened your whole career."

"It's not a career, it's a vocation."

"Whatever." I picked up a Bible from the table and held it out. "I don't believe in this any more, but I assume you do."

"You want me to swear on that that I didn't kill Lara?"

"Yes."

He placed his right hand on the black leather. "I swear, by Almighty God, that I had nothing to do with the murder of Lara Ramsey." When he took his hand away the sweaty imprint of his fingers remained. I was transfixed, watching the image evaporate in the over-heated room.

A wave of dizziness rocked me as I stood there. The room was like a hothouse. I had to get out of here before I combusted.

Father Thomas touched my hand. His fingers seemed to scald the skin. "Are you all right? Have you eaten anything today? Can I get you a cup of tea? A sandwich?"

I was suffocating. "No…" I hurried to the door, clumsily pulling at the brass handle.

"Let me, it sticks sometimes."

He brushed against my shoulder as he opened the door. He emanated heat like a radiator. I felt almost consumed, as if I'd flown too near the sun. I nearly fell into the corridor. It was a degree or two cooler here. Sister Veronica stuck her head out of the adjoining room.

"Is everything OK, Father?"

"It's fine. Make me a cup of coffee, will you?"

"Of course." She passed us on her way to the kitchen, keeping her eyes averted.

I was outside in the frosty air and Father Thomas was closing the door on me when I asked, "When the police finally release Lara's body, will you conduct the funeral?"

He looked calmer now, back in control. "Of course I will," he said. "She was one of my flock."

I rang Stan at his home number, assuming he wouldn't be back at work until next week. I was right. I asked him how he was.

"Not good, Jude. Neither of us can sleep. We look at

pictures of Lara all night, trying to remember the good times."

"I'm so sorry, Stan. Give my love to Carol."

"I will."

"Listen, there's something I should tell you, before you hear it on the grapevine." I explained that I had resigned from the paper, but before he could ask any more about it, I changed the subject. "Stan, I need to track down a film called *Scorching Desert*." It was possible the video was still in Lara's flat, but I assumed the police activity would make it impossible to gain access. I knew Stan was keen on old movies. He had a vast collection of videos and DVDs, his favourites being westerns, anything with Katharine Hepburn, and the films of Quentin Tarantino. He assured me his wife Carol had the same tastes. "Have you heard of it?"

"I don't know that one, Jude."

"Do you know where I can find a copy?"

He recommended a man in the market hall, a repository of every kind of film – the good, the bad, and the downright obscure.

"Thanks. Take care. I'll drop by as soon as I can."

The market hall had a roof as high as a cathedral. The sounds of stallholders shouting their wares echoed up to the rafters where the occasional pigeon fluttered. The place reeked of vegetables and fish and the aroma of the potent mugs of tea available from the café. I worked my way along the many aisles, threading my way past the cheap clothes and leather goods and highly coloured confectionery, trying to find the guy Stan had recommended. But the place was like a maze and all I knew was that the video stall was somewhere at the centre of it.

I turned a corner past a tottering pile of bird cages, and there it was. Half the stall was devoted to vinyl records and obscure CDs, and the rest to DVDs and videos ancient and modern. The stallholder was sitting on a stool reading a magazine. He had deep lines etched beside his mouth, which was twisted sideways in order to keep a cigarillo in place. With his dyed black quiff and long sideburns, it was clear his interest in style had stopped in the fifties. He took no notice of me.

The video cases were stacked in boxes like second-hand books, spines uppermost. I ran my finger along the first row. They didn't seem to be arranged in any kind of order.

"Looking for anything in particular?" A rich puff of tobacco wafted my way.

"Something called *Scorching Desert*," I said. "Ever heard of it?"

He rolled the cigarillo to the centre of his mouth, inhaled hungrily, then rolled it back. "1981. Starring James Alvarez and Rachelle Lamarr. Directed by…" He looked up to the roof as if the answer was written there. "John Harper."

"Very impressive. Have you got it?"

"Might have."

I swallowed my impatience, and together we trawled the many boxes, he starting from one end and me the other. We were getting close when I saw his skinny hand pluck a video out.

"Is that it?"

He turned the front towards me. *Scorching Desert*, I read. *Enter the Tent of Love But Be Prepared to Die for it.* An olive-skinned beauty was bent in the arms of an Arab. He had the required black moustache, and her bodice was well and truly ripped. It looked like complete bilge.

"How much?"

"I'll take a tenner."

"Pull the other one. I'll give you five."

"Call it seven-fifty."

I handed over my note and received my paltry change, feeling as ripped off as the heroine's blouse.

"What's it like?" I asked, as I turned to go.

The stall-holder chewed on his cigarillo in a passable imitation of Clint Eastwood in a spaghetti western. "It's bloody awful."

Twenty

He was right. And Lee Maddox hadn't thought much of it either. He had fast-forwarded it to see if there was any sex. There wasn't. Just a lot of smouldering between the Bedouin hero and the dusky Spanish girl who had ended up with him by unaccountably wandering into the desert and getting lost. Unfortunately I wasn't able to use the remote to hasten each trite interminable scene. I was trawling it for any link with Lara's death. I knew she had been watching it the night she died, possibly in the company of her murderer. It was a chilling thought, the only reason to keep going through each dull unconvincing second. There was plenty of the Arab music that Annie Molloy had heard, since the dialogue was woefully thin. There was a lot of riding about on camels in the desert, several episodes of pitching and dismantling tents, and a fair amount of staring into the fire.

After an hour or so of this trivial trash I was ready to chuck it in. Another five minutes, I kept telling myself. And another five. Surely it was nearly finished? A scene in the gloomy tent began. The man and the girl were pouting and heaving at each other, a bit cross because one of them had forgotten to wash the camels or something. No, wait – he was accusing her of getting the hots for the younger Arab who had been skulking about the camp, lusting after her.

He drew a curved knife from his belt. He heated it in the flame of the candle. She looked on, wide-eyed with horror.

"We Bedouins have a simple test for liars," he sneered. "I will place this hot knife on your tongue. If it sizzles you are telling the truth and it won't burn you. But if you are lying your tongue will be dry with guilt and it will blister. Open your mouth!"

He gripped her arm. She resisted, twisting this way and that. The knife flashed in the candlelight. She turned her head away. He grabbed her hair and tried again. But she kept her mouth shut, moaning behind her closed lips.

"Open your mouth!"

The knife touched skin with a hissing sound. She jerked away, her hand flying to the brand mark next to her full red lips.

I shot out of my chair and crouched on the floor, inches from the screen. There was a close-up of her blistered skin. I pressed rewind on the remote, watched the whole scene again, and the close-up several more times. Was this why Lara had blisters round her mouth? Had someone tortured her, to force her to spill some secret?

The phone rang. I pressed stop. Breathless with this revelation I hurried into the hall, ready to give the latest cold caller a right earful.

"Yes?"

"Is that Jude Baxendale?"

I ground my teeth. "So?"

"It's Norman Foley."

"Whatever you're selling I'm not interested." I was about to slam the phone down.

"We met in the park. We talked about the death of that poor young girl. Remember?"

I sighed. If there was anything worse than cold calling, I thought, it was being plagued by a psychic detective.

"I remember. What do you want?"

"I tried to ring you at work."

"I'm not there any more."

"So I believe. But I talked to a very helpful young man called Matt Dryden and he'd like to interview me for the paper."

How could Matt be so gullible? But as a professional journalist he didn't have to believe Norman Foley to write a feature on him. What mattered was copy and sales. What better for both than a medium claiming to know about Lara through paranormal means? It was a gift for the Ravenbridge Evening Post and they were welcome to it.

Then again, Norman Foley had known about the connection with satanism before that was public knowledge.

"That's great," I said as sincerely as I could manage. "I suppose you want me to take your photo? I'm sorry, I can't."

"It's not that. I feel I need to know more about the victim before I do the interview. Obviously the clearer my thoughts are, the more helpful they will be. It might even help to catch the killer." He sounded very pleased with himself.

"I don't see how I can help."

"You said you knew Lara. I wondered if you have anything belonging to her?"

"Why?"

"I need to make contact with her, and handling one of her possessions is a very good way of doing that."

"What sort of thing?" I asked, trying to keep the suspicion out of my voice. At the moment I couldn't be sure if he was a genuine medium, a pervert or a killer.

"Something she'd had for a long time and used regularly. Like a watch or a ring or a hair band."

"There's a bracelet she got for her birthday in December."

"Too recent."

"I don't have anything else. But I could ask my son.

He's the one who knew her best."

"I would appreciate that."

"Hold on."

I ran upstairs and looked in Daniel's room. He was yawning and stretching, no doubt woken by the phone.

"Daniel, do you have anything belonging to Lara – apart from the bracelet, I mean? Something she's had for a long time?"

He shook his head slowly. "No, nothing." I saw that the realisation made him sad. "Why?"

"I'll explain later."

He reared up from the pillow. "Mum, don't tell me you're going on with this?"

"Of course not."

I ran back downstairs and told Norman Foley the bad news.

"That's a shame. I don't suppose you have access to Lara's flat?"

"No." I didn't have a key, but I knew someone who had. I counted on my fingers. It was four days since Lara's body was found in the park. Surely the police had completed their examination of the murder scene by now? Suddenly I wanted to see it very badly. "Actually, there might be a way."

"Really? That's excellent. If you manage to get in and find a suitable possession, give me a call. You've got my number."

I hunted in the pocket of my jacket hanging by the door and found his card. "Yes, I've got it."

I rang off and called Annie Molloy. Her answerphone clicked on. "I can't take your call right now, but if you want to leave a message, please do so after the tone." This was followed by a snatch of k.d.lang singing a soulful ballad and a high-pitched bleep.

"Annie, it's Jude Baxendale. I was wondering if you still had the key to Lara's flat."

There was a click and Annie's non-recorded voice came through loud and clear. "Hi, Jude. Sorry about the answerphone. I've been plagued by reporters ringing me up. It's freaking me out. What do they think I've got to say? I've spoken to the local paper and that's it. I feel invaded. It's like your life's not your own. What it must be like for film stars and footballers I just can't imagine. Anyway, what's this about a key?"

"You still have it?"

"No one's asked for it back."

"Is there a chance you could let me into Lara's flat?"

"You don't want to go in there!"

"No, I don't want to," I lied. "But I've got a possible lead." My guess was that Annie would be into anything a bit off the wall. "It's a bit bizarre, but there's this psychic detective who wants to handle something Lara owned. He reckons he might be able to pick up vibes from it. I've spoken to him before, and he's quite impressive."

"That sounds amazing. I'd like to help, but I don't think I can go into Lara's place."

"That's OK, if I could just collect the key I'll take it from there."

"But what about the police? Forensic evidence and all that?"

"Haven't they finished their search by now?"

"I guess so. It's all gone quiet. And the tape across the gate has gone too."

"That proves it."

"All right. Are you coming over now?"

"If that's OK."

"Ring my bell at the front. I'll come down and let you in.

I'll give you the key to Lara's flat, but from then on, you're on your own."

I stood in the hallway with the key clutched in my hand, staring at the door. I didn't know how it would feel to be in a place where someone had been murdered. How would I deal with the sight of bloodstains? Had Lara fought back against her attacker? Would there be torn curtains or broken furniture? I hoped she had resisted, but I dreaded seeing the evidence of her struggle.

With a sense of foreboding I unlocked the door, hesitating on the threshold. The air smelt used up, as if all the oxygen had been sucked out of it. I stepped inside, leaving the door slightly open behind me from some primitive instinct. I didn't believe in ghosts, but so many of my certainties had been challenged lately I wasn't sure of anything any more.

The door led straight into the living room, which had the shabby look typical of rented flats – mismatched furniture and a swirly brown carpet. With a pang I saw that Lara had brightened the walls with Daniel's work, not just nudes but drawings of strange quirky objects and a large abstract oil done in searingly bright colours.

I glanced around nervously. No sign of a struggle. I wasn't sure if I was glad or sorry. I couldn't see any blood either. If it was there, it had blended into the brown blotches on the carpet, and I was relieved about that.

I circled the small room, glancing at books and ornaments and photos, not knowing what I was looking for. Trying to find evidence of the real Lara, perhaps, just like the psychic detective. That reminded me – I had to search for something to give Norman Foley, even though I was still unsure about his motives.

The most likely place to find her personal possessions

was in the bedroom, but hadn't Annie said Lara always kept it locked? I went through to the kitchen. The cupboards were a hideous shade of bile green, but Lara had customised them with stickers and posters, and arty-looking flyers for local bands. Everything was tidy, but looking closer I could see the silvery grey dust that the SOCO team had used to trawl for fingerprints. The fridge was empty. Either Lara never ate here, or the police had cleared it out.

I heard a noise like someone opening and shutting drawers. Was it Annie moving about upstairs? No, it sounded nearer than that. I hurried back into the living room. It was empty. Had Annie and I left the front door unlocked? I couldn't remember. I'd definitely left the door of the flat ajar.

I walked softly towards the bedroom. The keyhole had been bashed in with some sort of blunt implement, revealing splinters of fresh wood. I peeped in. Norman Foley was searching Lara's chest of drawers, pulling out tights, scarves, underwear. I drew back, my heart hammering with shock. Would Annie hear me if I screamed? It took several seconds to get my breathing under control. Then I stepped forward.

"What the hell are you doing?"

He straightened up without a trace of guilt or surprise. "I need to find the right thing."

"Who let you in?"

"You did. I assume it was you who left both doors unlocked?"

"How did you get into this room?" I pointed at the damaged door.

"It was like that already."

The police must have done it, too impatient to look

through Lara's things for the key. I glanced curiously around the room. So this was her bedroom, her most private space.

I don't know what I was expecting but it wasn't this.

The walls were papered with pictures torn from magazines. They made a kind of time line, starting with the earliest stages of the human embryo, then the developing foetus. There were graphic scenes of childbirth, and newborn infants still sticky with blood. Then babies in all their stages – asleep in prams, sucking their thumbs, sitting up, smiling and showing off two isolated teeth in their lower gums. Toddlers crawling, then pulling themselves upright, taking their first steps. It was a photographic record of the baby that never was, Lara's aborted child. It made me want to cry, especially when I saw that towards the end the line divided into two – small boys playing with cars, holding sticks like guns, and little girls absorbed in water play, digging in sand, making their earliest artworks with stubby paint brushes. Lara hadn't known if her child was male or female, so she had faithfully honoured both genders. The latest pictures were of children of around five, then the line stopped.

Reeling with shock, I took it out on Norman Foley. I demanded to know what right he had to waltz in here blah blah blah. He looked at me steadily as I blustered.

"When you said a personal possession I didn't know you wanted a pair of her knickers!" I snatched the panties from his hand, stuffed them and the others back in the drawer and slammed it shut. "What are you, some sort of perv?"

"No," he said patiently. "I have an unusual gift, but I'm not a sexual deviant. When I knew you were coming here I couldn't wait any longer. I have a strong feeling that we must act with the utmost urgency." He turned back to the chest. "Do you know if Lara kept a diary? It's something I forgot to mention to you."

"I've no idea. If she did, the police would have taken it away for close examination."

His face fell slightly. "You're right. Have you found her watch?"

"No. I've just been looking round, trying to capture the essence of Lara, but as usual she's proving elusive." I felt a sense of despair wash over me. "Have you picked up any vibes or whatever it is you do?"

"It's difficult…"

"You've no more idea than the police, then?"

"The problem is that anyone could become a murderer. In the right circumstances *you* might kill someone."

"No way!"

"It's true. What we need to discover is what the circumstances were that drove this person."

Kneeling down, Norman opened the bottom drawer. He looked through the contents briefly, then drew out a pair of gloves, woollen ones, each finger a different bright colour. He went very still.

"She wore these a lot."

"Yes, I've seen them before," I said, before I realised it hadn't been a question.

He closed his eyes. I kept quiet for once. What if he really could detect something?

"She was capable of great love, and fierce hatred," he said quietly. "The person she loved is associated with the letter… D… or B."

Or both, I thought.

"What about the person she hated?"

"That's the trouble. I can't see the name, or even a letter. It's as though she erased it."

"Did the person she hated murder her?"

"The hatred is trapped here, so yes, I think it's likely. She may not always have loathed him or her, but I feel an aura of intense dislike."

"You would feel that way if someone was trying to kill you."

"This wasn't an instant dislike. It had been there for a while."

"You're saying that Lara knew her killer?"

"Almost certainly." He stood up. "Is it all right if I take these gloves with me? Sometimes it takes time for the right message to come through."

"I guess so. Bring them back to the woman who lives upstairs when you've finished with them." I followed him out of the room. It struck me there was something I didn't know. "Where was Lara killed, in the bedroom, or in here?"

He looked around at the sad-looking furniture. "Neither."

"Then where?"

He turned abruptly, the way a robot might, and walked in a straight line towards the back of the flat. He stood in the doorway, breathing hard.

"It was here. She was murdered in the kitchen."

"Was it that bad?"

"Pretty awful."

I was sitting on Annie's leather sofa, the cat curled up on my knee. Annie had insisted I come in and have a coffee. It was only when I took my first sip that I remembered Annie's low standards of hygiene and the spiders' lair. But fear of a few bacteria was nothing compared to the chill that had made the hairs on the back of my neck bristle when staring into Lara's kitchen. It was Norman Foley's certainty that had unnerved me. How had he been so sure?

I explained to Annie about the psychic detective and the gloves he had borrowed.

"He was here? How amazing is that? I'm really sorry I missed him. There should be someone like him on every police force, I reckon. That would improve the clear-up rate, I'm convinced of it. *There are more things on heaven and earth, Horatio, than are dreamt of in our philosophy.* Not that I've got any idea who Horatio was."

"I think he was Hamlet's mate."

"Hamlet? The gloomy Dane. I saw it once. It all ends in a bloodbath." Her face became haggard. "It still haunts me, thinking about what happened downstairs."

"I didn't see any blood, if it's any consolation. Lara was strangled and the cuts were made later."

Annie flinched. "I hope her death was quick. I hope she didn't suffer too much. I hope the son-of-a-bitch who did this rots in hell!"

I'd given Father Thomas C minus for his performance. If Annie was simulating her grief and anger she was making a good job of it, B plus at least. Of course that didn't mean Father Thomas was lying, or that Annie was telling the truth.

"Did you know Lara had an abortion when she was fifteen?"

Annie sank back on her chair. "No, I didn't." She sounded disappointed. "She never told me. But that was Lara." Annie lit up and for a moment her face was lost in a cloud of grey smoke. "Why couldn't she tell me? I was her friend. She could have told me anything. I'm unshockable, you know."

"You loved her?" I asked quietly.

"Didn't everyone?"

"Maybe, at first. But Lara had been deeply hurt, and I suspect she left a lot of hurt in her wake."

"What are you saying?"

I closed my eyes. Exhaustion and shock were taking their toll. But the troubling images I'd seen in Lara's bedroom wouldn't go away. I was too tired to think of a roundabout way to ask Annie what I needed to know. "Did you sleep with her?"

"None of your business!" Annie stood up abruptly. The cat, reflecting her movements, reared up from my lap, and digging its claws in, prepared itself to leap on to the floor. But before it could let fly, Annie grabbed it from me and clutched it to her chest, her cigarette nearly singeing its ear off. It set off a yowling so primeval it made my skin crawl.

"She turned you down?"

She hurled the cat on to the floor. "We were friends, OK? If I wanted more than that she never knew it. I never told her. And now she's gone." She scrunched her cigarette on to a plate. "Satisfied?"

"Not till the person who killed Lara is caught and put behind bars, no." I zipped up my jacket. "I nearly forgot. Here's the key to Lara's flat."

"I don't want it."

I put it on the coffee table. "Nor do I."

There was no way I could ever go in there again.

Twenty-one

According to the estate agents' brochure, Chapel House was in the village of Gunnerston, about ten miles outside Ravenbridge. There was no address but in a small village like that it wouldn't be hard to find.

The recent snowfall had blurred the outlines of everything except the trees, which were etched with white against the pewter sky as if a child had outlined them with a thick white crayon. The gritters had been out so the road was clear. It looked like there would be more snow, but as I was going east rather than west where the darkest clouds were massing, I decided to go anyway. I reckoned I'd be there and back before it came on again.

Once out of town I wound my window down to get a blast of fresh air to blow away the staleness of 15 Stonebeck Avenue. As the road climbed up into the hills I hit a patch of sleet. I shut the window quickly. The sleet was thick and wet, forcing my windscreen wipers to work overtime.

As I drove, one image kept coming back to me – Lara's body, lying stiffly on the park bench, the front of her T-shirt drenched with blood. There was something odd about that, not just the fact it wasn't Lara's blood. What was it? I drummed my fingers on the steering wheel. There was too much of it all in one spot for the blood to be the result of someone else's dripping wound. She was already dead when the cuts were made and the human body doesn't bleed after death. But the way the pool of blood was concentrated on her chest made it look as if she *had* bled copiously from the wounds. The only explanation I could think of was that whoever killed her must have carefully added more gore to give that impression. But why?

I reached a crossroads. The signpost had been obliterated with snow but I knew Gunnerston was off to the right. The narrow road led past Scowgill Reservoir. I pulled in at a layby just beyond the head of the dam. This used to be one of my favourite places. Ben Greenwood and I had come up here a lot, but I hadn't been this way since we split.

To create the reservoir over a hundred years ago they had drowned the village of Scowgill. In dry summers the spire of the church could be seen rising from the receding water like Excalibur. In very rare drought conditions the abandoned houses were exposed too.

The sleet had stopped. Up here there were even a few breaks in the dark grey sky, the clouds broken up and pushed on by the icy wind. I walked along the concrete bridge so that I could look down on the vast sluice gates. The lake was full, but I couldn't help peering into the water, trying to detect the submerged village. For a moment I thought I could see the spire, or was it the bell tower of the old schoolhouse? The light changed and the mirage was gone, a trick caused by scudding clouds reflected in water. When I first learnt about photography, it had reminded me of Scowgill Reservoir, the way something hidden can emerge from watery depths, as if by magic.

I thought of going back to the car to get my Nikon, then remembered it was still in the stationery cupboard at work. In my haste to gather my few possessions together I'd forgotten all about my favourite camera. I cursed under my breath. Not having my faithful old Nikon with me felt like having a limb chopped off.

I stared into the lake for another few minutes but it

wasn't giving up any secrets and I was freezing. I trotted back to the car and drove on towards Gunnerston.

It was a beautiful village, built of mellow grey-gold stone, with a three-arched bridge over the river. In summer it attracted hordes of walkers and day-trippers. Even on an arctic day like this I wasn't surprised to see a middle-aged couple striding out in heavy waterproofs and stout boots.

I drove slowly past Gunnerston Mill, once a working mill powered by a great iron wheel. The wheel was still there, but motionless now, and the mill itself had been converted into holiday flats. I hadn't been up here for so long I couldn't remember exactly where the chapel was, but once I saw the stumpy church tower I turned round and drove back through the village. Anglicans at one end of the village, Non-Conformists at the other, that was the usual pattern in villages in these parts.

And there it was. Unmistakably a Methodist chapel with its dour flat front, the windows covered with grilles, giving it the grim look of a Victorian workhouse. I parked further along, in front of a rusty field gate that looked as if it hadn't been opened for decades, then walked back. There was a strong smell of pig slurry in the air, emanating from the farm opposite the chapel. A dead mole had been nailed to the farm fence, its fur dull like worn suede. With its spread-out limbs it reminded me of the way Hayley's ferret had clung to the tree trunk. I wondered if Rob had cremated it yet, if its ash was blowing in the wind down Weaver Street.

I crossed the road to Chapel House. A Kerwin and Black For Sale sign was propped up against the railings. A stone slab set into the wall above the double front doors read Wesleyan Chapel 1849. I rang the bell and listened to it ring hollowly through the building.

As I expected there was no response.

I walked around the converted chapel, trying to peer in the windows, but they were set high in the walls and the iron bars made it difficult to get near. I cursed myself for what looked like a fruitless trip when I should have been back in Ravenbridge following up other leads. Leads? Who was I kidding? I had fragments, impressions, niggling uncertainties, but no clear picture at all. Out here at least I was doing something.

Round the back the small garden was dark and neglected. I ploughed on through grass tall enough to poke through the layer of snow. I checked each window. At last I came to one that was at normal height and not covered by a grille, clearly a modern addition to the house to let more light into the dingy interior.

Peering through the dirty glass, I could see the original chapel, stripped of its pews and pulpit to make one large downstairs room. In the corner a spiral staircase led to the upper floor, which must have been converted from the choir loft. If this was where Lara brought her men, she must have revelled in desecrating what had once been a place of worship.

Moving on, I nearly tripped over a ladder lying flat in the long grass. I was tempted to heave it upright and take a look through the upstairs window, but I didn't fancy another ignominious fall. Having checked that the back door was locked, I returned to the front, rattling the handle on the main door, just in case I got lucky. It was locked too.

I stood on the footpath wondering what to do next. The village had a good pub as I recalled, but it was well past lunchtime and I wasn't sure it would still be open. There was only one way to find out.

I heard an engine being driven too fast down the narrow street. It was a Land Rover, rattling its way towards the farm.

I stopped to let it go by. But the driver pulled up beside me, braking hard. A tweed-covered elbow was sticking out through the window. The owner was a man with a square face and hard pink cheeks.

"Is that your car up there?" He jerked a thumb behind him. "The daft-looking thing with the shark's teeth?"

"Yes. Why?"

"It's blocking my gate. Get it shifted."

I was next to certain he never opened the gate. He was just enjoying being awkward. Strangers were always fair game. "Is it urgent? I thought I'd grab a sandwich at the pub."

"I need to get feed to my sheep."

"Right."

I started off in the direction of the Triumph Herald.

"Hey!"

I turned round and waited for the next round of Bait the Visitor.

"I saw you poking round Chapel House. You interested in buying it?"

I walked slowly back. "Might be. Depending how much they want for it, of course."

"Seen inside?"

"No, I just noticed it as I was passing."

"I can let you in."

Now I was really interested. "You mean, I can look round?"

"If you want to."

"How come you've got a key?"

"My sister used to live there."

I wondered briefly about the number of spare keys floating around the world. First Annie, now this apple-cheeked farmer. It was quite worrying. But it also meant I could take a look inside Chapel House. My trip wasn't fruitless after all.

"I'd really like to see it. Is that OK?"

He was already opening the door of the Land Rover and jumping down.

"No time like the present."

Strange that the feeding of sheep was no longer the urgent priority it had been two minutes ago.

I'd hoped he'd let me in, then leave me alone to look round. But he tagged along just behind as I wandered around the big open living room. I made the appropriate noises as if I was really interested in buying the place. In fact it was the last place on earth I would choose to live. There was still too much chapel about it and not enough house. The farmer didn't say much, just followed me like a shadow, towering over me as he dogged my every step.

"Has there been much interest?"

"A fair bit. They come and look but nobody buys. That estate agent, Gilmore I think they call him, the one with the bad skin, he brought a few people along, women mostly. But lately it was the girl, the one that was murdered."

I glanced at him. "Did you ever speak to her?"

"Once or twice." He looked uncomfortable. "There's a downstairs loo." He opened a door tucked behind the staircase.

I peeped in at the tiny room. "Very nice. Very useful." He followed me into the small kitchen down a couple of steps at the back of the house. "What kind of people have looked round so far?"

His eyes narrowed in an unappealing leer. "Funny that, how Mr Gilmore seemed to specialise in women clients, but the girl always seemed to bring men here."

"On their own?" I asked innocently. "I thought estate agents were meant to work in pairs?"

He laughed outright. "They did that too."

"Sorry?"

He tapped the side of his nose. "They came here together a few times, without a client I mean."

"Checking on the property, I expect."

"That'll be it," he smirked.

I shrugged, feigning lack of interest, but my mind was in overdrive. So Craig Gilmore had used this remote place to shag women, including Lara, and she in her turn had used it with her men. No wonder Gilmore had seemed so shifty.

I ran my fingers along the kitchen units. "Solid oak, I'd say. Your sister had good taste." I was lying. They were thinly veneered teak. I wouldn't give the ugly things house room. "Did anyone come back here more than once?"

The leer flitted across his face again. "Yep. Most of them seemed to want to take another tour. But like I say, none of them seemed interested in buying."

I left the kitchen and started up the spiral staircase. "I can manage up here. I won't be long."

I scuttled up the steps. The upper half of the chapel had been boarded to create another large open space and a bathroom. I looked up into the rafters, which I could almost reach up and touch. An original round window let light in at the front, and a larger modern casement did the job at the back. The room was bare, apart from an enormous wardrobe that looked impossible to get down the stairs, and a tatty old sofa.

Even though I had an antipathy for religious buildings I could see it would be a rather beautiful room when decorated and furnished. It was both spacious and intimate. As I walked around I could detect a faint smell, vanilla or jasmine. Drops of candle wax on the bare floor suggested perfumed candles. What the farmer had told me confirmed my suspicion that this was where Lara had had sex with a series of male clients. Then she met Daniel and put an end to such sordid liaisons. Had one of those men reacted badly to that? Badly enough to kill her?

I idly opened the wardrobe door. As I expected it was empty, just a few wire hangers rattling together in the sudden draught. As I closed it, I noticed something on the floor, almost hidden under the wardrobe. I reached down and picked it up. It was the metal top from a beer bottle, a brand I didn't recognise.

I felt the presence of someone in the room. Looking round, I saw the farmer looking at me intently. How had he come up so silently? I glanced at his feet. He'd removed his wellingtons and climbed the stairs in his socks. I slipped the bottle top into my pocket, stood up straight and closed the wardrobe door.

"What a lovely piece of furniture. Is it in the price?"

He didn't answer. He tugged his cap off and scratched his scalp. He was younger than I first thought. Mid-forties, I guessed. He came towards me slowly, still fixing me with his feverish stare. I stepped back.

"Lara – the girl who died – you know why she brought men here, don't you?" he murmured.

"I assume they were prospective buyers."

He gave a high-pitched laugh. "You could say that. She certainly put her wares on display."

"How do you know that?" But I'd already guessed the answer. He liked to climb the ladder I'd found round the back, and watch everything that was going on. There were no curtains at the window, and the candles must have lighted up the action like a stage set.

"You women are all the same."

"That's not true."

"My wife, for instance. She buggered off with a tractor salesman. Couldn't take the life, you see. Not enough parties, having to go all the way into Ravenbridge to shop. That's women for you, only interested in having a good time."

"That's your opinion." He came even nearer but I refused to give any more ground. "I've seen enough. I expect you want to feed those sheep of yours."

I tried to walk round him, but he stretched out and caught me by the arm.

"Let go of me," I said quietly.

He pulled me near to him. I could smell whisky on his breath. I could see the open pores on his nose. With his other hand he grabbed my neck, then planted a kiss somewhere in the vicinity of my mouth. I pushed him hard in the chest. He stumbled backwards, his legs ramming into the end of the sofa, and crumpled to the floor, flat on his back, a surprised look on his face. He tried to get up, but only managed to lumber on to all fours like a large arthritic dog.

"What did you do that for?"

"Excuse me?" I said incredulously. Perhaps Lara's behaviour had made him think that sex was the normal payment for showing someone round a house. Or perhaps he regarded himself as lord of the manor and me as a lowly peasant, and he liked to keep up the old tradition of *droit du seigneur*. Or perhaps he was just crazed with loneliness and drink.

He staggered to his feet, then fell against me, fumbling at my breasts. "You smell nice," he whispered thickly. The strength in his hands conveyed his desperate need. He nuzzled my neck.

222

"No!" I roared. But he wouldn't let go, and he was bigger and stronger than me. I knew with terrible certainty that I was out of my depth. I pushed and scratched but his hands were everywhere, ripping my shirt and clawing at my jeans. A feeling of powerlessness began to overwhelm me. I cursed my stupidity. But how was I to know? He had seemed a bit creepy, but not a potential rapist.

I thought as clearly as I could, even though my brain was beginning to go into panic mode. There was only one way out of this.

I went limp in his grasp. "All right," I whispered. "Shall we go back to your place?"

"No," he panted. "Let's do it here."

His eyes glistened like shiny brown buttons as I slipped off his tweed jacket with its milk and straw odour. I loosened the shirt from his trousers. He stood dumbly, like a child, while I unhitched his belt and let his trousers fall. I made my actions measured and calm, trying not to show how frightened I was.

I let my jacket slide down my arms to the floor, then started to undo the remaining buttons on my shirt, wriggling my hips lasciviously. He stared down my cleavage. Once his gaze was locked on to the dark line between my breasts, I brought my booted foot up sharply and kicked him in the testicles as hard as I could.

He yelped with shock then cried out in agony, collapsing to the floor, rolling on to his side and curling up like a foetus.

I grabbed my jacket and ran down the spiral stairs, nearly slipping and breaking my neck. Behind me I could hear cries of "Bitch!" I left the front door wide open, and ran to my car. Heavy snow had started to fall since I'd been inside Chapel House.

The car wouldn't start. "Come on, you bugger!" I yelled at

it, and on the third attempt the engine spluttered and turned over. I reversed into the track with the rusty gate, threw the wheel round and drove back towards Chapel House.

The farmer, dressed only in shirt and trousers, ran out of the front door and straight into the road, only twenty metres ahead. I don't know how long it took to make the decision – a matter of milliseconds. I pressed down hard on the accelerator. The car shot forward. The man froze, his mouth wide with shock. It took only another split second to cover the ground between us. In my mind I heard him scream, the crunch of bone. The broken body and all the terrible aftermath flashed before me. And inside my head I was yelling Serve you right, you animal!

He was only a few metres away when I slammed on the brake. The car skidded wildly on the fresh snow, stopping only a couple of centimetres from impact. He flopped on to the bonnet as if the force that had frozen him to the spot had been switched off.

I reversed at speed, the rear wheels barely making contact with the ground. The man staggered backwards as his support was suddenly removed, revolving his arms like windmill sails to keep his balance. I wound the window down.

"Get out of my fucking way, or this time I won't stop!"

The satisfaction I got from seeing him scuttle sideways with a scared look on his face was immense. I roared past him, not giving him another glance.

I screeched through the village and headed for home.

I drove as fast as I could in the worsening conditions. The Triumph didn't like it, making unhappy grinding noises in protest. I turned the heater on full but all I got was a few chilly blasts. I swore at the car, telling it not to let me down now, or else.

I was shaking, but not entirely with cold. For a while back there I knew how Lara must have felt at the moment she realised her attacker was about to take her life. I never had any real fear the farmer was going to kill me – it was rape he had in mind – but for several long seconds I'd felt robbed of my humanity, my power of choice, and it was terrifying.

The snow was falling fast now. White flakes were performing a frantic dance on my windscreen. I switched the headlights on, but the reflected glare made visibility even worse.

There was something else, something even more disturbing. I understood the enormity of what I had done, or nearly done. Another second and the farmer would have been dead. I tried to find excuses – my snow-encrusted boot had got stuck on the pedal, or I'd got confused between the accelerator and brake. Whatever the cause, it would simply have been an accident. Who could blame me for driving badly after what I'd just been through? The trouble with the accident theory was that, for a millisecond or two, I really had wanted the bastard dead.

It seemed that Norman Foley was right. We all had in us the capacity to kill.

Snow was being blown off the hills and already drifts were building up in the dips and curves of the road. I had to slow down and concentrate. But I was distracted by the feeling that I wasn't alone. Lara was there with me. I suppose it was the terror we'd both experienced, but I'd never felt so close to her.

Her murderer had hitched a ride too, not in the car but inside my head. For the first time in my life, I felt empathy with a killer.

Twenty-two

About three miles from Ravenbridge the grinding noises in the engine became continuous. I beat the dashboard, urging the car to carry on, promising that if it got me home I'd give it a hot bath, a slap-up supper, caviar and champagne, anything. Just get me there! I silently pleaded.

Shortly after, it jerked to a standstill.

"Shit!"

I got out. The wind cut across the open road like a blade. Cold white feathers fluttered against my face. The heavy pewter sky had lowered itself until it practically touched the hills, making the onset of dusk even earlier than usual. As best I could in the snowstorm, I checked the petrol, the fanbelt and, once the engine had cooled, the water and oil. Then I tried to start the car again. The key turned uselessly in the ignition.

I stood beside the car ready to flag down any passing motorist, but they'd clearly shown more sense than me by staying home. After twenty minutes not a single vehicle had passed in either direction. I was chilled to the bone and doing a fair impression of a snowman.

I got back in the car and slumped in my seat. I had set out to track down a murderer. It would be sadly ironic if I was found dead myself, killed by my own idiocy. What the hell was I going to do now? I needed to hear a friendly voice and someone to tell me I wasn't a complete idiot.

I fished out my mobile and phoned Matt.

"It's not even snowing here… Hold on." Matt paused, and by the changing acoustic I knew he was crossing the newsroom to peer through the venetian blinds. "Tell a lie. It's just started, but it's only a sprinkle."

"That's surprisingly unhelpful information."

"Do you want me to come and get you?"

"No, the conditions are terrible out here and getting worse all the time. I'll hijack the next passing car and get a lift back to town. Just talk to me, tell me what's going on."

"It's strange here without you, if that's what you want to know. Photographic's in a state of chaos. If you go in there you get shouted at, so I'm staying well clear."

"Any developments?"

"About the murder case, you mean? Kind of. I've been interviewed by Detective Inspector Laverack."

"What? Why you? You didn't even know Lara."

He coughed. "Actually… it was you he asked me about."

I was bewildered. "What did you tell him?"

"I tried to keep it tight… you know what the police are like. They twist your words. I knew exactly what he was up to, but when you're actually being interrogated — "

"For God's sake, anyone would think you told them I killed Lara."

"Don't be daft." He laughed, and it may have been the poor reception but he sounded nervous. "Nothing like that. But he did kind of get the impression that you didn't like her."

"That's not true."

"I know. But they kept asking me what you'd said about Lara, and how you felt about Daniel."

Now I was doubly bewildered. "This is ridiculous. But I've got nothing to hide. I'll straighten things out with Laverack when I get back."

"You did once say you'd kill her if she broke Daniel's heart." He sounded sad, apologetic. I realised Laverack had wheedled that little gem out of him and then distorted it to fit his own version of reality.

I exploded. "I didn't say that! It was something like *I'd wring her neck if…*" I stopped, appalled by what I'd said. Someone had wrung Lara's neck. "It's just a figure of speech. I didn't mean it in that way."

"I know. I tried to explain that to him. I'm so sorry, Jude. I didn't intend to land you in it."

"It's not your fault." I sighed. "I miss you."

"Ditto." His voice dropped. "Especially after what happened yesterday. Every time I go anywhere near the lift I start feeling randy."

"I'll be back soon and maybe…?"

"Sure. What were you doing out in the wilds anyway?"

"I went up to Chapel House in Gunnerston. It's where Lara took her boyfriends, I'm certain of it."

"Did you find anything?"

"I'm finding out a lot of stuff, Matt. I'm getting close, I'm sure of it. I'll tell you when I see you." A fluttery bleep on my mobile warned me that the battery was low. "I'll have to switch off. If nothing comes by in the next half hour I'm going to start walking."

"Don't do that, Jude. You know what they say, stay with your car and await rescue. Tell you what, I'll ring a garage for you. It's nearly dark. You shouldn't be out there on your own."

"OK. Try Raven Motors, the garage on Silver Street. They've got a big recovery vehicle."

"No problem. We'll soon have you back in civilisation."

It was a good half hour before I saw the welcome sight of headlights. A rescue truck with a powerful winch, giant tyres that gripped in snow and a friendly mechanic.

"You were easy to spot," he said, looking appreciatively at my bright red Triumph, the shark's teeth glowing in the lorry's headlights. He lowered the ramp, attached the car to a steel hawse and winched it on to the back of the vehicle with practised speed, clamping the wheels securely. Then we both climbed into the warm cab and set off for Ravenbridge.

The sprinkle of snow that Matt had mentioned had turned into a downy quilt, giving the town a quiet abandoned atmosphere. It was still snowing gently. A gritter lorry hurried past, heading for the ring road.

When we arrived at Raven Motors, my rescuer jumped out and detached the Triumph, guiding it into a service bay with the help of another mechanic.

"We're pretty busy, love, so we won't be able to fix it today."

"No worries." I gave him my phone number and he promised to try and get it up and running by tomorrow afternoon.

"I've never worked on an antique before," he smiled. "I'll use kid gloves, promise."

"No need. It's old but it's tough. Just beat it into submission."

It was dark when I walked out of the garage but enough light streamed out from the barn-like door to see the white car parked crookedly on the verge. I ran back inside.

"Who does the white Polo belong to?"

The mechanic emerged from under a bonnet lid, wiping his hands on an oily rag. "Why do you want to know?"

"Is it Lara Ramsey's? The girl who was killed?"

"As it happens, yeah."

"When did she bring it in? What's wrong with it? Do the police know it's here?"

"Whoa there, love. What's your problem? Course I rang the police when I heard what had happened."

"Have they looked at it?"

"Not yet. They said they would when they have time. They asked me to hang on to it for a while."

"You keep a diary?" I asked, moving across to the beaten-up wooden desk.

"Course I do." He grabbed it before I could, and pointed to one of the entries. "It came in late on Saturday December 30th. That's why the police weren't that interested. It was several days before she was killed. Just a regular repair job, nothing to do with the murder."

"How can you be so sure?" I strode up and down the concrete floor. "Do you know what's wrong with it?"

"Starter motor, most probably. That girl – Lara – she had it parked just around the corner from here while she was at work, and when she came to collect it, it wouldn't start. I remember a couple of us pushed it here. She was a lovely-looking girl." He shook his head sadly. "Who could do something like that?"

"Have you fixed it?"

"Well, no. What with the holidays, then when they found her dead – there didn't seem any point."

"Can you take a look at it now?"

His laughter wasn't encouraging. But I was used to being discouraged.

"I'm a friend of Lara's."

"Bloody hell… sorry."

I strode purposefully towards the door.

He sighed. "I'll get the keys."

"You'll need a torch as well."

"It's usually the starter motor," he told me as we walked towards the car. The bonnet opened with a struggle. "It's been standing idle for days in this weather, see." Once he'd cranked it into position he began examining the engine. "Could be the battery of course. Hold on…" He fiddled in the depths of the machinery, shining the torch beam on one spot in particular. "There's a loose connection… yeah, looks like the solenoid wire."

"Is that important?"

"When you switch on the ignition, the solenoid wire connects the battery to the starter motor, and that's what gets the car up and running."

"Just a normal breakdown, then?"

"Maybe… hold on, what's this?" He shone the torch on the coil of wire. "See that? It's been cut."

I rang home as I walked through town. No answer. Daniel must be out. I tried his mobile. A continuous bleep, then silence. He'd forgotten to recharge the battery. I stood in the market square, dithering. I thought of going straight to the police but the mechanic had promised me he'd ring them himself. I looked at my watch under a streetlight. Twenty past five. I was tired and hungry, but the thought of returning to an empty house was far from appealing. With what was left of my battery I called Matt.

"Are you still in the newsroom?"

"I've just got home. It *is* Friday night. I've been working like a dog all week. I need a break."

Music to my ears.

I explained about my car and the garage and the empty house. I didn't mention I felt bloody miserable and lonely, but he picked up on the subtext.

"Why don't you come over? Where are you? Shall I come and collect you?"

The snow had stopped but the roads were thick with churned slush that was rapidly turning to ice.

"No way. I'll walk."

"Good. That'll give me time to go round with a duster."

"You own a duster?"

"No, but I could improvise with a pair of dirty underpants."

I laughed, feeling better already. "Can you give me directions to your place?"

"Sure. It's Number 1, Raven Walk." He outlined the quickest route.

"Got it. See you in ten minutes."

We sat on a low squashy sofa and drank red wine, a full-bodied Shiraz that seemed to nourish and restore me as effectively as a three-course meal. Relaxing for the first time in what felt like years, I squirmed down into the sofa and told Matt about being pushed in the river and the dead ferret and the drunken farmer who tried to rape me.

"My God, Jude, that's terrible! You were lucky to come out of the river alive. And the farmer – what were you playing at? You can't go on with this amateur sleuth thing. It's too dangerous."

"You sound like Daniel."

"He's got the right idea, then." He leaned over and kissed me softly on the lips. "What you need is some TLC, and I'm your man. Let's have a bath together. Then I'll give you a massage. I'm pretty good at it. I've got some great perfumed oil, and I know just where to stroke you, how hard and how soft…" His tongue brushed my neck. "Then we'll get into bed and make love, very, very slowly."

I didn't argue. He began to undress me, tossing garments aside as if he was unwrapping a Christmas present, kissing and licking and biting each new bit of exposed flesh till my guts melted, and my blood turned to thick syrup. I pulled him up from the sofa. "Where's the bathroom?" I demanded.

It was a tight squeeze, but after a lot of hysterical giggling we found the best way was to sit like spoons, me lying back against Matt in the deep hot soapy water. When we were lobster-red and wrinkled like prunes we got out and dried each other. Matt patted my cuts and bruises tenderly. Then we went into the living room and lay on the rug. Outside I could hear the sound of the river flowing over one of the weirs. Here it was a soothing sound, not a terrifying one. I rolled on to my belly and Matt massaged oil into my back.

"Nice tattoo."

"Does it look like a leopard to you?"

"Of course not. It's a tiger."

I turned over and let him massage the rest of me. He played tease for what seemed like hours. When it got too much, I grabbed the bottle and ordered him to lie down and did the same to him until we were both crying out for release.

"I don't think we're going to make it to the bedroom, do you?" I whispered.

Matt answered with a groan.

Afterwards he switched all the lamps out. "I like talking in the dark," he said. "There are no barriers, no distractions coming between my mind and yours. We can be totally honest with each other."

"Talk? I haven't got a single active brain cell in my head right now."

We lay on the floor for a long time, holding each other. I closed my eyes and let the sound of water flow through my head, cleansing it. Sometimes it was delicious not to think.

"I like it here," I murmured.

"Me too. I was really lucky to get this place."

"You haven't got anything to eat, have you?"

"What do you like?"

"Something instant – fruit, nuts, crisps, anything like that."

"No nuts, I'm afraid. I've got this allergy. There might be a manky banana or two."

He got up and I heard him rooting about in the kitchen. He came back with a crinkly bag of sweets. "No bananas, in fact the cupboard's pretty much bare. But I'm never without these." He pulled the bag apart. "Chocolate raisins. I love them." He opened another bottle of wine and passed me a brimming glass. We drank and munched until the bag was empty.

"Tell me about Daniel's father."

"Why do you want to know?"

"Because I want to know about you. And I imagine having a child so young was a defining experience."

"Yes, it was. I was only eighteen when I got pregnant, nineteen when the baby was born. But Daniel's father... I don't think about him much."

"What was he like?"

"He was a bit older than me. Tall, dark and bloody good-looking. You get the picture."

"How did you meet?"

I sighed. I hadn't gone over this in a long time. It hurt too much. But Matt seemed genuinely interested and I owed him a lot for what he'd done for me today. And there was something liberating about the warm darkness and being naked in more senses than one.

"I was really into drama when I was young. I was no good at acting, so I used to help the set designer at Ravenbridge Theatre for nothing, just to get a taste of that strange other life. I think it was a reaction to the whole Methodist thing, a bit of glitz and glamour. I used to drag homeless actors back to our house and of course Mum and Dad always let them stay, even though they didn't really approve. These actors, they'd come to the theatre just for one production, or sometimes for a whole season – four or five plays – so some of them needed a room for several months."

"And Daniel's father was one of them?"

"He came for a short season – *Macbeth*, playing Banquo, some foppish twit in *The Rivals,* and Gus in *The Dumb Waiter.*"

"Was he any good?"

"At the time I thought he was wonderful. On reflection, I guess he was no more than mediocre. He seems to have sunk without trace, anyway."

"And he told you that you had fabulous cheekbones and a beautiful soul. He could see it in your eyes."

"Some crap like that. I fell for it. I was still at school, brought up in a Methodist household where drink and gambling were the devil's work. And as for sex…" I stroked Matt's thigh. "It didn't exist. It never happened. Or if it did, it was an aberration, best got over quickly, a necessary biological procedure like having a tooth filled."

"And at the end of the season he left, never to return, leaving you with a souvenir."

I punched Matt lightly on his bare chest. "No. I wasn't completely stupid, I knew about contraception."

"So what happened?"

"When he went back to London, I dropped out of the sixth form and followed him. I shacked up with him at first, but things quickly went pear-shaped due to his total inability to stay faithful and his ingrained habit of lying about it. So I moved out. I spent my time bumming around theatres, loving the life. About a year later I met up with him again, at a party. All that old hopeless passion flooded back. We got drunk, went back to my place…"

"And family planning was the last thing on your mind?"

I snuggled closer to Matt and let him circle me in his arms. "I refused to believe I was pregnant. I was five months gone before I came home and told my mother." I paused, remembering the bizarreness of those days. "She surprised me. She was really kind. She told me that if I wanted to keep the baby I should, and she'd support me whatever my dad or the old Bible-bashers at the chapel might say. And she did."

I realised I hadn't told Matt about Father Thomas and Lara's abortion. I gave him a brief outline of the facts, without mentioning the heartbreaking display of pictures in Lara's bedroom. After all, Matt never knew her, and I felt a strong desire to respect what was left of her privacy.

"I keep finding parallels between her life and mine," I said. "But there's one big difference – I got Mum's support when I fell pregnant. Lara's experience was quite the opposite."

"Is your mother still around?"

"No. She died a couple of years ago. Daniel adored her. He keeps losing the people he loves, poor kid."

"You've both had a hard time." Matt began to lick my neck.

I sighed and stretched. "I must go. Daniel will be getting worried."

"Give him a call from here. Tell him you won't be home. Stay the night with me." He stroked my naked breasts and all thought was put on hold for a few delicious seconds. Then my brain cells woke up at last. I stopped his hand. "I'd love to, but I better not."

"What are you going to do?"

"About Lara, you mean?"

"Yeah."

"I'm not sure. I haven't come up with anything concrete."

"What have you come up with?"

I told him about Harrison's pendant, the one shaped like a pentagram, and about the bracelet that had got into Daniel's pocket. And also the fact that someone had disabled Lara's car.

"But who?" I wondered.

"From what you say, Father Thomas has the strongest motive."

"Maybe. There is definitely a doubt over him."

"Anything else?"

"There's that missing print, but I'm not convinced it has anything to do with Lara's murder."

"Sleep on it, Jude. You know Daniel's right. It's time to give up this crazy search and leave it to the professionals. I don't want anything to happen to you."

"That's sweet." I stood up, switching on the nearest lamp and gathering up my discarded clothes. I found my pants behind the sofa and my bra draped over the TV. "But I can't stop now. Can you ring me a taxi while I get dressed?"

"You didn't say you'd be this late!"

"Daniel, it's been a hell of a long day. Can you recharge my mobile for me while I get something to eat? And sort your own phone out while you're at it."

"I've been frantic with worry."

"I tried to ring, but you were either out or unavailable. I had no idea which because of aforementioned defunct phone."

"Don't blame me!"

"I'm not blaming you for anything. In fact, I'm not aware there's been any transgression, so the concept of blame doesn't apply."

"What have you been doing all day?"

"Daniel, that's my business," I blustered. I'd never been much good at lying. Unlike Daniel's father, who'd been a professional. I'd had a jaundiced view of actors ever since. "I could ask you the same thing. You weren't answering the phone, so what have you been up to?"

Now he looked uncomfortable. "Nothing much."

He wasn't any good at lying either. I gave three silent cheers that he didn't take after his father.

"Tell me."

"I went to see Lara's mother."

"Was she OK?" I asked, recalling our last violent encounter. I wondered how she would feel about a visit from my son.

"She was in bed, too upset to speak to anyone. I talked to her dad instead. He seems like a nice guy. I don't think he'll ever get over losing Lara. Nor will I."

I hugged Daniel as hard as I could. "I know it's a cliché, but give it time. Time softens even the hardest blows. You'll just have to trust your poor grey-haired old mother on this one."

"You haven't got grey hair."

"No? I will have, by the time this is over."

Twenty-three

The first Saturday after New Year and the estate agents' was busy, as if the change in the calendar had made people restless to move house. A crowd of prospective buyers was milling around the property boards. Susan was dealing with a starry-eyed young couple about to embark on a lifetime of mortgages and leaky roofs, and two young men in loud ties were deep into transactions with clients too. Then a depressing thought struck me – had most of them had come to Kerwin and Black knowing that this was where Lara Ramsey had worked? Were they hoping for some sort of vicarious thrill?

The manager was nowhere to be seen.

"Is Mr Gilmore around?"

Susan looked at me as if I was something you find on the bottom of a shoe.

"He's in his office – no, you can't just barge in!"

"Is that right?"

Hemmed in by her desk and constrained to be the public face of Kerwin and Black, Susan stood even less chance of stopping me than Sister Veronica had.

Gilmore must have heard the raised voices. He was twisting round in his chair as I entered the office at the back, his skin mottled and raw-looking. I wondered why so many women had found him attractive enough to accompany him to Gunnerston. Perhaps they felt sorry for him, or perhaps he had a silver tongue and charmed them out of their knickers.

"Piss off!"

Or possibly not.

"I know all about the sordid goings-on at Chapel House," I said angrily, not bothering to lower my voice. "And were you aware that you and Lara and all the others provided hours of amusement for the farmer who lives opposite? He had a ladder."

Gilmore hurried to the door and shut it behind me. "We were doing nothing illegal."

"So you won't mind if I inform head office?"

He paled under his blotchy complexion. "I'll deny every word. After all, Lara's not here to support your story, is she?"

"But the farmer is."

"Who's going to believe some hick from the sticks? If he's a peeping tom, he won't want that broadcast around, will he? He won't say anything."

"You may be right about that, but can't you see that you and Lara were playing a very dangerous game?"

"That was half the fun."

I was infuriated by his smugness. "One of the men she took to Chapel House may have killed her!"

"The police have a list of her recent male clients. If it's one of them, they'll find him."

"You take no responsibility whatever for Lara's death?"

"No, I don't." He returned to his computer. "I've got nothing else to say to you. Now piss off and don't come back."

I opened the door and said loudly, "See you up at Chapel House, then. Shall I wear my French maid's uniform, or the naughty nun outfit? Or do you fancy the thigh-length boots and the whip?"

The milling crowd fell silent as I walked out. Susan had a bewildered expression on her face, as if she had been hit with a blunt instrument. The door rattled when I banged it shut.

Daniel had just got up when I arrived home. He looked at me suspiciously but I didn't share my thoughts with him. I dumped my shopping on the kitchen table.

"Vegetables, fresh pasta, salad, lemons, eggs and cream. Guess what we're having for dinner tonight?"

I spent most of the afternoon watching sport on telly with Daniel, as if everything was normal, then retreated to the kitchen to make a huge lasagne, and, after a great deal of swearing at the complicated recipe, managed to rustle up a *tarte au citron*. But though my hands were occupied, my mind was elsewhere, endlessly churning over the people associated with Lara, and the reasons they might have to kill her.

We ate late, opening a couple of beers, then a couple more. I chattered with Daniel animatedly about anything but Lara, in an attempt to reassure him that I'd kept my promise – no more amateur detective work. But occasionally I caught the same shadow of suspicion crossing his face. Beneath the banal chat I was debating with myself whether to go to the police to clear up that stupid comment about wringing Lara's neck. At the same time I could give them the information I had, but it all seemed so flimsy I was afraid DI Laverack would laugh me out of court.

In the end, they beat me to it.

We were watching a film when the doorbell rang. I glanced at the clock on the video. Quarter to ten. Who'd be calling this late?

We crept into the hall together. We could see the outline

of a figure on the doorstep.

Daniel whispered in my ear, "Don't answer it, Mum."

"Who is it?" I called out, trying not to sound scared out of my wits and failing.

"Detective Inspector Laverack."

I let out a sigh of relief. "OK, I'm coming."

"What does he want?"

"I can guess."

Laverack was wearing an elegant wool coat over his suit. His tie was plain turquoise silk. I was aware of my scruffy shirt and stained jeans, not to mention my worn-out sheepskin slippers. Behind him I could see DC Naylor.

"Come in," I said. "I think I know what this is about. When you spoke to my colleague – my ex-colleague – Matt Dryden, I think you got the wrong end of the stick."

"Actually, I'd prefer you to come down to the station."

"Why?"

"We'd like to talk to you," said Laverack.

"It's late. Why can't you talk to me here?"

"We can record it on tape at the station," said Naylor.

"I don't get this."

"We'd appreciate your co-operation in this matter," said Laverack smoothly.

Naylor chipped in, "The sooner we get on with it, the sooner it'll be over."

I couldn't deny the truth of that. I got my boots, which were still sodden with snow, and my leather jacket.

"My car's out of action."

"No problem. We'll take you in," said Laverack.

There was a pause before Naylor added, "And of course, we can bring you home when we're finished." But it sounded very much like an afterthought.

The table was pockmarked with clusters of burns, tiny overlapping circles scored deep into the surface. There was a cheap but serviceable green tin ashtray, yet cigarettes had been routinely stubbed out on the table. Perhaps the ashtray was a recent refinement. Or perhaps the occupants had chosen to ignore it, wanting to leave a tangible record of their presence.

I placed two fingertips in the depressions and walked my hand around the table from hole to hole. In the middle was an unmarked space, too wide to span. My index finger was stranded in mid-air. It felt like crossing a stream and running out of stepping stones.

Laverack and Naylor sat opposite, watching me through narrowed eyes. I pulled my hand back. We were waiting for my solicitor. There was something about the way I'd been ushered through the reception area and buzzed through a security gate, and the way the duty officer had barked questions at me – name, address, date of birth, occupation – and asked me to empty my pockets, that had made me anxious.

"I'm allowed to have my lawyer with me, aren't I?" I'd asked, trying to recall all those TV cop shows I'd watched with half a brain. Now I wished I'd paid them closer attention.

"That is your right," said the duty officer, without much enthusiasm for the idea. "Do you have your own representative or do you require the solicitor on call?"

The prospect of being represented by someone I didn't know unnerved me. I rang Charlie Tait, old friend and drinking buddy, specialist in conveyancing and divorce. A long time ago we became lovers for a while. He'd been married at the time, so it was an episode I was deeply ashamed of. My only justification had been that the marriage was already shaky, and the fact that Charlie was great in bed.

I was relieved when I heard Charlie's familiar voice, even though he sounded distinctly slurred. The Latin music in the background suggested he was in his favourite bar, El Paradiso in the Market Square. I explained where I was, and the connection between Daniel and Lara Ramsey. "The police want to ask me a few things and I'd really like someone with me." He said he'd be there as soon as possible.

"Put her in Interview Room Two."

With Laverack on one side and Naylor on the other, I was escorted down the corridor to the small cell-like room with the pock-marked table and we'd been waiting ever since.

I leaned against my jacket, slung over the back of the chair. Even in a shirt and jeans I was sweltering. At last the door opened and Charlie walked in, bringing a whiff of ten-year old malt with him. He sat in the vacant chair next to mine.

"You all right, Jude?" he mumbled. "You look terrible."

"Just tired. It's nothing that getting out of here won't cure."

"I meant your face." He peered at me in wonder.

I'd pretty much forgotten that I looked like a car-crash survivor. I hadn't had much access to mirrors lately, and Matt had somehow made me forget my scratches and grazes. He had made me feel beautiful.

"What's it all about then?" Charlie leant back and lit a cigarette. His hands trembled slightly. They had a purple blood-starved look about them, the sure sign of circulation damaged by alcohol. He'd lost weight too. I realised I hadn't seen him for quite a while. He'd always had a huge capacity for drink, but I'd never seen him like this. I'd no idea things had got so bad.

Laverack coughed. "Are we ready?" Attached to the wall was a large tape-recorder. His hand hovered over the controls.

"Sure," said Charlie. "Bring on the dancing girls."

Laverack pressed a button. "Recording an interview with Judith Baxendale. Friday, fifth of January. Time…" He checked the clock on the wall. "22.17. Also present in the room – DI Laverack…" He gestured for the others to speak in turn.

"DC Naylor."

"Charles Tait, Ms Baxendale's legal representative."

Laverack pulled a sheet of paper from a folder. Then he put his elbows on the table and steepled his hands as if he was about to pray.

"I understand you drove up to Gunnerston yesterday?"

"That's right."

"Why?"

"I… I was interested in a house up there."

"You're thinking of moving?"

"Maybe."

"Are you referring to Chapel House?"

"Yes."

"And are you aware that Lara Ramsey was familiar with that property and often took clients there?"

I hesitated. I didn't want to lie. After all I had nothing to hide. But Laverack's cool gaze put me on edge and I was tempted to bluff my way out of this with as many fibs as it needed. But I was too tired to think straight and I knew I'd only get in a muddle. In the end I decided honesty was the only way. Matt would be proud of me, I thought.

"Yes, I'm aware of that."

"And that's why you went there?"

"I'm trying to understand why Lara was killed, that's all."

"That's our job."

"You're not getting very far, are you?" I said angrily.

He glanced down at the sheet again. "Let's leave the matter of your son's girlfriend for the time being." He drew another piece of paper from the folder. "While you were visiting Chapel House you met a farmer called Brandon Hill."

"Is that his name? It sounds like some local beauty spot. Not exactly appropriate. Hold on, I didn't tell him my name, so how did you —?"

"He described your car."

I nodded slowly. This was the first time I had ever cursed Daniel's wonderful paintwork.

"He's made a serious allegation."

I was stumped for a moment. "Against me? That's ironic."

"He says you assaulted him."

"I kicked him in the bollocks, yes. Did he mention he was trying to rape me at the time?"

"He says you consented to sex."

"I… I was trying to find a way out of the situation."

Naylor leaned forward. "Did you consent to sex or not?"

"He might have thought so, but I —"

"This isn't the first time you've been involved in a fracas, is it?" Laverack interjected.

"What are you talking about?"

"There was a very unpleasant incident outside the police station a couple of days ago."

"You mean Patricia Ramsey? She attacked me! And I've got the scratches to show for it." I pointed at my ravaged face.

"I don't believe she was responsible for all those injuries."

"No… I slipped climbing down a wall, and… and I fell in the river."

The two detectives glanced at each other.

Charlie leant over towards me. "Jude, what's going on here? I'm slightly confused," he muttered.

"You're not the only one."

"You lose your temper very quickly, don't you, Judith?"

"My name's Jude! Only my parents and Methodist ministers ever called me Judith!"

He sat back with a smug look on his face. "Like I say, short-tempered."

Charlie put his elbows on the table and hid his face in his hands.

"Let's move on," said Laverack. He turned the sheet of paper over. "You seem to have set yourself up as some sort of vigilante in the case of Lara Ramsey."

"It's not like that at all."

He ploughed on as if I hadn't spoken. "You interviewed Annie Molloy at length the day after the murder. When we got round to speaking to her this morning she wasn't very helpful. *I've been through all this before* were her precise words. We had some difficulty persuading her to co-operate."

"It's a free country. I can speak to whoever I like."

"Unless by doing so you obstruct the course of a serious investigation."

"I didn't mean to. Perhaps you should have spoken to her sooner. You can't blame me for your..." The word *incompetence* hovered in the air. "For your lack of man-power."

"And yesterday you drove up to Gunnerston and interfered in our enquiry there as well."

"How?"

"By entering a potential crime scene – and by the way, we'll need fingerprints."

"What for?"

"To eliminate you from the scene," said Naylor.

"Lara wasn't murdered at Chapel House."

"There may be important forensic material and you've muddied the waters by blundering in. Not only by your presence, but by removing evidence."

Charlie seemed to be half-asleep, but he perked up when he heard that.

"What evidence?"

"Brandon Hill said he saw you pick something up and put it in your pocket."

I was about to vehemently deny it, then I remembered. He was right. I reached into my jeans pocket. It was still there. "You mean this?" I put the bottle top on the scarred table. "I wasn't stealing. I pocketed it without thinking. It's just litter, isn't it?"

Naylor poked at it with a biro. She read the unfamiliar brand name. "It's one of those European export beers. Dutch, I think."

"Put it in a plastic bag," said Laverack quietly. "Then send it to the lab."

While Naylor was dealing with the bottle top, Laverack gave me a sermon on the importance of every last piece of evidence, however small, and the irresponsibility of obstructing a police investigation.

"OK. I get the message. Though I can hardly believe you've brought me in here just to retrieve that bottle top and lecture me about my social duty. Can I go now?"

"My client wishes to go home, so if there's nothing else…" said Charlie, rising unsteadily from his chair.

"I haven't finished," said Laverack in a steely voice. "Ms Baxendale is accused of assault, remember? And there are some other things I wish to discuss."

Naylor returned to the room, nodded at her superior officer and sat down.

He pulled out a third sheet of paper, which could have been instructions on how to construct a bookshelf for all I knew. It all seemed part of the theatricality of the occasion, designed to intimidate me.

"Now we come to a very serious matter."

Charlie lit a cigarette. Naylor wrinkled her nose and waved the smoke away.

"How did you know about the marks on Lara Ramsey's body?"

I stared directly at DC Naylor. "*She* told me."

Laverack glanced at his colleague sharply. "Is this true?"

She coloured up. "I only asked whether her son had ever dabbled in black magic —"

"You said a black-magic symbol had been carved on her chest."

"I never said it was a pentagram!"

This was where I had to decide whether Ben Greenwood stayed out of trouble or not. "I made a lucky guess, that's all. Was it a pentagram? Well, what do you know."

"I didn't mention blisters either," Naylor protested. "I just said there were marks. I don't know where she got blisters from."

"So let me repeat the question," said Laverack. "How did you get this information?"

"You don't have to answer that," muttered Charlie.

"No comment."

The two officers were silent.

"I think my client needs a break," said Charlie.

They ignored him.

"You know exactly what the killer of Lara Ramsey did to her body. I repeat, how do you know?"

Still thinking about protecting Ben as long as possible, I shook my head.

"Ms Baxendale shook her head," Laverack said into the tape recorder, "which I understand to be a refusal to answer."

I stared at the burn marks on the table. Should I tell them about the video, about my theory that Lara suffered the same torture as the Spanish girl in the film? But thinking about it now, it seemed a lightweight premise, if not totally preposterous.

Then I remembered Lara's car. Surely the mechanic at Raven Motors had phoned the police by now?

"Your son Daniel…" Laverack said, going on to the next sheet of paper.

"What about him?"

"I think it's fair to say you're an over-protective mother?"

"No, it isn't fair. I'm a very slapdash mum."

"He's often at the doctor's, I believe. And he's just had a spell in hospital?"

"He suffers from asthma. The shock of Lara's death triggered a really bad attack. Apart from that one episode, he's been a lot better recently."

"You keep a close eye on him?"

"Do you have children?"

"I'm not married."

"Even so, you must realise that when your child has a serious illness you can't relax. But I do try to make sure he lives a normal life. There's just one thing I nag him about, and that's taking his medication with him wherever he goes. That hardly makes me over-protective, does it?"

He wrote a word or two on the paper, then looked up at me again.

"He'll be leaving home in September?"

"Yes. He's going to art college."

"How do you feel about that?"

"Fine." I'd been telling myself for months that I felt fine about it, in the hope that I'd start believing it.

"Will you miss him?"

"Of course. What do you expect?"

Laverack tapped the table with his pen. Behind his stony exterior I guessed there was a powerful ambitious streak. Had he made a conscious decision that marriage and children would get in the way of his progress? Then I wondered idly if he was gay.

"Was Lara his first girlfriend?"

"No. He's had one or two others, but no one significant."

"So Lara Ramsey was just another casual relationship?"

"This was different. He was serious about her and I know she felt the same way. I think they were very much in love."

"What was your impression of this girl?"

"I didn't know her that well." I reflected that the last few days had changed that. "Not when she was alive," I added.

"But you didn't approve of her?"

Charlie coughed into his fist. A warning.

"I never said that. She seemed nice. Daniel was happy and that's all that mattered to me. I didn't interfere. For all I knew, it could have been all over in a week or two. That's what teenage love affairs are like."

"Had his previous relationships ended like that?"

"Yes."

"And you were glad to see them end?"

"Neither glad nor sorry. He always got over the girl and moved on. That's life. Surely even you remember what young love was like?" Gay or straight, I thought, he must have felt passion at least once.

He pursed his lips but didn't answer.

251

Naylor took over. "You don't like the thought of Daniel having a serious relationship with a girl, do you?"

"Where do you get that from? Like I say, I just want him to be happy."

"Were you jealous of Lara?"

I looked at her in astonishment. "Jealous? Why on earth would I be?" Though my brain was fogged with exhaustion I began to see where this was going.

"I suggest you'd be jealous of any girl who took your son's affection away from you, especially one as attractive as Lara Ramsey."

"That's bullshit."

Charlie sat upright. "My client needs a break. Now."

"That's not possible," said Laverack. "But she can have a coffee. Do you want something to eat?"

The lasagne and lemon tart I'd eaten earlier were churning around my gut and the thought of more food made my stomach muscles contract. I didn't want to throw up over Laverack's expensive suit. "No thanks."

He gave Naylor instructions and we waited until she came back with four lidded paper cups on a tray. My hands felt so weak I couldn't lever off the plastic lid. Charlie stubbed out his cigarette and did it for me. I took a sip. It tasted disgusting, but the caffeine hit my bloodstream as effectively as the finest arabica.

Laverack read from the current sheet of paper. "If Lara ever hurt him I'd wring her neck. Do you remember saying those words?"

I knew he'd get round to this. It didn't mean I had an answer ready.

"I think you're misquoting me. I was talking to my friend, Matt Dryden, after Lara's death. I said something like, if she had hurt him or broken his heart, I think I

252

would have wrung her neck."

"Isn't that the same?" asked Naylor.

"No. I was saying that I liked her, that she and Daniel were good together. But if she had ever hurt him I wouldn't have liked her at all."

"Your actual words were, I'd have wrung her neck," said Laverack.

"It's just a figure of speech, for god's sake!"

"And we already know that you have a short fuse and can be violent."

Charlie coughed again.

"You're twisting everything to fit some ludicrous theory that I…" I couldn't say it. I didn't want the words *that I killed Lara* given any credence by being uttered aloud and recorded on tape. I started to pant, breathless from anger and frustration. Matt had said the police tried to trick you into saying things that made you seem guilty, and he was damned right.

Laverack sat there patiently, cool and unruffled. No doubt Chief Superintendent Rollins had told him they needed a quick result with this high-profile case. The local police force would look like incompetent fools in the full glare of the media frenzy if they didn't pin this shocking crime on someone soon. Laverack resented me for showing him up at the press conference, so who better to haul in for interview and beat into submission?

Only he'd picked the wrong person. In every sense.

"Where were you on the night of Monday, January 1st?" he asked.

"I was at home."

"Can anyone verify that?"

"Only Daniel."

Laverack put his papers together and tapped them into

a neat pile. He laid them squarely in front of him. "I suggest that you took a dislike to Lara, that you went to her flat that night to remonstrate with her – leave my son alone or else – that you lost your temper and strangled her."

I stood up. "I've had enough of this rubbish. My head's beginning to hurt, from banging it against a brick wall."

"That you know all about the marks on her body because you inflicted them yourself."

"I want to speak to my client in private," said Charlie Tait.

Laverack waited for a response from me. I began to sway, my ears buzzing. I gripped the pock-marked table to keep my balance. Now was the time to tell him about being pushed in the river, almost certainly by the person who killed Lara. But I knew exactly what his response would be. Were there any witnesses? Then why should I believe you? You could have jumped into the river yourself. *But I nearly died!* Then he would have checked my background and found I gained a 25-metre swimming certificate when I was eight, therefore I was a champion swimmer and just pretending I was in danger.

"She needs a break, dammit!" Charlie's words came from some distant echoey place.

Laverack loosened the knot of his tie. "Ten minutes."

Naylor came with me to the toilet. She stood outside the cubicle while I emptied my bladder. After I'd sat there for a while with my head in my hands I got my dizziness under control. I checked the window. Shut and barred. When we went back into the corridor, Charlie was waiting. Naylor stood at a discreet distance while we talked.

"Jude, I'm getting out of my depth here. Criminal law isn't really my thing. You'd better ask for the duty solicitor."

"How bad is it?"

He turned aside and took a swig from his hip flask. "He's got you in his sights and he's trying to build a case against you."

"How's he doing?"

"Pretty well, to be honest."

"Charlie, I had nothing to do with Lara's death!"

He raised one of his purple hands. "It's no business of mine whether you're guilty or not. I'm just here to advise you on matters of law."

But I saw there was doubt in his eyes. If I couldn't convince an old friend like Charlie of my innocence, I was lost.

"Do you think they'll charge me?"

"It's looking that way." He leant close. I caught the reek of whisky on his breath. "You do realise that if it goes to court and you're found guilty, it would mean a life sentence?"

"Are you suggesting I confess?"

"It might be a good idea."

"But Charlie, I didn't…" What was the point?

"Think about it." He took one more swig and put the flask away.

Naylor's mobile trilled. "OK. Right." She called down the corridor to us. "Mr Tait, please take your client back to Interview Room Two. I have to collect a file from the front desk. Tell DI Laverack I'll be there in a minute."

"All right," said Charlie.

She strode away importantly.

We were approaching the men's toilets when Charlie muttered, "I need a piss." He staggered into the gents, weaving like a boxer who'd already gone nine rounds.

I stood still for a moment, feeling abandoned. A cleaner, wearing a sleeveless blue tunic over her clothes, walked past me. She opened a cupboard, reached in, collected a bucket and hurried off. I looked up and down the corridor before opening the cupboard door. A spare blue tunic hung on the back of it. I stepped inside. I put the tunic over my head and pressed the velcro fastenings together at the sides. I grabbed a broom, then stepped back into the corridor, shutting the door behind me.

I walked quickly away, in the opposite direction from Interview Room Two with its diseased-looking table and air of defeat. As I turned the corner I heard the distant clatter of crockery and the murmur of voices – the staff canteen, no doubt serving the night shift endless bacon sandwiches and mugs of strong tea to see them through the small hours. Keeping my head down, I moved towards the noise, stopping to clean the floor every time someone went by. No one questioned my right to be there.

The corridor ended abruptly in an internal security gate. I started brushing the same patch over and over again, keeping out of range of the surveillance camera. I stole a glance at my watch. I seemed to have been at the station for hours but it was only ten to eleven. A woman in civilian clothes approached me. My heart pounded under the nylon tabard. She was reading from a file in her hand and didn't feel the need to acknowledge a scruffy-looking cleaner. It was strange how even a hint of a uniform took away individuality, especially if you were one of the lower orders of the hierarchy.

"Gate!" she called out absently, and with a click it slid open. I edged through behind the woman before it clanged shut. The canteen was very close now. I sniffed my way there, the odour of fried food increasingly strong.

I pushed open the swing door and walked straight past rows of tables and chairs, my head down, unchallenged. I was nearly through to the kitchen when two police officers, carrying loaded trays, came towards me, blocking my way. If I barged past they would look at me properly and see that I wasn't a regular. Game over. I turned sharp right, following a sign to the ladies' toilet. I marched in, looking purposeful.

One of the two cubicles was in use. I went into the empty one. The window had no bars, but the part that opened was far too small to squeeze through. I waited till I heard the toilet flush next door, the rush of tap water, the dragging of the roller towel and the squeak of sensible shoes on the tiled floor. Then I walked out and back into the canteen.

This time there was no obstruction in my way. The kitchen was a low-ceilinged area full of stainless steel. One bored-looking cook was flipping burgers with one hand and shaking a basket of chips in the fryer with the other. Eyes forward, I went through to the back where a jumble of rubbish bags and tins of oil nearly filled the narrow passage. I felt a blast of fresh air – the door at the end, slightly ajar to get rid of the greasy fug.

A few seconds later I was breathing in lungfuls of bitterly cold night air. My leather jacket was still hanging on the chair in Room Two, but there was no going back. I seemed to be in the staff car park. Bending low, I ran between the white police cars and vans until I found the exit.

I daren't go back home. I couldn't ring Daniel to tell him where I was – my mobile was in the pocket of my jacket, and I had no money for a public phone. But I had to find shelter before I froze. Who did I know near the centre of town who would offer me an unconditional welcome at nearly midnight?

It was obvious. I turned towards the river. Towards number 1, Raven Walk.

Twenty-four

I was fifty metres away when I smelt burning.

I ran round the corner into Raven Walk. At the same moment I heard a crack like something breaking. Strings of black smoke began to rise from the roof of Matt's house.

His car was parked outside. Which meant he was inside.

"Matt!" I screamed.

I shoulder-charged the front door, expecting it to be locked, but it gave way. I nearly fell into the hall.

"Matt, wake up! You've got to get out of here!"

I was about to run upstairs, but a ball of smoke and flame rolled down from the upper floor, beating me back. The smoke was choking me, the heat already intense.

"Get out! Jump out of the window!"

I backed out of the front door, pulling it shut to cut off the oxygen. I began yelling for help. Lights snapped on in the neighbouring houses. A man in pyjamas ran out on to the street.

"Phone the fire brigade – quick! And get everybody out of their houses!" I dropped to my knees, choking. He ran back inside.

When I opened my streaming eyes again, the whole house was lit up like a halloween pumpkin. Tongues of flame whirled upwards into the night sky. I heard more cracks – glass from the windows, splintering in the fierce heat. The small road was crowded with people now, subdued with shock. If the fire spread along the smart new terrace, their homes would go up in smoke too.

Then came the wail of a siren. A fire engine screeched to

a stop, disgorging fire officers. They unrolled a water hose like a big flat elastic band.

"Is anyone in there?" someone shouted.

"Yes," I croaked. "Please hurry," I said hopelessly. I knew Matt couldn't have survived the intensity of the fire.

"Keep back, love!" An officer shooed me out of the way to get to the water hydrant.

There was a crash that sounded like rafters coming down, and a shower of sparks from the roof. I closed my eyes, but the crazy dancing flames still played on my retina, along with other terrible things I hadn't seen, only imagined. It was better to keep my eyes open.

I watched until the flames were guttering feebly and the house was a hissing smoking ruin. Only then did I begin to understand what this meant. What if someone had seen me coming out of Matt's house last night? Someone who was shadowing me. Who else but Lara's killer? Having failed to get rid of me, they had turned to my friend. It was another warning, one that even I couldn't fail to ignore. And I had absolutely no doubt that they wouldn't stop till I was dead too.

The crew stood in a weary huddle, talking in low voices, even cracking jokes.

"Have you found anyone?" I asked.

A female officer turned to me. "Sorry, love, we can't go in there, the structure's too dangerous. But there's no hope of survivors from this one."

I found an empty bit of pavement and sat down on the kerb, noting vacantly that the heat from the fire had melted the snow. I watched the fire crew rewind their hose. Most of the people were allowed back into their houses. But Matt's next-door neighbours were wrapped in blankets and escorted into an ambulance. I had no idea where they were going to spend the night. For some reason it was their bewildered faces that set me off. I hung my head and wept till I was drained of tears.

It was only when a police car swung round the corner that I got stiffly to my feet. My disappearance from the police station must be well broadcast by now. I wasn't ready to go back into custody, to face more twisted questions.

I melted away like the snow on the pavement.

Stan Roguski lived in a bungalow on the west side of town. I knew plenty of short cuts through alleyways and ginnels, but I stuck to the well-lit streets, busy with cars and people. I kept looking behind me but I couldn't see anyone suspicious.

Eventually I came to the quiet suburban estate of trim gardens where life was simple in its predictability.

I reached the road I wanted. It was a weary trudge up a long slow hill, but my heart lifted when I saw that the lights were still on at Stan's place. On most Friday nights, he and Carol liked to watch a late film, or if there was nothing good on TV they rented a video or picked one from their huge collection. But this Friday night I was sure they weren't staying up late for pleasure. They would be talking about Lara, looking at family snaps, trying to delay the time when they lay sleepless side by side, remembering their beloved niece, and torturing themselves about her terrible death.

It seemed like hours before they responded to my knock. I wondered if Stan was finally going deaf from the clatter of machinery at the printworks. Eventually the door opened a crack, jerking to a stop on the security chain. Stan's round ruddy face peered out.

"Jude?"

He unhooked the chain and let me in.

I stumbled across the threshold. He caught me in his strong arms. "Carol!" he called out. She was already standing in the doorway of the living room, looking fearful. Her head cocked sideways, wondering if she really recognised this shivering wraith.

"Something terrible's happened!" I stammered.

"You poor love," she whispered.

Neither of them said another word, apart from the usual phrases of tender concern, until I was sitting on the sofa, wearing Stan's thick woollen cardigan. They watched in wonder as I slurped a steaming mug of tea, noting my trembling hands and my chattering teeth.

Carol was small and neat in contrast to Stan's beefy rotundity. They made an odd pair but a loving one. I hated to bring danger to their quiet respectable lives, but I didn't know where else to turn. And I needed to ask them about Lara.

"Jude, what is it?" Stan said at last.

"Stanislaus." Carol uttered the single word in a clipped schoolteacher voice. Stan had told me she only called him by his full name as a reprimand. Chastened, he leaned back in his huge leather armchair. She took the empty cup from my hand. "You look a bit better now. I'll get you more tea."

"No, really."

"It's no trouble." Carol actually was a schoolteacher. She taught a reception class at Stockhill Road Primary. I knew better than to argue.

"You're a saint," I said.

"Yeah, yeah, I polished my halo only this morning."

Stan waited until she'd gone before asking me again.

"It's hard to know where to begin." I paused, wondering how much I should tell him. "The police think I killed Lara."

"What? Are they mad?"

"There's worse… a fire."

"An accident? Were you there? Is that why you smell of smoke?"

"It was made to look like an accident, but someone's dead. It's Matt Dryden."

My voice cracked.

"That young journalist, the one doing the reports about Lara in the paper? That's terrible. You think someone started the fire deliberately? But why? It doesn't make sense. No, Jude. It must have been an accident."

"Maybe." If I explained that Matt had died because of his connection with me I would dissolve and be unable to function. I needed to function. I still had a lot to do. I also decided not to mention the fact that I had left police custody without official permission.

There was a photo album on the coffee table. I picked it up. The pages opened stiffly. Lara was in most of the pictures. Even as a young child she had a cloud of red-gold curls.

"She was a lovely girl," said Stan. "She didn't have an easy life, and things were just beginning to come right." He took the album from me. "There's one here of her and Daniel." The pages creaked as he turned them, then he laid the album flat in front of me. It was a classic pose, wonderfully ordinary – two young people in a bar some-where, paper hats on their heads, party poppers strewn around, raising their glasses to the future. Now, for them as a couple, there was no future.

"I wish I'd known her better," I said, brushing away tears. "I've found out a lot about her since she died. And do you know who she reminds me of?"

Stan shook his head.

"Me."

He smiled for the first time. "I hadn't thought of that, but you're right. She was full of life but stubborn, downright bloody-minded in fact."

"I'll take that as a compliment." I put the album carefully on the coffee table. "Daniel said Lara was anxious about something, or someone. Do you have any idea why?"

He frowned, thinking hard. "None at all. Lara often kept things private. It was to do with her mother, who always wanted to know her business, always trying to force her to be someone she wasn't."

Carol stood in the doorway. "It's true. I know Pat's my own sister, but I'm not like her. I'm pretty relaxed about the whole Catholic thing. That's why Lara liked to come here. Stan and I never tried to impose anything on her. She was always welcome in this house."

"I'm sure she appreciated that. In fact she came here for dinner, didn't she? That last day?"

Carol nodded.

"I know her car was in the garage, in fact I'm pretty sure someone sabotaged it so she couldn't use it." They both looked shocked. "With no car, how did Lara get here on Monday?"

"She walked. Stan offered to pick her up, but Lara said she wanted to clear her head after her night out. And it would give her a chance to think. I remember wondering what she meant by that."

"And when she got here, did she seem odd or nervous? Did she talk about anything out of the ordinary?"

Carol put the mug of tea on the table in front of me. "I can't think of anything."

"It might be something quite small, apparently unimportant. Please try and remember."

"What's this all about, Jude? The police have already

asked us the same questions. I know you quit the paper – have you started work as a detective or something?"

"Please trust me. I need to know Lara's state of mind that day."

"I suppose she was a bit jumpy." Carol picked a cigarette lighter off the table. "When I lit my cigarette with this after dinner she nearly shot out of her chair." She flicked the Zippo on and off, examining the flame. "I suppose it does flare up a bit. That's the only odd thing I can recall."

I felt a renewed sense of excitement. Lara had blisters round her mouth, like the girl in the film. Her attacker could well have heated a knife in the flame of a cigarette lighter. And if the killer had tried that particular trick *before* the night she died, she had every reason to be jumpy around flames. It was confirmation that Lara knew her killer.

"Anything else?"

Carol and Stan were silent.

"What time did Lara leave here?"

"Around nine."

"Did she say where she was going?"

"I think she was meeting someone," said Carol. "That's the impression I got because she said she was going into town, and she kept checking her watch from half-eight onwards."

I knew it wasn't Daniel. He'd been at home that evening, working on his A-level portfolio.

"Did she walk into town?"

"No. The town centre bus stops right outside here, so she took that. We waved to her from the window as she stepped on. That was the last time we saw her…" Carol's composure wavered.

"Jude, we've told the police all this," said Stan. "Why are

you asking us about it yet again?"

"For Daniel's sake," I said. "He needs to know as much as possible about Lara's last few hours. What do they call it… closure?" Carol looked at me oddly. I could tell I didn't fool her.

We sat in silence for a while, leafing through more albums. But half my mind was on what I had just heard. I was beginning to see the order of events unrolling, but there was a hole at the centre of it – the identity of the person Lara met in town. Was that person her killer? If so, how had they persuaded Lara to go back to her flat? From what I knew of her, she wouldn't have taken anyone there she wasn't a hundred percent sure of. An old trusted friend, perhaps. An image of Harrison's gangly frame superimposed itself over the pictures in the album.

That missing print could be significant after all. I needed to find it. I'd destroyed the negative, and I could hardly ring Harrison and ask for the file name.

At last Carol looked meaningfully at the clock.

"Would you like a lift home?" asked Stan.

"Thanks."

Stan drove an ancient but lovingly preserved Rover. He was notorious for driving at a snail's pace, cruising slow and proud in the middle lane of motorways, and turning left and right without indicating, leaving consternation and howling horns in his wake as he sailed blithely on.

I let him set off towards my part of town. But I had no intention of going home.

"Stan, can I ask you an enormous favour?"

"Well?"

"I need to get into Photographic. But I don't have a key card any more."

"You want me to let you in? Can't it wait till Monday?"

"I have to go there now. I promise I won't be long. I left my Nikon camera and I'm lost without it. And there's something else I need to do."

"It's important?"

"It could be very important." My concern was that Harrison had not only removed the print from the wall but had erased it from the system too. But he was a lazy sod, and now that I was no longer working for the Post he might not have bothered. So there was a slim chance the print was still on file.

"OK, I'll take you now. I was thinking of going in over the weekend anyway, to check on a faulty gauge. We've got a big commercial print run on Monday afternoon, and I don't want to be held up by a technical breakdown. What better time than a Saturday night when the presses aren't rolling?"

Twenty-five

The roads into the centre of town were quiet and we created no incidents, but the whole time I was silently urging Stan to get a move on. At last we reached the Ravenbridge Evening Post building, and drew slowly into the car park. Still wearing Stan's cardigan, I stood impatiently at the staff entrance, stamping my feet, while he fussed with the car's lights and switches and locks.

He finally swiped his card in the door and we took the lift. Stan got out at the first floor. "I'll go and take a look at that gauge. See you upstairs in about twenty minutes?"

"Sure."

The second floor was deserted. I hurried through the silent newsroom and into Photographic.

I took several deep breaths while I booted up one of the computers. With no reference number to help me, I had to track down the print I was looking for among several hundred in the system. Assuming it was still there.

First I called up the photo grid, but the images were so small, and my eyes so sore from exhaustion and smoke, that the patchwork of pictures began to stream together on the screen. I decided it would be quicker to do what reporters did – scroll through the list of file names. I had passed fifty or so without making any connection when I realised what a fruitless method this was. Harrison, after all, had filed a picture of Craig Gilmore, the estate agent, as Boringpic. No doubt he had chosen equally unhelpful names for the three prints I'd asked him to log.

I swivelled in my chair from side to side. To think like

Harrison I had to get inside that dim, fuddled, vacant place he called a brain. I tried scrolling down looking for Riverpic or Ravenpic, but without success. I got up and paced about. I thought back to the day when I'd shown him the prints. He hadn't thought much of the riverside picture, and when I'd explained the point of the image – how the For Sale sign made it look as though the river was on the market – he had replied with his usual incisive intelligence, "That's balls."

I rapidly typed in Ballspic, but the system rejected it.

What had I said to him then? *Cojones,* that was it, and I'd had to explain that *cojones* was Spanish for testicles, balls in other words. Understanding had dawned slowly on his face. In fact he'd referred to it again when we were in my basement darkroom. Excitedly I typed Cojopic and when a negative message flashed up I hit the computer with frustration.

Cojones, cojones…what else could it be? It looked as though Harrison had deleted the print, which meant he was deeply implicated in this mess. I thought about his vacant stare, the way he said '*Coho*-thingy?' Of course, he didn't know anything about Spanish pronunciation. He thought *cojones* was spelt *cohones.* Wasn't that what it sounded like?

I went back to the alphabetical list of picture files. Accidentpic, Alligatorpic, Browniepic, Bus-stoppic, Carbootpic, Cohopic. Yes! I called up the file, muttering through gritted teeth, "Please let it be, please."

And there it was.

"Yes!" I shouted.

With sweating hands I enlarged the picture on the scanner. I could see the swollen river, pouring over the stones of the weir, frozen by the lens into fine lacework, the For Sale sign leaning drunkenly over it. When had I taken it? There were leaves on the trees, but as the picture was black and white I couldn't tell if it was spring, summer or autumn. Over the New Year holiday I'd processed several rolls of film, some of them quite old. I had to face it, in my own darkroom, my filing system was no better than Harrison's. I tried to remember going for the walk that had resulted in this image. A blustery day… a lot of small branches snapped off trees… March or April… yes, my wool hat had blown off and I'd had to chase it down the street. A cold windy day in late April. Where did that get me? Abso-bloody-lutely nowhere.

I couldn't see anything odd about the picture. I examined it close-up in sections – the river, the weir, the buildings. Frantic now, I went back to the full image. I made it smaller, larger, brighter, dimmer. Still nothing screamed for attention.

I swivelled some more, paced about some more. Why would anyone have stolen this, and rearranged the other prints to hide the gap? There had to be something about this picture, I was certain of it.

I returned to the screen, increasing the enlargement on each part of the image. Then I saw it. With an almost audible click my brain made the final connection, the detail that my camera had objectively recorded and I had failed to see.

I sat back in the chair, winded with shock. Of course. Now I knew why the print had been stolen.

And who had stolen it.

It was nearly half an hour since Stan had left me. I tried ringing his control booth but there was no answer. Perhaps he was on his way. I remembered the other thing I had come here for, and retrieved my Nikon from the stationery cupboard. I switched off the computer and scanner, doused the lights and trekked back through the newsroom, taking the stairs down to the first floor. I walked up and down the corridor for a few minutes, wondering if I should ring Laverack straight away, or wait until I had more concrete evidence.

Still no Stan. I began to worry. What if he'd fallen on one of the narrow metal walkways above the machinery? It would be just like him to try and fix something on his own without calling out maintenance.

Hitching the camera strap on to my shoulder, I pushed through the double doors that led to the glass bridge, now only illuminated by streetlights and the occasional passing car. As usual it reeked of stale cigarette smoke. I could just see a tubby form leaning on the handrail, looking out through the window. Stan must be thinking about Lara. He'd lost track of time, remembering his beautiful niece.

"Stan," I called softly, but he didn't answer. I was right, he was going deaf. "Stan!" I said loudly. "Come on, I've got what I need. Let's go." Still no response. I began to walk towards him. Perhaps he was ill. My steps quickened.

"Stan, are you all right?"

Close up I could see a sheen of sweat on his forehead as if he'd been running. "Shake a leg, Stan. Time to get you to bed." I touched his arm gently so as not to startle him.

But it was me who jerked back in surprise.

He keeled over backwards, slowly at first, then accelerating as he neared the floor, landing with a soft thud, his arms spread wide. His eyes were bulging from their sockets. His tongue stuck out grotesquely. A length of black cable cut into his broad neck.

The contents of my stomach rose up into my throat in

an acid tide.

I cradled him in my arms, rocking back and forth, just as I'd held him several days ago, when I told him of Lara's death. Then, half-aware that it was a stupid and illogical thing to do, I took off Stan's cardigan, folded it and placed it like a pillow under his head.

I heard a noise. Faint but unmistakable. It was the stertorous breathing of someone gasping for air. I got up and stumbled forwards, my feet like lead weights. There it was again, the laboured breath, closer now. A sound I knew all too well.

The breathing stopped. I listened hard, turning my head to catch the faintest sound. Nothing. I moved forward into the gloom at the far end of the glass tunnel. The door was open.

I walked into darkness.

Twenty-six

My whole body ached from the tension of sitting still. I eased my legs forward from their cramped position. The huge roll of paper looked like a big white cushion, but it was as hard as steel against my spine.

I rubbed my aching back with two clenched fists. Time was playing its usual tricks. I had no idea how long I'd been hiding here. A few seconds? Ten minutes? An hour? It had given me time to work out some of the details that had eluded me before. I hoped it was only minutes. The painfully laboured breathing I'd heard on the glass bridge meant I didn't have long.

Without warning the voice boomed out, "I know you're there! I'm going to find you. Why don't you save me the trouble?"

Nothing to fear but…

Everything to fear. Fear flooded over me like a cold shower. I gulped in lungfuls of dusty air to control the shivering that gripped me from head to foot.

"I just want to talk, explain everything." The voice was softer now, more pleading. It was impossible to tell how far away it was. The press hall bounced the sound around its vast spaces before throwing it back, distorted and embellished with echo.

I rocked myself until the shivering stopped, clutching the camera to my chest like a baby. With the help of the Nikon the picture was complete, all the pixels had slotted into the right position. The image was still murky, the details lacked sharpness, but I knew enough. There was only one big unanswered question – why?

I heard a series of clicks. To my tired and confused brain it sounded like the underwater language transmitted by dolphins or whales. The shaking started again, but this time it came from outside myself, like the tremor of an earthquake the split second before it erupts.

With a great whirring groan the massive roll of paper I was leaning against began to move. I leapt up and away from it and clung to the wire cage. Behind me I knew what was happening. As if someone was pulling on a giant roll of toilet tissue, the paper was swooping towards the presses where it was snapped up, rolled, cut and folded into complete newspapers of pure blank whiteness.

The noise was deafening. Even with my hands clamped over my ears, my eardrums felt battered, swollen with the racket, ready to burst. Inching my way along the wire mesh, the relentless movement of the web at my back, I slowly eased myself into the narrow walkway between the machines.

Suddenly the giant toilet roll juddered and stopped.

The lights snapped on.

After such profound darkness the harsh fluorescent lighting dazzled me. I was paralysed. No doubt that was the intention.

But though my limbs refused to move, my mind raced on, flitting erratically. I was a fool to have run from my hiding place. Some hiding place. It must have been obvious all along. The presses had started rolling and I'd been flushed out like game.

I could see Stan's office thirty metres away, glowing with a faint green light. The machinery was controlled from that nerve centre.

"Such a waste of paper," came the booming echoey voice.

I stared at the stack of blank papers and silently agreed.

Nothing to fear but fear itself, I chanted in my head. It was only fear that froze my muscles and fractured my thinking. Why worry? After all, there was nothing to fear. Nothing. Apart from my violent death, of course.

"I won't hurt you, I promise."

Was I really supposed to believe that? Anger unlocked my limbs. I darted in a direction I hoped was away from the mocking voice.

Another click and the place was plunged into darkness. I began to run, trusting to blind instinct. My camera bumped against my hip in time to my pounding feet. It was so heavy and awkward I thought about ripping it from my shoulder and throwing it away. What use was it now? It had landed me in this shit, hadn't it?

"At last."

The voice wasn't booming now. It was quiet and calm. And very close.

I turned round.

At first I could see nothing in the darkness. Then I heard the shuffle of feet, the intake of a sharp excited breath.

"I'm here." It was no more than a whisper.

My eyes adjusted. The silhouette of a figure emerged from the gloom. I backed away. My bare heels made contact with a rough concrete wall. Nowhere to run. And anyway, I was tired of running.

"Jude. I'm so glad I've found you."

The familiar voice was a little hoarser than usual, slightly out of breath.

"Hello, Matt."

Twenty-seven

"It's good to see you, Jude."

"You can't see me, not properly. Why don't you switch the light on?"

"I'd rather not," said Matt. "I like the dark. I like talking in the dark, remember?"

I pushed aside the memory of Matt and me in a darkened room, sitting naked on the floor, limbs entwined. "Where's Daniel?"

"Ah… Daniel."

My heart lurched. "Is he dead?"

"He wasn't the last time I saw him."

"He's in the control room, isn't he?"

"Maybe." I heard the jingling sound of keys. "But it's locked."

"Take me to him." If we were both going to die I wanted us to be together.

"Not yet. I need to tell you everything, Jude. I know it won't go any further." He laughed drily. "Truth is a burden. It should be passed on. I pass it on to you, then I can live my days without the weight of it."

"All your talk of truth, but you lied to me, Matt."

"I never lied to you."

"We were in The Crooked Man after the police press conference. Remember? You told me you bought your house from Ravenbridge Properties. But that wasn't true. It was there all the time, on that missing print, almost too small to see with the naked eye – the name of your street – Raven Walk. The first house in the row, the one with the

275

bent over For Sale sign – that's yours, isn't it? And guess what's on that sign – Kerwin and Black. Why lie about it? Once I'd found the print and enlarged it, I knew exactly why. Because you knew Lara, and because you killed her."

His voice was so quiet now I had to strain to hear him. "She deserved it."

"No way."

"You don't know how strongly she came on to me."

"Lara was very mixed up. You weren't the only one she took up to Chapel House."

"I know that. But I thought I was special. And the way she insisted we keep it secret, that just made it even more exciting. We'd have a drink, then we went at it like —"

"Stop it!"

"Sorry, Jude. Sex with you was great, but let's face it, it was a matter of expediency. Lara just took my breath away."

Expediency? That got to me, but I shoved the hurt aside. "You shouldn't have left evidence behind."

"I didn't." He sounded stung by the accusation.

"But you did. I had time to think about it while I was hiding. It wasn't much, just a bottle top. Belgian beer, not Dutch like the police thought. The kind you were drinking in the pub that day. It may be just a little thing, but lots of small dots make the big picture. Never forget that."

"You sound so smug, Jude."

"Can't you take it, the fact that you've messed up?" I paused, trying to control my anger. I needed to get this truth-telling session over with fast, before it was too late. I knew what shock and trauma did to Daniel's breathing. I just prayed he had his inhaler with him.

"Then Lara wanted to end it," Matt went on. "I thought she'd found another bloke, but she denied it. I knew she was lying. I told her about the Bedouins —"

"Their test for liars – a hot knife on the tongue? I know all about that."

"You do?" He sounded genuinely surprised. "That's the trouble with you, Jude. You know far too much."

"You pestered her, hanging round her flat, leaving a video for her to watch – a warning about what she could expect. No doubt you liked to flick your lighter open and shut and threaten to heat up a knife. You really frightened her."

"Good! You see, when you love someone, and they let you down, the hurt is almost unbearable, and then, do you know what happens? It turns to hate. Very pure and clean, like acid."

I recalled what Norman Foley had said about passion turning cold. I had to grudgingly accept that the psychic detective had been proved right.

"And if you couldn't have her, nobody else would?"

Matt stepped closer. "You don't know everything, do you? It's not as simple as that. It could have been anyone."

"Anyone? What do you mean?"

"Don't you remember Tony Quinnell getting on our backs last autumn? Get the circulation up or else. Bigger and better stories, the more sensational the better."

There was a rush of bile in my stomach as I began to see what he was saying.

"If it bleeds, it leads." Matt imitated Tony's grainy London accent.

"You killed for *copy*?"

"You could say that. I needed a big story, Jude. I needed a murder. You've heard of self-help, haven't you? I decided to do it myself. But who would make the best headline – that fat woman who keeps taking my parking space on Raven Walk? One of the vagrants who hang around the town centre, who nobody will miss? Or a beautiful young girl, who by the way had messed with my mind and deserved everything she got?"

"You're sick."

"I'm ambitious, Jude, that's all. Do you think I'm going to spend my life in Ravenbridge? When I've milked this story dry I'll quietly hand in my resignation, and with the glowing references I'll get from Tony, I'll move on. I fancy TV. It'll make a change from print journalism. Do you think I'll look good in a khaki shirt, reporting from the latest war zone?"

"I've heard enough. Take me to Daniel. Let's get this over with." I was shaking with fury.

"I haven't finished. Don't you want to know how I did it?"

"No."

"I think you're lying. After all the effort you've put in, trying to track me down – of course you want to know."

The bastard was right, but I wasn't going to admit it. "I feel sure you're going to tell me anyway."

His dark shape leaned back against one of the iron legs of the high conveyor belt. "I phoned Lara last Saturday and asked if we could meet one last time. I'd already messed with the starter on the Polo while she was at work. All that reporting on car crime came in handy – I knew how to slide underneath, reach up into the wheel arch and cut the wire from the battery. But it nearly all went wrong right there – she couldn't see me that night, or on the Sunday because it was New Year's Eve. So we made it Monday night. Luckily for me, the garage was closed for two days so her car still wasn't fixed. I offered to drive her up to Chapel House, but she refused. She wanted to meet in a public place."

"I told you she was frightened of you."

He ignored me, speaking in a rhythmic monotone, as if he'd gone over these events in his mind many times. "We agreed to meet in a pub in town at half nine. Without her car, I knew she'd come by bus, so I waited near the bus station. It wasn't difficult to persuade her into my car – it was a bitterly cold night. But instead of going to the pub I drove to her flat. She wasn't very pleased, all that stuff about it being her own private space. But I spun her some yarn about not feeling well and needing an aspirin. Once we got inside, I insisted that we watch the video. I pulled her into the kitchen and took one of her own knives – nice touch, that – and heated it in the flame from my cigarette lighter. All I wanted was for her to tell me the name of her new boyfriend before I killed her. But she fought like a cat."

I cheered mentally. Lara had fought for her life and tried to protect Daniel. My respect for her soared.

"She ended up with blisters all round her mouth, and still she wouldn't tell me the name. All she would say was that yes, there was someone else, and he was special and he'd given her a bracelet." Matt's voice became more animated. "That made it easier, somehow. I used her own scarf to strangle her. I even thought about making love to her."

"Love?"

"But it wasn't that sort of excitement. And I had plenty to do once she was dead. My plan was to carve something to do with the occult on her body – newspapers like that sort of thing. I got the idea for the pentagram from that necklace Harrison always wears. And I wanted blood, plenty of blood…"

If it bleeds, it leads. I silently cursed Tony Quinnell.

"Only I forgot that the body doesn't bleed much after death. I was seriously annoyed about that. Should I cut my own finger and spill it over her T-shirt? No good because of DNA testing. Then I had a great idea. Where can you find blood, Jude?"

"The hospital?"

"Clever girl. It was after midnight by then. But the good thing about hospitals is that they never close. I grabbed a wheelchair from the entrance and pushed that about till I found the right department. The few people around just assumed I was a porter."

Like they'd seen me as a cleaner at the police station. Appearances were all, it seemed. But appearances could deceive.

"Once I'd stolen one of those pouches of blood, I went back to Lara's flat. A bit of blood spilled on the floor when I was cutting the corner of the plastic. But I got most of it on Lara's chest." He snorted. "Just think about it, Jude. The police are looking for some poor innocent sap whose only crime was to donate a pint of blood!"

I silently screamed at him to get on with it.

"With my trip to the hospital I was running late. And I still had to take her body to the park."

"Why? Why did you have to leave her there, like some discarded piece of rubbish?"

"Which she was!" Matt was breathing hard. "But that wasn't the reason. Don't you see why? If I'd left her in the flat it could have been ages before she was found. It was vital her body was discovered in the early morning, in time for the staff meeting."

"Not to mention the second edition of the Post?"

"Exactly. We had no decent front-page story – we never do just after New Year. I knew Tony would love this one. I wrapped her in a couple of bin liners, and as soon as the park gates opened at six-thirty, I drove over there. It was still dark and it was so cold I was pretty sure no one would be around. She didn't weigh much, but she was already stiff, which made her damn difficult to carry."

He made it sound as if Lara had deliberately inconvenienced him.

"I removed the bin liners and left her on the bench, jacket open, plenty of blood. Then I had to go back to the flat and clean up the spillage, plus any evidence of my fingerprints. It all took time, more time than I expected. Around half past eight I rang Charmaine, told her I was up at the hospital, which was almost true."

"There was no blood-contamination scare, was there?"

"OK. I admit fibbing is sometimes necessary. Satisfied? I got to work around the time some jogger found the body and rang the police. Fred rang Tony and the rest is history. It all worked like a well-made watch. But there was something I hadn't planned for."

"What?" I asked impatiently.

"You and I went to the park to cover the story, and only then did I find out what Lara refused to tell me."

"The name of her boyfriend?"

"And the fact he was your son. That was quite a shock."

"It didn't stop you trying to implicate him, did it?"

"No, Jude," he said coldly. "It didn't."

"You kept Lara's bracelet and planted it on Daniel. How?"

"When I heard about his asthma attack I went to the hospital, remember? Matt Dryden, the good guy, visiting the sick. Daniel was asleep, you were having a tetanus injection. So I just slipped the bracelet into the pocket of the jeans hanging up in the cupboard."

"If the police had found it they'd have arrested him."

"It would have been a sort of sweet justice, don't you

think?"

My blood boiled at Matt's notion of justice.

"Do you know what the most exciting feeling in the world is, Jude?"

I made a huge effort to keep my voice level. "Killing someone?"

"No. The best bit is afterwards. The police, the SOCO team, the doctor, the ambulance, the press conference, the sheer electricity in the newsroom, the buzz of excitement and fear in the whole town, and when the story's as big as this one, the whole country."

He fell silent, and I knew he was revelling in the mayhem that he had caused.

"Then you started interfering," he said harshly. "I wasn't too worried when you were just floundering about, but soon I could feel how close you were, like someone breathing down my neck. You only had to put all the pieces together —"

"And one of those pieces was the river print. So you stole it?"

"It showed my house for sale last spring by Kerwin and Black. Lara sold me the house, but I knew the police were only checking her work records for the last six months, so I reckoned I was in the clear there. That picture was the only thing that connected me to Lara."

"I might not have realised it was gone if I hadn't resigned and decided to take all my personal stuff home. Your luck ran out."

"I don't know about that. Having sex with you in a lift was a stroke of luck. An unexpected bonus of keeping you close."

I wanted to hit him but kept my hands by my sides. "Keeping me close? You pushed me in the river! You wanted me to die!"

"You just wouldn't give up, Jude."

"Why did you have to kill Hayley's ferret?"

"If I couldn't get rid of you I thought I could frighten you off. Then I had an even better idea. When Laverack turned up I knew luck was back on my side. It wasn't difficult to insinuate to him that you hated Lara. What I don't understand is, why did they let you go?"

"They didn't."

"I couldn't believe it when you turned up just after I'd set fire to my house."

"Wasn't that a pretty drastic way of deflecting suspicion?"

"I'm insured. And I love fire engines. It was all very exciting. Not least seeing you trying to rescue me."

"You were watching?"

"The whole time. I saw you choking your guts up. Miss Indestructible sat on the kerb and wept her heart out for me. I was touched."

"Then you followed me?"

"It was easy. When you called at that bungalow and Stan opened the door, I guessed you wanted his key card to get back into this building. And why else, but to find that bloody photo? So I drove straight here to beat you to it. I've been searching for it in the system so I could erase it for good. I'd have found it if Harrison didn't have spaghetti for brains."

He laughed, but there was no trace of amusement in the harsh sound. "Then I heard a car. I saw you and Stan get out. What took you so long, by the way?" Without waiting for an answer Matt carried on. "I realised you might find the print and make the connection, but I was going to make sure you never got the chance to tell anyone."

"This is between you and me, Matt. Why kill Stan?"

"I knew you were going to die, Jude, and I couldn't risk Stan seeing me. When I stepped out of the shadows on to the glass bridge he looked like he'd seen a ghost. Did you tell him I'd perished in the fire? He started yelling for you. He could move fast for a big man."

"You disgust me."

"I should care? It's odd – killing Stan was easy, much easier than Lara. Which is why I'm hoping dealing with you will be a picnic, possibly even a pleasure. I'm going to make it look like suicide. A dive from one of those walkways up there, I think. Just like Adam Keele and his high-wire act without a safety net. I'll even write your suicide note. I can see the headlines now: *I Killed My Son's Girlfriend – Mother's Shocking Message from the Grave.*"

"And Daniel?"

"Don't worry about Daniel."

"I've told the police."

"What?"

"I rang them. As soon as I realised the significance of the print. They'll be on their way soon."

"You're lying."

"I gave them your name. If anything happens to me… or Daniel…"

"You liar!"

"They'll be here any minute now. It's Saturday night – they must be snowed under with fights and vandalism, but they won't be long."

Matt stepped sharply up to me, blocking my way. I held my breath, wondering if he could hear the thudding of the blood in my veins.

"If you are telling the truth, I'd better get on with it."

Twenty-eight

He gripped me by the arm. He was young and strong and though I struggled I felt myself weakening. Lara had experienced this too, this sense of fear and powerlessness. But she had fought back. And she was smaller and lighter than me.

With a surge of fury I thrust my arms upwards. Matt was taken by surprise and almost lost his hold on me. I head-butted him in the chest. He expelled air like a punctured tyre. But his grip tightened. I twisted furiously, stamping on his shoeless feet, punching him with my free arm. As he dragged me along I resisted so that my arm was wrenched nearly out of its socket. I screamed with pain. I lowered my head again, aiming for his solar plexus this time. He must have guessed my plan because he hollowed his torso to avoid the blow. This brought his head down lower, and as I rose up from my abortive strike, the back of my head connected with his nose with a juddering crunch. It was his turn to scream. For a split second his hold on me loosened.

I darted away. I knew it was my last chance. If he caught me now that would be the end of it. They'd find my body and the note. The police would wrap up the case and stamp Closed on it. I couldn't let that happen, not only for my sake and Daniel's but for Lara and Adam and Stan. They deserved one last mark of respect – justice.

I kept running, staggering blindly in the dark, lurching under the elevated conveyor belt, trying to reach the control room. I heard heavy breathing up ahead. Matt must have dodged around the machines in front of me, cutting off my escape route. He'd be ready for me this time. If I tried to rush past, arms would grab me like tentacles. I could kick and scream for all I was worth. Who would hear me?

I pulled the Nikon forward, which even in the dark I knew better than my own face. I reached into the pocket on the strap, took out the attachment and slotted it on to the shoe on the left-hand side of the camera. I pointed it in the direction of the approaching figure and pressed.

The single flash was enough. Matt's hands flew up to shield his eyes. I bent low and barged forward, crashing into his knees like a front-row forward. I heard his head thud against the concrete floor. He moaned loudly. I stumbled over the flying legs and fell headlong, scrambled to my feet and began to zigzag between the machines.

Once again I heard his footsteps, more shambling now, running a roughly parallel course to mine. He stepped out ahead of me. Just beyond him I could see the glow of Stan's control room. I knew the door was locked and Matt had the key. To my right was the paper store. I veered into it. The towers of paper reared up in front of me like mountain peaks.

Behind me came the reek of fresh salty sweat and the sound of laboured breathing. Light flooded the room, picking me out like a target. I was trapped.

Only one way to go.

I ran towards the pillar nearest the back wall and dragged myself on to the first giant toilet roll. They weren't stacked perfectly, there were tiny footholds between each one. It meant taking huge steps, clinging on like a fly as my bare feet reached for each gap, then hauling myself upwards. Trees, cricket pavilions, now paper stacks. What next, Everest? My hysterical giggle nearly dislodged me.

I was halfway up the tower when I heard Matt's panting breath behind me. I glanced down. He was climbing awkwardly but frighteningly fast. There was only the depth of one web of paper between us now. I looked up. There was an open ventilation window in the wall between the paper store and the press hall, and I gauged it was just above the control room.

Something grabbed at my foot. I kicked out as viciously as I could. Matt screamed. I saw him take a flying leap backwards, his arms circling like propeller blades. He plummeted down on to the hard floor. He lay very still.

Gasping for breath, I struggled up the last few rolls of paper. By stretching up I could just reach the vent. I hauled myself through it, and lay balanced on my stomach on the frame, like a gymnast on a bar. I looked down. I was right. The glass roof of Stan's office was directly below me.

Holding the side of the vent to keep my balance I swung my legs over so that I was now sitting on the narrow frame. Taking a gasp of air I let my body hurtle downwards, feet first. A high-wire dive without a safety net. I smashed through the glass, praying I wouldn't land on Daniel. As I hit the floor I heard the sound of cracking bones and knew from the searing agony in my ribs and ankle that they were mine, not his.

The booth was empty. Daniel wasn't here. Bewildered, I started crawling round the floor looking for him, cutting my hands and knees on the broken glass.

I heard a key scrape in the lock. It swung open. Like me, Matt was crawling on all fours, his bloodshot eyes dark and murderous.

"What have you done with Daniel?"

A strange noise came from Matt's mouth, the same stertorous breathing I'd heard on the glass bridge. It ended in a hideous throaty chuckle.

"Pretty good imitation, eh? Made you come into the press hall, didn't it?"

"He was never here?" I didn't know whether to cry at being so easily duped, or cheer to the rafters because Daniel was safe.

"More's the pity. I'd have dealt with him too. Now that would have been fun. Still, soon he's going to find out that his mother murdered his girlfriend and then killed herself. He'll have to live with that for the rest of his life. I reckon that's punishment enough for taking Lara from me."

He began to crawl towards me.

Despite the knives of pain in my legs I dragged myself up. I pulled the camera strap over my head and held the huge heavy Nikon in both hands.

"I hate to do this to an old friend, but…" I smashed the camera down on his skull. "I meant the camera of course, not you."

Nothing to fear. Nothing.

Twenty-nine

"I'm going to miss you."

"I'll bring my washing home every now and then, promise," said Daniel.

"Can't wait."

He zipped up his holdall and heaved it from the bed on to the floor. He'd grown his hair over the summer and taken to wearing nothing but black. He looked every inch the art student. I could see from the excitement on his face that he was looking forward to college. Many months ago he hadn't believed me when I told him time healed almost anything. I knew he'd never forget Lara, any more than I would, but we didn't talk about her as much as we used to.

As for me, time had healed my lacerations and broken ankle and cracked ribs, but that night in the printworks still felt like yesterday. While my bones were mending it had been agony to laugh, and in just the same way, it hurt too much to think about the things I went through. That's why I tried very hard not to. And for about five or ten minutes a day, I succeeded.

I shivered. It was September. I'd soon have to put the heating on in this draughty old house and face another winter. When the media circus finally left town, and left me alone, I'd toyed with the idea of selling the place, maybe moving to the countryside. But I'd decided I loved this crumbling pile, or to be more exact, I loved being alive to see and touch all the old familiar things I thought I might never see or touch again.

"What are you going to do, Mum?"

"There are various options."

"Such as?"

"Let's see. I could open a cookery school…"

"Yeah, right. Lesson One: How to Open a Tin."

"And Lesson Two: Finding Your Way Round a Microwave."

"Not forgetting Lesson Three: The Best Way to Order Takeaway Pizza."

We laughed. We hadn't done that for a long time.

"Seriously, Mum. When I'm gone, you can't just hang around doing nothing."

"I don't intend to. Now everything's quietened down, I'll… I'll climb Kilimanjaro." No, not that. It reminded me of tall pillars of white paper. "Or I could open a shop. A really good photographic suppliers, with gallery space to display the best local photographers."

"Including you?"

"Why not? I'm pretty good." I took pictures that helped nail a killer, I nearly added. Don't go there, I told myself sternly.

"Hey, that's not a bad idea actually. Wait, I've got an idea for the name of your shop… Jude the Obscura."

More laughter. This was what I was going to miss more than anything.

I looked at the clock on Daniel's bedside table. "You ready?"

"Why not?"

Suddenly he looked nervous, aware he was going to be a new boy all over again. I held him by the shoulders.

"You'll be fine."

"What about you?"

"I'll be fine too." I thrust my hands into my jeans pockets. My fingers touched the letter, the one I'd received that morning. I caught my breath. The pain was always there, waiting on the threshold.

"Are you all right, Mum, really?"

"I was just thinking about Matt. He wasn't much older than you."

"He seemed such a nice guy," Daniel said bitterly.

"I thought so too."

"Do you remember when he came to see me in hospital? He was funny, he told me jokes and cheered me up. I thought he was really kind."

"He was kind to me too."

"Apart from trying to kill you."

"Apart from that, yes."

"It was all an act, wasn't it? Underneath he was completely ruthless."

"Psychopaths usually are. He sorted out what he wanted and the quickest route to getting it. He'd found being charming was an extremely efficient means to an end. The feelings of other people didn't come into it."

I stared out of the window into the back garden. The gap in the hedge had been filled in by the new owners, Howard and Tim, who worked in local government and bred West Highland terriers. Rob and Denise had got divorced and gone their separate ways, Hayley sharing her time between her parents. I hardly ever saw them these days, though I knew I would never get out of my mind the distraught look on Hayley's face when she realised her pet ferret was dead. Matt had no idea what he'd done to an innocent seven-year-old girl.

Daniel joined me at the window and hugged me awkwardly, all arms and elbows. "Don't think about it any more, Mum. It's over now."

I forced a smile. "You're right."

But he was wrong. I thought about little else and I didn't

know when it was going to stop.

"OK. Bring your bags down to the car. We'd better get a move on. It's going to be a long drive."

It was nearly midnight when I got back. Before I went to bed I checked my e-mails. I thought Daniel might have sent me a message to say he'd already made a dozen friends and got drunk in the union bar. He hadn't.

But there was an e-mail from Tony Quinnell, asking me to come into the office tomorrow. He wanted to have a chat.

I switched off the computer, wondering what that was all about.

I was still wondering the next day as I sat in his office, facing him across the wide wooden desk. He looked less wolfish and hollow-chested. I'd heard the rumour that his partner was pregnant, and the prospective new father was trying to give up smoking and get fit. But the nicotine stains on his fingers were still there, a souvenir of the past, inerasable.

A graph on a chart behind him showed how sales of the Ravenbridge Evening Post had gone through the roof. Murder was good for business, and how efficient to have your own in-house killer.

I'd done everything the police asked me to do, but when it was all over I'd refused all offers to do interviews, especially the ones involving money. Of course that didn't stop me being written about and discussed. I was praised for my dogged persistence and lack of concern for my own personal safety, and castigated for exactly the same things. Foolhardy was the word used most often, and the public were urged not to follow my example. I still occasionally got letters from people who wanted me to sell my story. Tony had practically gone down on bended knee, but I was adamant. He hadn't spoken to me since.

Until now.

"So, Jude, I expect you're wondering why I've asked you to meet with me today?"

"To thank me for helping boost circulation?"

"Not exactly." He smirked. "Though I have to admit, it's been a very good year so far, and you did make quite a sensational contribution to that." He leaned forward. "I know the brouhaha has died down, but it's still not too late if you want us to do a feature on your terrible experience?"

"No way."

He snorted. "You're one tough cookie, Jude."

Tough cookie? More B-movie stuff. That made me think about *Scorching Desert.* I mentally pressed *Eject* to rid myself of that memory.

"Right. I'll come straight to the point. It's Harrison."

I'd been wrong about Harrison. I felt guilty about that. The notion of guilt made me think of Carol Roguski, Stan's widow. Another casualty. One I totally blamed myself for.

"What's he done now?"

"He's left us in the lurch, Jude. Buggered off to India. He just went without saying a word. Young people today, what can you do with them?"

"So?"

"It's left us seriously short-handed. I'm offering you your job back."

I was stunned. I hadn't seriously thought about getting back into press photography. I'd been so busy recovering from my injuries, dealing with Lara's death and its aftermath, supporting Daniel through his A-levels, and gathering the pieces of my fractured life back together, I hadn't thought seriously about anything. No, that wasn't true. There was one thing I thought about constantly, and it wasn't the Ravenbridge Evening Post.

"You want me to return as Chief Photographer?"

"Buzz is doing a pretty good job in charge." Tony picked up a pen. He held it with the tips of his fingers, rolling it round and round. "How would you feel about a job share?"

"Have you asked Buzz?"

"No, but I'm pretty sure he'll be cool about it. We plan to expand the department again, now that sales are up." He grinned. "You know the old saying, a good picture is worth a thousand words." He looked at me expectantly.

I had to smile. I still wasn't sure whether I loved or loathed journalists. But I just didn't see any way a civilised society could manage without them. I'd been reading about journalists in Russia, murdered for uncovering organised crime and corruption. I was full of admiration for the brave people who took their place to carry on the fight. Free speech was a right that was dangerous to take for granted, and I never would.

Who was I trying to impress? Damn it, I missed the energy of a newspaper office. I missed having something to get up for in the mornings. I missed having places to go, things to do, people to meet. But I wanted to see Tony sweat.

"I'm not sure."

"We need someone really good like you. Harrison was hopeless. He did improve a bit, but you could never rely on him, do you know what I mean?"

"I could always rely on him." To be lazy, inefficient and puerile, thank god.

"He was a useless wanker. I'm glad he's sitting under a bloody banyan tree contemplating his navel. It's the best place for him. Come on, Jude. What do you say?"

"I don't think I can do it, Tony. The pay's terrible. I've got a son at college now. How am I supposed to keep him in beer money on what I earn here?"

He slapped the table. "All right. I'll get the board to give you a pay rise."

I thought about that, or pretended to. Eventually I raised my eyes to Tony's worried face.

"I'll do it."

He actually smiled. "When can you start? Tomorrow?"

"Tomorrow? That's Friday."

"So? There's a big backlog —"

"No, I can't do tomorrow. Previous engagement."

"Monday, then."

I picked up my bag and stood up. "See you next week."

"Welcome back, Jude."

Thirty

Next morning I woke early. I showered and dressed, e-mailed Daniel and drank two cups of instant coffee. I was too tense to eat anything. I was on the road by seven o'clock.

A light autumnal mist made visibility tricky. On the motorway there were heavy streams of traffic both ways, even at this hour. But I made good time. Every now and then I glanced at the letter on the passenger seat, complete with directions and hand-drawn map.

When I left the motorway I drove through a long featureless stretch of land until I saw the redbrick building emerge from the mist.

I left the Triumph in the visitors' car park and joined the trickle of people beginning to queue up outside the gates. They were mostly women, many of them with young children. From a van nearby came the smell of hotdogs and fried onions. I was hungry but my stomach clenched shut. In any case, I didn't want to lose my place in line.

When the gates finally opened we streamed through into a courtyard surrounded by tall cell blocks with small barred windows and razor-wire fencing. Warders with dogs patrolled the perimeter. We were marched through a mesh tunnel into the reception area.

I wondered whether to turn round now, get the hell out and never come back. But the surging bodies around me kept me moving forward. Then we came to an abrupt stop. One at a time we were shown into cubicles where we were bodysearched. I was even asked to open my mouth. The prison warder that dealt with me was quite young, blonde and friendly. But she was thorough. She riffled in my bag and pulled out all the cigarette packets. She shook the fags out of every one of them, looking for concealed drugs.

I'd brought plenty of chocolate too. In his letter Matt had told me that fags and sweets were valuable currency in here. He used a lot himself, the rest could be traded for small luxuries. The warder examined every chocolate bar and pack of sweets. I held my breath as she rattled the small box of chocolate raisins. Matt's favourites. She prised open the top flap and spread the contents on a tray. Satisfied, she sealed it shut again with sellotape and put it back in the plastic carrier with the rest. She hadn't noticed where I'd carefully opened and resealed the bottom flap.

After a long wait in a holding area we were ushered into a room full of tables and chairs. The women and kids swarmed in, each family grabbing a table and colonising it. I waited until the rush had died down before moving to a small table with just two chairs. The furniture was fixed to the floor. The table had the same scarred defeated look of the one at the police station. I sat there, feeling small and bleak, not knowing how I would react when I saw him.

The prisoners entered the visiting room in ones and twos. They wore navy trousers and blue shirts with bright green tabards on top. The noise level rose gradually, the shouts, laughter and tears blending together in a subdued human roar.

He isn't coming, I thought. He's changed his mind. He doesn't want to see me after all, despite his pleading letter. I got up to leave and that's when I saw him standing by the door, blinking in the brightly lit room. He looked pale. Even from this distance I could see the livid scar on his forehead. I had no regrets about bringing the Nikon down on his head, except for the damage to the camera. It had never been the same since, and I deeply regretted that. Another casualty.

He walked slowly towards me.

I knew I ought to spit on him, in full view of everyone, then storm out. But my feet were rooted to the vinyl floor, my throat parched of spittle. I put my hands in my pockets so I didn't have to touch him.

"Jude. Thanks for coming. Shall we sit down, or do you want to do it standing up?" His blue eyes were mischievous, but I knew the friendly sparkle was false. I sat down warily.

"How are you?" I asked.

"Pretty good. It's not that bad in here. And I'll be out in around… twenty years?"

"I thought the judge said *life* should mean life."

"Things change," he said blandly. "I'm working on it."

I believed him. He would spend those years charming everyone he met, convincing them that he killed Lara from pure uncontrolled sexual jealousy. That's how it was portrayed at the trial. I knew his motive to be colder and far more dangerous. There was nothing uncontrolled about Matt.

"Have you brought me anything?" he asked eagerly, and his eyes lit up like a kid at Christmas as I unpacked the cigarettes and sweets and a few well-used paperbacks I'd got at a charity shop.

He lined everything up until it filled the small table.

"Brilliant. Thanks, Jude."

He reached out to take my hand. Steeling myself, I let him hold it for a few seconds, feeling utter revulsion at his touch. He let go and I pulled my arm back quickly, knocking over the box of chocolate raisins. I bent down and picked it up from the floor. I shook it gently, making sure the neither flap had come open. I wondered which one was the chocolate-covered peanut I had inserted last night.

I held the box for a moment. It wasn't too late. I didn't have to do this. After all, justice had been done and seen to be done. But some primitive instinct told me it wasn't enough. That was public justice, but this thing between me and Matt, it was personal.

"Come on, hand it over," said Matt. "They're my favourites."

I placed the box in his palm. "Eat them when I'm gone and think of me."

His eyes narrowed as he contemplated me. "No," he said at last. "I want them now."

He tore the tape off the box and spilled a pile of sweets into his hand. He shoved them in his mouth in one gulp and chewed noisily.

"They're good. Want some?"

"No thanks. I brought them for you. Go on, you might as well finish them."

He tipped the rest into his mouth, staring at me all the time.

He suspects, I thought. He's eating them even though he's not absolutely sure they're OK. He reckons the odds are on his side. He's so arrogant he doesn't believe I'd ever do him any real harm. He thinks he's still in control.

Cups of tea in plastic beakers were brought round. Matt drank his greedily. I left mine untouched. It wasn't long before he began to cough. His eyes were watering as if he was crying. He pulled at his collar. His face grew red. He could hardly breathe. I saw the look of hurt and surprise on his face.

I watched him fighting for his life, resisting the urge to get help. I told myself this was for Lara and Stan and Adam

Keele. And for me and Daniel, too. He would have killed us without a moment's regret.

A woman at the next table leaned across. "Is he all right?" Her toddler was staring at Matt with wide-eyed horrified fascination.

I could let him die. It was up to me. I had the power now. The coughing fit grew worse. He was gasping, choking, no longer in control. I waited until he collapsed forward on to the table, jerking like a fish on a hook.

I scraped my chair back. "Can someone help?" I called out. A warder came running, then another. They laid Matt on the floor, where he writhed and twitched as he gasped for air.

"It's an allergic reaction – there must have been a trace of nuts in the sweets."

"It's OK, love. It's what they call anaphylactic shock. We know how to deal with it. He'll be fine, don't you worry."

As they stretchered him away, Matt opened his eyes. A hand fluttered in my direction. A farewell? A truce? An acknowledgement that I'd given him a fright?

Or a warning?

After all, he'd be out in twenty years.

But he didn't scare me any more. "Shall I come again?" I called after him. "I can bring more sweets. I know how much you love them."

He turned his face away from me and the door closed with a clang.

End

Printed in Great Britain
by Amazon

C000054189

A CAPFUL OF COURAGE

BOOK TWO OF THE NIGHTINGALE FAMILY SERIES

FENELLA J MILLER

Boldwood

First published in 2016 as *Count Your Blessings*. This edition first published in Great Britain in 2024 by Boldwood Books Ltd.

Copyright © Fenella J. Miller, 2016

Cover Design by Colin Thomas

Cover Photography: Colin Thomas

A CIP catalogue record for this book is available from the British Library.

Paperback ISBN 978-1-83518-693-0

Large Print ISBN 978-1-83518-692-3

Hardback ISBN 978-1-83518-691-6

Ebook ISBN 978-1-83518-694-7

Kindle ISBN 978-1-83518-695-4

Audio CD ISBN 978-1-83518-686-2

MP3 CD ISBN 978-1-83518-687-9

Digital audio download ISBN 978-1-83518-689-3

Boldwood Books Ltd

23 Bowerdean Street

London SW6 3TN
www.boldwoodbooks.com

NOTE FROM THE AUTHOR

A Capful of Courage takes place between October 1843 and August 1844. An account of the opening of the Thames Tunnel is included in this story. Keen history buffs may know that this happened on 25 March 1843, but will hopefully forgive me for moving the date to provide a dramatic backdrop for Alfie's final adventures in London.

1

COLCHESTER, OCTOBER 1843

With the children tumbling around her and an infant to cradle, Sarah was right at home. Her bedroom had no fireplace but there was a thick rag rug across the boards, which kept out the draughts that came up through the gaps. There were faded curtains pulled across the window, and they helped to keep the room warm as well. What she wanted was her patchwork quilt and other bits and pieces from her friend Betty at Grey Friars House. Should she go round and collect them after she'd got the money from the bank? It would make the place seem more like home.

Home? She mustn't think like that. She couldn't stay in Colchester – she'd never get a decent job without references. She had almost ten pounds saved, but it wouldn't last forever if she wasn't working. She didn't want to dip into her nest egg too much – that was for her future. Some of it must be used to find herself decent lodgings whilst she looked for a suitable position. Much better to leave her belongings where they were, let Betty keep them whilst she got on with writing her own references.

She needed to plan her trip to London. If she took a coach

she wouldn't have to walk three miles to the station, but the train only took a couple of hours, not all day to reach the city. Time enough to worry about that when she was ready to leave.

The house slowly quietened. The boys in the attic above her eventually stopped chattering. The church clock striking the hour kept her company during the long, sleepless night. When she left Colchester, as she must, she might never see Alfie again. He'd come back to look for her one day and she'd be gone. Once she was established in a decent position in London it might not be possible to return. She'd be lucky if she got a whole day off a quarter, and that was barely enough time to get to Colchester even on a train, let alone back again.

What was her brother doing at the moment? Was he happy? She prayed he'd had better luck than her, was prospering wherever he was. She rarely thought of her mother and stepfather now. They'd not considered her, so it was best she forgot them. She'd been around a few times to the churchyard and tidied up little Tommy's grave, put a few flowers in a pot under the simple wooden cross. She wished she could afford to get the stonemason to make him a headstone, but like other poor folk he'd have to make do with what was there.

Mrs Billings had told her she could eat breakfast with the family, or make her own with whatever was in the larder. The bank wouldn't let her withdraw her funds until the end of next week. That meant she had several extra days to spend in these unaccustomed surroundings. It wouldn't do to get settled. She must be off in a week or two.

She was determined to say goodbye to Betty before she left, but her friend didn't have an afternoon off until the end of November, which was nearly a month away. Should she stay until then? She had sufficient money in the bank to pay for her board and lodgings. Keeping herself busy helping out in the

house would make time fly by. Mrs Billings didn't need the room back until January; it was just possible Alfie would reappear before she left.

Downstairs it was cold and dark, the range almost out, the house quiet, apart from the occasional wail from baby Beth Billings. She glanced at the clock in pride of place on the mantelshelf. It was not quite seven o'clock. Good grief! At Grey Friars House she'd have been at work an hour by now. Deciding to get things going, have breakfast ready and the table laid by the time Mrs Billings came down, Sarah set about finding what she needed.

She was used to being up at six, couldn't understand why people would want to waste the best part of the day lying in bed. Still, Mrs Billings didn't look too good. This pregnancy was clearly taking its toll on her. Well, after eight children, it was hardly surprising.

Her eyes filled. The mistress at Grey Friars would be having her sixth child in December, but she'd never see the baby, nor the children she'd taken care of for two years. Rich folk thought more about their servants being honest than the feelings of their children.

At last, the range was hot. It was time to put the kettle on and start making the porridge. She'd make some bread, and, if she could find the ingredients, do a batch of buns as well. The dough was proving on the back of the range, the porridge simmering on a hot plate, the table laid and the room swept before the clatter of small feet told her the boys were coming down for breakfast.

* * *

So the pattern of her days was established. Each morning it fell to her to get up first, do all the jobs Mrs Billings ought to be doing. It wasn't her place to do this, but she liked to be occupied and her landlady was so grateful she hadn't the heart to complain. Idleness didn't suit her; action took her mind away from the emptiness of her life. There was no point sending a note to Betty to ask her to meet up – her friend couldn't read, and there was no one else she could ask to pass on the message. It was too soon to ask the housekeeper for a favour.

No, that wasn't quite true – the gardener's boy had a soft spot for her. She was sure if she sneaked round the back and found him he'd get a message to Betty for her. She'd slip up there this afternoon, when Beth was taking her nap. Maybe the boys would like to come? They could run round the castle bailey if the gate was open.

'I'm going out to take a message to my friend, Ada. Is there anything you'd like me to get you whilst I'm out?'

'I could do with a few vegetables and perhaps some mutton for a stew. It's very good of you, Sarah, but it ain't right you doing all this, not when I should be doing it for you. I'll not charge you more than a shilling a week in future, just enough to pay for your food.'

'That would be a great help. I need to save as much as I can. I know I have to leave here when Mr Billings and your boys come back, but I want to have enough to take me to London when I do go.'

She wasn't planning to stay that long. Whatever had prompted her to say so?

'That'll be grand, Sarah love. The baby is due the beginning of January. I would be happier having someone else in the house around that time. The ship's not due until after that, so if you could stay with me, I would be ever so grateful.'

Sarah nodded. 'That's settled then. I'll pay you a shilling a week for my food, so you won't be out of pocket and I'll help out wherever I can. But I need some time for myself. I'm helping out, not working for you.'

'I know that, love – you're not my drudge. I hope you're my friend. I think of you like a daughter already. My twins must be the same age as you. They'd do the same if they was here.'

Taking the boys with her, wrapped up against the biting wind like woolly parcels, she set off for Queen Street, a large basket on her arm.

'I shall shop on the way back, Charlie. I don't want to lug things around with me until I have to.'

'I'll carry the basket when it's full, Sarah. Me ma says I must. I'm the man of the house whilst Pa and me big brothers are away.'

He reminded her of Alfie at that age. Her brother would be a man now – two years was a long time when you were still growing. Look at her, she'd turned from a girl to a woman. She noticed men turning to look as she walked past. That hadn't happened last year. And that Bert Sainty – their old neighbour in Colchester – he'd be eager to fumble under her clothes given half a chance.

After what happened to Jane, she'd steer clear of entanglements, keep her knees together like Betty had said. She smiled. Well, if a handsome young man, with his own house and a regular job should offer for her, she might reconsider. There was a lot to be said for the security of knowing where your next meal was coming from.

'Charlie, take your brothers and wait for me by the castle. The gates are locked today so you can't go in, but you can have a good look over the fence. I've got to take a message to the place where I used to work. Don't wander off – promise me now.'

'We won't, Sarah. We haven't been up here this year. Will there be time to walk down to the river before we go home?'

'I don't know. The wind's bitter, and look at those clouds. I think there might be snow coming; it's a bit soon for that, so I might be wrong. We don't want to get caught out in a snowstorm do we?'

Leaving the children arguing about the prospect of snow and whether a jaunt to the river was worth the risk of being caught in a blizzard, she hurried down the pathway. She kept the hood of her cloak down over her head in case anyone might recognise her. She slipped round the back, but instead of going to the door she went to the poultry house.

'Robbie, are you in here?'

The resulting clucks and squawks indicated he was there. 'Crikey! You don't want to be caught round here, Sarah. I can't be seen talking to you.'

'I'm not staying long. I need a small favour. Could you tell Betty to meet me her on her afternoon off? I'll wait by the castle. Will you do that for me, for old times' sake please? I'd be ever so grateful.'

He couldn't resist, not when she put on her widest smile. 'Just this once. I don't dare do it again – not even for you, Sarah Nightingale.'

She bent and kissed him lightly on his grubby cheek. That was reward enough, certainly the only payment *he* was going to get. With a whirl of skirts she hurried back to find the boys waiting obediently where she'd left them.

'Well, do we risk it? What you think, Charlie?'

'Not today, Sarah. Ma wouldn't like me brothers out in the snow. We still got the shopping to do ain't we?'

Sarah was relieved; the last thing she wanted was to trek down to the river. 'I think that's a wise decision, Charlie. You're a

sensible boy. Now we have to buy provisions and there may be a copper spare to get you all a barley sugar twist as well.' This bribe was enough to make them forget the river.

Charlie insisted on carrying the basket. He was bent almost double by the weight, but didn't complain. She knew it would be wrong to take it from him; his pride would be hurt if she did.

They went down the side passage, through the gate in the wall and into the garden. She looked round – yes, it was definitely big enough to be considered a garden. There were flower beds down either side, a substantial vegetable patch and a few chickens in an enclosure at the far end next to the privy.

'Are there any eggs today, Charlie? I used the last making cakes this morning.'

'I'll go and have a look. They don't lay much now – I reckon it's the cold. And there ain't much to peck up off of the ground.' The boys ran down to the henhouse, leaving her to unlatch the kitchen door. Ada was rocking gently in a chair next to the range and there was no sign of the little one.

'We're back, Ada. The boys are looking for eggs. Is Beth having a nap?'

'She's just gone down. I'm having one meself. You go ahead, Sarah, don't worry about disturbing me. I'll doze in the chair. I reckon I'm that tired I could sleep through a thunderstorm.'

The boys burst into the kitchen, bringing a blast of icy air, and smoke puffed from the range. 'Close the door quickly. It's freezing out there. Was that snow in the air, Charlie?'

'It were, Sarah – it's coming down heavy now. We'll be able to build a snowman later.'

'I hate the stuff. It's cold, wet and creeps into your boots; but at least we've got enough in for the next few days. I'll not have to go marketing for a while.'

She wouldn't be able to go to the bank either, not if the

weather was inclement. It wasn't worth risking a broken ankle and anyway she wasn't leaving Colchester until January now. The money was safe and she had nearly a pound in her bedroom, more than enough to tide her over.

* * *

Colchester, November 1843

Two weeks later the snow had thawed and the weather was back to the more usual grey and damp you'd expect for November. Sarah was concerned about Ada. She had no energy and her ankles were so swollen by the end of the day she could scarcely walk. Sarah suggested they got the midwife in, but Ada insisted she was fine and couldn't afford to pay out unnecessarily.

There had been a letter come from Mr Billings. Ada couldn't read but her husband was literate. Sarah read it to her. His ship was making good time and he expected to dock in Harwich in the middle of December, a month earlier than planned. He expressed a wish to be home when the baby arrived.

She was pleased, even though this meant she had to change her plans. A woman needed her man about the place when a baby was born. She would make arrangements to leave for London a bit sooner. When she went to meet Betty she'd go to the bank, withdraw her money and buy the necessary paper to forge her references. She'd not take the coach. Now the weather was bad she'd rather go on the train instead and not risk getting stuck in a ditch.

The grand houses in London could be looking for extra staff for the Christmas season. Hopefully she'd get something, even if it was temporary.

* * *

It was Friday, the day of the cattle and corn market in the high street. She'd have preferred to go on a quieter day, but this was Betty's free afternoon so there was no choice. At least she could be certain the bank would be open – on market days there would be a deal of money changing hands. She'd just have to be extra vigilant whilst carrying her life savings with her; there were bound to be ne'er-do-wells and pickpockets about as well.

Ada smiled sadly as Sarah was putting on her cloak. 'I'm going to miss you, Sarah love. I wish we had room, but there ain't. And anyway, Billings wouldn't like it if you were here. He's not too keen on strangers, my man ain't.'

'I'm going to miss you too, Ada, and the children. But we both knew I couldn't stay when your family returned. It's much better that you have your husband home when the baby comes. I'm glad I've been able to be of assistance. I'd better get off – my friend will be waiting. She only has three hours.'

She tied her bonnet securely, checked her hair was firmly pinned at the back of her neck, and pulled on her mittens. She'd sewn an extra pocket into her waistband. This had a drawstring top so she could drop her money in and pull it tight. There was no way a thief could dip in *there* and get it.

Several passers-by greeted her by name. She'd been living in the neighbourhood long enough to have become a familiar sight in the surrounding streets. She had visited Mrs Cooke the first week to thank her for giving her Ada's address. She'd been round a couple of times since to take her a batch of cakes.

Sarah had been shocked to find the old lady lived in a neglected cottage, the limewash on the walls all but gone, the fire barely adequate to keep out the cold. No wonder Annie trudged up to the Wednesday fruit and vegetable market to buy

the leftovers. She'd visit again before she left the area and put a couple of pennies in with the cakes next time.

She'd not dwell on that; she had to think of herself, look to the future. She was determined to be optimistic, believe she would find herself suitable employment without spending all her savings. She would come back next spring to collect her belongings, see Betty, check if her brother had returned, and nip down to visit with Ada and the boys and see the new baby.

Although a day wasn't long, on the train it could be done. Mind, she'd have to find employment on the east side of the city; crossing London might well take longer than the fifty miles to Colchester.

She reached the corner of Queen Street and was shocked to find East Hill full of livestock, the bellowing and lowing of the cattle all but deafening. The street was littered with fresh dung and she was obliged to wait a good fifteen minutes whilst the drover herded the two dozen cattle down the hill. Betty was waiting for her, her face wreathed in smiles.

'I was beginning to think you wasn't never getting across, Sarah. You look well. I've been that worried about you since you went, but I can see you've found yourself somewhere decent to live.'

'I have, with a Mrs Billings. She lives just off St Botolph's Street. I've been helping her out, cooking and cleaning and so on. I've only to pay a shilling a week. But her husband and boys are coming home soon, so I've got to move on. That's why I wanted to see you, to say goodbye.'

Betty flung her arms around her. 'Sarah, don't leave Colchester. Even if we can't meet often at least I'll know you're there.'

'I have to. I'm going to write myself some references, and I'm not stupid enough to try and use them anywhere that the master's name would be recognised.'

'Then it has to be London? Ain't Chelmsford far enough?'

'No, I have to go somewhere no one has ever heard of Mr Bawtree. I'm going to draw my money from the bank today and buy the paper and envelopes to do the references. Tell me, what's been happening at Grey Friars in my absence?'

'You'll never guess – Sally's been sacked. She was caught pinching by Nanny Brown not long after you left. There's a new under nurse now, but she's not a patch on you, I can tell you. Still, that's not your concern. Let's get going. Shall we go to The Red Lion? If you're getting your money from the bank, you can treat me to a pot of tea and a cake.'

Sarah laughed at Betty's cheek. 'I'll do that, but I want to ask you a favour. Can you keep my things until I come down for them next year? Now there's the train, I've worked out I could get there and back in a day. I'll write and then you can get Mrs Hall to read it; I think she might be prepared to pass on a message by then.'

'I reckon she would. I heard her talking to Cook the other day, saying it was a shame you had to go, as you were the best girl she'd employed in years.' Betty grinned and squeezed her arm. 'I ain't told you the best bit – I've been keeping it for last.'

'Go on then, you're fair bursting to tell me.'

'I'm the under nurse. That's why I said she wasn't a patch on you. Nanny asked if I could have the job, and Madam agreed. I'm on a month's trial. I reckon I've done all right and I'll hear next week if my position's permanent.'

Sarah wasn't sure if she was pleased or envious of her friend's success. 'I'm glad for you, Betty. You deserve promotion and I'm sure you'll get good news. Did you move into my old room?'

'I certainly did. I've got your things hidden in the back of the chest. The two nursery-maids don't dare come in. They're

willing enough, but neither of them are much more than children themselves.'

'How are the children? No, tell me when we're having our tea. I must go to the bank. I won't be able to afford to treat you if I haven't got my money. I didn't bring anything with me.'

Sarah joined the queue at the counter, her bank book ready for when it was her turn. The clerk handed out the money without a murmur; she was the proud possessor of nine pounds eight shillings. It was a small fortune, more than enough to keep her out of the workhouse for a year or two even if she couldn't find employment. She was tempted to put some back, collect it when she returned, but there was a press of people behind her and she didn't want to draw attention to herself.

Surreptitiously she slipped the money into its special hiding place. With her cloak wrapped tightly around her, she was certain no one would notice the small bulge. She kept out a pound to pay for her train ticket and writing materials. She also wished to purchase small Christmas gifts for the Billings family, and something for the new baby as well.

Inside The Red Lion a huge log fire burnt brightly in the snug, but it was surrounded by farmers and traders. There was no room for them to find a table and order themselves a hot drink. The comments from the men made her cheeks turn red. In her haste to escape she trod on Betty's toes.

'We should have realised, it's too busy for us in here. Where can we go? We need to think of somewhere the farmers won't be, somewhere a bit further away from the market.'

'What about Mr Doe's Temperance Hotel in Wire Street at the back of The Red Lion? We can go through the yard here, then cut down Lion Walk easy enough.'

Sarah wasn't too happy about taking this route, not when she was carrying so much money. She'd be happier staying on

the main thoroughfare where there were people around, someone you could call out to if you were set upon.

'Look, Sarah, over there. I think that's Sally. She's got two blokes with her – surely she's not on the game already?'

'Quickly, I don't like the look of those men. Betty, they've seen us. They're coming over.' Sarah wished they hadn't come this way. It was far too quiet.

2

Sarah gathered up her skirts and ran, praying that Betty had the sense to follow. The sound of running feet behind her was reassuring, then she realised it wasn't Betty. She increased her pace. They were closer, too close. A blow from behind sent her stumbling forward to crash painfully on her knees. Instinctively she curled into a tight ball, protecting her precious money within the cradle of her body.

'No point in trying keep it, you stuck-up bitch,' a rough voice hissed in her ear. 'You've been to the bank. We've been watching out for you these past weeks. Give it us or we'll take it as hard as you like.'

They were not going to steal her money without a fight. Where was Betty? There'd been no cry. Had they struck her to the ground as well?

Her knees were bleeding, but so far she'd suffered no serious injury. Should she meekly hand over her money to avoid being hurt? Never! She had on heavy boots, when they came near she would lash out. If she screamed maybe someone would come to her assistance. She tugged off her

mittens, needing her hands free to scratch and gouge where she could.

Rough hands gripped her shoulders and shook her like a rat in a terrier's mouth. Her head jerked painfully from side to side and finally cracked against the wall. Dizzy from this treatment, but still conscious, she lashed out wildly, her feet making contact several times. It was a bad decision. Her actions enraged her attackers and a series of punches rained down on her. She screamed, but no one came. Then a final blow sent her spinning into blackness.

From somewhere far away a voice was calling her name. 'Sarah, Sarah, have they killed you? I've called the constables – someone's coming to help you. Be still until they arrives.'

It was her friend. Slowly she forced open her bruised eyes. Every bit of her hurt, and her mouth was full of blood, several of her teeth could be loosened. The waistband of her skirt was ripped apart, the money gone; even the pound she'd had in her cloak pocket had been stolen. Despair overwhelmed her. She closed her eyes again, willing the blackness to take her back.

They'd taken everything she owned. She was destitute, only a few shillings between her and the workhouse.

Betty called her repeatedly, but Sarah made no effort to respond. She wished she could die; she had no hope left. Unfamiliar voices were arguing above. A man spoke firmly to someone she couldn't hear.

'I ain't leaving this poor girl to freeze to death on the pavement. You two take the money back to Mr Hawkins. I'm stopping here to help.'

Sarah tried to sit up. She didn't want this man to lose his employment because he'd been kind enough to come to her assistance. 'I'll be all right in a minute; my friend can help me when I've got my breath back.'

A warm coat, smelling of wood shavings and tobacco, dropped around her shoulders. 'I'm Dan Cooper. Can you put your arm around my neck? I'll soon have you somewhere warm and dry.'

Strong arms lifted her from the freezing cobbles. Betty tucked the jacket tight. She wanted to protest but her head flopped onto the man's shoulder. She had no energy left and welcomed the darkness as it took her once more.

The overpowering smell of carbolic and the rattle of pans finally dragged her to consciousness. She must be in a bed in the hospital in Lexden Road. Ma had always said only a handful of those who went into hospital ever came out alive. Suddenly she didn't want to be one of the many, but one of the few who survived. She opened her eyes and pushed herself onto her elbows; a wave of agonising pain washed over her. She bit back her moan.

Betty was at her bedside, face chalk white and tear-streaked. 'Sarah, thank the good Lord. I thought you dead a while back.'

Sarah forced her broken mouth to smile. 'I'm battered and bruised, but I'll live. Where have they taken my clothes? I need them back. I'm not stopping here – I'm going back to Ada's. I'll stay there until I get well and can find myself some sort of work.'

Betty nodded. 'The constables were here. I told them what happened. That bitch Sally and her brothers took your money. She tripped me up, and sat on me so I couldn't get up and help you; but I saw it all and the police know where to look. I reckon they'll catch them and you'll get your money back.'

'I won't. They might catch the thieves, but the money will be gone. I'm destitute. I can't go to London. I'll have to find myself somewhere else to live before Mr Billings comes back and throws me out.'

'Don't worry about that now. You're not in any fit state to go

back to your lodgings. Don't cost you nothing to be in hospital. It's charity, right? You stop and get fed here. You can't expect the landlady to take care of you, not like you are.'

It was almost dark; Betty should be back at Grey Friars. If she was tardy on her first afternoon off since her promotion, she might not get her position confirmed after her month's trial. 'Betty, you're a good friend, but you must go. Take care of my things. I'll send word before long. Go, before you're late.'

'All right; that Dan Cooper took a real shine to you. He carried you all the way here, and he's coming tomorrow to see how you are. He said he'd do for those two what did it. I reckon if the law don't find Sally and her brothers he and his mates will.'

'I don't remember much about it, but he put his jacket round me, didn't he?'

'He did that, quite enjoyed the sight of him in his shirt-sleeves. Lovely broad shoulders and a fine head of curly black hair. Getting on a bit, about four and twenty I reckon. If I was you, my girl, I'd hang on here until he comes back. He might be the answer to your prayers.'

In spite of her desolation and injuries Sarah smiled. Trust Betty to think of something like that. 'I'm sixteen; far too soon to be thinking about that sort of thing. Anyway, if he's as old as you say, he'll be married already with a family to provide for.'

Reluctantly her friend gathered up her possessions, leaning over to give her a kiss. She promised to come down and visit as soon as she had time off. 'I know you won't be with Mrs Billings, but she'll know where you are.' The handsome stranger was not mentioned again.

Sarah didn't disagree. By the time the seasonal festivities were over she'd be long gone. She had no intention of telling

Ada where she planned to live; she didn't want anyone coming round to the slums where she was heading.

A nurse brought her a bowl of tasty broth and a cup of tea. She mumbled her way through both, and explained why she would like her clothes. Her tale was nothing new, and with her gone there'd be an empty bed for the next casualty.

The woman understood. Her clothes were fetched, but she needed assistance to an get them on. They were muddy, still wet from the time she'd spent spreadeagled on the cobbles. Fortunately, apart from the wrecked waistband of her skirt they were undamaged. The nurse told her she was lucky not to have been raped. Sarah didn't feel the slightest bit lucky.

Somehow she staggered back down St John's Road. She was exhausted when she reached her destination. Using the walls of the narrow passageway to hold herself upright, she unlatched the gate and tottered to the back door. Charlie opened it; his face fell. 'Ma, Sarah's come back. She's been beaten up something bad.'

Ada insisted she took the rocking chair by the fire, fussing and worrying about the awful ordeal Sarah had suffered. 'It could have been worse – you know what I mean. What you've lost can be replaced. Thank the good Lord for that.'

'So I've been told. I was too busy fighting for my money to worry about my virtue. I'd no idea *that* sort of thing happened in Colchester.'

'It happens everywhere, Sarah love. You're welcome to stay here right up until my Frank comes home. I don't expect you to help until you're better. Here, Charlie, you get Sarah up to her room. He'll bring you what you want on a tray tomorrow. I'll not have you put out on the streets just before Christmas; I'll make sure I find you somewhere.'

It took three days for Sarah to feel well enough to resume

what she considered as her duties. She'd got precisely nineteen shillings and sixpence, more than a lot of folk had where she was intending to go. It wasn't much, but she'd make it last. She'd find herself a cheap room somewhere in St Botolph's Parish. It was the poorest part of town, jammed with little lanes, alleys and courtyards. It would be vile, but unless she was prepared to pawn Alfie's watch, she had no option.

When Ada came down to find the bread baking, the porridge bubbling and the tea made, she smiled gratefully. 'You're stronger than I thought, Sarah love. I reckon you'll survive wherever you are. Most women would have gone under after the beating you took, and losing your life savings, but not you.' She collapsed into her rocking chair. The boys settled themselves around the table and Sarah took Beth on her lap to feed her.

'I've sent Charlie to see old Annie; she's going to ask around for you. You must visit her today, see what she's found out.'

Charlie noisily scraped up the last of his porridge. Ada waited for her reaction.

'That's kind of you and Charlie. I don't think I'll venture out until this afternoon. I'm still a little unsteady but I'm sure I shall be better later.'

However, the weather worsened, not snow but icy rods of rain. Snow would be preferable – at least it didn't drench a body to the bone the moment they stepped outside. She had no choice. She could be turned out of her comfortable room any day; she had to have somewhere to go when that happened.

'If it's all right with you, Ada, I'm going along to see Annie. I'd hoped the rain would ease off, but I daren't wait any longer.'

'You'll get drenched, but that can't be helped I suppose. When you get back you can dry your clothes in front of the fire. You don't want to leave with wet things.'

Sarah put on the garments she'd worn when she'd been attacked. She'd brushed them, but they were still dirty and she'd not had the energy to launder them. She might as well get them wet, and wash them properly tomorrow.

It was not far to Annie's home, but even in the fifteen minutes it took her she was soaked through. 'Here you are then, lovie. Sorry to hear about your attack, but the bruises will fade soon enough.' She stepped back and Sarah ducked her head and followed her into the cottage.

'Charlie Billings said you might have heard of somewhere suitable. I'd like to be able to see it before I take it, try and get it clean before I move in. I might only have a few more days where I am.'

'I'd ask you to lodge here, but I've already got me two regulars staying. I sleep by the fire when they're with me. I ain't sure you can go round until you take the room. It ain't like staying with Ada Billings you know.'

Thankfully the fire was more substantial than usual, in honour of the lodgers no doubt. 'Is it all right to hang my cloak by the fire?' The old lady nodded and poured Sarah a cup of tea.

'This'll warm you up. Put yourself on the stool. You look right poorly; the last thing you want is to get congestion of the lungs.'

'I'm sorry I haven't brought you any cakes today. Ada's not charging me anything for my board so I can't expect her to pay for extras.'

'Don't you fret, my girl – you've done more than enough for me already. It's me what owes you a favour, and I ain't let you down. I've been asking around, and there's a couple of places vacant. Mind you, that was two days ago. They could have been taken by now.'

'Where are they?'

'I ain't sure exactly. You've to go to The Prince of Wales, ask to speak to Ma Peck. She's the landlady there, but she's agent for Mr Hatch – collects the rents and that. She'll find you something suitable; she's a good sort. Mind you, it won't be what you're used to, but beggars can't be choosers.'

'I shall be grateful to have any sort of roof over my head. I only have a few shillings left, and I don't suppose any of those rooms will have furniture in.'

The old lady cackled. 'Bless you, course they don't. You'll need something to sleep on, a couple of blankets and a chair. I asked particular about rooms with a fireplace – you'll want to be able to do a bit of cooking.'

'I won't have enough to buy all that, not until I find myself some work. I don't care what I do as long as it brings me in a shilling or two. I don't suppose you've heard of anything going?'

'I ain't; sorry, love. But Ma Peck might know of something. Ask her when you go up there.'

'Well, it won't be today. I shall wait until I'm feeling better, unless I'm forced out earlier.'

Sarah said her farewells, promising to call in when she was settled. Annie might be the only friend she had once she'd left the security of Ada's house. Her cloak was still sodden, but then so were her clothes. The rain had eased off a little. She would hurry, try and keep warm that way.

Feeling a little more hopeful about the future she stepped into the kitchen to be faced by a giant of a man. He didn't look best pleased to see her. The house was silent, no sign of Ada or the children. She supported herself against the door, her heart pounding painfully. Mr Billings had come back too soon; she wasn't ready to go. Her clothes were wet and dirty, and she had no room arranged.

'You're not welcome here. Get upstairs and get your things

out of my boys' room. My wife had no right to take you in
without my say-so.'

There was no point protesting. This bad-tempered sailor
had made up his mind. Without a word she stepped round him,
her chin up, determined not to show her fear. Where *was* everyone? Surely he hadn't sent them out in this weather? And what
about the two older boys? Had they been on the same ship as
their father?

She expected her room to be ransacked but it was as she'd
left it an hour ago. There wasn't much to do – her carpetbag
was already half full. The remaining money was already
stitched into the lining of her cloak. Even the most determined
footpad would never find it there. As she dropped her
toiletries on top of her clothes something chinked. Pushing
aside the items she'd packed earlier she saw a small cloth
purse. Ada had given her a few coins extra, something she
could ill afford.

Her eyes filled. There were wicked people in the world. Life
was mostly unfair for poor folk like her, but there were also kind
and loving folk who were prepared to give their last penny to
help someone worse off than themselves. Betty, Annie, Ada and
Dan Cooper – they'd all been prepared to help her.

When Frank Billings returned to sea next year she would
return, thank Ada, see if there was anything she could do in
return. However, that was a long time in the future. For the
moment she had to concentrate on her own survival, find herself
a room, get employment, and one way or the other remain alive
until the spring.

On impulse Sarah decided to leave by the front door. She
wouldn't give that man the satisfaction of seeing her evicted.
Clutching her carpetbag to her chest she pulled her wet cloak
around it. She might look as if she was expecting. Even the most

hardened criminal would think twice about attacking a girl in the family way.

It took some time to locate The Prince of Wales. It was mid-afternoon, but almost dark already. The streets were quiet even here. The smell coming from one side of the building made her gag; men must relieve themselves somewhere round there.

She pushed open the door and was surprised to see clean sawdust on the floor, the few tables and chairs polished and the serving hatch as clean as a new pin. This wasn't like The Bugle Horn, although most of the customers were just as noxious. There were a few men supping their drinks, but no women. Her cheeks coloured – she should have gone around the back. Women didn't enter beerhouses, not respectable ones anyway. Curious eyes bored into her back, and she stiffened her spine as she walked across to the hatch.

She heard a noise behind the heavy bead curtain and a tall, thin woman, hair scraped back in a knot on top of her head, came through. Her high-necked brown dress had long sleeves and made her look more like a housekeeper than an innkeeper.

'I'm Sarah. Annie Cooke said I was to call and enquire about a room.'

The woman gestured for her to come through the curtain, lifting it aside for her, and Sarah walked through, glad to be out of the bar. The woman's living quarters were spotless. If this woman could keep herself and her premises as clean as this when surrounded by filthy hovels and even filthier customers, she must do the same.

'There's two still free. One has a fireplace – it's dearer, mind, but you'd be better there if you can afford it.'

'I'll take it. I have a bit of money left, and I'm hoping to find work. I don't suppose you need anyone here?'

The woman looked her up and down and then smiled. 'It

ain't pleasant work. I keeps the place clean enough but I ain't got no control over them that drink in here. One of me girls is off sick. You can take her place until she's back. It'll be busy over the festive season – folks like to drown their sorrows.'

Sarah couldn't believe she'd been able to find herself somewhere to live and paid employment within minutes of being thrown out. She must have a guardian angel after all. 'I'll take it. I've not done this sort of work, but I was in service before I lost my position. I'm a hard worker, and don't care what I do...' No, that was untrue. There was one thing she'd never contemplate, even if she was starving. 'I'm... I mean I don't...'

Ma Peck nodded. 'I didn't think you did. I'd not of taken you on if I thought you'd spread your legs for any Tom, Dick or Harry. This is a respectable establishment. None of my girls are on the game.' She smiled grimly. 'Mind you, the one what's sick is in the family way and no sign of the father anywhere.'

Sarah's optimism faded. She was out of her depth, had no idea how to manage in a place like this. The men who drank here were like those who had stolen her money. Although she might be safe when she was working, what about when she had to walk home in the dark through the stinking alleys to wherever her pitiful new lodgings might be? Who would look out for her then?

3

Ma Peck flung open the back door and shouted into the yard. 'John, I've got a young lady in here that's taking the room in the walk behind Bakers Row, off Magdalen Street. She needs someone to take her there. She'll never find it on her own and I'm short-staffed here.'

John Peck was a burly man, a fringe of gingery-brown hair around a bald pate. His eyes were kind, his cheeks rosy as polished apples. Sarah liked him on sight.

'Thank you, sir. I'm sorry to be a trouble, especially when the weather's so bad.'

'I never mind a bit of rain. I'll be happy to show you.' He shook his head, his lips pursed, and he stared sideways at his wife. 'Don't you have anything better? She's a sight too refined for the likes of them round there.'

Sarah quickly intervened. 'I shall manage, Mr Peck; I have so little money at the moment I must be satisfied with what's available. When I'm working, I can put a little by and find something better in the spring.'

'You got a job around here?'

Sarah looked for confirmation but Mrs Peck shook her head slightly. 'I've heard of something but I've to look into it yet. I'd like to get to my room, if that's not putting you out. I expect there's nothing in it, and I'll have to be out again and buy the necessities before it's too late.' It would be very unwise to be abroad in that neighbourhood at night.

Mr Peck insisted on carrying her carpetbag. He shrugged on a voluminous cloak and rammed on his felt hat.

Mrs Peck beckoned to her as they were leaving. 'You can start tomorrow. Be here at eight sharp. I'll give you the first shift. It's rough enough around here in the daytime and I'll not have my John complaining about you having to walk home at night. Taken a real shine to you, he has.'

Sarah smiled her thanks and hurried after him; first Mr Cooper, now Mr Peck. She must appeal to the older man. She needed a man's protection for her first foray into the slums that existed around Magdalen Street. The area was rife with prostitutes, lowlifes and thieves. She hoped there were others like her, women fallen on hard times, and that she wouldn't be totally surrounded by miscreants.

Since the barracks had been torn down after Waterloo the soldiers had gone – she wasn't sure if that was of benefit to her or not. Would military men have been more or less likely to accost her in the street? When full of beer no doubt they were just like any other man, foul-mouthed and vulgar; also a soldier would be trained to kill, would not think twice about taking what he wanted. The warning from both Ada, and the nurse at the hospital, about the possibility of being raped was constantly in her mind.

With the hood of her cloak pulled tightly over her head it served two purposes: it kept her precious bonnet secure and hid her face from curious passers-by. Even in her muddied garments

she was a deal better dressed than the majority she met. In spite of the appalling conditions, children huddled on street corners and cowered in archways, their clothes little better than rags. Huge eyes stared hopelessly out of gaunt, white faces; the thought of such little ones living in hardship without shoes or warm clothing filled her with anguish.

It wasn't right that people like those she'd once worked for lived in such luxury, threw away more each day than people round here had in a month. Someone ought to do something about it. Wasn't that what Parliament was for? Shouldn't someone be speaking up for the downtrodden and doing something to improve their lot?

Her lips twitched. She was becoming a radical. She'd read pamphlets written by the Chartists but had never thought she would experience what they were protesting about. The downturn in her fortunes made her aware of how things were for those unable to earn enough to live on. Looking back, her life in East Stockwell Street had been one of comparative luxury and comfort.

Magdalen Street was busy. Small roadside stalls sold tired vegetables, the pieman could be heard shouting his wares further down the street. There was a baker's shop, a general store and what could pass for a haberdasher's. These were not like the shops she was used to; they were little more than oddments set out in the window of a cottage. No doubt folks around here made a penny where they could.

There seemed to be as many beerhouses as food stores. It was small wonder the children were so thin if their parents spent what little money they had on gin and beer. Victuals would be purchased by those returning from work. With luck the shops would remain open until late, at least until she had found what she needed.

Many in this neighbourhood would be dayworkers, would spend what they had on the way home. Judging from the noise coming from the bars they passed, most of it went down the men's throats. Were the women obliged to wait to intercept their husbands in order to get any housekeeping?

'The walk we want is down here, miss. Mind where you step. Folk aren't too fussy what they throw out in these parts.'

Her stomach lurched. She clamped her teeth shut and swallowed vigorously. She must endeavour to get used to the stench. There was no point in pretending she was still the old Sarah Nightingale. Now she was another destitute young woman hoping to stay alive by any means she could. They turned right and left and then into an even more noisome alley, the houses so close together they seemed to be at loggerheads. A large man could touch both sides of the street with his arms outstretched.

Her guide stopped at a building at the end of the row with slightly less filth piled up outside than the others. The doorstep was clean, as were the windows, and the curtains, although faded, had been washed recently.

'Your room is in here. You've only got people on the left of you, so it's quieter than most.'

Sarah prayed her room might be the one with the clean glass and the curtains. Even looking out onto another house would be better than no window at all.

He put his shoulder to the door. It didn't need a lock; you'd have to be a strong man to open it. God knows how she would manage on her own. Why did no one see to it? The door had swollen with the rain. Surely it wouldn't be too difficult to rehang it so it closed properly? What nonsense! This was a different world, where doors didn't fit and nobody cared enough to mend them.

The passageway caused Mr Peck to turn sideways. 'You're

lucky, miss, your room's at the back, got a bit more privacy than the ones in front. You want to keep it locked at night mind. Although the lodgers in here are a bit cleaner than next door, they ain't nothing special, I can tell you.'

They shuffled past the stairwell. Sarah shuddered, relieved she didn't have to negotiate the narrow, twisting staircase. The smells that wafted down were almost as bad as the street. Human waste and unwashed bodies predominated. She'd just have to get used to it.

The key seemed overlarge for such a humble dwelling. It would be a nuisance carrying this about with her all the time. Mr Peck turned it easily. Thank God her room would be secure at night, her few belongings safe during the day whilst she was working.

'Right then, miss, it's not much, but better than nothing.'

He was obliged to step into the room so that she could see what was to be her home for the foreseeable future. Nothing had prepared her; her worst imaginings could not have conjured up such a dismal place. The window, if you could call it such, was no more than a foot square and so high on the wall it would be impossible to look out. Anyway it was thick with dirt. It might as well be midnight outside, the amount of light that came in through it.

Her companion had reached into his jacket pocket and removed a candle stub. Expertly flicking one of the matches against the wall, he lit it. By this single flickering light she surveyed the reality. The room was little more than the size of a store cupboard at Grey Friars; it *did* have a fireplace, but it was scarcely big enough for cooking. It might be possible to boil a small saucepan of water to make tea, and toast crumpets in front of the flames, but she'd never be able to make herself a meal.

The floor had no boards. It was beaten earth, the damp and

cold already seeping up through the soles of her boots. There was no furniture; the previous tenant had left nothing, not even a hook on the wall to hang her cloak on. She'd be better off in the workhouse than living here. Unable to speak, she held out her hand for her bag.

'I know it's not what you're used to, but look at it this way: it's so small even that piddling fire will keep you warm. You won't need much furniture, a couple of rugs across the floor, a bed and some nails to hang your clothes and you'll be all set.' On this cheery note he turned to go.

Panic engulfed her. She didn't want to be left in this dreadful place, had no idea how to proceed, where to go to buy herself what she needed. Did she even have enough money? She couldn't begin to find the way back to the main thoroughfare. She'd rather throw herself on the parish than remain here.

'Mr Peck, please don't leave me. I can't live here; I won't be able to manage. I'll go along to Balkerne Lane. At least they'll give me a bed and regular food in there.'

He reached out and squeezed her shoulder. 'You don't want go in there, not really. It's the shock talking; I know your sort. Girls like you can manage if they set their minds to it. I knew you were a survivor the minute I set eyes on you. Now tell me what you want, and I'll go and buy it.'

'That's kind of you, but I can't stay here. There's nothing I can do until I've got some furniture. I haven't thought this through. I haven't even a bucket for collecting water.'

'You want three really: one for water, one for coal and one for you know what. You don't want to use the privy in the yard, not if you can help it.'

'What about the water? Where do I get that?'

'That's one thing in Colchester – at least we got pure water. You'll not catch anything from drinking the water from your

pump. It's out back. It's another thing you share with this row of houses.' He stuffed her carpetbag into the empty grate so it wouldn't get damp on the floor. 'The water's on all day. You can go out when you want.'

She leant against the wall, the damp plaster making a cold patch between her shoulders. She had to be strong. After all, she had a few shillings in her pocket and was to start work the next day. She was a lot better off than some. If she kept her health, she would get through this and reach better times ahead.

'I'm steady now, sir. I have ten shillings to spend on furniture and food. I've paid a month in advance for this room and I'm keeping three shillings back. Will that be enough to get what I need?'

'More than enough. There's a second-hand yard in Magdalen Street that will have most of what you want. Here, take your key; you must lock the door. It's up to you to take care of yourself from now on.'

As they retraced their steps she took more notice of the landmarks. The walks appeared to be nameless; no doubt the post was never delivered in this area, so a real address wasn't needed. The wind had dropped, which was a blessing. She had an hour or so to get herself sorted out before the shops closed. Whatever she did to it, the room would never be her home.

* * *

Sarah frowned as she reviewed the improvements she had made. The room was less depressing certainly, but would always be little more than a furnished broom cupboard. However, she believed she had made a friend in Mr Peck. He was a true gentleman. He might be rough-speaking, but he had a heart of

gold. His good offices had meant she'd been able to acquire so much for so little.

She'd bought a china basin and jug, a rickety deal table and bentwood chair, a chamber pot and various pieces of cutlery and crockery. Mr Peck had cajoled the furniture seller into lending him a handcart. On this he'd wheeled back a bed frame, a new straw-filled mattress, two blankets and two dented buckets. He'd promised to come round first thing the following day with wood and a handful of nails to construct a shelf for her.

She had to be at work by eight. She'd be obliged to leave before he got there and this would mean handing over the key when they met in the street. On their second jaunt he purchased her a sack of coal. He'd insisted on paying for it, telling her it was much cheaper to buy it in bulk than by the bucketful. This was propped against the wall, alongside was kindling and half a dozen tallow candles. By standing precariously on her chair she managed to clean the tiny window. It wouldn't make much difference but things ought to be clean.

The square of tatty carpet, cadged for a few pennies by her benefactor, was against the damp earth, the two rag rugs on top; with her boots on it was like walking on a normal floor. The rudimentary bed frame would not support a heavier person; she would have to remember not to toss about at night. Her blankets were clean but threadbare. She'd have to place her cloak across as well if she was to stay warm. She couldn't afford to have the fire alight all the time.

With her first wages she'd purchase a length of material and make herself a bag. If she kept her spare underwear inside it would do very well as a pillow. Even the small saucepan took an age to boil. Her cracked china mug held a spoonful from a twist of tea. It was more dust than leaves, but better than nothing. Her stomach gurgled in anticipation of the hot meat pie she'd

treated herself to for supper. Tomorrow she'd be on short commons; she wasn't going to dip into her last three shillings in order to buy herself food. From now on she'd rely on the meal that was included in her wages at The Prince of Wales.

Mr Peck was right – there was something to be said for having this room. She *was* warm. The flickering light of the candle, plus the flames from the fire, were enough to dry her sodden garments.

She'd draped the wet clothes over the edge of the table and across the back of the chair. They'd not be laundered now. How did people manage to keep themselves fresh in these hovels? Laundering anything but the smallest items would be impossible. That was the least of her worries; she was fortunate to have a clean gown folded neatly on the table and the requisite underwear. She was better off than many, and she thanked God for it.

* * *

The clock at St Leonard's Church on Hythe Hill struck six. It was still dark, too early to get up. She couldn't afford to light the fire and it was much warmer in bed. A little after seven she washed in cold water, put her hair up by touch alone. This was the first time she'd attempted this without a glass to help her. With gritted teeth she removed her chamber pot from under the bed. It wasn't the emptying that bothered her; it was where it had to be emptied.

She had not stepped out of her room since her return the night before. One or two residents had already been outside to relieve themselves but no one was in the yard at the moment. The house was noisy: doors slamming, children crying and the shuffling and banging of feet on bare boards. During the night there'd been a disturbance next door; a hideous domestic argu-

ment, a woman screaming, the sounds of blows and a man's voice raised in anger. The walls were thin. Nobody could have any secrets living here.

That poor woman – to be woken by a drunken husband and beaten for no apparent reason. The married state was not for her. She didn't have the worry of children, or the fear of being mistreated. All she had to do was take care of herself and that suited her just fine.

Alfie would come back next year; together they'd make themselves a decent life. She would keep house; he'd bring her in a wage to supplement whatever she could earn. This was a daydream, she knew, but Mrs Hall had been fond of saying that it was good to have something to aim for.

A year ago her goal had been to save enough from her wages to set herself up in her own business, or take charge of a nursery in a grand house in the country. How things had changed. Now, it was to stay alive until her brother returned to Colchester.

So far she'd avoided a visit to the privy but she could have found her way blindfolded. The smell, even in the cold, was enough to kill a horse stone dead. It was impossible to hold her nose and carry the pot, so she held her breath instead. This meant the hem of her skirts trailing in the mud; it was small wonder everyone looked dishevelled.

She opened the door. The hole in the seat was so repellent she almost tipped the contents on her boots. Stepping forward she emptied her doings, glad she'd not had any breakfast. The scuttling of rats made the experience even more unpleasant, if that were possible. The night soil men should be called; this privy hadn't been emptied for a month. There was no way on God's earth she'd ever sit over one of those stinking holes. Heaven knows what might come up!

After slamming the door, she gathered her skirts and

hurried to the communal pump further down the yard. Rinsing her empty receptacle under the freezing water, she was just glad she'd completed this unpleasant task before anyone had observed her embarrassment. The pot vanished under the bed. She washed her hands and dried them on the cloth that served as a towel. There, that was the worst of the jobs done. She was just exiting when, to her surprise, Mr Peck turned up.

'Good morning, sir, so kind of you to help me out in this way.'

He beamed, his jowls wobbling. 'Ma tells me you're to work in the bar. It ain't the sort of work a girl like you should be doing, but needs must, I suppose. She'll keep an eye on you, and if anyone misbehaves, I'll flatten them.'

'I have to leave, Mr Peck, or I shall be late. That wouldn't do on my first day.'

'I've had a word with the missus. You're to come back with me today. Just you sit down out the way, and I'll get on. I'll have a fine shelf, with hooks underneath to hang mugs and such, and a few nails in the wall for your clothes, in no time.'

She felt a glow of happiness. Her situation was dire, but this man's kindness gave her hope. After a deal of hammering and banging the work was done. 'That's a splendid job – I have everything I need.'

He chuckled and pushed his tools into his bag. 'We'd best be off now, miss. Won't do to keep Ma waiting any longer.' He gestured to her clean dress. 'She'll be pleased you've made an effort. Raise the tone, it will, having someone like you working in the bar.'

In the morning light her surroundings appeared no better than they had yesterday. She made every effort to keep her skirts out of the filth, but her boots were sadly mired by the time she arrived at The Prince of Wales.

'Excuse me, sir, but I can't go in like this. Is there somewhere I can clean my boots?'

'We go round the back anyway; we've a decent yard where we store the empty barrels. You can use the pump out there. I'll fetch you a bit of rag.'

The alehouse didn't open until noon, so her work must be to clean up. After her experience this morning she thought she had the stomach to do anything without vomiting. Ma Peck was waiting impatiently.

'At last – make sure you're on time in future, my girl. Don't expect no mollycoddling from me. Remember you're on a week's trial.' Sarah curtsied and held her tongue. 'Here, put this over your gown. I want you looking smart when the bar opens.' Unexpectedly she smiled. 'Not that the rubbish that comes in here will appreciate the difference. I keep a clean house; no one gobs on my floor and gets away with it.'

The voluminous garment covered Sarah from head to foot. Obviously it had been worn by a far larger person. Fortunately her height meant it didn't trail on the floor. She was ready for whatever duties Mrs Peck might have. By the time she had removed the soiled sawdust from the floor, scrubbed the boards and sprinkled fresh, her hands were raw. Next the tables had to be scrubbed and polished and the wooden chairs wiped down.

By eleven thirty the place was spotless. However revolting the customers, this environment was preferable to her room. It smelled fresher and the winter sunlight streamed in through sparkling windows. There was a roaring fire to warm the room, and the smell of baking pasties and fresh bread drifted through from the kitchen. The outside cleaning was done by an old man, working for beer money and a hot meal.

'Right then, just got time for a bite to eat and a mug of tea before we start. You've done well, my girl. I'd not have thought

you'd have it in you. When you've eaten, you need to put on one of the aprons hanging behind the door. I supply those – I like my girls to look smart.'

Sarah found it difficult to swallow, but free food was not to be turned down under any circumstances. By swallowing a mouthful of tea after each bite she managed to finish the pasty. The apron wrapped around her twice, but the ribbons kept it snug at her waist. Mr Peck had vanished as soon as he'd delivered her. Ma Peck had told her he was a carpenter by trade and had a workshop at The Hythe. Sarah wished his reassuring bulk was there when Ma Peck unbolted the doors at noon. The sound of stamping feet, raucous voices demanding to be let in – accompanied by such hacking, spitting and swearing – made her knees tremble. How was she going to cope serving beer to men like these?

4

Mrs Peck had told Sarah the prices of the other things she sold. These were hot pasties, pickles, and occasionally bread and cheese or beef sandwiches. However, this was only when there was a spare girl to make them. The Prince of Wales was generally quiet during the afternoon and early evening; the busy time was after the men returned from work, then the bar would be heaving.

The girls who worked at night were paid more than her, but Sarah was just grateful her employer had taken pity on her inexperience and given her the daytime shift. Walking back through the streets late, even though the main thoroughfares were lit by gas lamps, would be a terrifying experience. She wasn't used to the sort of people who lived round here, and having been brutally attacked in mid-afternoon she was well aware what desperate lengths the criminal classes would go to in order to obtain money.

'You ready, girl? Start filling the jugs. Have them ready for when the men come in. Take no notice of their foul mouths. Most mean no harm; they know no better.' She smiled thinly.

'You do your job properly and I'll look out for you, don't you worry.'

'I will, ma'am.'

The woman nodded and marched purposefully across the boards, her feet leaving imprints in the fresh sawdust. The door was unbolted and she stepped aside. Sarah had expected a press of rough men to charge in demanding their beer, but this was not the case. Mrs Peck stood by the door, arms folded, like a schoolmistress watching her pupils enter. The men touched their caps respectfully, and headed for the tables. There was an empty square in front of the hatch. No doubt this was filled with standing drinkers at busy times. The lunchtime crowd had more than enough seats and tables to go round.

As soon as they were safely inside they reverted to type; voices rose, hobnailed boots clattered, and complaints that she get a move on with their beer were loud and insistent. Ribald comments burned her ears. She kept her head down, knowing her cheeks were scarlet. She'd have to get used to this, become immune to the coarse remarks about the size of her backside, the fullness of her front and all the bits in between. Nod and smile, fill the tankards with the foaming liquid, and ignore the people she served. If she made no eye contact, with luck none of the men would attempt to take liberties with her person.

She carried three empty tankards in one hand and a full jug in the other. The men waiting to be served shouted encouragement, causing her to slop beer onto the floor. With shaking hand she placed a mug in front of the customers at the nearest table as she had been told to do, then carefully filled each up. The beer was tuppence a pint. The coins were slapped down on the table as she poured the beer.

She had a special pocket in the front of her apron that reached to her knees; in this she was to drop the coins. Keeping

her face averted she murmured a soft thank you and moved on to the next group. Soon she was weaving in and out of the tables as if she'd been doing it all her life. A lot of the men reeked of stale sweat, but then they had been doing hard physical labour all morning. Some smelt downright foul, but at least half the customers were decent, hard-working men not much different from her stepfather.

After all it was Saturday – not every governor forced his employees to work that afternoon.

Men came and went. She ran back and forth to the barrels refilling her jug. Her feet were aching, her apron stained with beer and the pocket bulging with coppers. She'd have to ask where to put them; they were weighing her down and hampering her progress. How much longer did she have to work before her stint ended?

Mrs Peck had left most of the serving to her. She'd brought out the food and fetched down the pewter tankards for the regular customers. She also made sure the men kept their behaviour within acceptable bounds. There was a lull and she finally had time to ask about the money.

'I need to empty my pocket. I can't put any more in without bursting the seams.'

'Go into the kitchen. You'll see a metal strongbox on the table; empty it in there. Lock it and bring me the key.'

Sarah felt proud she'd been trusted with such a responsible task, having worked there only one day. She went into the kitchen hoping she'd meet Mr Peck, but the room was empty. All the pasties had gone, but the savoury smell lingered and her mouth watered. It was hours since she'd eaten.

It took her some time to empty the pocket. The heap of coins was most impressive; there could be more than a pound in the box. She closed the lid and turned the key. A slight movement

alerted her. She looked round to see Mrs Peck had been watching her throughout the procedure. Her cheeks flushed; so much for thinking she was trusted.

The woman nodded, satisfied Sarah hadn't been dipping into the takings. She held out her hand for the key. 'Good girl, I can see I shan't have to keep such a sharp eye on you, not like some of the others. Most of the regulars have gone home to give what's left of their wages to their wives. Start clearing the mugs; you need to take them to the scullery and get them washed for this evening. You'll have to fetch water from the yard.'

'Yes, right away, Mrs Peck. Is there any particular order you want the tables clearing?'

'Get on with it, girl. Stop asking daft questions.'

Sarah decided the table furthest away from the hatch would be a sensible place to start, especially as it was unoccupied. The one adjacent had a solitary drinker. Stepping past him shouldn't be a problem.

'Excuse me, sir, I need to reach the empty mugs.' She waited for the man to drag his chair closer to the table. He looked up. She knew him; it was Mr Cooper. She'd never forget his shock of black hair and twinkling blue eyes gazing down at her as she lay injured on the pavement.

'I never expected to see *you* in The Prince of Wales, Miss Nightingale. Are you fully recovered? I don't suppose the constables got your money back for you or you wouldn't be working in a place like this.'

She glanced over her shoulder. It wouldn't do to be seen socialising with the customers, but Mrs Peck was absent, which allowed a few moments to converse. 'I'm quite well thank you, Mr Cooper. And I'm so glad to have seen you again. I wish to thank you for helping me. As you guessed, I didn't recover my

savings and needless to say the perpetrators have not been apprehended either.'

'And this is the best you could find, I suppose?' His voice was deep, not rough-spoken like the others, and his eyes full of sympathy.

'I was left almost penniless, then I was turned out of my lodgings unexpectedly and obliged to find a room and employment or end up in the workhouse.' What had possessed her to tell a complete stranger such intimate details of her life? Her cheeks coloured and the empty tankards rattled in her hands. Something made her continue. 'Mr and Mrs Peck have been kind to me; I have a roof over my head and employment. *I'm* one of the fortunate ones, there are others far worse off than me in this neighbourhood.'

He smiled, his teeth white and even. She felt a strange flicker of something she did not recognise inside. 'I live at the bottom of Hythe Hill, but walk up here as this is the best alehouse in the area. Ma Peck keeps a decent establishment and a tight rein on her customers. You can get a quiet drink in this place without worrying if you'll be smashed on the head by a pot or a chair.'

Good God! She'd no idea that sort of thing went on in beer-houses. 'Excuse me, Mr Cooper, I must take the dirty pots. I'm to get them washed and ready for this evening's trade.'

'Do you work here after dark as well?'

She shook her head. 'No, I'm working the day shift only, but I'm on a week's trial. I daren't stand about talking any longer. Thank you again, sir, for your timely assistance the other week.'

Meeting Mr Cooper had brought back memories she'd much rather forget. It was a relief to busy herself in the scullery washing the stoneware tankards in the deep sink. The water was freezing, but at least she hadn't had to break the ice in order to do the washing-up. She left the mugs upside down on the

draining board and then returned to the bar to collect the rest of the empties.

Occupied with this task she was excused further work in the public area. Apart from the fifteen minutes she'd sat down to consume her meal at half past eleven she'd been constantly on the go. She was used to long hours and hard work, but the scrubbing she'd done first thing had exhausted her. It wouldn't be right to ask when her shift ended but it had been dark for hours and must be getting on for six o'clock.

She was drying the last of the mugs when loud female voices echoed around the yard. Thank goodness, she could go home now. Without asking permission she stripped off her soiled apron and left it folded on the end of the draining board. The bead curtain that kept her employer's private quarters free from prying eyes also meant she could leave without hindrance.

Two young women not much older than her were in the kitchen tying on their aprons. Her words of greeting remained unspoken. These girls looked as bad as some of the customers; their clothes were sweat-stained and muddied around the hems, but their hair appeared free of lice and, from what she could see, they were clean enough. It was their faces that made the girls so different. They had a knowing look about them. These were not innocents, but experienced in the ways of the world. It was small wonder the girl she was replacing was off because she was in the family way.

The young women exchanged glances but didn't speak. 'Good evening, I'm Sarah. I can't tell you how glad I am to see you both. It's not that busy at the moment, and the tankards are done. I can't remember ever being so tired in my life before.'

The taller of the two, a blowsy blonde, shook her head in disbelief. 'Bloody hell! Where did Ma find you? You're not from round here, that's for sure. Would you look at her, Daisy!'

Daisy cackled, sounding more like an old woman than a girl in her prime. 'Hoity-toity! I reckon Ma has you working first because the regulars would eat yer alive at night. You get off, love – we'd not want the likes of you around when it gets busy.'

Hastily Sarah grabbed her cloak, but didn't say goodbye to her employer in case she was called back and asked to do something else. Daisy and the other girl were common but not vindictive, and seemed genuinely concerned for her welfare if she hung around much longer. She got paid less than they did and had been working almost ten hours. These two barmaids worked from six clock and would be finished by two in the morning. Maybe they had to work harder than she did, put up with more abuse and the groping hands of customers as they got inebriated.

She paused for a moment under the flickering gaslight, trying to remember her route home; everything was different in the dark. This would be the first time she'd tried to accomplish the journey to her lodgings on her own. She couldn't stand dawdling here; she had to get back before the streets were filled with riff-raff. Pulling her cloak tight she rushed round the corner to collide with a solid object. She stumbled backwards, almost falling, but two strong arms shot out and grasped her elbows to steady her.

'Take care, miss, you don't want to fall over.'

She was relieved to find it was Mr Cooper coming to her rescue a second time. 'I thought you left some time ago. I'm sorry to have bumped into you. I wasn't watching where I was going.'

'I waited. I'll walk with you. A young lady like you shouldn't be out alone in the dark – not round here. I can't think what Ma's thinking of, letting you walk home by yourself.'

'Mr Cooper, I thank you for your concern, but I'm quite

capable of getting myself home safely. It's neither your nor my employer's responsibility. I bid you good evening.'

He was clearly not offended by her rebuff, as the rich, warm sound of his laughter filled the darkness. 'You're not in the High Street now, miss. Things are different round here. Being polite won't stop you being attacked. I'd have thought what happened to you a while ago would have taught you that.'

There was the sound of rough voices approaching. Four unkempt men swaggered down the pathway. Suddenly she was lifted to one side, Mr Cooper placing his bulk between her and them. She liked the feel of his tweed coat up against her cheek – she remembered his smell of wood shavings and tobacco. They passed with no more than a few vulgar comments. God knows what would have happened to her if she'd been unprotected.

'Come along, miss, the sooner you're off the streets the better. Here, take my arm. I'll be happier knowing you're by my side.'

Why was he taking such an interest? A handsome man like him, in his mid-twenties, must be married with a family of his own to worry about. Maybe his interest was neighbourly, but she couldn't take the risk. She'd not get involved with a married man, not for all the tea in China.

'Do you have children, Mr Cooper? I used to be a nurse at a big house on East Hill; I love looking after little ones, but as I was obliged to leave without references, I must do whatever I can to avoid the workhouse.'

He ignored the last part of her speech. 'I have three boys, little rascals, but I'm that proud of them. There's another expected next spring. Maria, my wife, is hoping for a girl this time. I'm not bothered either way, but if that's what she wants, then for her sake I hope it's a girl.'

She was obviously mistaken; she had no experience of men

– married or otherwise. He adored his family, loved his wife and was just being gallant. It must be pleasant being married to such a man. His wife was a lucky woman to have a husband who was not only attractive but also had regular work, a home of his own and was prepared to help those less fortunate than himself.

'Mrs Cooper must be wondering where you are; your boys will be wanting to see their father. I won't hold you up. Thank you for bringing me this far.'

He shook his head. 'I'll take you to your door. It's the back alleys that are the worst. You can't see where you're going, and anyone could be lurking, waiting to rob you. I know you don't have much, but a few pennies will buy a quart of ale. The beer-houses will be filling up, the men coming home with their wages. You don't want to be around on your own right now. Buy yourself a lantern with your first wages.'

The street lighting didn't stretch between the dilapidated buildings. The new gas lights only ran down the main thorough-fare. Light from these was enough for them to see the first few yards, but after that it was anybody's guess what they were walking in. She directed him down the next walk and pointed to the door of the end house.

'This is where I live; I'll be quite safe now. I have to learn to manage on my own, Mr Cooper. I cannot expect strangers to walk me home every night. I thank you for your kindness.'

'I hope you don't consider me a stranger. You know my name, and I know yours. Sarah Nightingale's a pretty name – it suits you. I shall be having a word with Ma next time I'm in. I shall ask her to get John to see you home safe.'

She let herself into her lodgings. It was scarcely warmer in the passage than it was outside. She was so tired, she'd not bother to light the fire or make herself a hot drink. She'd go straight to bed. It was cheaper being under the covers than

sitting around with the fire lit. It was so cold she decided to sleep in her clothes, piling her cloak on top of the thin blankets to keep warm.

Teeth chattering, she abandoned the idea and scrambled out of bed to light the fire after all. She was too soft for this sort of life. She'd not survive the deprivation unless she toughened up. Once she was nursing a mug of tea in front of the fire she began to feel more optimistic. The room wasn't so bad, the job bearable; if she could just think of a way to get herself home after work then she'd be fine.

5

COLCHESTER, DECEMBER 1843

Sarah had no time to think about her reduced circumstances. As Christmas approached even the afternoons were busy at The Prince of Wales. She was rushed off her feet most days and returned too exhausted to bother to eat a hot meal. Each night one of the customers was waiting to escort her home, Dan Cooper had spread the word around amongst the decent men who frequented the alehouse. Some family men, others unwed, but all happy to walk back with her when she finished her shift. She got to know each of her guards and through them had met one or two wives and daughters.

Her life was no longer lonely; she couldn't invite anyone back to her slum on a Sunday, which after her week's trial became her day off. Occasionally she was invited to visit one of these new friends for tea. Sometimes she considered sending a message to Betty. She missed her, and she'd like to let her know she'd found somewhere to live and wasn't on the streets. However, she couldn't bear to think of everyone at Grey Friars House knowing how far she'd slipped since she'd left there. No, it was better that they remembered her how she

used to be, smart and tidy, well-behaved and a credit to her employers.

Dan Cooper walked her back on a Saturday night, which was the only day he allowed himself the luxury of a few drinks. His family seemed more familiar than her own; Joe was seven, Davie six and John three. Maria and Dan had been married eight years. They'd been only seventeen when they let their love get the better of them and had been forced to marry in haste. From the way Mr Cooper spoke of his wife it was definitely not a case of their repenting at leisure. He loved her, and his three boys, but she detected a note of anxiety in his voice when he spoke about the current pregnancy. Maria was not as hale as she had been with the other three, was tiring easily, and in spite of having a woman in to do the heavy work was finding it difficult to take care of her three lively boys.

The weather took a turn for the worse and tramping backwards and forwards from The Prince of Wales ankle-deep in snow did nothing to improve Sarah's enjoyment of her job. She'd become a firm favourite with many customers. Even the drunks and ne'er-do-wells treated her with a modicum of respect. She still worked the day shift, but she was now getting the same amount as the other two girls.

Daisy and Josie were loud and vulgar but kind-hearted, not the sort of girls she'd have chosen to be friends with. They looked out for her, warned her about the regulars who would try and short-change her or would take a crafty grope under her skirts when she was bending down to serve another customer.

Sarah had expected to be given Christmas Day off, that at least on the Lord's birthday Ma Peck would show some respect and keep her establishment closed.

'Close on Christmas Day? I should think not, Sarah. It's one of the busiest days of the year – that and New Year. The men

don't have to go to work and the women want them out from under their feet, especially if they got the wherewithal to cook a special meal.'

'I'd hoped I could go to church, Mrs Peck. I've never missed attending on Christmas Day since I can remember.'

'Ain't there an early service? You can go to that before you come, my girl. I can't say fairer than that. I won't dock your wages neither – call it your Christmas box.'

Sarah tried to look happy. 'Ta, that's very generous of you. I believe there's a service at eight o'clock, which means I can be here a little after nine. Does anything different happen on Christmas Day? Do you roast chestnuts or serve mulled wine or something like that?'

Mr Peck walked into the kitchen and overheard her suggestion. 'Well Ma, what do you think? Roasting chestnuts and a hot toddy? That would bring the punters in and no mistake. You've always said you've got a better class in here. I've noticed, certainly of an afternoon, that things are quieter and more genteel.' He beamed at Sarah, who paused for a moment with her tasks. 'My dear, you've brought a bit of class to the place and that's for sure.'

Ma wasn't best pleased by this remark. As far as she was concerned her bar was a cut above the rest anyway. 'Get about your work, Sarah. I don't pay you to stand around talking.'

Sarah curtsied briefly, then dashed back to collect the bucket of clean sawdust and scatter it on the freshly scrubbed floorboards. This was a job she enjoyed. It meant the drudgery was over. When it was done she could sit down with mug of tea, a hot pasty and a slice of bread and cheese.

The only day for shopping was on Sunday; fortunately shops were open from first thing in the morning until eleven o'clock. Some men didn't come out of the pub until closing time on

Saturdays, and *their* womenfolk didn't get their housekeeping money until they staggered back. If the shops weren't open, families would have gone without their Sunday dinner.

Her clothes hung from her. Not being able to cook in her room was a major handicap to good health. Being provided with a decent meal at midday was not enough to prevent her losing weight. She'd given up eating breakfast and only occasionally bought herself fried fish or a hot meat pie for supper.

She thought longingly of the food she'd been given whilst working at Grey Friars. What she wouldn't give for a plate of Cook's tasty mutton stew. Strangely the image of her little brother Tommy had faded. It was Alfie she wanted to see; it was he she kept close to her heart in the hope that one day he would walk into The Prince of Wales and take her away from this miserable life. Her brief conversations with Dan Cooper, hearing about his happy family, just made her miss her brother more.

Attending church on Christmas Day meant she had to be ready earlier than usual. It was unpleasant trudging through the slush; the snow was thawing and the pathways were even more treacherous. This morning was the first time since she'd been making this journey that the shops were shuttered, few folk about, and she was able to reach the haven of St Leonard's Church without being accosted.

She was a regular there, but being a poor working girl could no longer sit, and must remain standing in the empty space at the back throughout the service. It was colder inside the ancient building than it was outside. Instead of thinking joyous thoughts, it was all she could do to stop her fingers turning blue and her teeth rattling in between the droning from the vicar and the congregation's responses. Thank God there were no hymns

to sing. The sooner she could get to work and warm up the better.

The reverend gentleman galloped through the service, obviously as eager to get away to his vicarage as she was to leave. She arrived at The Prince of Wales, for the first time pleased to be there. As she stepped in through the kitchen door the heavenly smell of roasting chestnuts greeted her. Good heavens! Why were they doing these now? The doors didn't open until midday; the chestnuts would be shrivelled and ruined by then.

She hung her cloak on its customary peg and picked up her overall. Mr Peck appeared carrying a basket. 'Happy Christmas, my dear girl. Sit yourself down. Ma and I intend for you to share a festive breakfast with us today. See, I have here the chestnuts you suggested. I bought a sack at the produce market last Wednesday. We're going to offer them to the customers when they come in, for a halfpenny a plate.'

Ma Peck appeared from the bar and Sarah looked at her nervously. This was so out of character. She didn't like to be idle when she would normally be working.

'Sit down, girl, before I change my mind. Now, I've got boiled eggs, hot muffins, and fresh beef dripping for the toast. It will be a feast, and to finish we'll have the chestnuts. I reckon they'll be cool enough by then.'

This was the first time since leaving Ada's house that Sarah was so full she couldn't eat another morsel. She licked her fingers, sighing. 'I can't tell you how much I enjoyed that breakfast. That was the best present I've ever had in my whole life.' She blinked furiously. 'I know I'm not the sort of girl you usually employ, but you gave me a chance and I hope I've not let you down.'

Mr Peck banged on the table making the crockery jump. 'I should say not, my dear. Word is spreading you know. It started

with Dan Cooper coming up the hill because he liked a place he could drink without getting his head bashed in. He spread the word, and others followed. Still a bit rough on Saturday night, but the rest of the time it's a respectable place.' He beamed at her.

'We're thinking of turning the kitchen and scullery into a saloon and catering for those with more money to spend. Dan Cooper has suggested we have a savings club in here, somewhere a workingman can put his money of a Saturday before he's spent it all on beer.'

'I'm sure that will be much appreciated. I'd like to put a few pennies a week away in a savings club. I had all my money stolen from me when I took it out of the bank.'

The two exchanged glances. 'We thought as much. You're a hard worker and the customers like you. Your misfortune was our gain.'

Sarah cleared away the debris from the table. She wasn't going to outstay her welcome. It might be Christmas Day but there was still a floor to scrub and tables to do. They wouldn't polish themselves. Whilst scrubbing, she began to wish she'd eaten rather less, but having a full stomach was worth the discomfort. She had more energy than usual this morning. The aroma of hot chestnuts filled the room with a festive feel and this mingled with the apple logs bought specially for today. The tobacco smoke and the smell of unwashed bodies was less evident. She could almost believe the bar was already catering for the middling folk instead of rough workmen.

It was a pity that Mrs Peck had not wanted pitchers of mulled wine standing around the fire as she could have done with a drink to help her keep going. Daisy and Josie had the day off. The Prince of Wales was closing when her shift ended. All very well for them, but it meant she had to wait until the last

customer left as she had to wash all the tankards up before she could go.

An elderly man remained behind. 'I'll hang on for you, love; I'm walking your way. You don't want anything to spoil your day.'

'That's very kind of you, Mr Davies. I'll be as quick as I can. You sit by the fire; there'll be a fair old draught as I'm going in and out to the scullery.'

Her employers had already retired upstairs, leaving her to finish on her own. They'd taken the strongbox with them, so that was one less thing to worry about. She was to call when she'd done, and Mr Peck would come down and lock up after her. Tonight she was to leave by the front door; the yard and kitchen were already bolted for the night.

It was nearer seven when she eventually stepped out into the crisp night air. 'Would you look at that, Mr Davies, a carpet of stars up there! I wonder which one is the star that the three wise men were supposed to have followed.'

'I don't reckon it's one of those, love. It were nigh on two thousand years ago. It was sent just to guide them and the shepherds. What would we want with a guiding star now?' He struggled to button up his coat, his gnarled fingers refusing to obey. Her interference would not be appreciated. Eventually he managed one and then wrapped his muffler tightly around his neck and tucked the ends in to cover the gap. Pulling his cap on firmly he held out his arm.

'Here, take my arm. We can hold each other up. This pavement's sheet ice, and we'll be on our arses if we're not careful.'

Tom Davies had no children at home. He'd told her one son had taken the Queen's shilling; the other was at sea. He lived in a tiny cottage with his wife a couple of hundred yards from the

turning she took to her lodging house. 'I hope Mrs Davies will not be put out because you waited for me.'

'Bless you, child, she was glad to see the back of me. It was she suggested I go for a pint and walk you home. I'm to ask you to come back with me, if you'd care to, and share a cold collation with us.'

'I would love to. How kind of you to think of me. I was dreading going back to my room.'

'Well, that's grand. The missus has been saying ever since I mentioned you starting that she's eager to meet you and hear how a nice girl like you ended up round here with the likes of us.'

'It's the usual story, Mr Davies, but I shall be happy to share it if you really want to know. I seem to remember you live not far from me.'

'That's right, my dear, you'll only have a few hundred yards to go back. We're almost neighbours, ain't we?'

'At least I didn't have to light my lantern this evening. The moon makes things as bright as day.'

One of the first things she'd purchased, at Mr Cooper's insistence, was a small lantern. This made the last part of her journey less hazardous as she could see where she was putting her feet. The stinking alleys were no longer such a nightmare, the light seeming to scare the rats away. Occasionally she saw shadowy faces peering out at her from doorways but so far no one had stepped forward to molest her.

Apart from the drunks this wasn't such a bad area. The inhabitants were almost destitute, their children neglected and barefoot, but most wished her no harm. She'd not heard of any girls being raped or of anyone being murdered. Maybe she was worrying unnecessarily.

'Here we are, love, home sweet home.' Mr Davies knocked

loudly and the door was pulled open. A wave of heat welcomed them.

A tiny lady, her face so wrinkled it had the appearance of a prune, drew her inside. 'There you are, Tom. I have supper waiting for us in front of the fire. Come in, my dear, it's not often we get a visitor.'

They stepped directly into the room. It had proper boards on the floor, a generous fireplace and two comfortable armchairs either side. As she removed her cloak and bonnet, Mrs Davies slammed the door and pulled across a thick curtain. It was cosy and made her realise just how much her own room lacked.

She spent a pleasant hour or so in the cottage and when she rose to leave, Mrs Davies insisted on wrapping up what was left of the supper for her to take back with her. Several slices of cold meat, a piece of plum cake and some freshly baked bread all went into a small basket.

'Drop the basket back on Sunday when you have your day off, Sarah love. I'll have a nice tea ready for you and plenty for you to take home.'

On impulse Sarah leant forward and gave the old lady a hug. 'I have really enjoyed myself, Mrs Davies, and I should love to come to tea next Sunday.' The old couple reminded her of her grandparents in West Bergholt. How long would it be before she could see them again?

Mr Davies had fallen asleep in his chair half an hour since and Sarah decided it would be unfair to make him go out again. It was only a few hundred yards back to her room; she'd be there in no time.

The sound of the bolts being pushed across the door behind her made her feel more alone than she had for weeks. It was getting on for nine o'clock. The sound of revellers celebrating came from various beerhouses close by. She shivered. Rough

men were flocking from the alleys and cuts, heading for the beerhouses.

There were so many, some little more than a room at the front of a cottage. To be a proprietor the tenants merely had to have enough to buy the licence. Mrs Peck had said there was no restriction on the whereabouts or facilities of these places. There must be half a dozen at least within a stone's throw of where she was standing and all of them filled with men she'd rather avoid.

This was the first time she'd been out on her own so late. Why hadn't she made a move earlier, when the streets were quieter, the hostelries less raucous? This was ridiculous. It was not far to her turning and the pathway was lit by gas lamps. All she had to do was negotiate the dark areas between the lamps safely. Wasn't that why she'd bought the lantern in the first place? She wished the moon had stayed out just a little longer.

It was dark here, the next pool of light fifty yards ahead, and then it was her turning next. The sound of breaking glass and raised voices from the establishment over the road made her set off briskly. Unsteady footsteps behind her warned her that a group of inebriated men were approaching.

She melted into the shadows letting the group walk by, positive she hadn't been spotted; she'd been most careful to keep her lantern within the folds of her cloak. The sooner she got home the better. It might be Christmas Day, but those three men were full of the wrong sort of Christmas spirit.

Over the weeks she'd developed her own way of walking fast, but not running which would draw attention to herself. Only tonight she had a basket of food over one arm and was obliged to hold up her skirts with the same hand. This was awkward as the path was slippery. She was concentrating on remaining upright and not paying attention to the men in front.

Before she realised it they had stopped. She was surrounded, one behind and two in front. They'd chosen the spot carefully. It was dark; the light from the two gas lamps didn't reach this far.

'Look here, Bill, it's that pretty little girl what works at The Prince of Wales. Never has a kind word to say to the likes of us.'

The speaker moved closer. She wanted to step away, but if she did she would be pressed up against his equally repellent companion. The stink from the three of them made her gag; she felt her stomach lurching. She prayed she wouldn't vomit over their boots.

'Well then, where's your fancy man now to protect you? I bet you spread your legs quick enough for him of a Saturday night.' A groping hand cupped her backside and started pulling up her skirts.

Bill, the man to her right, reached out and touched her cheek with his rancid finger. 'Who's having her first then? Grab hold of her, Freddie boy, put yer hand over her gob. We'll take the stuck-up bitch down the alley. Nobody will bother us there.'

There was no point in screaming; her cries would go unnoticed in the row coming from the beerhouses nearby. Gripping her basket firmly in one hand and her lantern in the other, she readied herself. She was trapped between them. Their filthy hands would soon be on her body. She'd been robbed and evicted but she was damned if she was going to be raped on Christmas Day.

From somewhere came a rage, a surge of madness that gave her the courage to act. She swung the lantern back and smashed it into the face of the man in front. The glass broke, the oil spilled, and suddenly her attacker was on fire, his muffler and jacket ablaze.

Snatching her skirts from the ground she took to her heels, praying it would take the man's companions several minutes to

beat out the fire. She hoped it looked worse than it was, that the small amount of oil would not do serious damage.

She skidded round her turning, not pausing to catch her breath, the sound of her pursuers growing closer. It was pitch-dark at the end of this alley, but she'd made this journey so many times she would have an advantage over those brutes. Almost there. Turn right, then the length of the walk between the overhanging houses and she would be safe. She ran pell-mell to her front door, thanking God Mr Peck had rehung it and it opened and closed without the need of a hefty shoulder.

At any second they could appear at the corner. She had to be inside before they saw which house she lived in. She pushed the door shut, not banging it – the sound would echo in the night. On tiptoes she crept to her room, key ready in her hand. It took several attempts to turn it, her fingers refusing to allow her to insert it in the lock.

Finally it turned. She fell into her sanctuary. The bolt was across – she'd escaped. She was safe. Her breathing ragged, she waited in the freezing darkness. Would the rapists have seen where she lived? Coarse male voices shouting in the street made her legs buckle. She could do no more. She drew her knees up under her chin, and huddled, as she had in the candle cupboard at Grey Friars House all that while ago.

6

The sound of mice scratching behind the wall and the occasional thump and shout from another tenant were the only sounds in the darkness. Sarah had no idea how long she'd been cowering on the damp floor praying to a God she wasn't sure existed. Well, the men had gone, so perhaps her prayers had been answered.

She inched her way up the door until she was standing. With her eyes open there was enough moonlight filtering in through the window for her to move around freely in the freezing darkness. She needed a fire; she was chilled to the marrow. The warmth and cheerfulness of a blaze might help restore her.

Her tinderbox was resting on the shelf. She'd seen men using the new lucifers – the little stick with its phosphorescent head bursting into flames when struck against a rough surface. They were expensive, but maybe when she was settled she'd invest in a small box. It would certainly make life easier. Having to fiddle around striking a flint onto a bit of fluff was tiresome

and all but impossible when your hands were so cold they weren't working properly.

With the fire finally lit, her pan balanced precariously over the flames, the room was warm enough to risk removing her cloak. She draped it over the table hoping it would be dry by the time she wanted to spread it across the bed. Lighting a second candle was extravagant, but one wasn't sufficient tonight. Anyway, it was the Lord's birthday, a time of celebration and rejoicing, although she didn't feel much like doing either at the moment.

It was fortunate, certainly, that she'd escaped from her encounter with no worse than a scare and a lost lantern. But those men would not forget what she'd done; they didn't know her exact address but they had followed her to the walk outside. She'd heard them shouting. How long would it take for them to discover the exact house? They could be waiting for her tomorrow night, break in and rape her and then slit her throat.

There was no option; she'd have to find herself a position in a different part of town, fresh lodgings, make another life for herself. She'd only been working at The Prince of Wales for a few weeks. Her employers had been kind to her and it wouldn't look good leaving so abruptly. Mrs Peck might not give her a reference, and she'd not find work so easily a second time without one. Writing her own reference was not an option any more – the cost of the materials was beyond her meagre resources.

She wouldn't be sorry to leave this room, but it was cheap and she'd managed to add a few coins to her savings every Saturday. Whilst she waited for the water to boil she reached under her pillow and withdrew her purse; there was a satisfying clunk as she shook the contents onto the table.

She counted it most nights. It gave her the reassurance she

needed that her savings were growing and not shrinking. Occasionally an extra farthing or halfpenny was left on the table; at first she'd not known what to do with it, but Daisy had told her it was hers. Some regulars liked to reward a barmaid for good service. As long as they didn't expect favours in return she was happy to drop it into her skirt pocket.

These coins, and her frugal diet, meant her wages were more than adequate to live on. She balanced the last penny on the pile; there was almost two pounds. Not a fortune, but surely enough to keep her from destitution until she found employment elsewhere. Next time she hoped to afford a more salubrious lodging; it might be better not to inform Mrs Peck she was giving in her notice until she'd done so.

She didn't enjoy bar work, but she'd come to like her employers, especially Mr Peck. Perhaps he'd give her a reference and she could find herself a job in a better class of hostelry. A big place like The Cups or The Red Lion would be ideal. There might be board and lodging included at a coaching inn, which would solve the problem of finding suitable accommodation.

She shuddered, remembering the red-faced, loud farmers who had packed out the bar the day she'd gone into The Red Lion with Betty. She'd hated the way some of the customers deliberately brushed against her as they passed, made lewd suggestions, leered at her over the top of their tankards. She wasn't *that* sort of girl. The very thought of one of those men touching her filled her with disgust. It might well be even worse with middling folk. They thought themselves better than those less fortunate and they might believe that they were entitled to take liberties.

The girls she worked with had been talking about Mary, the one she'd replaced. As soon as the baby was born it would be given up. The unfortunate girl was already within the confines

of the workhouse. Daisy had assured her Mary hadn't been casual with her affections; the young man concerned had promised her a cottage and a ring on her finger before she'd agreed. As soon as she'd caught on he'd vanished, leaving her to throw herself on the parish.

A handsome face and a winning smile would not make *her* forget how to behave. And even if a girl got wed, a constant stream of babies would surely follow. Look at Ada Billings – she was worn down by all the children she had borne. She hoped her friend was managing without her; she hadn't liked the look of that Mr Billings. He didn't seem the sort of man to offer his wife any assistance.

The tea was black, but she'd become used to this; milk and sugar were luxuries she couldn't afford. The rustling above her head reminded her of the basket of food Mrs Davies had given her. She was amazed she hadn't dropped it during her flight. It couldn't be left where it was – the mice she could hear scampering in the ceiling would devour it whilst she was in bed.

There was never any food left over. She bought just enough to feed her after work and had stopped eating breakfast altogether so this was the first time she'd been faced with this problem.

Collecting the basket, she removed the folded napkin and placed it on the table. Inside were three slices of ham, a wedge of cheese and a twist of paper in which were three pickled onions. She was tempted to eat it straight away, not risk her nocturnal visitors getting it first. However, her stomach was more full of food than it had been in weeks; she couldn't force another morsel down.

In a separate package was a generous slice of plum cake and a piece of apple tart. It was sufficient to last her for several days if somehow she could protect it. There'd not been droppings on

the shelf so this must be the safest place in the room. She removed her clean petticoat from inside the pillowslip and wrapped it several times around the food and then replaced the bundle in the basket.

Tomorrow was a normal working day so she'd better get herself into bed. She smiled and stretched contentedly. The room was warm enough to remove her outer garments without turning blue; in fact she could put on her nightgown. The thought of being so vulnerable made her decide to leave it where it was, inside the pillowslip.

As usual it was her drawers and petticoats. She grinned as she snuggled down beneath the blankets, recalling something Daisy had told her. Her mother had used to sew the unfortunate girl into her undergarments for the winter. It didn't bear thinking of; her childhood had been luxurious compared to those she worked with now. Although it was impossible to wash her gowns, her underclothes and stockings were clean and she regularly rinsed the hems and scrubbed the sweat stains from the armpits of her two dresses.

Sarah had expected to lie awake, but she slept well, the warmth of the room making her relax. She woke suddenly, not sure what had disturbed her. She'd been deep in a nightmare, standing at the head of a flight of stairs whilst her brother had been climbing towards her. But the faster he ran more stairs appeared in front of him. It was a relief to be awake.

It was dark, but the small square of moonlight from the high window gave sufficient light to see. The house was quiet, not even a child wailing in the darkness. Something had woken her. Then she heard the scrabbling above her head. The mice had discovered her food and were having a festive feast of their own.

She scrambled out of bed to snatch the basket from the shelf, holding it at arm's length, not sure what she should do

next. Determined to save some of the food, but loath to have the livestock in the basket tumble out over her bare feet, she gingerly stretched out and placed the object on the table.

The scrabbling had stopped. It was ominously silent. She would take them outside, but first she must put on her boots and cloak. Hopefully, if she upturned the basket the rodents would fall out and what was left of her food would remain behind. The petticoat would have to be washed; she didn't fancy wearing it when the mice had made free with it all night.

In unlaced boots, her cloak securely clasped around her neck, she grasped the basket handle and carried it from the room, having unbolted the door already. Leaving the door ajar – she wasn't going to be gone more than a few moments – she stepped out into the freezing darkness of the narrow passageway.

It was a struggle opening the back door one-handed but eventually she was outside. Placing the basket on the ground she pushed it sideways with the poker she'd had the forethought to bring with her. Three small grey shapes tumbled out and vanished. She straightened the basket, prodding it a few times to see if anything else jumped out.

Satisfied the livestock had abandoned their meal she hooked the handle over the poker and carried it back into her room. She rattled the basket a few more times until she was satisfied the mice had gone. The ham and cheese were untouched; however, the mice had made severe inroads into the plum cake and apple pie. She was tempted to throw it all away but this would be a disgraceful waste. She couldn't bring herself to eat it. She had not been living in penury long enough to lose her own fastidiousness, but there were children starving in the street who would think this a feast.

She removed each item, shaking off any droppings, then cut

away the nibbled pieces. She rewrapped what was left in the napkin and put it back in the basket. No doubt the mice were already making their way back into the house. There was no point in leaving the food in the room – she would take it with her and give it away.

Dealing with the mice pushed her attack to the back of her mind, and when she set off for work hoping to find recipients for her bounty, she quite forgot to check if she was being followed. It was so early there were no children abroad; she'd have to find someone on her return. Laughing she explained to Mrs Peck what had happened with the mice.

'Put it in the pantry. My tomcat makes sure we have no mice in here. You want to get yourself a cat; they don't cost much to feed and it would be company of a night.'

'I'll think about it, Mrs Peck. I'll get on with the floor. There'll be chestnut peelings all over it this morning.'

She was so busy, what had happened the previous night was all but forgotten. There were chestnuts to roast and serve, and the bar was full. She got a few peculiar looks but didn't take any notice; however, when two of the less pleasant customers snarled at her she was forced to admit things had changed.

She tried to avoid the corner of the room where these two sat. They didn't have the wherewithal to order a refill, thank goodness. Mr Cooper came towards the end of her shift; she felt safe now he was there, nobody would take liberties with him about. The width of his shoulders, the strength of his fists and the steely glint in his eye would discourage all but the most determined.

The bar was quiet, everyone gone, apart from one or two dozing by the fire reluctant to return to their cold lodgings. Dan Cooper, as always, was last to go. He waited for her to finish so he could walk her home. He beckoned her over. Sarah checked

that Mrs Peck was elsewhere. 'Sit down a minute, Sarah. I need to talk to you.' She sat and waited. He grinned. 'I've been hearing all about you, that you set fire to Fred Paterson last night. Is it true?'

The way he described it, it seemed funny, and she returned his smile. 'Three men stopped me. They said they were going to...' Her cheeks flushed scarlet.

His smile vanished. 'Did they indeed. We'll see about that. It's not safe for you around here any more. My Maria has been asking me to persuade you to come and work for us. Ever since I told her you were a trained nursemaid she's not let up. I didn't think it a good idea, but now things are different.'

'Mr Cooper, are you offering me employment? Will I be living in?'

He nodded. He didn't appear too keen on the idea – perhaps employing a girl without references worried him. 'I can't pay much mind, but you'll get board and lodging and you'll be safe under my roof. There's a woman comes in to do the heavy work; you'll take care of the boys and do the cooking.'

She couldn't believe she'd been given such a wonderful opportunity. 'I promise you'll not regret this, Mr Cooper. I don't eat much and I'll do the heavy work as well. You can give me what you gave her.'

He frowned, shaking his head. 'I'm not putting someone out of work; the money she earns keeps her off the parish.'

She hung her head; she hadn't meant to offend him. 'I beg your pardon, Mr Cooper. I meant no harm by the suggestion.'

'Good, that's settled. The sooner you're out of that room the better. I've spoken to Ma Peck and she's in agreement. You're not safe here any more. John Peck will come with us. He's bringing a handcart for your belongings. Your room will be the attic. It ain't big, but it's clean and dry, and warmed by the chimney breast

that runs through it. Anything you've got by way of furniture of your own will be helpful.'

She wanted to reach out and shake his hand, to embrace him, but he didn't look the sort of man who'd take kindly to such a gesture. She detected he was only taking her on to please his wife, that if she hadn't been in such a perilous position he would never have spoken. Betty had been wrong; Dan Cooper certainly hadn't taken a shine to her. Indeed, he seemed most reluctant to take her on.

'I thank you, sir; I'd already decided to start looking for employment elsewhere. I never thought things would fall into place like this. I won't let you and Mrs Cooper down. I love children, and I can read and write. I'd be happy to teach them their letters if you wish me to.'

'My older boys already attend infant school most mornings so that won't be necessary. Now get a move on, the sooner we get your things the quicker I'll be home to my family.'

Flanked by two substantial men, Sarah was in no danger from anyone. Mr Peck had a lantern tied to his cart, and using this they were able to find their way to the front door of her lodgings without mishap. She led the way, belatedly remembering she had her damp petticoat draped across the table. Too late to worry about such niceties. She unlocked the door, stepping in front of them in order to snatch up the offending garment and toss it on the bed.

'Bugger me! I can't believe you've been living in this rathole all these weeks, Sarah, and still turning up at work cheerful and smart.'

'It's all I could afford, Mr Cooper. As you can imagine, I shan't be sorry to leave.'

He chuckled. 'Compared to this, the room you'll have will seem like luxury.'

In little less than half an hour they were retracing their steps, she still clutching the basket of food. When would she have time to return it to Mrs Davies? She'd been invited to tea next Sunday. 'Mr Cooper, I went to visit with Mr and Mrs Davies last night. It was on the way back from their cottage that I was attacked. She's invited me to tea next Sunday when I'm to return this basket.'

His brow creased. 'I ain't a hard taskmaster, Sarah, but you're not to come up here again, even to return a basket. I'll give it to him when I see him next. He'll understand when I explain the circumstances.' His voice was abrupt. She felt rebuffed and less certain of her welcome in his house.

A group of ragged children were watching wide-eyed as they passed. Quickly she removed the food and held it out to the largest. 'Would you like this? There's ham and cheese and a few other things as well.'

He didn't need asking twice; the urchin clutched the bundle to his chest. He was not much more than five years old, and he grinned. With his siblings beside him he raced back into the alleyway; she hoped the children would all get a fair share of the food.

She had two pounds in her purse and was to work with children again. This was the second time she had somehow managed to avoid disaster. It was nothing short of miraculous. As they trundled past St Leonard's Church she closed her eyes and sent up a prayer of thanks. She'd never doubt the existence of the Lord again.

7

LONDON, JANUARY 1844

More than two years had passed since he'd left home and Alfie no longer thought about returning to Colchester. He'd built up a steady business and sometimes employed an extra boy to push the third cart. He and Jim had replaced the money they'd spent and there was a small fortune put by to rent themselves a cottage with a yard sometime in the spring.

He stayed away from Bishopsgate and had all but forgotten he'd ever belonged to a gang of thieves. Jim was thriving; he was taller and had filled out a treat. George Benson from upstairs had become a good friend as well. He'd been learning him how to use the carpentry tools of a Sunday and Alfie reckoned he was a natural. They might even suggest to George that they shared a yard. It made good sense.

After the holiday season things wasn't as busy, but there was a steady trickle of business, and if they had to go further afield to find it, then so what? They was fit and healthy and the more they worked the more they had to put in their savings. Alfie was tempted to stick it in one of them savings clubs he'd heard about. The Pig and Whistle, his local hostelry, ran such a thing.

The weather was foul. More ice, snow and sleet plagued them until the middle of January. Even with thick coats, extra socks to wear inside their boots, and gloves on their hands they were near frozen to death.

Alfie no longer looked over his shoulder. It was eighteen months since they'd split away from the gang and something would have happened before this. Jim was confident enough to work on his own. Sometimes Alfie sent Buster, but the dog preferred to remain at his side. When the weather was inclement the animal had to be persuaded to leave his warm spot on the rug in front of the fire.

He couldn't credit that this huge, friendly dog was the same vicious tyke what had spent the first few years of his life living on a coal barge. The snow thawed but was replaced by a bitter east wind, and Jim developed a hacking cough. Alfie decided it wouldn't hurt for both of them to take the day off. They had nothing booked until the following week; why not stay in the warm and toast crumpets in front of the fire?

'You know, Jim, I've been living in London almost two years and you're the only friend I got apart from George and Buster. The man on the coal lighter I ran away from, that bastard Black Ben, he'd slit my throat, or do me in with a shovel, if he got the chance. I reckon Ginger and the others from our old gang would do the same, and Silas the fence would be right behind them. I seem to have a knack of making enemies not friends.'

Jim was coughing so hard he couldn't answer. Alfie handed him a mug of tea. 'Thanks, Alfie. My chest feels as if someone's sitting on it. I don't reckon I'll be well enough to work tomorrow. I'm right poorly and no mistake.'

'You don't have to work, not if you're ill. We've done so well this past year we can afford to take it easy. You stop in the warm;

I'll go to Finsbury Market on me own. Pity to miss the chance of making a few bob.'

'You'd better take the dog. I'll be fine here. Buster could do with the exercise; he's getting right lazy nowadays. How old is he, do you know?'

'Ain't the faintest idea, but he must be five or six. You hear that, Buster? You're coming with me tomorrow. Jim's stopping here in the warm for a change.'

Several times he was woken by Jim's coughing. If his friend were no better in a couple of days he'd have to find a quack. He'd try some cough syrup first; he'd get it on the way home tomorrow. He crept off the next morning without waking his friend who had finally fallen into a restless sleep an hour or two before dawn.

The market was poorly attended; most folk must have thought it better to stay at home than come out in this weather. He got two deliveries and made two shillings, enough to spend on medicine for Jim. He jogged the last mile; he couldn't feel his fingers or toes but the thought of a warm room and a hot mug of tea drove him on. Buster was limping at his side looking sorry for himself.

The wheels banged and rattled on the cobbles. He was too cold to care if he caused damage in his haste. It was dusk when he trundled his barrow into the yard. There was no candle flickering behind the curtain. Jim must still be asleep. He'd hoped he'd have the kettle on.

'Come on, Buster, let's get out of the wind. I've got hot pasties and fresh bread and cheese for supper. And I got something tasty for you as well.'

Jim would have bolted the door, so he raised his fist to knock loudly. To his surprise it was open. The room was icy, the fire out, and there was no sign of his friend. The dog

trotted into the room showing no sign of disquiet. Alfie's stomach returned to its normal place and he unclenched his fists. For an awful moment he'd thought Ginger or Silas had finally discovered them and Jim had been abducted. If this were the case the dog would be bristling and growling, would have known at once that someone strange had been in the room.

'Where the hell has he gone, Buster? I think he ain't been here for a while, else the fire would be burning.'

He shivered. The first thing to do was get it going again. Wherever Jim was, he'd not want to come back to a freezing room, not when he were feeling so poorly. Eventually it was rekindled and the room warm enough to take off his overcoat. He pulled the kettle over the flames; it wouldn't hurt to have a cup of tea, thaw out a bit, whilst he thought about what to do next.

The window rattled and a gust of icy air swirled around his feet. Where on earth was Jim? What had possessed him to go out when the weather was so bitter? Only then did he see his friend's overcoat hanging where he'd left it the night before. He scrabbled under Jim's bed and pulled out his boots. His friend only had the one pair. He must have gone barefoot. It didn't bear thinking of, being without footwear tonight.

The kettle hissed and he pushed it off the heat. He couldn't settle until he'd found him. He'd nip upstairs and enquire off Mrs Hunter – his landlady – and George. Maybe they'd seen something. She had the right-hand side of the house and her kitchen window overlooked the backyard; her front parlour faced the street. 'You stop here, Buster. Take care of things. I'm just going upstairs to see if anyone knows where Jim's gone.'

The dog thumped his tail and flopped down in front of the fire, not bothered about going outside again in the cold and

dark. He could hear voices in the rooms. Good, someone was in. He knocked on the door and waited.

'Alfie, what can we do for you?' The daughter, Elsie, smiled up at him, her ruined teeth spoiling her appearance.

'I was wondering, miss, if you'd seen Jim. I left him behind today – he was not too well – but when I returned just now the room was empty. He's gone out without his boots or his coat on. I was hoping you might have seen him leave, what direction he went, if there was anyone with him?'

The young woman turned and called to her mother. 'Ma, did you see Alfie's friend go out earlier?'

'No, I've only been in meself a little while. I thought he weren't well and was stopping behind today.'

Alfie stepped forward in order to speak directly to Mrs Hunter. 'I left him with a high fever, but he's gone outside with no boots and no coat. The room was icy, the fire out. I reckon he's been gone all day.'

She shook her head, her expression sad. 'You'll not find him in the dark, Alfie. Let's pray a kind soul took him in. He'll not survive without shelter, it's that bitter. I don't envy no one on the streets tonight.'

'That's what I thought. I'm hoping someone from one of the poorhouses might have took him in. I ain't going down there now; I'll visit tomorrow. I'm going to have a look round the area with the dog. If Jim's still in the neighbourhood Buster will sniff him out soon enough.'

He spent a fruitless two hours peering in shop doorways, calling down dark alleys, but to no avail. 'I don't reckon he's round here no more. He's wandered off right and proper. Let's get back, no point in freezing to death.'

In spite of his worry he ate heartily. Buster gobbled down the stale bread and cheese rind then settled in a corner to gnaw

his bone. Alfie put the second pie and the iced buns on the shelf alongside the cough mixture he'd bought. He hoped Jim would be back to take some. Each time there were footsteps in the yard he got up, but it were just other residents using the privy.

He slept little, tossing and turning restlessly. In the year they'd been together he'd become accustomed to Jim's snuffling and snoring; the room seemed quiet without him.

Next morning he was up before dawn. He poked the embers into life and threw on a few lumps of coal. He'd get something down him and set off at first light. The back door was frozen solid. He reckoned he'd woken half the house by the time he'd prised it open. A pale sun shone down from a cloudless sky, and everything was thick with frost. Even the privy sparkled; pity the smell didn't match its appearance. Mind you, it were a lot better when the contents were frozen solid.

His breath steamed in front of him; his feet crunched on the ice. It looked pretty, but he pitied the poor buggers who'd not found a bed last night. He was determined to find his friend today, even if it meant knocking on every door until someone told him something. Going so close to the dosshouse, even after so long, meant there was a risk he might be recognised. His enemies would be on him before he could return to the safety of his own place. Taking his dog with him would keep him safe from attack, but the animal was a dead giveaway. If anyone *was* still looking, it would be for a youth and a big brown dog. The animal was better guarding the money.

'I'll not be gone long, old fellow. I'm going to find our Jim and bring him home. Don't you let anyone in, you understand?'

The dog cocked an ear and lazily opened one eye, then settled back to snooze. He'd been out in the yard to cock his leg and do his business. Alfie had scooped the mess up and tossed it in the privy. There were old ladies who collected dog shit, sold it

to the tanneries or something. It was free and plentiful on the streets of London, but it weren't something he'd like to do.

In his thick coat, muffler wrapped around his face, his cap pulled down over his ears, he was unrecognisable as the boy who'd lived in Half Moon Street. He was a man now. He took the route along Norton Folgate, which led into Bishopsgate Street, mingling with the crowd. No one would pick him out as anyone particular. He'd try the London Workhouse first and then go to Bishopsgate after.

He crossed the road; strolling on the side furthest from his old haunt gave him added protection. The pathways were busy – it was business as usual around here. Folks had to get to work, housewives had to shop, never mind the weather. Still, the city looked pretty enough, soot-streaked buildings silver-coated like something out of one of them picture books Ma had read to Tommy.

He blinked; losing Jim so unexpectedly reminded him of his little brother's death. He kept his eyes skinned for his friend. His heart stopped when he saw a huddle of old clothing in a shop doorway. He bent down to look more closely. It was an old man, stiff as a board. He'd obviously been dead some time, but no one took no notice.

A bit further on he saw two children, clinging together like sparrows in a nest, their scrawny bodies clothed in rags, their lips and feet blue with cold. He dipped into his pocket and handed them a shilling each. They were too cold to speak, but the gratitude in their eyes was enough to make him feel a bit better about finding Jim. If he could help children in distress, then maybe someone had done the same for his mate.

Jim wasn't a child, but then he weren't an adult grown neither. He reckoned his friend was about his age, fifteen, but he looked younger because of his size. Mind you, Alfie looked

several years older, already a head taller than most women and eye to eye with a lot of men. His shoulders were broad, his arms well-muscled from the year he'd spent shovelling coal. Sarah wouldn't recognise him, but then maybe he'd not know her either.

He screwed his face up trying to fathom how old she was. She must be seventeen this year. For a girl that was fully grown. She could be courting. Ma had been married not much older than that. Would he ever see her again? He squared his shoulders and raised his head. His business were doing well, he'd got decent savings hidden away, and in a month or two he could start looking about for his own premises. Maybe he would take the train to Colchester one fine day.

He was so lost in thought he was at his destination before he knew it. Half Moon Street was opposite and the turning to the workhouse the next one. He must risk his neck and cross the road busy with diligences, carts and hackney carriages. He waited for a decent gap in the traffic and, after dodging through, arrived safely on the other side. His boots were liberally smeared with manure. He'd better get rid of that before he knocked at the workhouse.

He wasn't sure how he should do this. Did he bang on the door and ask if they'd taken someone in? Did you have to be a relative to enquire after an inmate? He dithered, gazing in despair at the grim building. Its high wall made it look like a prison, the heavy wooden gates adding to this impression. The inmates were kept as secure as prisoners – that's for sure. He saw the tall hat of a constable approaching and without a second thought Alfie stopped him.

'Excuse me, sir, me friend wandered off yesterday from Hog Lane whilst I was out working. He was right poorly, had a fever and went off without his boots and coat. I've searched every-

where but I ain't found him. I was wondering if he might have been taken in there. Where do I go to enquire?'

The man pulled his whiskers. 'If you go to the side door, you'll see it plain enough. Just ring the bell and someone will come. You can ask them. Let's hope you find your friend safe, young man. It wasn't a night to be out, especially if you ain't got your boots on.'

'Thank you, sir, I'll do that. I see the gate now.'

The peeler tipped his hat and strode off. Alfie approached the gate, not sure if he wanted to know if Jim *was* in there. He had a bad feeling about this; the constable had shaken his head like his landlady. They didn't hold out much hope. The London Workhouse was a bleedin' long way from Hog Lane. Was it likely Jim could have ended up here?

He rapped on the door, his knuckles making little sound. Then he spotted a metal rod hanging from the archway. He grasped the knob, wincing as the metal burned his hand. A hideous clanging echoed behind the wall. He was about to ring again when a flap in the door was wrenched open. A pasty-faced woman glared out at him, her eyes like currants in a bun, her greasy grey hair stuffed under a filthy cap.

'What you want?'

'I was wondering if you'd taken anyone in last night. This is the only place I can think my friend could have ended up.'

'Wait here, I'll make enquiries.'

The opening slammed shut. He danced from foot to foot in an effort to keep warm. It was an age before the mean face stared at him again.

'No one came in last night. I should try the hospital – he's more like to have been taken there.'

Alfie wanted to ask where the hospital was, but considering her duty done the slattern crashed the hatch shut. He'd have to

try to Bishopsgate Workhouse next. He'd cut back down Bishopsgate and turn left into Dunnings Lane. This time he knew the drill and located the door he needed without assistance. No one had seen Jim there either.

His last hope was gone. What he needed was to find another peeler; they seemed to know what's what. He didn't think Jim could have ended up in the London Hospital. He'd not have staggered that far the condition he'd been in yesterday. He shivered, remembering something he'd heard when he was working on the coal lighter. Someone had said the boy who'd worked for Black Ben previously had been so badly beaten he'd had to go to the hospital but died within its walls. No one came out of those sorts of places alive.

No, he was missing something here. Jim must have been taken in by someone nearby. He'd get back directly and start banging on doors. He'd come on a wild goose chase; should have been going in the opposite direction, to the shops as well, making enquiries there. He retraced his steps, stopping off briefly at his lodgings to collect Buster. Maybe the dog would sniff his friend out for him. He'd had no luck last night, but it was a bit warmer now and that might help.

He spent the rest of the day asking. Folks shook their heads sadly; no one had seen Jim and no one had much hope of him having survived the cold. Alfie was mystified – ill and dressed as he was, how could Jim have left the neighbourhood?

The store was quiet. Most folk would be at work or at home eating their midday meal. It would do no harm to enquire in here – he'd asked everywhere else already. The proprietor, Mr Beamish, whose name belied his nature, was busy emptying the last grains of rice from a sack into a tin on the counter.

'Not come back then, Alfie?'

'You know I'm looking for my Jim? He's been gone two days now and not a sign of him anywhere.'

'The whole street knows he's gone. Word spreads fast. You're both well thought of round here. You know what's a mystery to me? Why no one has seen him. Mind, as he wandered off in the dark, sensible folks would have been inside keeping warm.'

'But he didn't, mister, he left in broad daylight, when I were out working. I can't understand why no one saw him at all. There was folks around on the streets, there always is, and walking as he was without his coat and boots he'd have stuck out round here. Not many folks without no footwear in this part of the city.'

'True enough. I've been asking customers this morning, but nothing doing so far. They'll spread the word. Someone must know where he is. You'll find him eventually – don't fret.' The shopkeeper swept up the few spilt grains and polished the counter with his shirtsleeve. 'Have you tried at the rectory? The rector's wife and daughter do good works and they might have taken him in out of charity.'

Alfie thought this unlikely. He'd seen these two, a hatchet-faced woman and her daughter no better. They rarely walked around here; the folk were too common for the likes of them. They travelled in style and always had a maidservant with them. Hardly the sort of women who'd take someone off the street, more likely to drive on past. He'd go and ask, but good Samaritans were in short supply there in his opinion.

'Ta, Mr Beamish, I'll nip along right away. Whilst I'm here, any deliveries need doing?'

'Not today. Come in again on Friday – might have something for you then.'

The visit to the rectory proved another wasted journey. He got no further than a maidservant at the back door who sent

him packing double quick. He was told in no uncertain terms that the master weren't in the habit of taking people off the streets. There was a perfectly good workhouse for *that* sort of person. God-fearing they might be, but full of Christian charity, they certainly wasn't.

It was too late to go out now and tomorrow he must go back to work. He'd have to hope that word was sent round to him about Jim's whereabouts. There was a hospital, but it was at least forty-five minutes' walk from here, not worth checking to see if his friend had managed to stagger that far. It were more likely he'd collapsed nearby – he'd been too sick to get any further.

Alfie prepared to spend a second night without his friend for company. He reviewed what had happened. What was he missing? Was it possible Buster didn't react because it had been one of the gang who'd taken Jim away? Wouldn't they have stopped to give him his coat and let him put on his boots? It didn't make sense no matter from which way he looked at it. People didn't just vanish into thin air, did they?

He flopped back on his bed too dispirited to hook the curtain across the window or eat the last remaining pasty. He gave the one that had been meant for Jim to Buster for his supper. The temperature dropped. His windows were as icy inside as they were out. He couldn't afford to waste heat by not pulling the curtain across. Using extra coal didn't make sense, especially now he was the only one bringing in money. A freezing draught came under his door as someone braved the elements to use the privy before turning in.

George had offered to help to look on Sunday when he had his day off. With luck Jim would have been found before then. Tomorrow there was a market where the middling folks purchased goods. He'd tried the Saturday night market where

the poorest bought the makings for Sunday dinner, the women-folk waiting outside the beerhouses to get their housekeeping after their men had been paid. These, although busier than the one he was going to next day, were frequented by those what carried their own goods. Their money was so scarce they hadn't even a copper to spare for him to take their laden baskets home on his barrow.

He couldn't afford to sit moping about. He'd done all he could; he must get on with his life or he'd go under. There were a few regular customers who looked out for him, knew he was honest and wouldn't filch their goods on the way back. There were no grand establishments in this vicinity but there were a fair few well-to-do with substantial properties. It was them what were happy to have him deliver stuff. He'd have to find another boy to help with the big barrow at the next furniture sale. Too soon to think of replacing someone he'd begun to think of as a brother and not just a business partner.

He kept busy until dusk, had no time to think about his loss. The room that had once seemed like home now seemed cheer-less and empty. Even Buster failed to make it a happy place. His enquiries had uncovered no further news of Jim. All that was left of him was his overcoat and boots, and his share of the money they had put by. He began to think he might have imag-ined he'd ever had a business partner.

George Benson rapped on his door that evening. 'Alfie, I'd like to borrow a barrow again tomorrow, first thing, if that's all right? I've a nice bit of timber put by and the gaffer needs me to clear it out or some other bugger's going to get it instead. We could keep an eye out for Jim on the way.'

'You're welcome. I ain't got much on, and without Jim I only need a small one. You need a hand? I'll be glad to come along and help.'

'I reckon the big one would be better, because I could do it with one journey. I works in a yard about half an hour from here. If I get there early the master says I can take it then. As long as I'm back at starting time he'll not dock me wages.'

'Suits me – I can tout for work after.'

* * *

It took the two of them to push the laden barrow back over the cobbled streets. It was piled high with off-cuts, broken planks and bits fit only for burning. When they arrived Alfie was gasping, had to support himself on the handle. When he recovered his breath sufficiently to speak he straightened, mopped his face on his sleeve, and turned to his new friend.

'I reckon there's enough to make a couple of tables and a bench and maybe a bookshelf as well. Shall I get started planing the wood for you? I don't have the heart to go to the market at the moment.'

'There's two ladies down Worship Street after bookshelves – make a start on that. It's bloody cold to work outside, but I suppose you're used to it by now.'

'I'll light the brazier, use the off-cuts. I'll be warm enough. I think I'm best cut out for carpentry. Jim says he'll run the delivery side of things and I can concentrate on making furniture with you. I reckon we could start looking for premises as soon as Jim's back.'

George nodded. 'You learnt more in the past year than I did in three. I'll start looking for somewhere suitable right away.'

* * *

London, February 1844

As the days passed Alfie had almost resigned himself to never seeing Jim again. He folded his friend's coat carefully and put it on his empty bed along with his boots. He wouldn't get rid of any of it, nor consider the money his, not until he was sure his mate had gone for good. It was as if Jim had never existed; the small space he'd made in the world had closed up.

He was scraping the last of his vegetable stew from his bowl when Buster raised his head, his lips curled, and a deep, threatening growl filled the room. There was a knock on the door. It was a person his dog didn't know.

8

Alfie hesitated, taking his dog's adverse reaction to indicate it was someone who wished him ill outside the door. The knock was repeated.

'Open the door, if you please. I have urgent news for you.'

This was no villain, not the usual type any road. With Buster at his side ready to spring to his defence if necessary, he'd risk it. He stood behind the door, his heart pounding, his mouth dry. 'Who is it? Name yerself.'

'Mr Hudson. I've come about your friend Jim.'

Alfie flung the door open. Facing him was a sombre gentleman in a many-caped overcoat, his hat pulled down low over his ears and a woolly muffler around his face. Toffs didn't look like this. Had he made a dreadful mistake?

Buster stopped growling and his tail thumped the wall. He trusted his dog's instinct and relaxed, stepping aside to let the man in.

'I'm Alfie Nightingale, Mr Hudson. I've been that desperate for news about Jim but given up hope of ever hearing.'

'I am the benefactor and trustee of a charity that takes care

of street children. Your friend Jim was picked up by one of the wardens.'

'Why would he leave his warm bed, mister, when he was so poorly? I can't understand how he ended up in the street; he could scarcely move when I left for work that morning.'

'It was his delirium, young man. It would appear that he set out looking for someone called Ginger. He reached Worship Street and collapsed. If Jarvis had not been driving past at that precise moment he would surely have perished where he fell.'

Jim found, and snug and warm in some mission? Alfie could hardly believe it, could feel his spirits lifting, his face cracking in a smile. 'If you care to take a seat, sir, I'll get me coat and such, and collect Jim's things; he'll need them to come home.'

The gentleman had removed his hat and loosened the scarf around his face. He cleared his throat. 'I should leave those here, my boy. They'll likely go missing if you take them at the moment. Fetch them later, when Jim's able to accompany you.'

'How did you find me? Did Jim give you my direction?'

'No, a constable brought in two children he'd found freezing to death in a shop doorway in Bishopsgate Street. When he called back to enquire after their welfare we mentioned having found your friend. He recalled speaking to you outside the London Workhouse a while ago. After that it was a simple matter of asking a shopkeeper for information. It seems that everyone knew you were searching for your friend.'

'I was that. I can't tell you how happy I am to see you, mister. I'm ready to go. No, Buster, you stop here. They'll not allow dogs where I'm going. I'll be back later with news of our Jim.'

In the icy passage he hesitated a moment, not sure if he should lock his door or leave it as it was. If there was a fire no one could release his dog, but if the door somehow came open

Buster might well come out to look for him. He couldn't risk their secret hoard being taken.

He locked the door. Mr Hudson had already vanished into the yard, retrieving a lantern he'd left burning just outside. It were odd the gentleman coming to the back gate, not knocking on the front door, but not to worry. All that mattered was he was going to see Jim, and when he was well bring him home again. They went down the narrow side passage and waiting outside was a hackney carriage.

'Crikey! I ain't never been in one of those. We're to travel in style then, sir?'

'We are indeed, young man. It is too far for us to walk.' He smiled, his teeth flashing white under the flickering gas lamp. 'At least it is too far me – I'm not as young as I used to be, as no doubt you have observed.'

The gentleman was past middle age, but not elderly by any means. When he'd removed his hat, his hair had been grey all right, but thick, and it matched his handsome side whiskers. He was otherwise clean-shaven, and smartly, if sombrely dressed. His trousers, what could be seen of them, were of a dark material, his boots black and well made.

Alfie scrambled into the hackney carriage, clutching the strap as it rocked. Briefly the interior was illuminated and he looked around with interest. There was a scuffed leather seat, more than room enough for two, but it smelt of stale tobacco and sweat. He reckoned he'd rather be walking in the fresh air than cooped up inside one of these vehicles.

This cove must be wealthy – it weren't cheap to travel in a hackney cab. He'd said he was the benefactor or some such of this charitable home; he was obviously not short of a few bob. Jim had been lucky; this mission place sounded a sight better than a workhouse.

'Does we owe you anything, mister? As you can see, we ain't badly off. Jim and me – he's my business partner – we own three barrows and do a decent trade. We reckon to rent our own premises next year if we continue busy like what we are now.'

'You are a hard-working young man. I was aware of that the moment I saw you. And a good and loyal friend to Jim.' He cleared his throat again, and Alfie heard him shifting in the darkness. 'I must warn you, Alfie, Jim is not at all well. However, we must not dwell on that now. He will be much restored to have you come to visit. He's been asking after you constantly these past days.' He cleared his throat for a third time; it was beginning to annoy Alfie. 'I can assure you, we require no recompense from you. It is a charity and most of the people we assist are completely without funds.'

He stopped talking as the vehicle swayed and bounced around the corner before straightening, the jarvey cracking his whip and urging his nag into something resembling a trot.

'It was because Jim came out without his boots and coat we thought he was destitute. But as soon as he was able he quite forcibly disabused us of this fact. But as our mission is in Wood Street, and he had no recollection of where he was, he found it difficult to tell us exactly how to find you.'

Alfie cursed his decision not to tell Jim the name of the street they lived on. He'd thought that if Jim was ever waylaid by Silas Field, or Ginger and the gang, he'd be unable to give away the whereabouts of their lodgings. If Jim had known he lived on Hog Lane he would have been returned to him days ago, not have been left among strangers all this time.

It was a full thirty minutes before the vehicle shuddered to a halt. They were outside an imposing building with stone steps and a portico. It looked too grand to house foundlings. Mr Hudson waited until the jarvey dropped down from his perch to

open the door. Coins exchanged hands and then the cab moved off.

He was to make his own way back then. Bugger that! He could read the street signs, but he had no idea where Wood Lane was; he'd never find his way in the dark. He'd face that problem when he came to leave. He didn't want to go anywhere without Jim, but he weren't well enough to leave – that was obvious. He frowned. What about Buster? He couldn't abandon his dog for more than a few hours. He'd have to return at first light whatever happened.

He shrugged, running after Mr Hudson as he ascended the front steps. Why not go around the back? He'd not be admitted roughly dressed as he was. The gentleman rapped sharply on the door. It was opened by a uniformed servant. She curtsied and they were ushered in. This weren't like any hospital he'd ever heard of. It was set up like the residence of some toff. He hovered uncertainly behind Mr Hudson, glancing sideways at the family portraits hanging on the wall, the clean carpet that ran down the centre of the wide hallway. Then he got a whiff of something he recognised, carbolic soap, and then boiled cabbage and unwashed boys.

The gentleman handed his outer garments to the maid; she waited patiently whilst he did the same. He weren't so sure about this. He hoped he saw them again, that they didn't disappear forever. He felt out of place. Someone like him should have been taken in the back like other common folk.

Mr Hudson saw his disquiet. 'No doubt you are surprised by this building. The front rooms are occupied by the warden and his wife and, when I'm in town, I stay here also. The house servants reside in the attics. However, as you will see, the rear of the house has been substantially extended to accommodate dormitories, wards and recreation spaces for our children.'

He sniffed and his eyes crinkled at the corners. 'Although we keep separate, you are always aware of the real purpose of this place. Come along, Alfie, you must be desperate to see your friend after having given up so much of your valuable time searching for him.'

He led the way along the corridor and down a short flight of stairs. Facing them was a substantial door. He knocked, and hurrying feet arrived behind it. There was the sound of a bolt being undone, a key turned and the door swung back.

This time it was no uniformed maid, but a skinny woman in a starched cap, long white apron and shiny gown. She curtsied. 'Good evening, sir, we've been expecting you. I take it this is the young man Jim has been asking for?'

Mr Hudson nodded. 'Indeed it is, Mrs Jones. May I introduce you to Alfie Nightingale.'

The woman smiled, and Alfie saw her stiff appearance was misleading. She had kind eyes and her smile was sympathetic. 'I'm so pleased to see you. Come along with me. Your friend is in a side room.'

The corridor looked and smelled like an institution. This was obviously a hospital wing, but noisy feet and the sound of laughter came from somewhere further away. If there was laughter in here, it weren't such a bad place; no one laughed in a workhouse. The nurse stopped outside the door. It was slightly ajar, but he could hear no sounds from within it. Jim must be asleep. It was after nine o'clock, but he'd soon wake up to speak to him.

He stepped into a small room, just large enough for a large metal bed, a chair and washstand. A decent fire burned in the grate, an oil lamp stood on a side table, but this must be the wrong place. That couldn't be Jim resting so still in the centre of the white sheets.

He clutched the door frame. They hadn't told him his friend was at death's door. No wonder Mr Hudson had been so keen to get him here that he'd been prepared to pay for a hackney cab. He rushed forward, dropping onto the edge of the bed, the only sound in the room the rasp of Jim's laboured breathing. The heat from his body burned through the thin coverings.

'Jim, Jim, it's me. It's Alfie come to see you.' There was no response. He clasped his friend's skeletal hand and tried again. 'Jim, wake up. I ain't going to sit here talking to meself all night.' The blue eyelids flickered and opened.

'Alfie, I'm right glad to see you. You took your time. Almost missed me, you did.' The words were little more than a hoarse whisper and the effort tired him. His eyes shut and the hideous sound of his breathing continued.

He gently squeezed Jim's hand. It was little more than a week since he'd seen him; how could he have lost so much weight that his shape barely made a dent under the sheets? 'Don't you fret, Jim, I'll see you through this. We've got plans, you and me; you're me business partner. I want you back beside me fighting fit.'

The faintest flicker of a smile crossed Jim's face. 'Promise me, you ain't going to leave me on me own? I'm scared. I need you with me.' His voice was a thin thread in the silence. Alfie's eyes brimmed over.

'I ain't going nowhere, Jim. You're as good as a brother to me. You're the best mate I've ever had. I'm not leaving without you – you have my word on that.'

'Remember, Alfie, everything I got I leave to you and Buster. You get that yard, keep me name on the barrows so you'll not forget me.'

There was a brief pressure on Alfie's hand, then Jim – exhausted by the effort – went quiet again. The nurse and Mr

Hudson had left him alone. He was glad of that. He and Jim didn't need anyone else; they were a team, weren't they?

He sniffed, but his nose continued to run. His cheeks were wet, but he wasn't going to let go of Jim's hand to rummage for the rag. 'Don't give up, Jim. Don't you dare die on me. You're me best mate. We're going to make a fortune, find ourselves two pretty girls one day and get married. I can't do it on me own; it won't be the same if you ain't here.'

The grip on his hand tightened briefly, and then with a final shuddering breath the room was silent. Alfie waited, willing his friend's chest to rise, for him to take another gasp, but nothing happened. Instead, the hand in his went slack. Just like that – his life was snuffed out.

He collapsed across the body, his grief far worse than it had been when Tommy had drowned. He sobbed, inconsolable. His dreams had ended with the death of his friend.

Then he felt movement behind him and gentle arms reached round to remove him from the bed. 'Come along, Alfie, Jim's gone to a better place now. Thank the good Lord that you got here in time. He was hanging on until he could speak to you.' Mrs Jones drew him away from the corpse that had once been his friend. 'When he was able, he talked of nothing else but how you'd rescued him. You made him very happy.'

Alfie choked and wiped his nose and eyes on his sleeve. He didn't care what they thought of his manners – his best friend in the world was dead. He couldn't imagine carrying on the business on his own.

'I am taking you down to the kitchen. Cook will take care of you, and when you're recovered Mr Hudson wishes to speak to you.'

He slumped into a chair and a hot mug was placed in his grip. He tried to lift it, but the contents slopped onto the table.

'Let me do it for you, Alfie. Here, swallow this down; it'll make you feel much better.'

It was lifted to his mouth and he drank. The hot tea warmed him, the sweetness a pleasant surprise. Jim had given everything he owned to him. He didn't need it; he wanted nothing without his friend to share it. He'd use the money to give Jim a good send-off – that's what he'd do.

He finished his drink, replacing the mug carefully on the table. The cook nodded and refilled it from an enormous brown china teapot. 'Have another one, and then I'll get you something to eat. Shock can do funny things to a body.'

'Thank you, madam. I'm feeling more meself now.' His voice sounded strange, as if it was someone else speaking. He was in a large kitchen sitting at a scrubbed pine table. All around him were gleaming pots and pans. A massive kitchen range filled one end of the room. It was similar to the one Ma had used back in Colchester but many times bigger.

Sitting opposite him was Mr Hudson, not fussing nor prosing on about heaven, just waiting quietly until he'd finished his tea and was ready to listen. There was another cove beside him, in waistcoat and shirtsleeves; they were both drinking tea from the same sort of mug he was using.

'Mr Hudson, it's all my fault. If I'd taken Jim to the hospital, not gone to work that day, he wouldn't have died.'

'It wasn't your fault, Alfie. The physician said he had congestion of the lungs. It was so far advanced when we found him he would have died wherever he'd been. Do not blame yourself. He was weakened from his years of living on the street. Console yourself with the thought that his last years on this earth were the happiest he'd experienced.'

The other man nodded solemnly. 'It was his time. We cannot

question God's will. He is in a place without pain or suffering. Rejoice in that, my boy.'

Alfie didn't want to hear this hogwash about a better place, a wise and a benevolent God. If that were true, why did he let children die of starvation in the streets whilst others lived like kings?

'I have enough to pay for the funeral. I've got to get off home now; I'll come back tomorrow with the money.'

Mr Hudson shook his head. 'That will not be necessary, Alfie. Jim wouldn't want you spending any of his precious savings on that. The foundation is here to help. It's what we do. No one gives up their life under this roof and gets a pauper's burial. They are all buried decently, and given a small headstone to mark the grave. Tell me, what would you like written on his?'

For a second time Alfie was overwhelmed by his loss. He stared at the table, swallowing the lump in his throat and willing his tears back. 'Put, "*Here lies Jim, the best friend anyone could have. Rest in peace.*" That'll do, thanks, mister.'

He glared, daring them to contradict him. The man in the waistcoat smiled. 'Very fitting. Your words shall be exactly what is carved on the headstone. You will be able to visit the grave and see for yourself later on. Do you wish to spend the night here or return to your lodgings?'

Having something practical to think about helped him gain control of his emotions. 'I have to be back at first light. Me dog's shut in the room and won't take kindly to being left.'

The men exchanged glances. 'That's what we thought. Mr Hudson dismissed the hackney carriage. It doesn't do to keep a beast standing about in this weather. However, we shall summon another to return you to your lodgings.'

Alfie interrupted him. 'I'm happy to walk back. You've done more than enough for us already. Give us the directions – I'll get

back all right. And I'll find me away back for the funeral too. Just tell me when it will be.'

Mr Hudson pulled his whiskers. 'You're a fine young man, Alfie Nightingale. Your attitude does you credit. Do you read, by any chance?' Alfie nodded, for the first time truly proud of his accomplishment. 'Excellent, I shall write the directions down for you. I don't suppose you've eaten tonight so I insist that you eat some supper before you leave. Are you quite certain you wish to walk back? It will take you an hour or more and it's already past ten o'clock.'

'I spend all me time outside, in all weathers, sir. I ain't familiar with the streets round here, but I'll soon learn them.'

'Your friend's funeral will be tomorrow; it is best these things are done immediately. Can you be back here at noon? We have our own chapel. The service shall be conducted there, then the hearse will transport the coffin to the cemetery.'

The mention of a coffin caused Alfie to shudder. He stared at the table, gripping his chair to steady himself. A large plate of beef stew, dumplings floating on the surface, was plonked in front of him. He thought he wouldn't be able to eat, that his grief had stolen his appetite, but the savoury smell wafting up from the plate made his mouth water. He'd not eaten anything so tasty since he'd left Colchester. Maybe this was a sign from the Almighty that it was time he returned and found his family.

9

LONDON, MARCH 1844

Alfie felt numb. He survived by filling every minute of the day with work. He trundled his barrow from place to place, market to market – dropping his rates when he didn't get immediate work. He returned to his lonely room each night too exhausted to mourn; even Buster began to look thin and dejected. When he wasn't delivering he was making tables and benches for George.

The weather deteriorated. Although the snow made things more difficult for pedestrians and carriages alike, more folks were eager to have their groceries and such delivered. Carrying large baskets of vegetables, household provisions and other paraphernalia become an exercise fraught with danger. The cobbles and pathways were permanently icy; one slip could mean a broken limb and no work. Then it would be the work-house for everyone in the family.

The only glimmer of hope, the one thing that kept him sane, was his friendship with the man upstairs. George Benson got him to shift stuff regularly; sometimes it was completed pieces of furniture from the yard he worked at, but more often it was a

load of off-cuts. Of a Sunday they worked together building bookshelves, tables, and the occasional cradle.

They were obliged to do this in the backyard of the lodging house. Mrs Hunter wouldn't hear of them working indoors. Buster refused to remain outside when they were hammering and banging; he snoozed by the fire, content as long as he could hear his master close by. Alfie noticed his dog had become more possessive, quicker to snarl at a stranger, since Jim had died. It was as if the dog was worried his special person might disappear one day like Jim had done.

George told him he was a competent carpenter now, had learnt better than most apprentices did in five years. Alfie took pleasure in making something solid. But often the tools, even with their wooden handles, became ice-coated and too slippery to use safely.

One day, on impulse, he walked the hour and a half to the cemetery to leave a bedraggled bunch of violets on the mound of earth. Jim's grave was still marked by a simple wooden cross with a number painted on it. The headstone wouldn't be positioned until the ground settled.

By the middle of March he'd begun to rent out the spare handcarts; he wouldn't make as much renting out, but he had no need for more than one. He charged two shillings a week for the smaller, three shillings and sixpence for the big one. He would still be adding to his savings. When he'd got a pony saved, he'd pack his bags and go back to Colchester.

He'd had enough of city life, the dirt and grime, the constantly looking over his shoulder in case one of the gang, or one of Silas Field's bully boys, was creeping up behind him. More often than not Buster opted to remain at home. The snow split and cracked his pads, the ice freezing between his toes. His beloved companion might well be feeling his years. If anything

happened to the dog that would be it. He wouldn't want to live without him at his side; it would be unthinkable.

He spoke to George about his plans one Sunday. Compared to the bitter months that had gone it was pleasant outside in the yard. Buster had deigned to join them today, was gnawing on a large bone one of the neighbours had chucked him. The dog was well liked by everyone in the terrace. They reckoned there'd been no pilfering of coal from the yard since he'd moved in. They were putting the finishing touches to a dresser ordered by the newly married couple in a cottage over the back.

'George, I'm going to back to Colchester in a few weeks. I'll need to sell the barrows. Are you interested?'

'I am. With all the extra I've been making since we've been working together I've got more than enough to pay three months up front on a decent yard. I found one that has a cottage goes with it. The place is near derelict and will need a deal of work before I can move in.'

'Good for you! I'm happy to give you a hand doing it up, but I'm off the end of April – come what may.'

George put down his rag. 'Why don't you still come in with me? You could organise the deliveries, employ a couple of boys to work for you. You can work alongside. You'll be a real asset to me, and we could take on bigger jobs together.'

'That's kind of you to offer, but no. I want to get back. I've been away too long already. I have a sister in Colchester. We was always close, and I need to know how she fares. I thought I'd set myself up as a carpenter. I reckon I can make tables and such as good as you nowadays.'

'Fair enough, but I'll miss you, Alfie. You're a mate. If you stick to what I've learnt you – don't go for anything fancy, mind – you'll do well enough.'

They continued to polish the dresser. George was a good

bloke to work with, didn't natter on all day, left you to your own thoughts unless he had something useful to say. It was getting chilly by the time they'd finished.

'There, let's get this on the big barrow and deliver it before it gets dark.' George waited whilst Alfie removed the two smaller carts and wheeled the large one over. When they were trundling down Hog Lane, Alfie paused to check the rope was secure.

'Jim and I had intended to go to the opening of that new tunnel what goes under the river.'

'The Thames Tunnel? I'd like to see that. When's it open then?'

'On the 25th March. You can buy a penny ticket and go right inside. It will be my final farewell to Jim. His headstone's going up in a couple of weeks. After that I reckon I can think about leaving.'

'We'll go together, make a day of it, have supper out and a pint or two to celebrate. I'll give in me notice and finish the day before. Will you help me do up me cottage before you go? I only need two of your barrows really, but I'll take all three. I can rent them out like what you do. You'll give me a good deal, as I'm your mate, won't you, Alfie?'

He slapped his friend on the back. 'You can pay what I did, and they were in a shoddy state then, not painted and running smooth like what they do now.' He rubbed his back. Pushing a laden cart over the cobbles weren't easy. 'I'll help until I leave. Will that do you?'

He told his landlady he was leaving at the end of April. She'd agreed to buy back his furniture when he went, which would give him a few more bob to add to his savings. He would have surpassed his target of £25 by a considerable margin by then.

Each week, when he had five pounds, he'd been exchanging

his coins for paper notes. These he intended to stitch into his waistcoat lining – no thieving bugger would find them even if he was done over. He scratched Buster's head. No one would dare do that, not with his dog at his side, but better safe than sorry.

* * *

Spring rushed in. Flowers appeared in patches of bare soil, a haze of green covered the hedges where he walked first thing with his dog. With the end of the hard winter, his optimism returned. He yearned to be back in the countryside; to stroll in open fields, to breathe air that wasn't heavy with soot, to walk on pavements that were clean.

In his mind's eye he saw Colchester as the perfect place – prosperous and well-cared-for. Streets gaslit, with a brand-new hospital, workhouse, and other municipal buildings. He'd rent himself lodgings before he went to look for Sarah. He smiled. No, he'd get himself a little cottage in Maidenburgh Street, behind the castle. If he remembered rightly, there was a row of decent places along there and more often than not there was one or two vacant. It was close to the river meadows as well. He couldn't recall if any of them had a yard big enough to put a handcart.

'You'll like it in the country, Buster. Rabbits to chase, the ground soft under your paws, friendly faces everywhere and our own home to live in. I'll put me money in the bank, set meself up proper and then go round to see Ma.'

He thought maybe he'd stopped growing. He hadn't had to replace his boots this year because his toes was being crushed against the end. His trousers weren't halfway up his ankles; they remained where they should be, resting on his boots. He was

only an inch or two shorter than George, and his friend was a fine-looking man.

He ran his fingers across his upper lip and felt the roughness of hair. It wouldn't be long before he had to buy a razor and start shaving. He was a man. He could take care of himself. He couldn't wait to get back home and show Sarah how well he'd done. He'd have so much to tell her, and he could start with the opening of the Thames Tunnel.

* * *

The morning of March the 25th dawned sunny. No cold east wind – it was a perfect spring day. Alfie had bought himself a smart carpetbag ready for his return, plus a new suit of clothes. He was the proud possessor of three cotton shirts, two waistcoats, spare trousers and three pairs of socks. He now had all his vests and underwear laundered regular and took himself off to a bathhouse. He enjoyed immersing himself in hot water, being completely clean and fresh. He bore no resemblance to the half-formed boy who had run away from Black Ben.

'You stop here, Buster. I ain't taking you with me today. You'll not like the crowds, and I don't want to be picked out by anyone. Ginger and the gang will be working and they'd spot you soon enough. You stay in the yard and eat your bone.' His dog had had a long walk that morning and would be happy to snooze the rest of the day away.

There was savings clubs for the likes of him run by the unions, but he weren't going to get involved with any of that political stuff. The Chartists might be right – rich folk had everything and the poor a rotten deal – but marches and protests wasn't his style. He'd leave the toffs to get on with it if they left him to live his life the way he wanted.

He checked the dog's water container was full and the yard gate shut, and he was ready. He ran up the stairs and banged on George's door. It opened immediately.

'Alfie, you look a real gent. If I'd known you was putting on your Sunday best I'd have made more of an effort.'

His friend looked his usual dapper self. His yellow cravat neatly tied, his brown tweed jacket and trousers freshly sponged and his boots good and shiny. 'Fishing for compliments? I reckon we'll turn the heads of a few young ladies today. I don't want to be back too late. I'm off first thing tomorrow to an auction and it's a fair distance away.'

'I'll be glad to get started on the cottage. My governor weren't too happy about me leaving, I can tell you.' He grinned, looking more Alfie's age than a young man of almost twenty. 'It won't be the same here without you and that Buster. I'm going to make the most of the next few weeks. I reckon with your help I'll be well set up by the time you go.'

'It'll make a change slapping a bit of distemper on the walls. Now, let's get off – there'll be thousands with the same idea. It ain't supposed to be open to the public, according to the leaflet, until six o'clock, but I reckon we're right to go this afternoon. We'll probably have to queue, so the sooner we get there the less time we'll have to wait.'

This was the first time Alfie had ventured near the river. Without his dog, and a head taller and dressed smart, he doubted – even if he came face-to-face with Black Ben – that he'd be recognised. He would enjoy the spectacle today. It would be something to tell his grandchildren about. 'I gave Buster a bath yesterday. He weren't too keen, but I ain't taking him back next month covered in soot.'

'Stop talking about leaving. Let's enjoy ourselves today and not think about the future. I've money in me pocket; I'm ready

for anything. We'll join in the fun, watch the fireworks, listen to the band and buy a decent meal and a couple of pints of beer before we go home.'

As they approached Wapping, the streets were bustling with like-minded people. There was a festive atmosphere amongst the crowd, children skipping and laughing, men and women exchanging jokes; everyone in their Sunday best determined to enjoy themselves. It was a wonder and no mistake – a tunnel running right under the Thames.

He could hear the sound of a brass band playing in the distance. He checked the pamphlet again. There were two entrances to the tunnel on this side of the river and the same at Rotherhithe.

'It's a shame folks can't go through in a vehicle – that it's pedestrians only what can use it. Fancy taking all these years and spending all that money and not being able to take goods across as was first intended.'

George nodded solemnly. 'I heard there was problems and the only way they'd got to finish it was by putting spiral stair-cases at each end. Still, I'm going under. Imagine, being able to walk under a river. It's a blooming miracle – that's what it is.'

There were thousands of other folk ready to experience the novelty. The colourful flags decorating the surrounding streets added to the excitement. He heard a lady in front of him telling her children that people were coming on omnibuses, on horseback, in carriages and specially chartered boats.

Penny tickets were being sold, so fast Alfie was glad he'd had the foresight to purchase his the previous day. There were two marquees, he heard someone say, erected in Cow Court where the dignitaries and their guests were to sit through the speeches. He was enjoying the warm spring sunshine, the feeling of

excitement in the air, the thought that the world was changing and he wasn't being left behind.

As they were ticket holders they joined the rear of the crowd pressing towards the entrances. It was a little after two o'clock when suddenly the queue forced itself past the waiting inspectors and began to descend into the tunnel, brandishing their tickets to prove they were not there illegally.

He and George had no choice – they were carried along in the press of people until they reached the top of the spiral staircase. They went down willy-nilly, the folks in front and behind making it difficult to stay upright. Alfie pitied the women in their full skirts with all them layers of petticoats. It was hard enough to negotiate for a gent.

The walls were brilliantly whitewashed, sparkling in the gaslights. He marvelled at the spectacle – and to think he'd seen it before it was officially opened. The ceilings were vaulted, and high. He almost expected to hear the sound of the river running overhead. The glittering globes attached to either side of the walls made it light enough to see down the tunnel. Ahead of him, set in small alcoves, were women selling cheap souvenirs and bits and pieces. He had more sense than to waste his hard-earned money.

There must have been a couple of thousand in the tunnel before they were supposed to be there. They milled about admiring what they saw. He lost sight of his companion in the crowd. He'd find him soon enough when he got out.

By the time it was his turn to ascend on the far side he'd had more than enough of tunnels. He realised he didn't like being underground. Halfway through he'd begun to feel the walls pressing in on him. Perspiration was trickling between his shoulder blades and his hands were clammy, his heart racing.

It was an effort not to fight his way up the stairs, so desperate

was he to get back in the fresh air. George was waiting for him. 'I'm mightily impressed. I can't wait to go back later on today, but we'll have to wait until it's officially opened, and that won't be until after six o'clock.'

'I'm going back by London Bridge. You'll not get me down again for love nor money. Done it once – that's enough for me.'

'Fair enough. There's a coffee stall ahead and I could do with a cup. I'll see you there.' His friend strode off and the crowd closed around him. He sniffed. The distinctive aroma of coffee brewing would make it easy to meet up with George again.

There were as many awaiting the treat on this side of the river as on the other. He felt someone bump into him and instinctively grabbed the hand that had tried to dip into his pocket. His hold was strong, no match for the pickpocket who'd hoped to remove his cash. He spun round and found himself face-to-face with Nelson.

His erstwhile friend seemed to have shrunk since he'd last seen him. He was still dressed in the garments he'd been given the day they'd moved from Half Moon Street. These were as dirty as the ones he'd worn before, his hair as full of crawlers. The real change was in his eyes. They were sunk into his head. How could he be in such dire straits? The boys had had enough money to live like lords for a year or two.

'Nelson, it's me, Alfie. Don't you recognise me?' Immediately he stopped whining and protesting his innocence and his face lit up.

'Bugger me! I'd never have spotted it was you. You look like a toff. Done all right for yourselves then, you and Jim?' He glanced over Alfie's shoulder hopefully. 'Where's Jim? Ain't he here?'

Alfie felt the familiar stab of pain. 'He died a while back, congestion of the lungs. What's happened to you and the rest of

them? I didn't think to see you here like this. Last time I saw you, you were well set up. What's going on?'

He checked George was out of earshot, then drew Nelson to one side to continue the conversation. He wanted to find out what calamity had occurred to reduce the boy to such a state.

'Sorry to hear that. Jim was a good friend.' Nervously Nelson glanced over his shoulder before crouching down so he wouldn't be visible in the crowd. 'We all work for Silas now. He got Ginger. We told him to wait, not to try and move that stuff, but you know Ginger, he wouldn't listen.' The boy wiped his snotty nose on his hand. 'Ginger took everything one day, all of it, inside his coat, saying he'd be back with the money that night. We never saw him again. Two days later Silas and his boys turned up. They took what was left. We got beaten something cruel, and well, here we are.'

'What happened to Ginger? Did they kill him?'

'They did, slit his throat, murdered him in cold blood. We was forced to move. We live in a worse dosshouse than Ma Bishop's. There's a dozen of us. We manage the best we can, but it ain't like it used to be, I can tell you.'

'Buy yourself something to eat, Nelson. I wish you well. I'm sorry things ended like this.'

Nelson looked down at the half crown in his grimy hand. 'You're a gent. I always said so – not like us. Good luck to you, Alfie.'

He was gone, slipping through the crowd like an eel. Alfie would never see him again. There was nothing he could do for any of them. They'd chosen their path; he'd chosen his. He was sorry that Ginger had been murdered, the boy had taken him in when he'd been desperate. No one deserved to die that way you. Saddened by the meeting, he turned and forced his way through the crowd to the coffee stall. Today had certainly been a final

farewell in more ways than one. George was waiting for him, two mugs in his fists.

'Crickey! You look as though you've seen a ghost. Drink this, Alfie – it'll make you feel more the thing.'

After a few swallows he was restored. 'I could do with something to eat. It's hours since we had breakfast. Shall we go and find a place?'

It was after nine when Alfie finally staggered down the stairs to rescue his dog from the backyard. 'Buster, I got you a meat pie to make up for it. Come on, let's get in. I need to get me head down; I've had one too many beers tonight.'

He tottered over and collapsed onto his bed. 'Here, I didn't forget you when I were out. See, what do you think of your smart red collar and lead?' He buckled on the collar. Buster took umbrage and jerked away. He deigned to gobble up the pie but then turned his back and went to sleep.

The next morning when he attempted to attach the lead the dog growled and shook his head. Alfie thought it prudent not to insist. 'It's for the best, old fellow. They won't let you on the train next month unless you're tied up.'

Happy once the hated leash was removed, the dog wagged his tail. The smart red collar looked grand against his freshly scrubbed fur and the animal seemed proud to be wearing it.

'Right, let's make a bit more money to take home with us. Only a few more weeks and we'll be off. I can't wait to see Sarah's face when she meets you.'

10

COLCHESTER, MARCH 1844

Sarah crept down the attic stairs. She was unwilling to disturb the three Cooper boys who slept in the bedroom on the right of the landing, or Dan and Maria Cooper who slept in the larger bedroom on the left.

As always on laundry day she would have to light the fire under the copper in the scullery. Nelly would be here in an hour or so and would expect the water to be hot. It was light enough to see without using candles or the oil lamps. Her first task was to riddle the grate and get the range back to full heat. She traced her fingers lovingly across the embossed writing that ran boldly across the top – *Hewens' Patent Range*. This had cost Mr Cooper the princely sum of five pounds and fifteen shillings according to Joe Cooper. It was a pity his wife didn't appreciate the wonders of the cooker. The money he'd spent on it was the same as Sarah's wages for a year.

She had been alarmed to find this beautiful object dull and encrusted with grease when she'd arrived in December. This cast-iron contraption was her pride and joy; now it was black-leaded every week and the brass attachments polished to a rich

shine. She could produce perfect bread, scones, wonderful stews and anything else she had a fancy to make. It even had a tap on the left-hand side from which she could draw hot water. It made bathing a pleasure instead of a chore.

The kitchen was *her* domain; the Coopers sat in the front room of an evening, leaving her to rock happily in a wooden armchair exactly like the one her ma had used. The boys (Joe, the eldest at seven; Davie, a year younger; and the youngest, John, almost four) drifted back and forth, welcome in either room. She couldn't stand here daydreaming – she had tasks to perform before she went up at six o'clock to tap on Mr Cooper's door.

The dough she had left to prove on the back of the range was well risen. It was the work of moments to knock it back and put it in the greased bread tins. By the time she'd finished her early morning chores, the oven would be hot enough and the bread ready to go in. This morning they would have porridge with sugar *and* cream. It had taken her a while to get used to the fact that in this household there was no shortage at the end of the week. Mr Cooper earned excellent money in his position as foreman at Hawkins timber yard.

He gave her the housekeeping money on a Saturday. Anything left over at the end of the week was hers to keep. He was generous to a fault, a kind and loving father and affectionate husband. She valued the time she spent in his company first thing in the morning; the more she got to know him and his wife the happier she was.

The fire under the copper was taking longer to light than usual; if she didn't hurry she'd be late waking up her employer. She poured out his mug of tea, set his bowl of porridge at his place on the long, scrubbed table and added a small jug of

cream. The sugar pot was always in the centre. Both her employers liked to have it in their tea.

She checked her appearance in the shiny base of a large copper pan. Her cap was straight, her apron clean and her face free of smudges. Good – she would go up and knock on the door. Mrs Cooper liked to sleep in. The baby was due in three weeks and the midwife insisted she rested as much as possible. The boys came down after their father had left for work. They were all good sleepers, thankfully.

When Mr Cooper appeared she was just removing the first loaf from the oven, the kitchen filled with the aroma of freshly baked bread. Not something they had been accustomed to until she'd joined the family three months ago.

'Good morning, Mr Cooper. Would you like toasted bread or fresh this morning?'

He yawned and smiled at her. 'Toast, and some of that dripping you made yesterday to go with it, Sarah.'

'How's Mrs Cooper this morning? Did she get any sleep?'

'Not much. I shall be glad when this baby arrives. Maria's not been well throughout her time. But these past weeks she's been much better. It was a godsend you turning up at The Prince of Wales when you did.'

Her cheeks coloured at his praise. 'That's what I say about you, sir, every day since I came to live here. I have a decent position and because of your generosity am able to put a few coppers each week into the savings club.'

He said no more, merely nodded and picked up his spoon. Whilst he munched contentedly she made his toast at the open fire in the centre of the range. There was no need for her to pack him up a midday meal. His place of work, just over the bridge, was no more than ten minutes' distance from the house and he always returned to eat with his family. *He* insisted Sarah sat with

them; *she* insisted that Sarah called her by her given name and treated her more like a younger sister than an employee.

The weather was harsh, as cold as it had been in December, but the nights were lighter now, and the promise of spring was in the air. When she returned from checking that the fire under the copper was burning he'd gone. It was six thirty, another hour before the boys woke up and Nelly arrived to do the laundry.

She prepared the vegetables for the midday soup and the evening meal. Tonight they would have shepherd's pie, a firm favourite with the boys. All she had to do was mince the leftover lamb and her chores for the day would be done. She glanced at the little brass clock that stood in pride of place in the centre of the dresser. There was still time for her to eat her breakfast at leisure before taking a tray to Mrs Cooper; she could not bring herself to think of her as Maria even after three months of being asked to do so.

The boys needed little help to dress themselves nowadays. Even John wanted to be like his big brothers and do it himself, sometimes with comical results.

'Joe, I've put out your porridge. I'll pour the tea when I come down. Mrs Beeson is busy in the scullery. Don't be going in there and getting in her way – promise me.'

He grinned. With his mop of dark curls and twinkling blue eyes he was the image of his father. 'Promise, Sarah. How's me ma this morning?'

'She had a restless night, Joe, so I doubt she'll be getting up today. She needs to build up her strength for when the baby comes. It could be any time.'

'We'll draw her picture, won't we, boys? We can take it up when we get back from school.'

'John can come too,' the youngest screeched.

'If you're a good boy we can feed the ducks on the way home. What do you say to that?'

The little boy's frown vanished. 'I like duckies, Sarah.'

Joe and Davie attended the infant school most mornings, but they didn't seem to learn much there. No doubt because there were over forty in the class and only one harassed schoolmistress.

The tea was getting cold – she must take it up. She rested the tray on a small side table outside the marital bedroom. She tapped on the door but didn't wait to be invited in. More often than not she had to wake Mrs Cooper up. It didn't seem natural, sleeping so much and still feeling tired all the time.

'Maria, I have your breakfast here; why don't I help you to sit up?'

'I'm not that hungry, Sarah love, put it down and I'll drink the tea. I feel like a beached whale. The sooner this nipper appears the happier I'll be. The midwife says I'm carrying a lot of water. The baby's small and I thank the Lord for that.' She waved Sarah away and slowly edged back until she was propped against the pillows. Her cheeks were flushed and puffy; she didn't look at all well.

'Here you are, drink this. Nothing like a strong cup of tea to brighten you up. I'll leave the bread and butter here. You might fancy it later.' Sarah knew better than to offer anything more substantial. It was a mystery to her how Mrs Cooper was so big when she ate barely enough to keep a fly alive. 'Nelly's here; I'd better get back to the kitchen. John isn't safe around the hot water.'

* * *

The mistress retired early complaining of a headache. The boys had gone to bed without a murmur, and Mr Cooper had gone up soon afterwards. She liked having the downstairs to herself – she wandered into the front parlour to tidy and check the fire was safe. It was a pretty room, full of knick-knacks and bits and pieces, but not somewhere the boys could play unsupervised without breaking something precious. Satisfied the room was as it should be, she returned to the kitchen.

She was making a shirt for Joe and would finish that before she went upstairs to her attic bedroom. She loved her eyrie at the top of the house, especially the two windows that looked out across the river. She could stand and watch the barges at the quay, the dock workers and the casual labourers hurrying about their daily business. Somehow this made her feel a little closer to her brother Alfie, as he'd left Colchester by boat.

Lost in thought, she was dozing in front of the range when she heard a door bang and hurrying footsteps on the stairs. Instantly alert, she was on her feet when Mr Cooper burst in.

'Maria's taken real badly and I'm going to fetch the doctor. I want you to stay with her whilst I go.'

'Have her pains started, sir? Shall I get things ready?'

He didn't answer, stared at her as if he'd not understood. His face was pale. Something wasn't right; this wasn't a normal labour or he wouldn't be looking so anxious.

'I need to talk to you whilst I get my boots on.'

Sarah handed them to him and shivered. It wasn't the cold that made her tremble. There was something dreadfully wrong – she just knew it.

'It's too soon. The baby's not due for another three weeks and Maria don't have big babies – John was not much bigger than a rabbit and he were full term. She's been poorly these past few days and I reckon that's why it's started.'

'But the baby's been active. She was complaining about being kept awake only yesterday.' She tried to look calm and encouraging, but when her ma had Tommy she'd not been allowed in until afterwards so knew little about what actually happened.

'Mrs Cooper said it might be early this time. A lot of movement, it's a sign of a healthy baby, isn't it?'

He nodded. 'Let's hope so, Sarah. But I'm still getting the doctor. Maria reckons it's a girl this time and if anything happens to the baby she'll take it hard.' He stood up, shrugging on his heavy work coat, tying his muffler around his neck. Then, reaching into a deep pocket, he removed his cap and jammed it on his head. 'I'll be as quick as I can; I'll stop by the midwife's on my way – she lives in St Botolph's Street, so I reckon she'll be here first. The doctor's in Queen Street. It'll take me an hour or more to get there and back. Can you manage on your own?'

'Yes, I'll be fine. I'll wait upstairs. Please take care, Mr Cooper. The roads are slippery – it's freezing again tonight.'

In the bedroom there were several candles burning, but the fire had been allowed to go out. Mrs Cooper was lying propped against the pillows, her cheeks flushed, her hair wet with perspiration.

'Maria, I've come to sit with you whilst Mr Cooper fetches the midwife. How close are your pains? Have your waters broken yet?' This was something she'd heard the midwife ask her mother all those years ago. Giving birth was difficult at the best of times and downright dangerous when the mother was already unwell.

There was no response. Maria's eyes flickered and closed again. Sarah rushed to her side, feeling the unnatural heat radiating from her. The baby was coming, but she'd also got a high fever; this could prove fatal to both her and the infant. More

women died from childbed fever than anything else. That was one thing she did know, for Nanny had told her.

Perhaps if she made the room cooler it would help. What they wanted in here was a fresh breeze, not more heat. The window stuck a little, but she managed to force it up and was gratified to feel the temperature drop. She must sponge Maria down. Looking round she saw there was a water jug standing half-full on the washstand.

'I think you need to be cooler, Maria. It'll make you more comfortable.' Again there was no answer. It was going to be a long and difficult night. She prayed the boys slept through; she didn't want them awake if the worst happened.

More than half an hour passed before Maria was able to speak. Sarah had seen the mound of her stomach contract three times. She thanked God the pains weren't coming any closer together. When they did would be the hardest part. To expel a baby was bad enough at the best of times; it wasn't called labour for nothing. To try and do it when you were desperately ill might well prove too much for both infant and mother.

'Sarah? What're you doing here?' Maria turned her head and seeing the empty space beside her tried to push herself upright, flopping back, too feeble to manage it.

'The boys are fast asleep, and Mr Cooper has gone for the midwife. Your baby's coming and I'm trying to reduce your fever before you have to push.' Ringing out the cloth for the umpteenth time, she wiped her patient's face, glad to see that a combination of fresh air and cold water had brought her skin temperature down to almost normal.

'I'm that thirsty, Sarah love. Could you fetch me a drink?'

'I have some here – I haven't used it all.' She was about to tip some of the water into the glass but stopped. 'I'll go down and

get you some that's been boiled, and check on the boys whilst I'm about it.'

The contractions continued at five-minute intervals for another hour, but Maria was a lot better in herself. She couldn't imagine why Mr Cooper was taking so long. The midwife and the doctor must have been out on other calls or one of them would surely have been here by now.

'As you're feeling so much better, Maria, shall I go down and make you a cup of tea?' She crossed the room to close the window before taking the jug and cloth away with her.

* * *

The kettle was hissing over the flames when she heard someone on the cobbles outside. Thank goodness! He was back and he had at least one person with him. The back door opened and two muffled figures stepped in.

'Sarah, how is she? I've got Nurse Digby with me. The doctor's out but his housekeeper's promised to send him as soon as he returns.'

'Her fever's broken, thank God, and the contractions are still five minutes apart. She's sitting up and taking notice now, and has drunk two glasses of water and is asking for tea.'

Nurse Digby removed her cape and bonnet. Sarah was impressed by the woman; she was spotless, her apron pristine, her greying hair neatly coiled at the back of her head. Mr Cooper handed over the carpetbag he'd been carrying for her and she nodded.

'Thank you, Mr Cooper. I can find my way upstairs, and you know what I'll need.'

'Is there anything else you'd like me to do?' Sarah asked.

'I shall examine Mrs Cooper. You look rather young; do you

have experience of these matters?' Sarah shook her head. 'In which case, my dear, you will be more use to Mr Cooper. I'm sure he could do with a nice cup of tea; it's fair freezing outside.'

Mr Cooper followed the nurse upstairs. She couldn't remember her stepfather even being on the premises when Tommy was born.

The tea was brewed when he returned looking a deal happier than earlier.

'You did well, Sarah. I can't believe Maria's so much better.' He picked up his mug of tea and drained it in one swallow. 'I could do with some bread and cheese. I'm famished after traipsing around all over Colchester looking for that dratted doctor.'

'It won't take a moment, sir, and there's some rock cakes I baked this morning to have afterwards.'

She was busy in the pantry, on edge for news, but Mrs Digby was still upstairs when she carried in the plate.

'Has Nurse Digby not been down yet? What's keeping her so long?'

'She's thorough, that one. Don't worry, she'll be here soon enough.' He'd finished his meal before they heard footsteps on the stairs. They stood up fearing the worst.

Nurse Digby smiled, and Sarah's fingers unclenched. 'Everything's progressing as it should; Mrs Cooper's still weak after her bout of fever but I'm expecting a happy outcome, although not until the morning.'

'Thank you, I was that worried. Sarah brought the fever down; when I set out to fetch you she was real poorly.' He rubbed his eyes and collapsed back in his chair.

'Would you like a cup of tea, nurse? And what about Mrs Cooper – perhaps she could eat something? She'll need her strength for the morning.'

'That would be nice. I'll be getting back, but I'll not be needing hot water for a few hours yet.'

Maria looked a lot better when Sarah went upstairs with the tea and some dainty cheese sandwiches. 'You're a good girl, Sarah. I bless the day that you moved in with us. I'm feeling stronger now, and the pains are regular, but not getting any closer. The boys all arrived in a rush. I reckon this one's a girl; ladies like to take their time.'

'Try and get some sleep. You'll need to be rested later.'

'Listen to her, nurse; you'd think she'd delivered a dozen babies and her only sixteen years of age.' Maria reached out and squeezed Sarah's hand. 'You run along, love, get some sleep. There'll be plenty to do in the morning.'

'As soon as I have everything prepared for tomorrow, I'll go up – that's if Mr Cooper doesn't object.'

'Course he don't. You get a bit of kip. No point in all of us being awake is there?'

Sarah hesitated outside the door. She'd just check the boys were sound before returning to the kitchen. She found Mr Cooper slumped across the table fast asleep; she left him there and went to her own bed.

11

_____

Sarah was in the kitchen the next morning when the three boys trooped in. Mr Cooper had gone out. She prayed it wasn't to fetch the doctor. She'd already told them the baby was coming, but not how gravely ill their mother was. 'Good morning, you're just in time. I have porridge and fresh bread and butter ready for you.'

'How's Ma? Is the baby here yet?' Joe asked anxiously. 'Do we have to go to school this morning, Sarah?'

Davie shook his head, yawning widely. 'Pa's not here. There's someone upstairs with Ma, but I didn't hear no baby crying.'

'I expect your pa's gone out to stretch his legs. He spent the night in the kitchen.' Should she take the boys or would they be better at home? 'I'll ask your pa about school when he gets back.'

She glanced at the clock and saw it was almost seven, high time for the baby to have been delivered. Something had gone wrong – it must have done. She closed her eyes for a moment to send up a fervent prayer.

'Come along, I'm ready to dish up. Why don't you make

some toasted bread this morning? I've got a bowl of dripping from Sunday's roast you can spread on it.'

Her suggestion distracted the boys and, in the excitement of browning the bread on the end of a long fork, they forgot about their father's absence and the lack of a new baby in the house. But she didn't; her thoughts turned constantly to what was taking place upstairs. She wished she knew what was happening.

Mr Cooper returned through the front door and he had someone else with him. He didn't come down to join them in the kitchen. Keeping the children entertained occupied her thoughts, although her eyes kept turning anxiously to the clock. The hands moved remorselessly around and still there was no news. School had been abandoned this morning.

At nine o'clock someone left the house. What was going on up there? If it was bad news perhaps Mr Cooper would wish to tell her first.

'I'm going to take some tea upstairs. Behave yourselves whilst I'm gone.' She smiled at Joe. 'I'm relying on you – you're in charge.'

She hesitated in the small vestibule at the bottom of the stairs. The cups rattled on their saucers. The thin wail of a baby filtered through the floorboards. Thank God! The baby was alive. Mr Cooper must be upstairs admiring the new arrival. He appeared looking drawn, but smiling.

'It's a girl. It was touch-and-go, but everything's fine now. Maria can't wait to show you the baby. Is that tea you have there? I'm coming down. I'll have mine in the kitchen with the boys; give them the good news.'

'I'm so glad for you. Have the nurse and doctor gone? Were there complications?'

'You'd better ask Maria. All I know is, I'm glad it's over.' He

rubbed his eyes. For the first time since she'd met him he was unshaven. 'We've got our daughter now – there'll be no more. I'm not having her go through that again.' He stepped round her, removing a cup and saucer from the tray as he passed. He didn't seem overjoyed at the arrival of the much-longed-for girl.

Maria was lying propped up in bed, looking exhausted but radiant, the infant cradled in her arms. 'I'm so glad everything turned out well. I've brought you and Nurse Digby a cup of tea. Shall I bring it in?'

The midwife bustled over. 'Good girl. Exactly what Mrs Cooper needs and I must say a cup of tea will do me good as well.'

Sarah put the tray down and took a cup over to the bed.

'Would you like to hold her, Sarah? I daren't drink tea with her in my arms.'

The baby was so small, and there was a strange blue tint around her mouth. She stroked the baby's velvet cheek, tears pricking at the backs of her eyes. She could recall holding Tommy in just this way when he'd been only an hour or so old. This baby seemed so tiny by comparison. Perhaps they'd got their dates wrong. It often happened. 'What are you going to call her? Have you decided?'

'Emily. It was my own ma's name. What do you think?'

'I think it's lovely, and so's she.'

Maria patted the empty side of the bed and Sarah sat down beside her, dismayed to see the flush across Maria's cheeks – the fever had returned. She didn't like to suggest the window was opened, not with the new baby.

'Mr Cooper's telling the boys. They'll want to see you and Emily. Are you up to a visit?'

'Of course I am. They'll be as pleased as punch. Did Dan tell you what happened – why we had to send for the doctor?'

Sarah would prefer not to know the details. It wasn't her place to be told such things. 'No, I gather there were complications.'

'She was a breech delivery; if she'd been any bigger I reckon neither of us would have survived. The doctor couldn't turn her, and I've got a lot of stitches, but we're both here. I'm going to need you to help with Emily this next week, Sarah love.'

'I'll be thrilled. I don't have enough to do as it is; Joe and Davie are at school of a morning, and John's no trouble. Nelly does all the hard work round here.'

The boys, once they were sure their ma was well, took little interest in the baby. Mr Cooper went back to work. He couldn't take further time off or he'd have his wages docked. His position was a responsible one and he took his duties seriously.

It was left to her to change the baby and launder the rags used to keep her backside clean. Maria still had a fever, but she insisted it was only a bit of a cold and she'd be right as ninepence in no time at all. It was the baby Sarah was most concerned about. Emily was too quiet, was a poor feeder and didn't seem to be thriving the way Tommy had.

Mr Cooper didn't come in any more to eat with the boys; when he returned at lunchtimes he got on with some project in the capacious shed at the bottom of the yard. She was obliged to take his soup and sandwich out to him. However, he always went upstairs to greet his wife and see the baby before he went back to work. Did he realise there was something not quite right with Emily? Was that why he was so distant? If the baby was ailing surely he would send for the doctor?

* * *

A few days later Sarah took the midday meal upstairs as usual. Maria was tossing about restlessly on the bed, her breathing harsh. Her fever hadn't returned; it was something different this time. She almost dropped the tray. 'Mrs Cooper, Maria, what is it? You should have banged on the floor. I'd have come up straightaway.'

'I feel right poorly, Sarah. My leg hurts something rotten and I can't catch my breath.'

'I'll fetch Mr Cooper. He's in the yard.'

She fled through the kitchen, ignoring the open mouths of the boys. Something was dreadfully wrong. Mr Cooper must run and fetch the doctor. He looked up from his carpentry.

'The baby?'

'No, sir, it's Mrs Cooper. I don't know what's wrong. She's desperately ill. Please come at once.'

He took one look at his wife and his face paled. 'Maria, Sarah will sit with you and Emily. I'll fetch the doctor. He'll soon sort you out. Don't fret, love. You rest quiet until I get back.'

It could be an hour or more before he returned. She had to trust the boys not to do anything silly in her absence; she daren't leave Maria on her own. All she could do was hold the patient's hand and murmur nonsense to her, but it seemed to help. She'd been sitting by the bed for half an hour when the door opened slowly and Joe's face peeped round.

'Is Ma poorly, Sarah?'

She hurried over to him, hoping he hadn't seen his mother's struggle to breathe. 'Yes, Joe, I'm afraid she is. Can you be a big boy and take care of your brothers for me? I have to stay here until your pa gets back.'

'I can do that. We can play spillikins – Davie and John like that.'

'Good boy.' She gathered him close, kissing his curls, praying

he wouldn't have to cope with the misery of losing his beloved mother. 'You can get down the biscuit tin. You may have two each. Make sure you put the lid on tight after, won't you?'

His worried frown vanished at the promised treat. Biscuits were only for Sundays. 'I will. We'll be quiet as mice, then Ma can have a nice rest.'

It was a further dragging twenty minutes before the front door opened and help arrived. It wasn't the doctor who had come back with Mr Cooper.

She smiled encouragingly at Maria. 'Mrs Digby's here now. She'll know what to do.' Sarah was relieved to leave the patient in expert hands.

'If you would care to wait downstairs, Mr Cooper; I'll call if I need you. Doctor Andrews will be here at any moment.'

He followed Sarah out of the sickroom. He gestured for her to accompany him to the parlour and closed the door behind them. 'Sarah, Emily is as sick as Maria. The doctor told me she has a heart condition, will not live much longer.'

'I thought she was too quiet; if anything happens to the baby, Mrs Cooper will be heartbroken.'

'That's why I haven't told her. I wanted her to be stronger before I broke the news.' His throat convulsed, and he brushed his hand across his eyes. 'I'm trusting you to take care of my boys; whatever happens today they'll need you more than ever. You're like a second mother to them already. Get them ready and take them for a walk along the river. I don't want them here this afternoon.'

He expected his wife to die. Sarah couldn't speak, feared she would break down if she tried. She had to be strong. Now was not the time to give in. He didn't require an answer, merely nodded and patted her shoulder, then with heavy feet returned to his wife. Pinning on a false smile she joined the children.

Joe looked up from the game. 'I saw the doctor go in a while back. That's a good thing, ain't it, Sarah?'

'I'm sure it is, Joe. Now, I thought we could go and feed the ducks. Davie, can you fetch your coats and mufflers from the scullery? Joe, will you and John bring in the boots?'

With a basket of stale bread over one arm, and John's hand in the other, she took them away as instructed. In spite of the sun it was cold by the river. Even the ducks seemed dispirited. It was no good; she couldn't keep them out any longer.

'Sarah, John's wet himself. He never asked like what he normally does.'

She scooped the miserable child into her arms. 'Never mind, sweetheart, accidents happen. Let's get back into the warm and I'll put nice dry clothes on you.'

They'd been away almost two hours. The clock had just struck three. Joe carried the empty basket; Davie held his other hand. John grizzled all the way back. The house was quiet, too quiet. She stripped off his wet clothes and replaced them with the fresh that were kept downstairs for such an eventuality. She got down the Snap cards and found them a barley twist to suck before going to investigate. She could hear someone in the parlour. She tapped on the door. Mr Cooper opened it; his face was ravaged, his eyes tear-filled. He shook his head and turned away to continue his pacing back and forth.

Sarah rushed upstairs dreading what she'd find. Nurse Digby was bending over, a still figure in the bed. She didn't need to ask – Maria was dead.

The nurse straightened, her eyes glittering. 'Mrs Cooper seemed better. Her breathing was easier and she fed the infant. I was changing the baby when she suddenly collapsed. It was a congestion of the lungs. It's not uncommon when a new mother has been poorly.'

Sarah could hardly take it in. The three boys were mother-less. How would Mr Cooper manage on his own? She walked over to the bed – forced herself to look for the last time. Maria's face was already cold as a marble slab, and as white. What she must have suffered to have died like this.

The nurse sniffed and dried her eyes. 'Doctor Andrews will call in at the vicarage on his way home. I shall stop by the undertaker's...' The woman looked uncomfortable and cleared her throat before continuing. 'The baby will be joining her any time now. I'm surprised she has survived so long.'

Poor Mr Cooper, to lose his wife and infant on the same day. 'How long?' She couldn't manage any more, hardly dared look in the cradle.

'This evening – no longer than that. I'm glad Mrs Cooper didn't know about the baby. They'll be together in heaven soon.'

Sarah wasn't certain about that. But they'd be together in a coffin – that's for sure. Leaving the midwife to do what was necessary she slipped out. She braced herself against the wall, forcing down her grief. This family needed her. She must hold firm for their sake. They'd taken her in when she'd been desper-ate; she must do everything she could to help the boys and Mr Cooper come to terms with the double tragedy.

Downstairs she discovered him slumped in an armchair, his shoulders no longer heaving, but shudders travelled up and down his spine at intervals. What he needed was a strong mug of tea with plenty of sugar. He would have to pull himself together; he needed to tell his sons before the undertakers appeared. He must know about the imminent demise of the baby. Was he delaying things until he could give them both pieces of bad news?

The children were sitting round the table playing Snap. It was the quietest game she'd heard them play. 'I'm making a nice

cup of tea. I'm sure you could do with one to warm you up after our long walk.'

Fortunately they were too engrossed to ask questions. She placed a mug of milky tea in front of each boy and then carried another into the front room. This time she didn't knock.

'Here you are, Mr Cooper, drink this. Maria needs you to be strong. The boys have to be told and arrangements made. I can't do it for you.'

He pushed himself upright rubbing his face on his sleeve, not bothering to reach for his handkerchief. His eyes were red and puffy, his nose running. He had to get himself straight before he could go next door. She handed him the damp cloth she'd had the foresight to bring with her. Like an automaton he cleaned his face and took a few slurps from his mug.

'Thank God you're here, Sarah. The boys will not take it so hard having you to comfort them. I'll go and tell them. Will you come with me?'

'I'm going to hold Emily. She can't be allowed to die on her own.' Not waiting for his response she went back to the bedroom. The midwife had finished laying out the body. Maria looked as if she was sleeping now, her arms folded across her chest, a fresh nightgown on and her hair neatly braided. It was kind of Nurse Digby to do this for them – Sarah wasn't sure it was usually her task.

'I thought I'd sit and hold the baby...' She couldn't continue, couldn't ask what she should do when the child drew her last breath.

'You're a good girl, Sarah. Just place the baby in her arms when she's gone. I've left room for her. Doctor Andrews will be along later to write the death certificates. I'll see myself out. It's a very sad day, but Mrs Cooper told me she knew you would take

care of her family when she'd gone. There's not many women can pass over confident of that.'

The room was silent and unpleasantly cold. She supposed it made no sense to waste coal. She reached into the cradle and picked up the infant. She placed one finger on Emily's tiny cheek; it was still warm. She was glad the little one wouldn't die alone.

Downstairs the boys were crying, Mr Cooper consoling them. It was better they were with their father. She rocked the bundle gently, murmuring words of love, telling the baby she would soon be with her mother in heaven. After a while she loosened the shawl and reached in to take the baby's hand. Maybe physical touch would give her comfort in her final hours.

It was dark in the room when she realised she was holding Emily's mortal remains. The baby had died as quietly as she'd lived. Dry-eyed she wrapped the little body up and carried it across to place it gently in Maria's arms where she belonged.

It was quiet downstairs. She daren't cry. The loss was too great; if she let down her defences for a second she would be overcome. Maria was relying on her, but it was a heavy burden on someone not yet seventeen years of age. She was committed to the Cooper family. She must forget all hope of joining Alfie or setting up in a business of her own. Sarah had dreamed of having her own dressmaking business one day, but that must be forgotten as her life was now here.

12

LONDON, MAY 1844

'Have you got your ticket for tomorrow, Alfie?'

'I got it this morning. You know, George, the bugger made me pay the same for Buster. He ain't going to sit on the seat; he'll go under it. It's a blooming cheek making me pay twice.'

The dog, hearing his name, got up from the cobbles and wandered over, shoving his huge head under Alfie's arm slopping his tea over his trousers. 'Get on with you, stupid animal. Good job we're outside in the yard. George wouldn't be best pleased if we got it all over his clean floor.'

'I reckon we've made a good job of this cottage, Alfie. It's a regular little home from home; my girl's coming to see it tomorrow. It's a shame you won't be here to meet her.'

'I'm catching the first train from Bishopsgate Street station. I need to get to Colchester in plenty of time. I want to find meself a bed for the night and then have a look round for somewhere permanent to rent.' He drained his mug and set it down on the windowsill. He was more than ready to leave the city. Already the stench was worse even though the choking smog had eased as people burnt less coal.

'Still, we've got this evening to spend together. I'm taking you for a slap-up meal and no arguments. I couldn't have got the place ready if you hadn't moved in with me like what you did.'

'Happy to do it. That's what mates are for, ain't they? Moving here saved me the rent on the room for a couple of months and I've learnt a whole lot more about this carpentry business. Them tables I made last week were a bit of all right, weren't they?'

His friend grinned. 'I reckon you're more than ready to set up on your own; if you stick to tables, benches and dressers you'll have no complaints.' George collected the empty mugs and turned to go indoors. 'The water will be hot enough for us to have our bath. If you finish putting things away out here, I'll get myself washed and then it'll be your turn.'

'Well, Buster, we'll be smart as paint tomorrow. You with your fine collar and lead, and me all spruced up in me best togs. You'll love the country, you wait and see.'

* * *

It was a fair old walk from George's drum to the station so Alfie left at sunrise. He paused as he turned out of the yard. He doubted he'd ever see his friend again. He had no intention of coming back to London; he'd done with it now. If Jim hadn't died, things would have been different.

Buster had become accustomed to being led and made no protest when he clipped the lead to his collar. The dog in one hand, his carpetbag in the other, he headed for the east side of London. He wasn't too sure about going back in that direction; it had unpleasant memories for him, but that's where the train left for Colchester so he had no choice.

Bishopsgate Street station was like a place from hell. The

clanking and groaning of the massive steam engines, the shouts, wails and whistles from the guards, made him wish he'd decided to travel all the way on foot. Buster shivered at his side. He hoped the dog would consent to getting on the train when the time came to embark.

He reached into his waistcoat pocket and withdrew his two tickets. There were three classes: first for the toffs, second for the middling folk and third class for the likes of him and Buster. The carriage was open to the elements, sides and seats the only comfort provided. If it rained he'd be drenched, but he weren't spending his hard-earned cash to sit inside. He could imagine the uproar if Buster farted; no he was better off in the fresh air.

His seat was towards the end of the train. There were already a handful of passengers ahead of him. He was relieved he didn't have to take his dog any closer to the hissing engine – he'd never have got him aboard then. He found his allotted space and Buster needed no encouragement to wriggle under the seat. Amazing how small he could make himself when he tried.

Promptly at seven o'clock the guard blew his whistle and waved his green flag. The train shuddered and heaved and rumbled forward. After a few miles the novelty of travelling at such speed wore off. His arse was black and blue from being bounced up and down on the hard seat and he was covered in soot from the engine's smoke. He'd look like Black Ben by the time he arrived.

For all that, it was nothing short of miraculous travelling fifty miles in less than two hours. It would have taken him all day in the mail coach and three days to walk. Being covered in soot and having a sore arse seemed a small price to pay when he stepped onto the platform of Colchester station. He glanced around. It weren't up to much, not much more than a wooden shed really.

He was back home. Nearly three years had gone by since

he'd left with that bastard captain. He'd been a boy then; he was returning a man. This had nothing to do with age; he'd taken care of himself, learnt a decent trade and come back with his waistcoat filled with five-pound notes. Ma would be proud of him. Even Jack Rand would think twice about knocking him about.

His lips curved. It were Sarah he wanted to see. She'd not recognise him, but then she'd have changed as well. He'd find himself a billet for the night, somewhere at the bottom of North Hill, then he'd cut along the river and up to Maidenburgh Street. It was there he was going to look for a cottage to rent. It was a stone's throw to the water meadows where Buster could roam around freely.

Like the other passengers he took a few moments to bang the worst of the city smuts from his person. Buster, who had spent the entire journey cowering under the seat, was relatively clean. 'Are you ready, Buster? This is where I come from. It's going to be our home from now on.'

'That's a fine dog you have there, mister; don't see many as big as him round here.' The speaker was a young man not much older than himself, similarly dressed, an almost identical carpetbag under his arm.

'I've been away a few years. Are you local, then?' The man followed him down the slope to the road that would lead them into Colchester.

'I am. Sam Foster's the name, been up the Smoke on business.' Foster fell into step beside him.

'Alfie Nightingale, and this here's Buster. I've been working in the city, made enough to set meself up in a little business. What line of work you in?'

'Family business; we buy and sell, and lend a bit to those who need it.'

'I'm a carpenter by trade, and aim to run a delivery service along with that.' They were over the bridge at the bottom of North Hill. 'I'm turning off here. Good to meet you, Sam.'

'Good luck to you, Alfie. I drink at The Red Lion most nights; maybe I'll see you there?' He tipped his cap and strode off.

The kind of business Sam Foster was involved in sounded like the same kind of business Silas Field had run. He didn't look Jewish – if he had, he would have supposed his pa to be an *uncle*, to run a pop shop. It weren't any of his business, but he'd make sure he stayed away from The Red Lion, find somewhere else to wet his whistle.

As soon as he was along the river path he released the dog. 'Go on, old fellow, have a sniff about. This is your patch now.' The dog didn't dash off as he was wont to do, but hovered nervously a few yards from him. Alfie smiled; this was the first time in the two years they'd been together he'd seen Buster unsure of himself. 'It's countryside, Buster, it won't hurt you. Go and have a look-see – find yourself a coney.'

They met no one in the water meadows; it could have been in the depths of the country not on the outskirts of a bustling market town. Alfie leant against the stile that separated the fields from the path that led to the bottom of the street where he hoped to find a vacant cottage. The clean air and early summer sunshine refreshed him. He was confident he'd made the right decision.

'Buster, time to go. Better put your lead back on; don't want people to be put off when we're looking for somewhere to stay tonight.' The dog had soon got over his anxiety and had spent the past half-hour galloping through the grass, barking at any wildfowl he came across. He turned towards the area of Colchester he'd grown up in. It was only then he recalled he'd just

walked past the stretch of river where his little brother had drowned. He'd all but forgotten that tragedy. He'd been a different person then; it was in the past.

* * *

The very next day he found what he was looking for. The man what owned the place was a Mr Hatch. He was to meet him that afternoon to seal the deal.

'This will suit me fine. I'll take it. Three months in advance do you, Mr Hatch?'

'Let's shake on it, Mr Nightingale. Pleasure to do business with you. The outbuildings need a bit of doing up, but being a carpenter, that'll be no problem to you. The kitchen range was installed this year. Most of the furniture is in good order. You've paid a fair price for it. If you need anything else, you know where to find me.' Money exchanged hands and Alfie had his first rent book. One day he'd have the deeds to a property in his hand, be beholden to no one, but this was a good start.

He'd only given the place a quick glance-over to know it was perfect for him. The previous tenants had left the place clean; although sparsely furnished, what was there would do him for the moment. It was a bit more than he'd intended to pay, but when he'd seen the yard and the row of dilapidated sheds he'd known it was ideal. It was at the end of the terrace, the back gate opening onto the path that led down to the river.

He hadn't thought he'd find something as quickly. He'd only had to spend one night in a lodging house. Rattling the two keys, he called the dog to his side. 'Buster, come and see our new home. You can go out again later once we're settled.'

The landlord had left the place unlocked. Alfie hung the keys on the hook inside the back door, tossing his carpetbag

onto the kitchen table. The range was the same as the one they'd had in East Stockwell Street. Many's the time he'd had to light that for his ma. Then he examined it more closely. It weren't the same. It had no open grate, the fire was behind a metal door, and there was a place to put your pots and pans to heat up. He saw a small brass tap poking out of the metal. He turned it without thinking.

'Bleedin' hell! Would you look at that, Buster? I've got a boot full of water. I reckon when this is lit we'll have hot water to wash in whenever we like.'

He must stop talking to his dog as if he were a human. He needed a mate, someone to share his life with, someone like Jim. No, he'd not want a friend again; what he wanted was a family of his own. He'd go and see Ma tomorrow, find out where his Sarah was, try and persuade her to move into his cottage. Then they could start a life together like what they'd always planned to do. He weren't ready to find himself a sweetheart; that was for the future. What he needed was company of a night. Who better than his sister?

His home had a good-sized scullery attached to the left of the kitchen. Although it had a door into the yard this had to be unbolted from the inside. The kitchen had shelves either side of the range, more than adequate for his needs. There was a table, not as good as he could make himself, and two chairs. The door to the right of the range opened inwards. There was a tiny hall-way, with the stairs leading up to the two bedrooms. He crossed the hall in one stride and entered the front room. This opened onto Maidenburgh Street. Being at the bottom of the hill it didn't require more than a single step outside.

The room was a decent size, had a fireplace, a stone mantelshelf above it and a window overlooking the road. There were boards on the floor, but no furniture. He'd purchase

himself a rug, a comfy armchair and make himself a side table to put an oil lamp on. He'd not use this room until Sarah came; then she could furnish it the way *she* wanted.

The stairs, although steep, were straight. A matching hallway at the top; to the left a bedroom above the kitchen, to the right a bedroom above the parlour. Both had bed frames, washstands and hooks to hang his clothes. He chose the one at the back; it would be quieter and gave him an unrestricted view of the yard.

When he'd got a couple of handcarts out there he'd want to be sure no one stole them. His years of living in London had made him wary. Hadn't the very first person he'd met been someone outside the law? Colchester was no better than anywhere else in that respect – there were always folk ready to steal instead of work.

* * *

He'd get himself settled; buy what he needed and stock up his larder before taking himself round to his old home. It was too hot for his tweed suit; he'd put on a clean shirt and his spare trousers. His hair was clean. He'd got George to trim it the other night, and he'd not had crawlers since he'd parted company with Ginger and the gang.

There were pots and pans, crockery and cutlery on the shelves now. He'd bought a meat safe, put it in the scullery and covered it with a wet cloth. His milk, butter and cheese should stay fresh enough like that. He'd not bothered to light the range, but it was laid and ready, the coal he'd ordered safely stored in the one shed with a decent lock on the door. His position on the end of the row meant he didn't have to share his privy with anyone, but he still had to go into his neighbour's yard to get his

water. At least what he pumped up was fresh enough to drink, not like the pumps where he'd been living.

'You stop here, Buster; take care of things for me. Your water's by the back step, and you got your bone to chew on. I don't think Ma's ready to meet you straight off.'

He locked the kitchen door and put the key behind a loose brick in the wall of the scullery. He'd no worries about being burgled, not when his dog was in the yard. The key were too cumbersome to lug around with him. He'd find somewhere better to hide it later.

The walk up the hill to the High Street took him five minutes longer than usual, for he stopped every few yards to stare. Everything looked exactly as it had when he'd left three years ago. He was the one who'd changed, not Colchester. He stepped into the High Street and gawped. Crickey! There must have been a fire at the far end. He crossed the road, standing outside The Red Lion in order to get a proper look. St Peter's Vicarage had gone and there was a smart new building in its place.

He dodged back between the hackney carriages, the diligences and private vehicles and entered East Stockwell Street, surprised how nervous he felt. The house he'd lived in most of his life was a third of the way down, the end of a row of ancient cottages. Should he go round the back, or knock on the front door? He'd do neither. He'd call at Mrs Sainty's, see how the land lay before he risked a confrontation with his stepfather.

Shuffling footsteps approached, bolts were drawn back and then the door opened. She hadn't changed, still as stout and dishevelled as ever. 'Can I help you, young sir?'

'It's me, Alfie, Mrs Sainty. I'm back to find my Sarah.'

Her eyes widened, she clutched the doorjamb for support. 'Good God! I never knew you, Alfie. You're a real toff now, made your fortune in the city did you?' She stepped to one side.

'You come along in. I've got the kettle on. Things have changed around here. I'm glad you called here first.'

By the time she'd finished he was as dumbfounded as she'd been earlier. Fancy Ma doing a vanishing act, not bothering to tell his sister she was going. 'Has Sarah been around lately?'

'I've not seen her since, let me see, spring last year. She's too busy, I reckon, what with her promotion and all. You go on round to Grey Friars House, let her know you're back. She was that desperate when you didn't return. Imagine, working on a coal barge all those months.' She smiled and prodded his arm. 'That's where you got those muscles from, so it weren't all bad news.'

'And your boys, what are they doing with themselves nowadays?'

'Bert's taken the Queen's shilling and George's moved in with his fancy woman on Balkerne Hill.'

'Maybe I'll look him up now I'm back.'

'Promise me you'll come round and see me, give us news of Sarah won't you, Alfie?'

'I will, Mrs Sainty. I'm going round right away to Grey Friars.'

No time like the present; he couldn't wait to see his sister's face. Would she be as shocked as Mrs Sainty to see the change in him? His old neighbour had told him Sarah was a young lady now, head nursemaid at this grand house. It was good news for her, but he doubted she'd want to leave her position to join him in Maidenburgh Street.

He'd not ask her to until his business was prospering and he had a steady income. She could do a bit of sewing – she was always good with a needle – make herself some extra. He didn't want her to work in a factory, do something menial. He wanted to provide for her, give her the little luxuries she'd never had.

There was no point in having all this money if he couldn't share it with someone else.

The sound of voices coming from the coach house behind Grey Friars House attracted him. He'd ask whoever it was in there if he could speak to Sarah. He didn't fancy knocking on the door – they might send him away without asking him his business. Grand folks didn't take too kindly to people like him banging on their back doors uninvited.

A girl, her blonde hair neatly coiled at the back of her neck, had her back to him as she was talking to a groom. Her smart grey dress told him she was a senior servant. His Sarah would be a senior too.

'Excuse me, miss, I'm looking for Sarah Nightingale. I was told my sister worked here.'

She spun, and smiled at him as if he was a long-lost friend. 'Alfie, you've come back at last. Sarah's not working here any more. I can't tell you how glad I am to see you. Can you come back tomorrow at two o'clock? I have the afternoon off and I can explain everything to you then.'

Too stunned to do more than nod, he watched the girl run lightly back towards the house. He didn't want to talk to the groom; he needed to get away, try and understand what the girl had said. He didn't even know her name. She must be a friend of Sarah's to know all about *him*. Somehow he was back on the pathway walking the wrong way, down the hill instead of back past the castle.

Ma gone, and now Sarah – he couldn't believe he'd come back to find his family scattered. He was more alone here than he'd been in London, for at least there he'd had George's companionship.

13

COLCHESTER, MAY 1844

'When Mr and Mrs Davies come, I thought we'd take a picnic along the riverbank for a change. What do you think boys?'

Joe paused in the game of marbles he was playing with Davie. 'We ain't been on a picnic in years, Sarah – perhaps Pa will come with us?'

'I don't know about that, Joe. He's very busy at the moment.' There was a tug on her skirt.

'He don't go to work on Sundays, do he, Sarah? So where's he gone then?'

'I expect there's something special he had to do. Remember your father has a very important position at the timber yard. It's his hard work that gives us all the extras we wouldn't have otherwise. Now, who's going to go and get the eggs from the chicken run for me?'

Joe and Davie ran off, a basket held between them, leaving her alone with John. She crouched down beside him, quickly collecting up the little painted clay balls and returning them to the cloth bag. She didn't trust the child not to push one up his

nose or try to swallow it. 'Come along, young man, you can measure the ingredients and mix up the sponge cake.'

After settling him on the chair beside her, she handed him a pudding basin and wooden spoon. There was no need to weigh the butter or flour. She'd made scones so many times she could do it blindfold. The sponge cake also; she used her ma's recipe – a cupful of each ingredient two eggs and a little milk.

The weeks had slipped past since that dreadful day. The first two weeks had been the worst, John wetting the bed every night, Joe calling out every half an hour for her to come. Stumbling up and down the attic stairs so often she was surprised she hadn't broken her neck.

One afternoon she came back from a walk to find everything had changed. Dan had been sleeping in the parlour; now his bed was in the attic along with his clothes. Her rickety bed frame was in the marital bedroom with all her belongings. He'd left the drawers, the commode, washstand and clothes cupboard for her use.

He said the children needed her close by; he didn't want to sleep in the room his wife and baby had died in, so it was the perfect solution. He'd packed away Maria's ornaments and knick-knacks. The front room was for the boys in future. They could play in there, get out from under her feet whilst she was working.

John rapped her on the knuckles with his spoon. 'Sarah, what I do next?'

Laughing, she tipped the beaten eggs into the cake mix. 'Sorry, sweetheart, I was wool-gathering. There, you stir, and I'll help you put it in the tins. Your brothers are back with the rest of the eggs. We're going to hard-boil those to take on the picnic.'

Mrs Davies and her husband had been coming every Sunday

for lunch or tea since she'd moved in here. It was Dan's suggestion. She treasured the afternoons she spent in the company of the old folk. It was hard to make friends when you didn't get any time off. She couldn't even go and see Betty, but Dan kept insisting she wasn't an employee but a member of the family.

She wasn't entirely comfortable with this new arrangement as it meant she was tied indefinitely to the Cooper household. Didn't he realise one day she might wish to leave, to get married and set up a home of her own? Or maybe he'd wish to find himself another wife. The next Mrs Cooper wouldn't take kindly to a servant being treated like a blood relative. Whatever he said, she *was* still a servant and didn't want it any other way.

He still gave her far more than she needed for housekeeping, told her to put anything left over in her savings account for a rainy day. Maybe this was his way of saying he understood that one day she would leave, but not yet. The children must come first at the moment.

The food was packed, two rugs rolled up and ready when the visitors arrived. John greeted the elderly couple with the news they were going on a picnic.

'My word! We ain't been on one of them since I don't know when. It'll be a rare treat being out in the fresh air on a lovely day like this. What have we got in this here picnic then, young John?'

The children listed the contents of the two baskets and the elderly couple exclaimed appropriately. Sarah was returning from the privy with John when Dan returned.

'We're going on a picnic, Pa,' Joe shouted. 'You can come with us, can't you?' The child grabbed Dan's hand. Sarah held her breath, praying he would agree. He glanced up, catching her eye, then grinned and nodded.

'I wouldn't miss it for the world, son. A picnic's just what we

need on a day like this. Give us a minute to change out of me work clothes and I'll be ready to come with you.' He ruffled the boy's hair. 'You and Davie fetch your ball. We can have a kick-about if we can find somewhere safe.'

She knew he was referring to her brother Tommy. She'd told the children about this in order to stop them running too close to the bank on their frequent walks by the water.

* * *

When they returned John was asleep, his head lolling on his father's shoulder. Mrs Davies carried the empty baskets and her husband the rugs. Sarah walked with Joe and Davie. Even they were subdued, the fresh air and riotous game of football having tired them out. They said farewell to the old couple outside the house. She hoped they'd manage the long trek up the hill to their own cottage without mishap.

She unlocked the back door, Dan standing beside her. 'I'll give you a hand putting this lot to bed. I reckon you'll not hear a peep from them tonight. About time you got a good night's rest.'

'Thank you, Dan. We'll just take their clothes off. I'm not bothering to wash them all over tonight, just a quick wipe with a wet flannel will have to do.'

Between them this task was accomplished smoothly. He patted her shoulder. 'I'll get the kettle on, Sarah. We could both do with a cup of tea.'

He clattered down to the kitchen, leaving her to give them a final goodnight kiss. They were all asleep before she left the room. She removed her boots and bonnet, slipping on her indoor shoes. These were another little extra Dan had insisted she bought. Her cupboard was full of gowns, shawls and petticoats; why, she even had *two* bonnets now!

He was too generous. It wasn't right for him to treat her like this. She feared she was becoming more and more beholden. Tonight she'd explain how she felt, get things back on a more formal footing. It would make things easier later. She hadn't given up hope that Alfie would come back for her one day.

The kitchen was empty. He must be locking up the chickens. The tea was brewing, the milk, sugar and two cups waiting on the table. With the window and back door left open, the heat from the range wasn't too bad. Her rocking chair was by the open door most evenings. Listening to the nightingales was a treat after a long day's work. Usually Dan sat in the parlour reading the paper. This was the first time since Maria's death they'd spent any time together.

His shirt glowed white in the darkness as he returned from the far end of the yard. 'That broody hen has a clutch of chicks under her. They must have hatched today. The boys will be excited when they see them tomorrow.'

'She was sitting on more than a dozen. I wonder how many will be hens.'

'It don't matter either way – the cockerels make good eating.' He collected his tea from the table and brought a chair to join hers. 'I enjoyed myself today, Sarah, thank you for arranging it. You're a good girl. Maria would be happy to know you're here being a mother to her boys.'

Her cup rattled against the saucer. She placed it down beside her. Keeping her head lowered she had to explain. 'It's not right, treating me as one of the family. I'm not a relative; I'm an employee. One day you'll want to get married again and your next wife will not take kindly to this arrangement. I might even want to get married myself. What then?'

She raised her head, daring to look at him. He wasn't angry

or offended; there was a faint gleam of something she half-recognised in his eyes.

'You're quite right to remind me, Sarah. I'll not say it to the boys any more. But you're a friend, I hope, not just an employee.'

'Dan, it's an honour to call myself your friend. I'm glad you understand my position. I don't want there to be any misunderstanding in the future.'

He grinned. For some reason her cheeks coloured. 'Sarah, is there something you've not told me? Do you have someone in mind?'

She frowned, not understanding.

'A young man? Are you leaving to get married soon?'

'I should think not. I'm not seventeen until October, far too young to be thinking about that sort of to-do.'

'Promise me you won't leave for any other reason and I'll be content.'

'I promise. I'm very happy here and I love the boys.'

'Good. Now, Joe and Davie have their birthdays at the beginning of August, and John will be four in July. Let's have a party to celebrate their anniversaries. Maria wouldn't want us to grieve any more. It will be nearly six months by then. Time to move on. Don't you agree?'

'I suppose so, and the boys would love it. Do you mean a *real* party? One with cake and guests and party games? I've never even been to a party, let alone arranged one.' She smiled, that wasn't quite true. 'Although I did attend one when I was working as a nursemaid.'

'In which case, you're the expert. Can you make a birthday cake, buy the extras and things? We must think about gifts as well.'

She yawned, covering her mouth apologetically. 'Of course I can, but not now – we've months to plan it. I think I'll retire,

Dan. It's been a long day and all the fresh air has quite worn me out.' She stood up, ready to do her usual chores, but he shook his head.

'No, you go on up, Sarah. I'll do what's necessary.'

It was some time before she could settle in spite of her fatigue. Had she said enough? Did Dan understand her position? He'd seemed unperturbed by her request, not at all upset by her suggestion that one day she would be leaving. She had no intention of getting married yet.

Unless he found himself a wife she'd be quite content to stay where she was. But she wished she hadn't made that promise. If Alfie came back, things might be different then. But why should she live with her brother when she had such a good position here? Whatever he might offer couldn't possibly match what she already had in comfort and security.

Alfie spent far longer on his appearance than was customary. He checked his cravat was neatly tied, shirt clean and waistcoat unstained. He gave a last rub to his boots confident they couldn't be any shinier. Today he wore his jacket, a bit warm for anything apart from shirtsleeves, but he intended to make a good impression. He'd thought of little else but the girl he'd met briefly the day before. She was small, barely came up to his shoulder, but her pale blue eyes sparkled and her blonde hair had shone around her face.

Leaving Buster at home, he set off up the hill taking a shortcut around the bailey of the castle. He waited opposite the rear entrance to Grey Friars. The church on the hill struck two. Moments later the girl emerged. He caught his breath. She was even lovelier than he'd remembered. Out of uniform today, her

pretty straw bonnet caught his eye. Her dress, in a soft pink material, fitted snugly over the finest bosom he'd ever seen.

He was about to cross the road when she waved back, then dodged expertly in and out of the traffic to arrive laughing and breathless at his side. 'You must think me daft, Alfie Nightingale. Inviting myself to meet you and you not knowing who I am.' She dipped in a mock curtsy. 'I'm Betty Thomas.'

Laughing, he bowed solemnly. 'Pleased to meet you, Betty Thomas. I'm desperate to know what happened to Sarah. Let's find somewhere quiet we can talk.'

It wouldn't be proper to invite her back to the cottage, be on their own like; he didn't know much about how things were done, but being alone with a girl wasn't something he'd suggest so early in their acquaintance.

'I know somewhere in Wire Street, Mr Doe's Temperance Hotel – we'll go there. You look the kind of gent who can afford to take a girl out for a cup of tea.' Without being asked, she placed her arm in his. 'Mind you, we can find a wall to sit on if you ain't comfortable going to a place like that.'

'No, much better inside where we can get a bit of privacy.' He marched off, following her directions, feeling ten feet tall. He'd never been in a hotel, so left matters in her capable hands.

The waitress ushered them to a quiet corner. Betty ordered tea and cakes. He waited for the girl to leave before asking about his sister. For some reason he'd not wanted to spoil the mood on the walk through Colchester.

'Now, what happened? Why were Sarah turned off?'

'In a minute, Alfie. First I've got something to give you; she left this with me. I've other things of hers, books and such. Next time we meet I'll give them to you.'

He wasn't sure he liked being ordered about by this slip of a girl. Maybe she felt superior because she was a bit older than

him. He'd not bother at the moment, but it would be best to put her straight when they met again.

She put a small white parcel on the tablecloth. He raised his eyebrows; she said nothing. He unfolded the material and his eyes filled. Pa's gold watch. He remembered being shown it when he was a nipper. Beside it was a guinea – Ma hadn't quite forgotten him after all. He flicked the coin, dropping it in his waistcoat pocket.

'I'd forgot about this. It belonged to my pa; it were his pride and joy. It were promised to me when I was grown. I wonder if it's still working.' He twisted the winder a few times and was gratified to hear a regular ticking.

'Go on then, put it on. You're just the sort who should have a gold watch in his pocket. I can't wait to see you wearing it.'

He pushed the end of the chain through his buttonhole and dropped the watch into the top pocket. He liked the solid feel of it against his chest. He grinned, feeling like a young boy again. 'I reckon I'll be lifting it in and out every five minutes to show it off to folk.'

The waitress appeared with their order and over tea Betty explained what had happened to Sarah. He was horrified to think she had been robbed and beaten, and him not there to protect her. He'd make it his business to find the bastards what done it. He knew their names and where they lived. He might not get Sarah's money back, but they'd get what was coming to them – he'd make sure of that.

'At least we know she's living with Mrs Billings somewhere down St Botolph's Street. It shouldn't be hard to find the house.'

Betty shook her head. 'She won't be there now, Alfie. Remember, she had to be out of the room by Christmas. Don't look so gloomy – we'll find her. Sarah's a survivor.'

'I know what me own sister's like, thank you. We went

through enough together over the years. But this ain't the same. It's different for a girl on her own. That parish is little better than the backstreets of London.'

'Shall we go and look right now, Alfie? You pay the bill; I have to go out back a minute. I've still got a couple of hours. It's no more than fifteen minutes from here. That gives us plenty of time to start searching.'

He resented paying out so much for a pot of weak tea and slice of cake his Sarah could have made a lot better. He wasn't sure he wanted Betty along with him; it weren't the sort of place a nice girl like her should go.

Sarah had promised to get in touch with Betty, to send for her belongings, but it were over six months and not a word. Surely, if things had worked out, she would've contacted her best friend? But it was impossible to feel downhearted as he strolled in the sunshine with a pretty girl on his arm. He weren't accustomed to escorting young ladies, but with Betty it were all right – she did all the talking for him. In spite of his worries he found himself laughing at her sallies, enjoying her company more as the afternoon went by.

He enquired at a grocery store and was given the exact direction to the house he sought. They waited together on the doorstep for someone to answer their knock. A large bloke, dressed in the navy woollen of a seaman, filled the doorway. He smiled pleasantly enough.

'Can I help you?'

'It's me sister, Sarah Nightingale – I believe she lodged here last year.'

He looked puzzled. 'I think you've got the wrong house. We don't take in lodgers – there's no spare rooms. Sorry I can't help.'

The door was closing when Betty jumped forward. 'Please, ask Mrs Billings about Sarah. She lived here, last year, when

your ma was expecting her last baby. She looked after your little brothers and sister. She was sleeping in your bedroom, I reckon, and left before you got back.'

His expression changed to concern. 'Wait a minute, I'll fetch Ma.'

He left the door ajar and shuffling footsteps, like those of an old woman, approached. He was shocked to see the state of Mrs Billings. She was unkempt, as was the fractious infant cradled in her arms.

'Yes, your Sarah did stay with me. But my husband turned her out when he got back. He locked me and the children upstairs so I couldn't speak to her. I didn't dare go out and look, and then I had a new baby to take care of as well as the other little ones. I've not had time to breathe since then.'

'Look, I'm sorry, mate – I'd no idea about this. If I'd known that bastard had turned a girl out that way, I'd have searched for her, made sure she was all right. I'm Robert Billings. I'll come and help you look.' He placed his arm around his mother. 'You go and sit down, Ma. The boys can take care of Beth. Tell them I'll bring them back a candy twist.'

The woman smiled tiredly and shambled off down the corridor. He came out to join them in the street. 'There's no love lost between me and my father. He's a right bastard, and my younger brother's little better. I only come back to see the kids and give my ma a hand. I hope your sister's came to no harm because of what happened here.'

Alfie liked this bloke. There was no blame on him. 'I'd be glad of your help. I don't know this area; I came from the north.'

Robert eyed Betty's outfit. 'I don't think you should come with us, miss. It's not the sort of place a young lady like you should go.'

Alfie understood exactly the sort of place he was referring to;

he'd lived somewhere similar himself. 'I'll take you back, Betty. Robert's right – I don't want you going in them filthy places.'

She stood her ground. 'Don't you dare say I can't go somewhere Sarah might be living. I don't care if my dress gets dirty. All I care about is finding my best friend.' She glared at him and he gave in.

An hour later they'd drawn a blank. People round here were too miserable to take much notice of anyone else's misfortune. No one had heard of Sarah and no one cared either way. He shook hands with Robert and agreed to meet him the next afternoon to resume the search. He walked Betty back, this time taking her to the door.

'Thank you for coming with me, Betty. It makes all the difference knowing Sarah has such a good friend to stand by her.'

'I'd have gone looking on me own, but didn't dare to. I wish we'd found her, Alfie. I have a whole day off at the beginning of June. It's on a Tuesday for a change. Shall I give you her things then?'

'Yes, I've got a decent place. I'll take you round to meet me best friend – Buster. What time shall I be here?'

She tilted her head, working out when she'd be free. 'Be here at half past nine. I'm looking forward to seeing your dog. I like him already. After all he kept you safe in London, didn't he?'

She squeezed his arm, then with a flick of petticoats vanished through the gate. He walked back in a daze, past the castle and into Maidenburgh Street, scarcely noticing where he was. He didn't know if he was worried about Sarah's whereabouts or pleased that he'd met her best friend.

14

COLCHESTER, JULY 1844

Alfie gave a final rub to his table. It weren't too bad in the yard. Most of it was in shade by this time of the day. Betty was in the kitchen baking, but came at his call, a mug of tea in her hand for him. She walked over to admire his work, then sat on the back step, patting the space beside her, inviting him to sit there.

In the last two months she'd taken to dropping in, turning up whenever she had an hour or two free. She tidied the cottage, baked pies and cakes, ironed his shirts. He was beginning to feel hemmed in; he wasn't ready for this sort of commitment. He liked escorting her around on his arm, walking in the country-side and such, but she seemed to think he was courting her. He weren't ready – not by a long shot.

'I got some tea here, Alfie. What time's Mr Hatch coming to look at the table?'

He couldn't help smiling back. Even with her cheeks flushed from working in the hot kitchen she was still as pretty as a picture. 'Later on this evening, on his way round from collecting rents. If he likes it, I'll get the other work, not have to do so much of the delivering.'

'He'll love it. It's the best bloomin' table I've ever seen. I can't believe how quickly you've got yourself set up here, Alfie. All the sheds mended, a handcart and orders for furniture. Not many men twice your age could have done as well.' She handed him his tea, not suggesting they sit together a second time.

'I ain't sitting next to you, Betty, not until I've had a wash. It's sweaty work, carpentry, and no mistake.' She didn't pull a face, just sat down on her own quite happily. He drained his mug. Funny really, how tea was just as good even when the weather was baking. 'I'll have another one, if there's one going.'

He wished it were Sarah making his tea. He'd still not come to terms with the fact that his sister wasn't going to be found. After two weeks of fruitless searching he'd had to accept she was gone. She must've left Colchester or he would of found her by now. The alternative was unthinkable: that she was dead and lost to him forever.

'I have to go down to The Hythe one of these days to buy me timber; I reckon it'll be cheaper from Hawkins than getting it at that Fred Allcock's near where you work.'

She called from the kitchen. 'It'll make a nice day out. We could take a picnic. I've got a day off at the beginning of next month; I'm not sure which one but I'll tell you next time I come round.'

He wandered up the steps, sniffing appreciatively. 'That smells tasty. What you made me this time, Betty?'

She beamed. 'I've made you steak and kidney pie, and as the oven was already hot, I've made a plum pie as well.' Where she'd got plums from this time of year he didn't like to ask. She'd been bringing stuff round every time she visited; he hoped they were given to her. He'd not want her to lose her position on account of him.

He took his refilled mug, ready to return outside. Was that

what her game was? Liquid slopped over his fingers. His eyes narrowed and he stared at her. Had he misjudged her? Was she trying to get herself dismissed knowing he'd be obligated to take her in?

'These things you bring from Grey Friars, you don't pinch them, do you?'

'Don't be daft, Alfie. The housekeeper had a soft spot for Sarah; when she knew I was looking for her, doing a bit of cooking and such for you, she was keen to help. She finds me something left over from the pantry. Don't worry yourself – I'm not about to lose my position over any lad. Especially not one as young as you.'

His laugh echoed round the empty yard. He'd been put in his place right and proper. 'Young? I've done more in my almost sixteen years than you have in seventeen. It's a matter of experience, my girl, not how many birthdays you've had.'

She left soon afterwards, promising to come back to let him know exactly when her day off fell. He was glad he'd not been wrong about her. He'd miss her company. Since Robert had returned to sea he'd not had anyone else to talk to. He drew himself a bowl of hot water and took it through to the scullery. He preferred to be clean nowadays, reckoned he washed more than most folk did.

It was hard leaving his supper under the cloth, but he'd not eat until Mr Hatch had been. The flimsy table that had been in the kitchen when he moved in was now in the back bedroom. The one he'd made to replace it was superior in every way. The parlour was furnished. He'd let Betty come with him to purchase the curtains, armchairs and rugs. There seemed little point in leaving the room unused, just waiting for his sister to come and help him choose things.

At least Sarah hadn't been in the workhouse. According to

their records she'd never been an inmate. Robert Billings had taken a three-month run on a ship that sailed from Harwich. He didn't like to leave his mother while she was so unwell. Alfie had promised to keep an eye on Mrs Billings. Once he'd got to know her, heard her talking so lovingly about Sarah, he'd really warmed to her.

Next time Robert was home he was coming with him to find the men who had robbed and beaten Sarah. The least he could do was keep an eye on his ma, do a few odd jobs when he was there. She now had a slovenly girl in to help out with the heavy work; better than nothing he supposed. The younger brother was on the same ship as Robert's pa. This meant they rarely met, which suited his friend.

Buster sat up. His low growl filled the yard. The dog hadn't taken to his landlord for some reason. 'Enough of that. You behave yourself.'

Mr Hatch appeared, his smile wary. 'Good evening, Mr Nightingale. Is that the table you've made for me?'

He got straight to business – that's one thing he liked about the man. 'It is, Mr Hatch. There's two side tables and a dresser to look at as well.'

The man ran his fingers over the surface of the table, tipped it to check the joints, then leant his weight on it to see if it would wobble. 'Fine workmanship – plain, sturdy, exactly what I need. Show me the rest. If it's anything as good as this, you've got yourself a deal, young man.'

When he left, they'd shaken hands on an arrangement that should prove beneficial to them both. He was to deliver the table to an address near St Mary's the following day. The only drawback being he'd have to make two side tables, a further kitchen table and a couple of stools, but wouldn't get paid until they were done. He should have asked for a deposit. If he spent

out on materials and then didn't sell the items he'd be out of pocket.

He ate his supper, a paper at his side as he scribbled out designs and added measurements. Although he'd not put money in the bank since he'd returned in May, he'd not drawn any out either. He'd made a couple of tables and sold them locally. With this he'd had enough to buy a dilapidated hand-cart. By the time he'd mended it, and added a little paint, it was as good as new.

That was another problem. Doing carpentry meant he wouldn't have time for delivery jobs. Market days he was run off his feet. He didn't charge much, and although there were others plying their trade, the womenfolk liked his cheeky grin. He reckoned it was Buster that got him so much business; the dog had turned into a right old softy. It was only with Mr Hatch the old Buster showed. That was enough for tonight. He'd turn in early for a change.

* * *

The joint birthday celebrations were well in hand. Dan was no longer distant from his boys. He was eating his lunch with them two or three times a week. His interest made all the difference. There were no more wet sheets or disturbed nights, for which she was thankful. A week before the party he came to find her whilst she was washing up.

'There's something I want to show you in the workshop after the boys are in bed. I'd value your opinion.'

Sarah looked up from the sudsy water. It was the first time he'd followed her into the scullery. 'I've almost finished, then I'll put John to bed. I'm afraid it'll be another hour before Joe and Davie will be asleep.'

He grinned, making him look younger. He'd changed these past weeks, was almost unrecognisable from the man she'd met last year. Sometimes, when he was playing with the boys, rolling around whilst they jumped all over him, he seemed no older than her Alfie. She'd worked out he must be about ten years her senior, but at times like those she seemed the more grown up.

The boys settled. She only had to read two stories before they were ready to sleep. There was usually a cool breeze in the evening coming off the Colne. With the windows open front and back it wasn't too hot upstairs. Mrs Davies had suggested she buy herself a corset, telling her she was letting herself down by not wearing one. Imagine having that on in all this heat! She was still a bit thin – she didn't eat much in summer. Her waist was quite small enough without donning such an instrument of torture.

Dan had knocked up an outdoor table and a couple of benches for the yard. Most days they ate outside now it was so warm. With a nice tablecloth over the top, and a jar of wild flowers the boys had picked along the water meadow, it looked a treat. The children had helped her make a flower bed on the far side, and there was a border full of marigolds, forget-me-nots, daisies and cornflowers to brighten the space. Her spirits lifted every time she came out. One day when she got married, she'd like a real garden, grass to sit on and somewhere to grow vegetables.

She'd also like to have her own things, not be wearing Maria's refurbished clothes. He'd said she could sell them or make them over. It had seemed a pity to sell the clothes when she could make use of them herself. This was why her cupboard was full. Was she becoming the woman whose clothes she was now wearing?

John often called her ma, and although she corrected him

gently, he continued. Six months was a long time when you were so small. She headed for the yard, the golden glow of the lamps guiding her to the workshop. What was it that Dan was so eager to show her?

He was standing outside watching the skylarks in his shirt-sleeves and bare feet. Good gracious! What had possessed him to work with his boots off? If he dropped a hammer on his foot, it didn't bear thinking of. He turned and smiled.

'There you are, Sarah. Come and see what you think of this.' He threw open the double doors. Her eyes widened. On his workbench was the most wonderful wooden castle; it even had a crenellated top, a drawbridge, and little windows and doors. Next to it was a box of tin soldiers. She clapped in delight. 'Dan, it's beautiful. I'd no idea you were so skilled. The boys will love it – I can't wait to see their faces.'

'I've been searching out soldiers these past few weeks. Some were a bit battered, but I've touched them up; I don't think they'll know which are old and which new.'

She picked up two and placed them on the platform that ran round the inside. There was also a flight of stairs, and a grand hall with miniature furniture. 'I must make wall hangings and curtains. What about adding three flagpoles? I'll make flags to fly on them.' She examined one of the little tin men more closely. 'I shall make them tabards to match their flags, then there will be no arguments when they're playing.'

It was late when they returned to the house. The chickens had gone to roost long ago. She couldn't remember spending such a pleasant evening. 'I've been making them a kite. Mr Davies cut it out for me. They'll be so excited. I can't wait to see their little faces next week.'

That night she fell asleep, her head full of party planning. Mr and Mrs Davies were coming, and Dan had invited a couple

of friends from work with their families. That would be nine children and eight adults to cater for. She was making fairy cakes, a blancmange and a junket as well as meat pasties and sandwiches, but pride of place would be the birthday cake.

She'd been horrified how much everything was costing, but Dan had told her to spare no expense. She was going to put sugar paste on the cake and then decorate the top with flowers from the garden. The boys had been making party hats and wanted *blind man's buff* and *pin the tail on the donkey* for the games.

She would soon turn seventeen. Three years ago she'd not been much more than a child – look at her now! Running a household, responsible for three children, and with Nelly to do all the hard work for her.

The boys were beside themselves with excitement about their shared birthday party. They'd put up bunting made from scraps of material. The kitchen table was going out to join the picnic table and all the other chairs. The white sheets were ironed and ready to use as tablecloths and the crockery and cutlery stacked up in the scullery.

A voice called from across the landing. 'Is it morning yet, Sarah?'

'No, John, it's not. It never will be unless you go to sleep right now.'

She brushed her hair in front of the open window. Dan was moving about in the attic. She liked to know he was close by. They'd been lucky with the weather. It hadn't rained for several days; rain would be a disaster because the yard became a quagmire when it was wet.

It wasn't right the master of the house slept up there and she had the best room. Looking around, it was as though Maria had never existed. She'd dropped from their lives like a stone into a

pond, the ripples of her life no longer visible. Sometimes Sarah felt she was being dragged down beneath the water herself. The children looked to her for everything. All of them treated her as though she was their mother. Now the fort was completed Dan was spending his evenings in the kitchen with her, no longer sitting on his own in the front room. He'd read her articles from the *Essex Standard* and then they'd discuss the news together whilst she got on with her sewing.

They were settling into a routine. He'd no feelings for her of *that* sort and she most definitely didn't for him. But they were comfortable around each other, shared the same sense of humour. If she was honest she thought he was happier now than he had been when Maria was alive.

* * *

August 1844

Alfie gave Buster a final brush. 'There, you'll do. Want you to look your best today – we're taking you on a jaunt.' Betty would be here soon. The food was ready, and he'd bought the basket specially for today. Hythe was a fair way to walk in this heat, but they'd go along the river path, then the dog could run free until the last half mile.

'Crickey, you made the picnic yourself?' Betty stood grinning in the open doorway.

'Hard-boiled eggs, cheese sandwiches and some of that fruit cake you made. It's a feast. But I ain't carrying the basket – that's your job.'

The walk was pleasant, and they'd picked out a place to stop on their way back for the picnic. 'Will there be anybody to speak to on a Saturday morning, Alfie?'

'I hope so. It's a long way to come for nothing. I need to know if it's worth me while trekking down here; with a full cart it'll be no fun going back up the hill.'

'Go on with you. You're getting fat and lazy like your dog. The exercise would do you good.'

'Ta very much, nice to know I'm appreciated. I'll tell you something – I've not enjoyed a day out so much since I...'

'You went to the opening of the Thames Tunnel. You've told me so often, Alfie, I don't reckon I'll need to go there myself.'

They were like brother and sister. He felt happy with her, treating her as if she was Sarah. He no longer believed she was after him. She had no family nearby and seeing him gave her something to look forward to.

It was after eleven o'clock when they arrived at the bridge. They crossed it and turned down towards Hawkins timber yard. It was quiet, not like a weekday. One of the labourers directed him to a brick building where he would find the foreman. Alfie could see the man he needed was tall with a head of dark curly hair and shoulders even broader than his own; he could see him in the office.

'Betty, I can't take the dog into the yard. Will you be all right waiting here?'

'Go along, Alfie, I'll be fine. No one looks sideways at me with his fine fellow at my feet.' The dog flopped down next to her. Buster had taken a real shine to her, but he weren't sure if it was Betty, or the treats she brought him, that had won him over.

He strode across the yard to bang on the door and was beckoned in. 'I've come to enquire about the price of your timber. I'm a carpenter. Me own yard's in the north, but I reckon it might be worthwhile to bring me cart down here, rather than buy it local.'

The man nodded. 'It will be; the sort of timber you want will

come from off-cuts. Dan Cooper, I'm foremen here. Tell me what you're looking for and I'll give you a rough price.'

'Alfie Nightingale, pleased to meet you.'

Cooper's jaw dropped. He looked as if he'd been punched in the guts. 'My God, I can't believe it. Today of all days. Alfie Nightingale, you come with me. There's someone I want you to meet.'

15

COLCHESTER, AUGUST 1844

'Look at this, Sarah, it's nearly long enough to go right across the archway. Can I put it up?' The boy waved at the row of misshapen rags tied haphazardly to a piece of string.

She laughed. 'You're too small, Joe. If I stand on a chair I think I can do it for you.'

The boys hadn't seen their birthday gift yet. The castle would be revealed at the start of the party when all the guests were there to appreciate its magnificence. The boys were wearing the shirts she'd made and very smart they looked too. Today she was wearing a new gown. She'd treated herself to a length of cornflower blue cotton and somehow found the time to get it completed for the birthday party.

'Sarah love, I thought we'd come down a bit early; see if we could give you a hand with anything.'

'You're very welcome, Mrs Davies. Look who's here, boys. They can help you finish off your flags whilst I put the kettle on.'

Dan was working as usual this Saturday morning, but he'd promised to be back before noon, giving himself time to wash and change before the first guests arrived. The party was starting out at

twelve thirty – a bit early for a tea party but the boys wouldn't be able to contain themselves until the afternoon. Their excitement might well turn to tears and fractiousness. The kitchen seemed unfamiliar without the central table and chairs now these were outside as well.

Mrs Davies joined her. 'Lovely day you've got for it. Whose birthday is it today?'

'Actually, Joe and Davie have birthdays next week, and John's was last week. Made sense to pick a date in the middle.'

'Is everything ready? Nothing I can do to help?'

'When everyone gets here, I'd be glad to have a hand taking out the food. I can't do it too soon; it's too hot out. The birthday cake's a surprise. I finished decorating it last night after they'd gone to bed. And you wait and see what Dan's made them.'

Mrs Davies glanced over her shoulder to see they weren't overheard. 'Something I need to tell you – it's about you and Dan. There's tongues wagging about the pair of you. Gossip has reached as far as The Prince of Wales.'

Sarah was speechless – why should anyone be talking about them?

'It's like this: you're living here, a member of the family not a servant any more. Folks are saying you're his fancy woman.'

The teapot smashed on the flagstones, sending scalding liquid across her ankle. The boys raced into see what the fuss was about but returned to the yard once sure she was not badly injured. Mrs Davies collected a wet cloth and helped her hobble to the front room, by then it was too late to reply to her outrageous suggestion. She and Dan sharing a bed as well as a house? How could people think such a thing?

Mrs Davies cleared up the mess before sending her husband out to purchase a new teapot; this was one article they couldn't manage without today. There had been the odd sideways look

recently, the occasional sly wink or nudge when she'd been out shopping, but she'd taken no notice.

How *could* she have been so stupid? She was even sleeping in the bedroom he had shared with his wife a few months ago. Nelly must have been talking, making something out of nothing. It just hadn't occurred to her to mention that Dan slept in the attic now.

She couldn't think straight, didn't know what to do. She'd promised not to leave unless she was getting wed, but surely he wouldn't want her good name to be destroyed? She couldn't think about this at the moment. It was the boys' special day – it might well be the last one she shared with them.

Voices outside on the pathway roused her. Dan was here – she'd recognise his laugh anywhere. Then a woman spoke. Surely not? It couldn't be! Betty here? This must be the surprise he'd promised her. Forgetting her worries she rushed through the empty kitchen and into the backyard just as Dan appeared through the archway. Sure enough, walking beside him was Betty, her arm through that of a handsome young man who looked vaguely familiar.

'Betty, I can't believe it – you're the best surprise I could possibly have.' The young man grinned. She rocked back on her heels. It was her Alfie. She'd not known him until he smiled at her.

Ignoring Betty's outstretched arms she flung herself at her brother. He swept her from the ground. He was so tall and handsome. He was supposed to be her younger brother; somehow they'd changed places.

'Sarah, I can't believe it. When Dan said there was someone he wanted me to meet, I'd no idea it was you.' He twirled her around like a small child, her petticoats flying everywhere

revealing her bare ankles. It had been too hot to wear stockings this morning.

'Alfie, put me down. Let me give my best friend a kiss.' Then she was in Betty's arms, laughing and kissing, tears of joy streaming down her face. Dan was standing quietly, watching her excitement. 'Dan, I can't believe it. Thank you so much for bringing them. When you said you had a surprise for me, I'd no idea it was something as wonderful as my long-lost brother and best friend.'

'Glad to be of service, Sarah love. I'll leave you to catch up; I'll go in and get myself spruced up. Come along, boys, you can find your ball.'

Fortunately Mr Davies returned, clutching a shiny brown teapot, just in time for his wife to make everyone a cup of tea.

'Come and sit down. Don't use the benches – they're for the children. Use a chair. Where have you been all this time? I can't believe how much you've changed.' She looked across at his smart jacket and saw a gold chain protruding from his button-hole. 'You've got Pa's watch on. He'd be proud of you – you've obviously done well since you left Colchester.'

Alfie grinned, making him look more like the boy she remembered. 'I'm sorry, I didn't bring anything for the party.'

Betty interrupted him. She seemed to do a lot of that, Sarah noticed. 'We didn't know we'd be seeing you. You don't expect anything, do you, Sarah?'

'Of course not. We can't talk now; the guests will be arriving soon and I've got food to bring out. Everyone should be gone by teatime. Can you stay on till then, Betty?'

Her friend smiled. 'I don't have to be back until nine o'clock. I can't believe my first full day of this year and I find you safe and sound and living with Dan Cooper.'

Sarah's cheeks crimsoned. Betty's smile faded and Alfie's expression turned to a scowl.

'I didn't think to ask what you're doing here. That little one called you ma, didn't he? I can't believe me sister would move in with a bloke without being wed. I'm going to have words with Cooper.'

This was a disaster. 'Please, Alfie, don't. Whatever it looks like, I'm not sharing his bed. He sleeps in the attic; I sleep next to the children. I was housekeeper before his wife died in March. John calls me ma because he can't remember his own any more.'

He sat down, but kept staring at the kitchen door as if he was planning to go in and confront Dan at any moment. Betty reached over and squeezed her hand.

'It's my fault – me and my chatter. I should have thought before I spoke. You're the last person to do anything they shouldn't; in some ways you haven't changed at all.'

The boys erupted from the back door holding their ball. Suddenly, Alfie was on his feet and vanished into the kitchen.

'Betty, this is awful. I only realised today what folks are saying. It didn't occur to me anyone might think I was sharing a bed with my employer. He's not shown the slightest interest in me in *that* way. We're good friends, we get on well together, and that's all there is to it.'

'I believe you, Sarah, but it's not me that matters. You've got two choices: you've either to leave, move in with your Alfie – he's got a lovely little cottage in Maidenburgh Street. He could do with someone to take care of him.'

'Or? Are you suggesting that I must marry Dan if I want to stay here?'

Alfie appeared in the doorway. The day was ruined. Even

having her brother and her best friend back couldn't make up for this.

'Dan's in the front room. He wants to speak to you. Go on, it ain't as bad as it looks, I promise you.'

This wasn't the Alfie she remembered. She didn't know him any more. It had always been *her* role to take care of *him*.

Dan was standing by the window, his face in shadow. 'Come in, love, this shouldn't have happened, not this way. But I'm glad it has. I should sit down. I've got to talk to you, and we don't have much time before the guests arrive.'

She folded herself in the armchair, the dark red mark clearly visible across her foot and ankle.

'How did you burn yourself? Let me look.' He was at her side, his hands gentle as he picked up her foot to examine the scald.

'It's not as painful as it looks, Dan. I dropped a teapot and it splashed over me. It's nothing, I promise you.'

He moved across to sit opposite. 'Betty wasn't the surprise I promised you, Sarah. I was going to speak to you this evening, after the party, but things have changed. I shouldn't have left things so long.'

She stared at him, beginning to get his drift. 'You don't have to marry me, Dan. I don't care what other people say. We know there's nothing going on, and anyway, I can move in with Alfie and come here on a daily basis. If I'm not sleeping overnight the gossips will have nothing to talk about.'

'That's the point, Sarah, I don't want you to leave, not now, not ever.' He reached into his shirt pocket and held out a small velvet box. 'Sarah love. Will you marry me? I didn't want to ask you until you were seventeen, but I've no choice now the gossip's started.'

'I'm not sure. I'm not ready to be married to anyone. I

don't...' Her voice faded away. She turned away, unable to continue. He was back beside her, taking her hands.

'I understand, love. You don't want me in your bed. *I* don't want any more children. I don't want anything to happen to you. I want to take care of you, keep you safe from harm, but I don't want to share your bed.'

She risked a glance. 'Things can go on as before? The only difference will be I'll have a ring on my finger?' He was marrying her so that she could take care of his children. The boys loved her as if she was their mother. He was giving up his chance of happiness with someone later on, doing it for the sake of the boys and to keep her safe.

He was a good man, a kind and gentle one. It would be madness not to accept. She'd never get a better offer. She didn't love him in *that* way, but he didn't think of her like that either.

'Thank you, Dan, I'd be proud to accept under those conditions.'

He opened the box, removed a pretty silver ring and slid it on her finger. 'There's something else. As soon as we're married, we'll start looking for somewhere else to live. You shall have your own house, with a garden for the boys to play in, where you can grow vegetables and flowers.'

Tears filled her eyes. 'But you have to get to work, Dan. I'll not have you walking miles just so I can live in the country.'

'I thought Greenstead Road would be the place to look. I can walk in from there easy enough. I want you to be happy, want us all to start afresh.'

A dog barked in the yard. 'You must go out, Dan. There's a dog, and the boys will be terrified.'

'That'll be Buster, your Alfie's animal; he's a monster but soft as butter. Listen, they're laughing. I reckon they're playing ball with him. I'm surprised you didn't notice him.'

'I was so shocked to see Alfie and Betty I'd no time for anything else.'

Outside the children were rolling about with the biggest dog she'd ever set eyes on. The animal appeared to be enjoying it as much as they were. Alfie and Betty were chattering to Mr and Mrs Davies and all were clutching mugs of tea.

She looked at Dan, and he slipped his arm around her waist. 'It's for show, love. What we've decided is nobody else's business.' She relaxed against him, and he raised his hand and called for quiet. 'Joe, Davie, John, we've something to tell you, come over here, quickly now.'

The three boys stood in a semicircle gazing at their father. He touched each one in turn. 'Sarah and I are getting married as soon as we can; she's going to be your ma.'

They flung themselves, not at him, but at her. She drew them into her arms. She was doing the right thing; she loved these boys as if they were her own. She'd be comfortable and secure for the rest of her life. Alfie didn't need her – he'd got Betty at his side, hadn't he? Her brother walked across and slapped Dan on the back. Mr and Mrs Davies joined in with their best wishes. Only Betty remained silent; she knew how things were.

The party was a huge success, the cake admired, the castle the best thing anyone had ever seen, the spread more than enough for everyone. By the time the guests departed, each carrying slices of cake, it was getting dark. The boys were exhausted and with Betty's expert assistance they were washed and into their nightshirts within half an hour.

Dan and Alfie cleared away and did the washing-up whilst they were upstairs. Alfie then insisted on taking Dan out to celebrate; after all he was going to be his brother-in-law very soon.

Betty was waiting to express her concern, but Sarah was determined to speak first.

'I'm not like you, Betty. I don't have a romantical bone in my body. I never really understood how Jane felt about that groom. I don't think I'm *that* way inclined. Dan's a good man. I shall live in my own house, will be secure and comfortable for the rest of my life. How many other women can say the same?'

Betty shook her head. 'But you don't *love* him. That's all very well at the moment, but what happens if you meet someone and fall for *him* later on?'

Sarah laughed. 'I'll tell you what happens: nothing at all, because if ever I *do* fall in love it will be with my husband.'

'I told you he thought you were a bit of all right when you was robbed and he came to look after you. I reckon it won't be long before you change your mind. I wouldn't say no to a bit of how's your father with him, I can tell you.'

Sarah hastily changed the subject and they spent the remainder of the evening planning the wedding. When Alfie returned with Dan he took her to one side. 'He's a good man, Sarah. He loves you and will make you a fine husband.'

'I'm sure he will or I wouldn't have agreed to marry him. I want to bring the boys up to see your cottage. What about tomorrow? We can come after we have attended church.'

'I've not got enough in to give you dinner – but we'll manage.'

She embraced him and then kissed her friend. They walked off, the huge dog by his side, and she thought they too made a perfect match. Perhaps there would be a second wedding later in the year.

For some reason Dan hadn't come into bid her goodnight but wandered off into the yard again. She made her way

upstairs, her heart so full she couldn't remember ever being so happy.

She checked the boys were sleeping soundly and then retired to her own room. Once comfortably settled between the sheets she let her mind wander – thought about what the future might hold. When Alfie had told her that Dan was in love with her she'd thought this was just something that had been said to smooth things over.

Now she recalled all the little things that he'd said and done over the past few months, how happy he'd been, and she began to believe that whatever he'd said, his offer hadn't been one of expedience, but because he truly wanted to spend the rest of his life with her.

A warm glow started at her toes and spread rapidly until she was tingling all over. One day she would share her bed with him, hopefully have a baby of her own to hold in her arms, and be living in the house of her dreams. She was the luckiest girl in Colchester.

Was it possible she already had feelings for him but had been keeping them at bay because of their situation?

There was no rush – she had the rest of her life to fall in love with him.

ABOUT THE AUTHOR

Fenella J. Miller is a bestselling writer of historical sagas. She also has a passion for Regency romantic adventures and has published over fifty to great acclaim.

Sign up to Fenella J. Miller's mailing list for news, competitions and updates on future books.

Visit Fenella's website: www.fenellajmiller.co.uk

Follow Fenella on social media here:

facebook.com/fenella.miller

x.com/fenellawriter

ALSO BY FENELLA J MILLER

Goodwill House Series

The War Girls of Goodwill House

New Recruits at Goodwill House

Duty Calls at Goodwill House

The Land Girls of Goodwill House

A Wartime Reunion at Goodwill House

Wedding Bells at Goodwill House

A Christmas Baby at Goodwill House

The Army Girls Series

Army Girls Reporting For Duty

Army Girls: Heartbreak and Hope

Army Girls: Behind the Guns

The Pilot's Girl Series

The Pilot's Girl

A Wedding for the Pilot's Girl

A Dilemma for the Pilot's Girl

A Second Chance for the Pilot's Girl

The Nightingale Family Series

A Pocketful of Pennies

Sixpence Stories

Introducing Sixpence Stories!

Discover page-turning
historical novels from your
favourite authors, meet new
friends and be transported
back in time.

Join our book club
Facebook group

https://bit.ly/SixpenceGroup

Sign up to our
newsletter

https://bit.ly/SixpenceNews

Boldwood

Boldwood Books is an award-winning fiction publishing company seeking out the best stories from around the world.

Find out more at www.boldwoodbooks.com

Join our reader community for brilliant books, competitions and offers!

Follow us
@BoldwoodBooks
@TheBoldBookClub

Sign up to our weekly
deals newsletter

https://bit.ly/BoldwoodBNewsletter